CONSENT TO SEXUAL RELATIONS

When does a woman give valid consent to sexual relations? When does her consent render it morally or legally permissible for a man to have sexual relations with her? Why is sexual consent generally regarded as an issue about female consent? And what is the moral significance of consent? These are some of the questions discussed in this important book, which will appeal to a wide readership in philosophy, law, and the social sciences. Alan Wertheimer develops a theory of consent to sexual relations that applies to both law and morality in the light of the psychology of sexual relations, the psychology of perpetrators, and the psychology of the victims. He considers a wide variety of difficult cases such as coercion, fraud, retardation, and intoxication. We can all agree that "no" means "no." This book suggests that the difficult question is whether "yes" means "yes."

ALAN WERTHEIMER is John G. McCullough Professor of Political Science at the University of Vermont. He is the author of *Coercion* (1987) and *Exploitation* (1996) and has published articles in *Ethics, Philosophy & Public Affairs, Law and Philosophy,* and *Legal Theory.*

CAMBRIDGE STUDIES IN PHILOSOPHY AND LAW

General editor
Gerald Postema
(University of North Carolina, Chapel Hill)

Advisory board
Jules Coleman (Yale Law School)
Antony Duff (University of Stirling)
David Lyons (Boston University)
Neil MacCormick (University of Edinburgh)
Stephen Munzer (UCLA Law School)
Phillip Pettit (Australian National University)
Joseph Raz (University of Oxford)
Jeremy Waldron (Columbia Law School)

Some other books in the series:

ROBERT F. SCHOPP
Automatism, Insanity, and the Psychology of Criminal Responsibility

STEVEN J. BURTON
Judging in Good Faith

JULES COLEMAN
Risks and Wrongs

SUZANNE UNIACKE
Permissible Killing
The Self-Defense Justification of Homicide

JULES COLEMAN AND ALLEN BUCHANAN (EDS.)
In Harm's Way
Essays in Honor of Joel Feinberg

WARREN F. SCHWARTZ (ED.)
Justice in Immigration

JOHN FISCHER AND MARK RAVIZZA
Responsibility and Control

R. A. DUFF (ED.)
Philosophy and the Criminal Law

LARRY ALEXANDER (ED.)
Constitutionalism

CONSENT TO SEXUAL RELATIONS

ALAN WERTHEIMER

University of Vermont

PUBLISHED BY THE PRESS SYNDICATE OF THE UNIVERSITY OF CAMBRIDGE
The Pitt Building, Trumpington Street, Cambridge, United Kingdom

CAMBRIDGE UNIVERSITY PRESS
The Edinburgh Building, Cambridge, CB2 2RU, UK
40 West 20th Street, New York, NY 10011–4211, USA
477 Williamstown Road, Port Melbourne, VIC 3207, Australia
Ruiz de Alarcón 13, 28014 Madrid, Spain
Dock House, The Waterfront, Cape Town 8001, South Africa

http://www.cambridge.org

First published 2003

Printed in the United Kingdom at the University Press, Cambridge

Typeface Adobe Garamond 10/12.5 pt.   *System* LaTeX 2$_\varepsilon$ [TB]

A catalogue record for this book is available from the British Library

Library of Congress cataloguing in publication data
Wertheimer, Alan.
Consent to sexual relations / Alan Wertheimer.
p.   cm.   (Cambridge studies in philosophy and law)
Includes bibliographical references and index.
ISBN 0 521 82926 7 (hardback)   ISBN 0 521 53611 1 (paperback)
1. Sexual consent.   2. Sexual ethics.   3. Sex and law.   I. Title.   II. Series.
HQ32.W463   2003
176 – dc21   2003046030 CIP

ISBN 0 521 82926 7 hardback
ISBN 0 521 53611 1 paperback

To Susan

Contents

Preface

Although this book ranges more widely, its central organizing question is this: when does a woman give valid consent to sexual relations? Put slightly differently, when does a woman's consent render it morally or legally permissible for a man to have sexual relations with her? Some very special cases aside, I take it to be uncontroversial that it is morally impermissible and should be legally impermissible to have sexual relations without consent. What should count as the sort of consent that is morally or legally transformative is a more complicated question. Or so I shall argue.

Most philosophical discussions of sexual consent have taken different tacks. Some have focused on the "ontology" of consent. They have asked whether consent is a state of mind or an action. And, if consent is an action, they ask whether consent must be explicit or verbal, or whether tacit or nonverbal signals are sufficient. Many other discussions have been prompted by some infamous cases in which defendants claimed that they mistakenly believed that the woman consented. Were they guilty? Can there be rape without rapists? These are all interesting and important questions, but they are not the questions with which I shall be primarily concerned. Assuming that everyone knows what is happening, when should we regard a male's behavior as morally impermissible or as a legal offense?

I have long been interested in consent. My doctoral dissertation, "Consent and Elections in American Politics" (1968), asked whether the electoral process is sufficient to support the view that we are ruled with the consent of the governed. I argued that it does not.

After a period in which I worked on the philosophy of punishment, a project on plea bargaining and retribution brought me back to consent in ways that I had not anticipated. It has been argued that when a prosecutor threatens a much more severe punishment if a defendant is convicted at trial than if he should plead guilty, it follows that a defendant's subsequent guilty plea is coerced and involuntary. I thought that the argument must be mistaken, but I was not sure why. Having found that the case law on plea bargaining provided important grist for my philosophical mill, I decided to cast my philosophical and legal nets more widely. When are contracts made under duress? Marriages? Confessions? When does someone commit a crime under duress? I tried to answer these questions in *Coercion* (Princeton: Princeton University Press, 1987). I did not consider rape or coercive sex in that book. Because I was younger and less courageous (wiser?), I was reluctant to enter what I took to be the sensitive waters of sexual coercion.

My work on coercion transmogrified into a project that resulted in *Exploitation* (Princeton: Princeton University Press, 1996). I argued there that it was important to distinguish consensual and mutually beneficial exploitation from nonconsensual and harmful exploitation, and that we should be reluctant to interfere with consensual and mutually beneficial transactions, exploitative though they might be. Although I did consider sexual exploitation in psychotherapy as a paradigm of harmful exploitation, I continued to shy away from a more direct analysis as to when sexual relations were consensual or exploitative.

Before I could settle on another project, I was invited to participate in an informal symposium on sexual consent at the University of San Diego Law School in 1995. I had not written explicitly on the topic, but I decided that if Larry Alexander thought I might have something to say, then maybe he was right. It has taken a long time, but this book is the result. I could not think of an appropriate one-word title.

Acknowledgments

According to what John Rawls calls the Aristotelian Principle, human beings enjoy the exercise of their capacities and the enjoyment increases with the complexity of the task. I suppose that I must be motivated to write, but I cannot say that I always enjoy it, save for the opportunity to acknowledge publicly the help and support that I have received.

The stimulating presentations and comments by the participants at the University of San Diego Law School symposium were crucial at the formative stage. I thank Larry Alexander, Donald Dripps, Heidi Hurd, Heidi Malm, Joan McGregor, Stephen Schulhofer, and Emily Sherwin. Stephen Schulhofer also gave me extended comments on parts of the manuscript.

My colleagues in the Department of Political Science at the University of Vermont, Pat Neal and Bob Taylor, read a draft of the entire manuscript and were, as always, enormously generous with their time, comments, and encouragement. Colleagues in the Department of Philosophy allowed me to present several chapters to our informal discussion group. I thank David Christensen, Arthur Kuflik, Don Loeb, and Sin-Yee Chan.

Friends and colleagues at other institutions were also extraordinarily helpful. Albert Dzur provided me with detailed comments on every chapter. Peter Westen kindly allowed me to read a draft of his own manuscript on sexual consent. Arthur Applbaum was crucial. I did not keep the meter running, but over the course of several years, we must have spent the equivalent of several full days discussing this project. He convinced me that I should write this book and then showed me at least some of the places where I had gone wrong.

Gerry Postema, the general editor of Cambridge Studies in Philosophy and Law, was both supportive and appropriately critical. An anonymous reader saved me from numerous errors and forced me to rethink several issues. It has been a pleasure to work with Hilary Gaskin, Alison Powell, and Jan Chapman of Cambridge University Press.

When I try to consider matters from an impartial point of view, it is truly amazing that one can actually be paid to engage in this sort of philosophical reflection. I am grateful to the University of Vermont for a sabbatical leave during which I held a fellowship from the National Endowment for the Humanities.

Finally, nothing that I do would be possible without the love and support of Susan.

Abbreviations

EEA	environment of evolutionary adaptation
FH	formula of humanity
NMN	no means no
PTSD	post-traumatic stress disorder
PVC	principles of valid consent
PVC$_L$	principles of valid consent for the law
PVC$_M$	principles of valid consent for morality
RVNS	rape is about violence, not about sex
SSSM	Standard Social Science Model

CHAPTER ONE

Introduction

It is commonly thought that we should regard it as morally and legally permissible to engage in sexual relations if and only if the parties consent to do so. With appropriate qualifications, I think this view is correct. But, as with many other principles, it raises more questions than it resolves. Among those questions are the following.

First, *what is the moral significance of consent to sexual relations?* A law professor is reported to have remarked that "consent turns an act of rape into an act of lovemaking."[1] That seems improbable. Acts of prostitution can be consensual, yet fall quite short of acts of love. If consent is not sufficient to render sexual relations a positive good, is it sufficient to render sexual relations morally permissible? Does consent render sexual relations consistent with Kant's formula of humanity, the principle that we should always treat others as ends in themselves and never merely as a means?

Second, *in what ways are nonconsensual relations harmful or wrongful?* And are harm and wrong identical? In posing these questions, I do not mean to imply that nonconsensual sexual relations are not (almost always) harmful or wrongful. Still, it may be less clear precisely why this is so. Consider forcible rape. Is it a simple harm to the body, similar to the harm of a nonsexual assault? Or is it a harm in virtue of its contact with the victim's sexual organs? If so, why is such contact especially harmful? Is it harmful because of the victim's psychological reaction? Is the harm of rape (at all) a function of cultural norms, of the way in which a particular society views the act? Would it be a better or worse world in which rape was viewed and experienced as less harmful? Or is the harm of rape an "objective" matter because it is a violation of the victim's autonomy or rights, independent of the way it is experienced by the victim or viewed by society?

---

[1] Jean Hampton, "Defining Wrong and Defining Rape" in Keith Burgess-Jackson (ed.), *A Most Detestable Crime: New Philosophical Essays on Rape* (New York: Oxford University Press, 1990).

Third, *in what does consent fundamentally consist?* Is consent (solely or primarily) a state of mind or is it an action? Can one consent to sexual relations by adopting the relevant mental state? If an act of consent is necessary, is it sufficient? Can one give (valid) consent to sexual relations that is not accompanied by the relevant mental state? If consent is an action, what sorts of actions are required? Is verbal consent required? Is tacit consent possible?

Fourth, and perhaps most importantly, *when is consent valid?* Some think that we can define nonconsensual sexual relations as those cases in which A has sexual relations with B even though B says "no" or fails to say "yes." I disagree. I shall argue that the important question is not whether "no means no," but whether "yes means yes." When is consent *valid* or *morally transformative* or *legally transformative?* When does someone's "token" of consent to sexual relations render it permissible for the other party to proceed? It is often said that valid consent must be suitably competent, voluntary, and informed. How should we understand those criteria? Can minors give valid consent to sexual relations? The mentally retarded? Can one give valid consent while intoxicated? What about coercion? It is un-controversial that one's consent is not valid if it is offered in response to the use or threat of physical force, but what about other threats? Is one coerced by the threat to be abandoned in a remote area? By the threat to end a dating relationship? By the threat to be fired (or not promoted)? Can one be coerced by an attractive offer? Does inequality or economic pressure compromise the validity of consent? And what about deception? Does fraud or misrepresentation invalidate consent? If not, why not? If so, when?

Finally, and with some trepidation, I want to ask a question about consent to sexual relations within the context of long-term relationships. *Given that the parties may have asymmetrical desires for sexual relationships, when should someone consent to sexual relations?* Does the less desirous party have moral reason to consent to sexual relations that one does not (otherwise) desire? Might there be something like a just distribution of sexual satisfaction among intimates?

The purpose of this book is to develop a theory of consent to sexual relations, one that begins to answer the sorts of questions I have described. I say *begins*, because even though the book is clearly quite long, full answers to many of these questions require moral and empirical analysis that are beyond the scope of this project. The most important task is to develop a general account of what I shall call the *principles of valid consent* (PVC), a set of principles that itself can take two forms: the principles of valid consent for the law (PVC_L) and the principles of valid consent for morality (PVC_M). Both PVC_L and PVC_M are *moral* principles, but the moral principles that indicate when consent should be regarded as legally valid are not identical to the principles that say when a person's consent renders another's action morally permissible.

The book is primarily analytic not programmatic. I shall not be advocating particular legal reforms nor shall I defend a single or general substantive thesis about the conditions under which consent to sexual relations should be treated as valid. Indeed, I will be at pains to argue that no analysis of the concept of consent can answer the questions in which we are interested. The criteria for what constitutes valid consent will always involve moral argument and empirical evidence that is sensitive to the reasons for adopting a more rigorous view of PVC_L or PVC_M as balanced against the reasons for adopting a less rigorous view of PVC. And the reasons go both ways. There is a deep tension between what we might call the positive and negative dimension to respecting an agent's autonomy. We respect an agent's negative autonomy when we say that it is legally or morally impermissible for others to have sexual relations with her that do not reflect her competent, informed, and voluntary consent. We respect an agent's positive autonomy when we make it possible for her to render it permissible for others to engage in sexual relations with her. Unfortunately, we cannot simultaneously maximize both dimensions of autonomy. To the extent that we seek to protect an agent's negative autonomy, we should set high standards for what qualifies as valid consent. We will say that she does not give valid consent in many marginal cases (for example, when she is retarded). On the other hand, setting high standards for what qualifies as valid consent may encroach on the agent's ability to realize her own goals and desires. It may, for example, prevent a retarded woman from experiencing sexual pleasure and intimacy. And that is why it is very important to properly understand in what ways nonconsensual or marginally consensual sexual relations are harmful. For we cannot determine just how far we should go towards protecting a woman's negative autonomy unless we understand in what ways she is harmed when we fail to do so.

And that leads me to mention several "methodological" commitments that underlie much of what follows. First, I share Martha Nussbaum's view that "philosophy cannot do its job well unless it is informed by fact and experience."[2] To say that facts matter is not to say that they determine the best moral view in any straightforward way. There is no naturalistic fallacy

---

[2] Martha C. Nussbaum, "Public Philosophy and International Feminism," 108 *Ethics* 762 (1998), 765.

here. It is to say that the most defensible normative positions cannot be developed in the absence of the relevant set of facts. In particular, I do not think that we can develop a satisfactory theoretical account of the distinction between consensual and nonconsensual sex without first examining the experience of nonconsensual sex from the perspective of perpetrator and victim. And that is where I propose to begin. More specifically, I think it is impossible to think sensibly and sensitively about consent to sexual relations without a clear and honest understanding of human sexual behavior and psychology. Although I shall not resolve these issues (to say the least!), I hope to say something about them and to point to the relevant sorts of data and the way in which different assumptions about the data might support different views about the validity of consent.

Unfortunately, much writing on the issues that lie at the center of this project is, in my view, highly ideological. To take an example, almost at random, D. Kelly Weisberg writes that there is a "consensus among feminists...that rape is quintessentially a crime of aggression and hostility, not a form of sexual release."[3] I will consider this particular claim in some detail later on. The present point is simply that the question of what motivates those who engage in nonconsensual relations with others is fundamentally an *empirical* question about the psychology of perpetrators. This is not an issue about which feminists – defined as those committed to gender equality – need to have a position. Similarly, the question whether women frequently say "no" when they desire to have sexual relations or are likely to change their mind is an empirical question, the answer to which may or may not be important in shaping the best set of principles with regard to what should count as valid consent to sexual relations.

Second, and related to the previous points, I believe that biology matters. It is an old but true saw that sound normative theories must be rooted in a sound understanding of human nature. And this applies to a theory about sexual relations as much as it does to politics or economics. There is considerable evidence that there are important psychological differences between males and females with respect to their sexual attitudes and behavior, and that these differences can be partially explained in evolutionary terms. Biology is not destiny, and biology never justifies or excuses. But it matters. I hope to show how and why.

Third, I argue that whereas facts matter a lot, words do not matter much at all. In particular, I shall argue that no linguistic analysis of the concept

---

[3] Editor's introduction to section on rape in D. Kelly Weisberg (ed.), *Applications of Feminist Legal Theory to Women's Lives* (Philadelphia: Temple University Press, 1996), 412.

of consent or related concepts will answer the legal and moral questions in which we are interested. We will not settle anything by determining what consent "really means." If, for example, someone wants to say that a woman does not "really" consent to sexual relations if she agrees to sex in response to a man's threat to break off their relationship, then one can say that if one wants.[4] But that leaves open the question whether we should regard A's behavior as morally or legally impermissible. Similarly, one can say that one cannot give genuine consent if one is intoxicated, but if a woman unambiguously tokens consent to sexual relations after voluntarily consuming several drinks, that leaves open the question whether we should regard the man's behavior as morally or legally permissible. The question is whether PVC_L or PVC_M would regard such consent as valid and not what consent means or how the word should be used.

SOME DISTINCTIONS AND CAVEATS

The bad, the wrong, and the criminal

A full moral theory of sexual relations would answer at least three questions: (1) when are sexual relations morally *unworthy*, or *bad*? (2) when are sexual relations morally *impermissible* or *wrong*? (3) when should sexual relations be *illegal* or *criminal*? Sexual relations can, of course, also be evaluated in nonmoral terms, for example, aesthetically, hedonically, or medically (safety). Moreover, the moral and nonmoral are by no means independent. One may have moral reason to attend to another's sexual pleasure. The present point is that we can distinguish between the three moral questions that I have posed. They are all moral questions, but they are different moral questions.

By contrasting moral impermissibility and legal impermissibility, I do not intend the completely obvious distinction between what is wrong and what *is* illegal as a matter of positive law. Rather, I intend the somewhat less (but still) obvious distinction between what is wrong and what *should be* illegal. It is ordinarily wrong to break a promise or tell a lie, but there are good reasons – good *moral* reasons – why it should not be illegal to break some promises or tell some lies. The law is a blunt and expensive instrument, to be invoked with great reluctance, even at the cost of refusing to sanction some behavior that is clearly wrongful. Similarly, it may be wrong to obtain

---

4 Charlene L. Muelenhard and Jennifer L. Schrag, "Nonviolent Sexual Coercion" in Andrea Parrot and Laurie Bechhofer (eds.), *Acquaintance Rape* (New York: John Wiley, 1991), 119.

another's consent to sexual relations by lying about one's marital status or one's affections. There may or may not be good moral reasons to regard such behavior as illegal.

Just as what should be legally impermissible is a subset of what is morally impermissible, the morally impermissible (wrong) is a subset of the morally unworthy (bad). The distinction between the bad and the wrong may seem problematic because we have moral reason not to do what is bad as well as what is wrong. But there are moral reasons and moral reasons, and the distinction between the bad and the wrong is meant to capture a distinction among them. Our common-sense morality distinguishes between reasons of justice, obligations, and rights, on the one hand, and a motley variety of other ways in which acts can be morally defective or vicious, on the other. To use Judith Thomson's example, a boy who refuses to share his box of chocolates with his brother may be stingy, greedy, and callous, but it does not follow that he has an obligation to share, or that the brother has a right to the chocolates, or that he treats his brother unjustly.[5]

To put the point in familiar terms, common-sense morality distinguishes between the claim that A *has a right* to do X, and the claim that A *is right* to do X. On common-sense morality, A may have a right to do bad. Some think that there is something deeply problematic about this. If doing X is bad, all things considered, how can A have a *moral* right to do X? Perhaps A does and should have a *legal* right do X even though doing X is bad. That we can easily grant. But, it may be thought, it does not make sense to say that one could have "an all-things-considered moral right to do what is, all things considered, morally wrong."[6]

It is true that if it is bad for A to do X, all things considered, then A has moral reason not to do X. So if the claim "it is morally impermissible for A to do X" is equivalent to "A has moral reason not to do X," then the objection is sound. It is simply true by definition that it could not be morally permissible to do what is bad.[7] But they are not equivalent, or, if one wants to insist that they are, then the moral distinction I mean to highlight can be expressed in other terms. As Brian Barry puts it, "people do say things like 'I think you ought not to do such-and-such but I concede that you have a right to do it.' "[8] In saying such things, we sometimes signify

---

[5] Judith Thomson, "A Defense of Abortion," 1 *Philosophy & Public Affairs* 47 (1971), 60.

[6] William Galston, "On the Alleged Right to Do Wrong: A Response to Waldron," 93 *Ethics* 320 (1983), 320 (emphasis added). This article is a critique of Jeremy Waldron, "A Right to Do Wrong," 92 *Ethics* 21 (1981).

[7] This is Alan Donagan's position in "The Right Not to Incriminate Oneself," 1 *Social Philosophy and Policy* 137 (1984), 147.

[8] Brian Barry, *Justice as Impartiality* (Oxford: Clarendon Press, 1995), 79.

that they have (as a matter of fact) or should have (as a matter of morality) a legal right to do it. But, as Barry suggests, such claims often signify that the action is permitted by the moral rules of our society – the rules that define our obligations, rights, and demands of justice – and that we think those moral rules are not "radically defective" or, I would add, that the action would be permitted by what we think *should* be the moral rules of our society.[9]

In addition, we miss the point of the distinction between the wrong and the bad if we focus solely on the participants. To say that A has a moral right to do X or that it is morally permissible for A to do X is often best understood not as a claim about what *A* has moral reason to do, but, rather, as a claim – perhaps only a placeholder – about what *others* have moral reason to do with respect to A's doing X, to wit, that others have moral reason not to interfere with A's doing X.[10] Suppose we think that A has a right to read smut. A cannot appeal to his right to read smut as a reason to read smut. If it is bad for A to read smut, then A has moral reason not to read smut. Yet we can also say that there are moral reasons why others should not interfere with A's reading smut – for example, that A is not harming others or treating others unjustly or violating anyone's rights.

The distinctions among the bad, the wrong, and the illegal are purely schematic or analytical. They are neutral with respect to the content of those categories. We could all agree that there is a distinction between unworthy sex, impermissible sex, and illegal sex, but disagree whether (say) prostitution is morally unworthy, or morally impermissible, or should be illegal.[11] A full moral theory of sexual relations would provide the content of these categories. Not surprisingly, I shall not be offering such a theory. In particular, I shall have relatively little to say about morally unworthy sex. I shall have more to say about the wrong and the illegal. On the view that I shall defend, the content of the morally impermissible and the legally impermissible can be captured by the concept of consent. The hard work will be to say what that means.

(Non)gender neutrality

I shall generally prescind from any attempt to frame the issue of consent to sexual relations in gender-neutral terms. I shall generally assume that the

---

[9] *Ibid.*   [10] Jeremy Waldron, "Galston on Rights," 93 *Ethics* 325 (1983), 325.
[11] One might think that prostitution is not bad at all. One might think that prostitution is bad, but not wrong if consensual. One might think that prostitution is wrong (for the customer or the prostitute or both), but should not be illegal. And one might think that prostitution is bad, is wrong, and should be illegal.

person whose consent is at issue is female and I shall refer to her as B. I shall generally assume that the person who requires such consent is male, and I shall refer to him as A. There are several reasons for adopting this approach. First, it makes things simpler. Second, it reflects empirical reality. With the exception of minors and prison inmates, it is extremely rare for males to claim that they did not consent to sexual relations, whereas this claim is frequently and rightly made by females.

Rape and nonconsensual sexual relations

Although there will be numerous occasions on which I shall invoke the word "rape," that term plays little role in the analysis. Because "rape" is emotionally freighted, it is best to use more neutral language. I do so for two principal reasons. First, we should not assume that if a situation is not well described as rape, then it follows that B has given valid consent to sexual relations, that A's action should be regarded as legally or morally permissible. Second, we should not assume that if B does not give valid consent to sexual relations, then it follows that A has raped B. There may be good reasons to distinguish between nonconsensual sexual relations that involve the use of physical force, or where the victim is unconscious, and a motley range of other situations in which B does not give valid consent. And it is distinctly possible that what we traditionally call rape is a more serious offense than many other cases of nonconsensual sexual relations. The present task is to make some progress toward identifying the criteria for valid consent and not to say what is and is not well described as a case of rape.

Generalizability

There are numerous contexts in which issues of consent arise. Do citizens consent to obey the law? Can prisoners consent to participate in medical experiments? Should adolescent females be able to consent to an abortion (without parental permission)? Given that many women undergo profound changes during pregnancy, can a potential surrogate mother give valid consent to relinquish her child after birth? And so on.

Although this book focuses on consent to sexual relations, I believe that the general structure of the argument is generalizable to any context in which issues of consent arise. It is possible that the principles of valid consent remain relatively constant at an extremely abstract level, but I believe they will demonstrate considerable variability when applied in different contexts. There is, for example, no reason to assume that the informational requirements of valid consent to a medical procedure are identical to the informational requirements of valid consent to buy a television or to engage in sexual relations. To put the point in now familiar terms, while the *concept* of the principles of valid consent may be identical across contexts, we will find different *conceptions* of those principles in those contexts. It would be easy to explain why this is so on a consequentialist moral theory. I shall suggest that this can also be explained on a contractualist account of morality.

Plan of the book. Those are my aims. This is the plan. In chapter two, I briefly review the law of rape – history, statutes, cases, reforms, scholarship. I start with the law because it provides a literature that defines the issues that an adequate theory of sexual consent must confront. Chapters three, four, and five examine the psychology of sexual relations insofar as it bears on issues of consent. In chapter three, I sketch that psychology in general terms and also discuss the evolutionary psychology of sexual relations. Chapter four examines nonconsensual sexual relations from the perspective of the perpetrator. Chapter five examines nonconsensual sexual relations from the perspective of the victim. Because the character of the harm of nonconsensual sexual relations depends on a theoretical account of harm as well as empirical phenomena, chapter five is more philosophical than chapters three and four.

I then turn from sex to consent. I do not think we can say what counts as giving valid consent to sexual relations unless we first understand why consent is valuable. In chapter six, I consider the value of consent to sexual relations. In particular, I consider whether (valid) consent renders sexual relations compatible with the Kantian principle that we should always treat others as ends in themselves and never merely as a means. I also consider whether appropriately robust consent is sufficient to render sexual relations permissible. Chapter seven considers what might be called the "ontology of consent." In particular, I consider whether consent is best understood as a "performative" or as a mental state. In chapters eight through eleven, I try to sketch an account of the principles of valid consent by considering three sorts of potential defects of consent in those cases where a woman unambiguously "tokens" consent in one way or another. Chapter eight considers defects in voluntariness or coercion. Chapter nine considers defects in information or deception. Chapters ten and eleven consider defects in competence. In chapter ten, I consider issues of age, mental retardation, and false preferences. I devote chapter eleven to an extended discussion of intoxication.

Chapter twelve switches gears. Assuming that we know what counts as valid consent to sexual relations, I consider an issue not unknown to many couples: when should one consent to sexual relations? Assuming an asymmetry of desire for sexual relations, are there moral reasons for the less desirous partner to consent to sexual relations more frequently than she would otherwise prefer?

CHAPTER TWO

Law

Legal controversies

I begin with the law because it provides us with a rich and varied literature of statutes, cases, and scholarship that bring the central issues of the project into sharper relief, although the law's understanding of sexual consent must be sensitive to issues of evidence and standards of proof that are not entirely replicated in our moral thinking. And to begin with the law of sexual consent is to begin with the law of rape.

For many years, rape was defined by common law as sexual intercourse "by a man with a woman, not his wife, by force and against her will."[1] That definition found its way into the statutes of many states. There are three features of this definition worth noting: (a) the marital exclusion; (b) the force requirement; (c) the no-consent (or "against her will") requirement. First, a man could not rape his wife, whatever the degree of force or absence of consent. Second, rape required the use or threat of physical force. If a man did not use or threaten physical force, he did not commit rape even if the sexual act was against a woman's (expressed) will or without her consent.[2] Third, the phrases "by force" *and* "against her will" were supposedly regarded as jointly sufficient but independently necessary conditions. If a man used or threatened physical force, there was no rape if the woman consented to sexual relations, implying that the use or threat of physical force is not incompatible with the victim's consent.[3] Call this the *conjunctive account.*

---

[1] Richard A. Posner and Katharine B. Silbaugh, *A Guide to America's Sex Laws* (Chicago: University of Chicago Press, 1996), 5.

[2] The phrases "against her will" and "without her consent" were effectively synonymous. See *Corpus Juris Secundum* (St. Paul, MN: West Publishing Company, 1936). It might be argued that "against her will" denotes a psychological state, whereas "without her consent" refers to an action or performative, but it appears that the law did not reflect any such distinction.

[3] "If she consents to the sexual intercourse, although that consent may be reluctantly given, and although there may be some force used to obtain her consent, the offense cannot be 'rape,'" *Black's Law Dictionary*, fourth edition (St. Paul, MN: West Publishing Company, 1951), 1427.

Contemporary commentators typically argue that we have moved and should continue to move toward a conception of sexual offense that is based on the absence of (valid) consent rather than the presence of force. But appearances to the contrary notwithstanding, I believe that consent rather than force was always the central concept underlying the traditional conjunctive account. Consider the marital exclusion. It appears that a man commits no crime if he has nonconsensual sexual relations with his wife. But this ignores the rationale for the marital exclusion. Anglo-American law once held that the marriage contract involved a permanent and irrevocable consent to sexual relations on demand: "[T]he husband cannot be guilty of a rape committed by himself upon his lawful wife, for by their matrimonial consent and contract, the wife hath given up herself in this kind unto her husband, which she cannot retract."[4] From this perspective, the marital exemption does not permit men to engage in nonconsensual sexual relations with their wives. Rather, it perversely maintains that marital sex is always consensual. A wife could, of course, refuse to give concurrent consent to sexual relations, but, *ex hypothesi*, she has consented to sexual relations in advance, and the force of her prior consent trumps her subsequent nonconsent.[5] This is not a good argument, but it is consistent with a general prohibition of all admittedly nonconsensual sexual relations.

It is arguable that force and nonconsent are not actually independent requirements in the (supposedly) conjunctive account. It is not clear whether a woman could consent if the man used what was regarded as the requisite forms of force or coercion. *Corpus Juris Secundum* says this: "The female must not at any time consent; her consent, given at any time prior to penetration, however *reluctantly* given, or if accompanied with mere verbal protests and refusals, prevents the act from being rape, *provided the consent is willing* and free of initial coercion."[6] The argument here is not that A's use of force is compatible with B's valid consent as the conjunctive account seems to imply, for the statement says that consent must be "willing and free of initial coercion." Rather, the argument seems to be that if A does not use considerable force, then we can assume that B does consent, albeit

---

[4] 1 Matthew Hale, *The History of the Pleas of the Crown* 629 (S. Emlyn [ed.] 1778). Although the marital exemption survived into the twentieth century, it probably did so for different reasons, for example, the difficulties in evaluating testimonial evidence, concerns about false accusations, and worries about introducing the prospect of criminal sanction into the marital relationship.

[5] It could be argued that the wife has agreed to have sexual relations on demand, but that she has not agreed to be *forced* to have sexual relations on demand. And it could be argued that even if the wife "owes" her availability to her husband, it does not follow that he has the right to take by force that which he is owed.

[6] 474 (emphasis added).

perhaps reluctantly. The presence of force precludes willing consent; the absence of force is evidence of willing consent.

To illustrate the point, consider a case in which a man does not use or threaten force, but a woman says no. So a woman who does not physically resist penetration while verbally expressing her dissent is behaviorally consenting to the penetration. To sustain a charge of rape, the offender was required to use a degree of physical force sufficient to overcome resistance or to use the "constructive force" of the threat of severe bodily injury.[7] Precisely because a woman of virtue would regard sexual relations with a man to whom she was not married to be abhorrent, it was assumed that penetration was voluntary unless the male had to overcome her resistance.[8]

There is an additional reason to think that the traditional account of rape is better understood as nonconsensual sex (for which the presence of force is not necessary) than on the conjunctive account, on which the presence of force is an independent requirement. For in common law and many statutes, force was required only "where the female is physically and mentally able to offer resistance..."[9] Rape could be committed without force on those who are not "capable of giving consent or exercising any judgment in the matter."[10] One need not use force or coercion to have intercourse with a woman who is "insane or idiotic" or with one who is unconscious because "drugged, intoxicated, or asleep."[11] In addition, sexual intercourse with a minor was generally illegal, although only children under ten were protected in the antebellum South.[12] This can easily be explained on a consent theory if we assume that the unconscious cannot token consent and that the insane or minors cannot give valid consent, but it cannot be explained on a definition of rape in which the use or threat of force is a necessary condition.

One thing is clear: the traditional law of rape defined sexual offenses in very narrow terms. The motivation for this narrow construction is less clear. It is often said that the traditional law of rape was misogynistically designed

---

[7] Susan Estrich, *Real Rape* (Cambridge, MA: Harvard University Press, 1987), 29. In the words of a Nebraska case, a woman was expected to display "utmost resistance" if she was to deny that she consented – "voluntary submission by the woman, while she has power to resist, no matter how reluctantly yielded, removes from the act an essential element of the crime of rape ... no matter how tardily given, or how much force had heretofore been employed ..."; *Matthews v. Nebraska*, 27 N.W. 234 (1886), 236.

[8] Joan McGregor, "Force, Consent, and the Reasonable Woman" in Jules Coleman and Allen Buchanan (eds.), *In Harm's Way* (Cambridge: Cambridge University Press, 1994), 239.

[9] *Corpus Juris Secundum*, 474.   [10] *Ibid.*, 468.   [11] *Ibid.*, 468.

[12] See Diane Miller Sommerville, "'I Was Very Much Wounded': Rape Law, Children, and the Antebellum South" in Merril Smith (ed.), *Sex without Consent* (New York: New York University Press, 2001), 136.

to give men relatively free rein for the exercise of sexual aggression while demonstrating little regard for a woman's bodily integrity (and no regard for their sexual agency).[13] But misogyny may only be a small part of the story. According to Ann Coughlin, the law's understanding of nonconsensual sex was directly tied to the extant social and legal condemnation of nonmarital consensual sex. It is not so much that the law of rape was designed to protect a woman's sexual autonomy, but performed the task inadequately. Rather, the law of rape was primarily designed to determine whether a woman should be *excused* for the wrongful action of adultery or fornication and thus not an appropriate candidate for criminal punishment.[14]

From this perspective, some traditional but waning features of rape law – the requirement that the perpetrator threaten bodily harm or death and the requirement that the victim actively resist her attacker rather than acquiesce – make some (perverse) sense. The criminal law allows a defendant to claim that he committed the (otherwise criminal) act under "duress," but the criteria for duress as a defense to a crime are generally quite stringent, much more stringent than the criteria for duress as a basis for invalidating a contract. The law expects one to endure more suffering when the alternative is to deflect one's suffering onto others than when the alternative is to suffer harm oneself. If a thug says "Sign this contract or I'll break your arm," the contract would be regarded as invalid. But if a thug says, "Drive my getaway car or I'll break your arm," B might well be found guilty of aiding a crime if she goes along.[15] So if a woman were ostensibly to commit the crime of fornication or adultery and then seek to show that she should be excused, she had better be prepared to show that she was under considerable duress. In principle, this view of rape does not persecute targets of sexual aggression to the advantage of the aggressor. The male is on the hook either way: if the female does not consent, he is a rapist; if she consents, he is a fornicator or adulterer.[16]

Was rape viewed as a serious matter? It is difficult to say. On the one hand, rape was typically punished by long prison sentences and was regarded as a capital offense in many states (a *wide* range of offenses were once punishable

---

[13] Anne Coughlin, "Sex and Guilt," 84 *Virginia Law Review* 1 (1998), 5.   [14] *Ibid.*, 8.

[15] For an extended discussion, see my *Coercion* (Princeton: Princeton University Press, 1987), chapter 8. "To overcome the will, so far as to render it incapable of contracting a civil obligation, is a mere trifle compared with reducing it to that degree of slavery and submission which will exempt from punishment"; *McCoy v. State*, 49 S.E. 768 (1887), 769.

[16] Else Hambleton observes that there was a risk to accusing a man of rape, for if the charge did not result in a conviction, a woman might be subsequently charged with fornication. See " 'Playing the Rogue': Rape and Issues of Consent in Seventeenth-Century Massachusetts" in Smith (ed.), *Sex without Consent*, 36.

by death).[17] On the other hand, some evidence suggests that there were relatively few prosecutions for rape. Only fourteen men were tried for rape in Massachusetts between 1630 and 1692.[18] In Pennsylvania, only fifty-six prosecutions for rape appear in court records between 1682 and 1800 – less than one prosecution per year.[19] Indeed, despite or perhaps because of the severe punishments for rape, it appears that courts were quite (too?) concerned to protect defendants against false accusations and wrongful convictions. In the (in)famous words of Lord Hale, rape "is an accusation easily to be made and hard to be proved, and harder to be defended by the party accused, tho never so innocent."[20] Although it is currently fashionable to dismiss worries about false accusations as male paranoia, it is arguable that the fear was not outrageous at the time. As Lisa Cuklanz puts it, "women had strong, socially based motivations to lie about rape…when a woman's character was so closely related to her reputation for chastity."[21] Moreover, and as I have noted, women who engaged in nonmarital sex were at risk for prosecution for fornication and a charge of rape was one of few available defenses.

Although I do not know of any systematic historical evidence about the frequency of false accusations, the intense concern about false accusations persisted well into the twentieth century. Many states adopted a "corroboration" rule: conviction on a rape charge required the testimony of an independent witness or physical evidence supporting the victim's claim, although it also appears that "the corroboration handicap meant that courts allowed prosecution evidence which was generally inadmissible in other crimes."[22] And the need for such rules was supported well into the twentieth century. A 1967 article in the *Columbia Law Review* maintains that the uncorroborated testimony of an alleged victim should not be accepted, because "stories of rape are frequently lies or fantasies."[23] Along similar lines,

---

[17] Stephen J. Schulhofer, *Unwanted Sex* (Cambridge, MA: Harvard University Press, 1998), 18. On the range of offenses punishable by death, see Stuart Banner, *The Death Penalty* (Cambridge, MA: Harvard University Press, 2002).

[18] Hambleton, "Playing the Rogue" in Smith (ed.), *Sex without Consent*, 28.

[19] Jack Marietta and G. S. Rowe, "Rape, Law, Courts, and Custom in Pennsylvania, 1682–1800" in Smith (ed.), *Sex without Consent*, 86.

[20] *Pleas of the Crown*, 635.

[21] Lisa Cuklanz, *Rape on Trial* (Philadelphia: University of Pennsylvania Press, 1996), 19. In addition, it seems that there was a common belief that rape charges were frequently used as a form of blackmail; Antony E. Simpson, "The 'Blackmail Myth' and the Prosecution of Rape and Its Attempt in 18th Century London: The Creation of a Legal Tradition," 77 *Journal of Criminal Law and Criminology* 101 (1986).

[22] See Hal Goldman, " 'A Most Detestable Crime': Character, Consent, and Corroboration in Vermont's Rape Law, 1850–1920" in Smith (ed.), *Sex without Consent*, 195.

[23] "Corroborating Charges of Rape," 67 *Columbia Law Review* 1137 (1967), 1138.

a 1952 article in the *Yale Law Journal* argued that women are frequently in denial about their own behavior, that women frequently believe that they do not (or did not) consent to sexual relations when their behavior (and unconscious desires) suggests otherwise, that their recall about their sexual behavior is "tailored to fit personality needs which become dominant after the act."[24]

At least on the surface, a good deal has changed. The past several decades have witnessed changes in the statutory definition of rape (or sexual crimes under different labels), changes in what is required and permitted as evidence, and increased attention to the phenomenon of date rape or acquaintance rape. The general thrust of the changes and proposals has been to relax the criteria for what constitutes a sexual crime, to create two-tiered or multi-tiered statutory distinctions among more serious and less serious sexual offenses, to make convictions for sexual crimes somewhat easier, and to make the legal process less burdensome for the victims.

Statutes

I will begin with the statutes. There is considerable variation among the statutes of the fifty states, although it is less clear to what extent statutory variation is associated with practical variation in the behavior of police, prosecutors, judges, juries, and citizens.[25] The marital exemption has been abolished in most places, although it survives in a few states for spouses living together (marital rape frequently involves separated couples).[26] In any case, I have seen no data on how many husbands are charged with or convicted for sexual offenses against their wives. As a matter of statutory law, it is simply not true, as Catharine MacKinnon has written, that "The law of rape divides women into spheres of consent according to indices of relationship to men."[27]

---

[24] "Forcible and Statutory Rape: An Exploration of the Operation and Objectives of the Consent Standard," 62 *Yale Law Journal* 55 (1952), 66.

[25] See David Bryden and Sona Lengnick, "Rape in the Criminal Justice System," 87 *Journal of Criminal Law and Criminology* 1194 (1997). In one experiment, George C. Thomas III and David Edelman found that there was no difference in artificial jury outcomes between cases in which A commits a sexual offense if he does not have explicit affirmative permission and cases that define the offense as nonconsensual intercourse. See "Consent to Have Sex: Empirical Evidence about 'No,'" 61 *University of Pittsburgh Law Review* 579 (2000).

[26] See Posner and Silbaugh, *A Guide to American Sex Laws*. It survives in Kentucky, South Carolina, and Texas.

[27] Catharine A. MacKinnon, *Toward a Feminist Theory of the State* (Cambridge, MA: Harvard University Press, 1989), 175. No statutes exempt defendants who have a nonmarital prior relationship or acquaintance with the victim.

The core of most current statutory definitions of rape is organized around either "forcible compulsion" or "consent," although some statutes continue to use the conjunctive phrase "forcibly *and* against her will."[28] As I suggested above, however, there is much less than meets the eye to the distinction between the forcible compulsion model and the consent model. Most "forcible compulsion" statutes also regard it as an offense to have sexual relations with someone who is unconscious, where force need not be used, or with those who are not competent to give consent. It is still true that in some states a man commits a felony against a woman who is capable of giving consent (adult, competent, and conscious) only if he uses or threatens physical force that is "likely to cause serious personal injury." Simple disregard of the victim's explicit refusal is not sufficient. But this does not show that force is required *in addition* to nonconsent. For as we have seen, it was once thought that if a woman did not *really* want to have sexual relations, then she would offer "utmost resistance" to her attacker, and acquiescence in the face of less force implied a form of tacit consent. Most states have now abandoned a statutory requirement of "utmost resistance" and some have explicitly abandoned the need for any resistance at all, although it is not clear to what extent fact finders implicitly continue to apply some sort of resistance standard.[29]

It is typically a felony to engage in sexual intercourse by way of a threat to use physical force even if no physical force is actually used.[30] What about threats of non-physical harm? Here there is greater variation. Arizona's statute makes reference to threats of force against "property." In Delaware and New Jersey, one commits a sexual offense if the offender instills the fear that if the sexual act is not performed, he will cause physical injury to any other person, cause damage to property, engage in other conduct constituting a crime, make statements (true or false) that would subject anyone

---

[28] Washington and Wisconsin make it a felony to have sexual penetration "without the victim's consent" where the consent must be "freely given," but leave the latter phrase undefined. Some states, such as Georgia, make it a felony to have sexual relations by force, but a misdemeanor to have sexual relations "without that person's consent," where what that entails is undefined. See Posner and Silbaugh, *A Guide to American Sex Laws*.

[29] Alabama defines forcible compulsion as that which would overcome "earnest resistance" and North Dakota requires a threat "that would render a person of reasonable firmness incapable of resistance". Alabama does not require actual resistance in the face of a threat (express or implied) of death or serious physical injury. On the other hand, New Mexico states that "physical or verbal resistance . . . is not an element of force or coercion." Vermont states that lack of consent "may be shown without proof of resistance." And Delaware states that the victim "need resist only to the extent that it is reasonably necessary to make the victim's refusal to consent known to the defendant"; *ibid*.

[30] Some statutes make explicit reference to other sorts of physical threats, for example, a threat to kidnap the target or anyone else, or to retaliate against the victim or another person in the future.

to hatred, contempt or ridicule, or "perform any other act which is calcu-
lated to harm another person materially with respect to his or her health,
safety, business, calling, career, financial condition, reputation, or personal
relationship."[31] Although it is not clear how these broadly worded statutes
have been implemented, they have the potential to criminalize a range of
sexual interactions that were historically immune from prosecution.

By contrast with the use of force and threats, it is generally not illegal to
secure consent to sexual relations by fraud, misrepresentation, or deceit.[32]
There are three major exceptions. First, it is a sexual offense in many states
to have sexual relations obtained by what is called *fraud in the factum*,
as when a woman gives a doctor permission to insert an instrument into
her vagina and he then inserts his penis. Second, it is a felony in several
states for a person infected with one of several sexually transmitted diseases
to engage in sexual relations without disclosing this information, although
some states limit this to HIV.[33] And in some states, it is a felony to obtain the
victim's consent by fraudulently inducing the belief that one is her husband,
although this provision is probably motivated by a desire to protect the
victim (and her husband) against an unwitting act of adultery rather than
fraudulently induced sexual relations, *per se*. These sorts of exceptions aside,
one does not commit a criminal offense if one induces another to engage in
sexual relations by lying about one's marital status, one's intentions, one's
identity, one's affections, one's economic status, or one's other relationships.
Caveat amator is the legal norm.

Most states also make special provision for various forms of "incompetence," broadly understood – incapacitation, mental deficiency, age, and
role or relationship. It is generally a felony to have sexual relations with a
woman who is mentally incapacitated, which is often taken to mean that
she is unconscious, whether the incapacity is induced coercively or fraudulently by the defendant or voluntarily self-induced by the woman herself.
For the most part, however, it is not illegal to have sexual relations with a
woman whose judgment is distorted by self-induced intoxication. There
are some exceptions. In some states, it is a felony to have sexual relations
when the victim "is prevented from resistance" by an intoxicating substance, but only if it were administered by the offender (Idaho) or without

---

[31] Indeed, it is a misdemeanor in Delaware to engage in *any* form of sexual contact that "is offensive to
the victim or occurs without the victim's consent." See Posner and Silbaugh, *A Guide to American
Sex Laws.*

[32] Alabama makes it a misdemeanor to obtain consent "by the use of any fraud or artifice."

[33] In some states, the victim's informed consent is not a defense to the charge. See Posner and Silbaugh,
A Guide to American Sex Laws.

the victim's knowledge or against her will (Delaware).[34] An Ohio statute makes it a felony to engage in sexual penetration when the offender knows that the "victim's ability to appraise the nature of or control her conduct is substantially impaired," although it is not clear how that provision is applied.

In most states, it is a criminal offense to have sexual relations with someone who is "incapable of consent" because she is "mentally defective." In some states the crucial terms are undefined. In other states, a victim has the relevant mental capacities only if she is "incapable of appraising the nature of the conduct."[35] On this criterion, a woman might lack the competence to make a contract, because she cannot understand its terms, but have the capacity to appraise the nature of sexual intercourse.[36] States vary with respect to the seriousness with which they view sexual relations with a mentally deficient person. In some states, such conduct can constitute a felony, but in other states, it is only a misdemeanor if sexual relations are otherwise consensual.[37]

Many (not all) states make specific provision for those who abuse a position of "trust or authority." Some states are quite specific, and refer to such positions as school employee, guardian, physician, foster parent, and prison employee. Several states make detailed provision concerning sexual relations between psychotherapists and patients, and some such provisions explicitly state that "consent is not a defense," in part because it is widely thought that psychotherapy patients are not capable of giving competent consent.[38] As a general proposition, then, many statutes recognize that even an unambiguous token of consent to sexual relations does not constitute giving *valid* consent to sexual relations.

And then, of course, there is (otherwise) consensual sexual relations with minors, where states have a varied and complicated array of provisions involving age, age spans, virginity, reasonable belief, and seriousness of the offense. In Michigan, it is a felony to engage in sexual relations with a person under sixteen. Period. In Alaska, it is a *felony* for a person sixteen or older to have sexual relations with a person fifteen or younger and at least

---

[34] Under some statutes, "administration of the substance without the woman's knowledge or consent is essential . . . where the female voluntarily drank the substance alleged to have excited or stupefied her . . . the act is not rape"; *Corpus Juris Secundum*, 483.

[35] See the Colorado statute as quoted in Posner and Silbaugh, *A Guide to American Sex Laws*, 10.

[36] Some statutes specifically build in the *mens rea* requirement of a sexual offense. In Michigan, it is an offense to have sexual relations with someone who is mentally incapable of giving consent only if the offender "knows that the person is mentally incapable"; *ibid.*, 18.

[37] See the West Virginia statute; *ibid.*

[38] See my *Exploitation* (Princeton: Princeton University Press, 1996), chapter 6.

three years younger than the offender, but a *misdemeanor* for a person *under* sixteen to have sexual relations with a person under *thirteen* and at least three years younger than the offender.[39] In Alaska, it is an affirmative defense that the offender believed the victim was of age to consent. By contrast, in Arkansas, whose statute is extremely complicated, sexual relations with a minor is a "strict liability" offense if the victim is under fourteen, but it is an "affirmative defense" that the offender reasonably believed the victim to be older than sixteen.[40] In two (southern) states, a male commits an offense under some age-related conditions only if the female is of "previous chaste character."[41]

Cases

There is always a gap between the law on the books and law in practice, but the gap may be particularly large with respect to rape. In some states, social changes have outpaced the statutes. It is difficult to believe, for example, that males in Florida are frequently, if ever, charged with having sexual relations with seventeen-year-old virgins. In other states, the statutory revisions may have outpaced social changes, defining nonconsensual sexual relations in broader terms than prosecutors and juries are willing to apply. Although the statutes enable us to see the principles that have guided legislatures, it will prove useful to examine the way in which some cases have been adjudicated.[42]

Consider *State v. Rusk*.[43] According to the complainant, Rusk met Pat in a bar and asked her to drive him back to his rooming house. He invited her to come into his apartment, and, when she declined, he took her car keys. Pat testified that she would have otherwise have been left alone in an unfamiliar neighborhood. After entering Rusk's apartment, Pat asked if she could leave, but Rusk said no. Instead, he pulled her onto the bed, began to undress her, and demanded that she remove the rest of her clothing. Pat says that she started to cry and that Rusk then choked her "lightly."[44] Feeling scared, she said, "If I do what you want, will you let me go?" When Rusk

---

[39] Eighteen–fourteen and twenty–fifteen would be a felony, but sixteen–fourteen would not. Fifteen–twelve and fourteen–ten are misdemeanors, but thirteen–eleven is not.

[40] Posner and Silbaugh, *A Guide to American Sex Laws.*   [41] Florida and Mississippi.

[42] Appellate courts may appear more "pro-defendant" than they really are. Because acquittals cannot be appealed, there will be no cases in which an appellate court rules that the jury wrongly acquitted.

[43] 424 A.2d 720 (1981).

[44] In describing cases and testimony, I will generally omit saying that a party "alleged" that something occurs. We should not necessarily assume that Rusk did choke Pat, although there is no reason to doubt that he did.

said yes, she performed oral sex on Rusk and they then had intercourse. At this point, Rusk said that Pat could leave, returned her keys, walked Pat to her car, and asked if he could see her again. Pat said that she agreed, but that she "had no intention of meeting him again." After a short while, she reported the incident to the police.

Rusk was convicted under a Maryland statute on which it is a felony to engage in sexual penetration "by force or threat of force against the will and without the consent of the victim." The Court of Special Appeals reversed the conviction, arguing that "force" is an essential element of the crime and there was insufficient evidence "that the victim resisted and her resistance was overcome by force or that she was prevented from resisting by threats to her safety." The court conceded that Rusk's possession of Pat's car keys "deterred her vehicular escape," but claimed that this did not deprive her of other options, such as seeking help in the rooming house or in the street.[45]

Rusk raises several issues, and it is important to distinguish between them. First, there is a question of fact. Not surprisingly, Rusk's story was different. Two witnesses (his friends) maintained that Rusk and Pat left the bar walking arm in arm. Rusk maintained that they engaged in petting in Pat's car after arriving at Rusk's apartment, and that she came up to his apartment willingly. He denied choking her or using any force or threats. Second, there are issues of statutory interpretation. Assuming Pat's version of the facts, we can ask whether Rusk had used the requisite level of force, given that he only choked her "lightly," given that he made no explicit threats to harm her physically, and given that she did not scream or physically resist or try to escape.

But this is to raise a third and normative issue: what sorts of threats *should* be sufficient to create a charge of rape? Statutes and court decisions have historically drawn a bright line between the threat of bodily injury and other threats, perhaps reflecting the view that "no fear justifies a woman's surrender of her body 'against her will,' except the fear of physical harm."[46] Whether we should accept that distinction is another matter altogether. Let us assume, arguendo, that Rusk did not use or threaten physical force, that he took Pat's car keys and told her that he would not return them unless she did what he wanted, and that Pat acquiesced because she was fearful of being stranded in a dangerous and unfamiliar area. The pre-reform view was that it is not rape "where the threats are merely to abandon the female in

---

[45] Rusk's conviction was subsequently reinstated by the Court of Appeals on the grounds that the question whether force was used was a matter of fact, not law, and was properly decided by the jury.

[46] "Forcible and Statutory Rape: An Exploration of the Operation and Objectives of the Consent Standard," 65.

the road after an automobile trip."[47] But this does not resolve the normative issue as to whether this *should be* the sort of threat that renders someone liable to conviction for a sexual offense.[48]

This normative is well illustrated in two other cases. In *State v. Thompson*, a high-school principal was convicted under a Montana "without consent" statute because he threatened to block a student's graduation if she did not submit to sexual intercourse.[49] The conviction was reversed on the grounds that the statute defines "without consent" as a case in which "the victim is compelled to submit by force or by threat of imminent death, bodily injury, or kidnapping..." The court indicated that while it would have been happy to apply a statute under which the alleged acts would qualify as an offense, Thompson was not guilty under the existing statute.

Commonwealth v. Milnarich concerned a fourteen-year-old girl who had been committed to a juvenile detention home and was subsequently placed in the defendant's home when he agreed to assume custody for her. The victim submitted to the defendant's sexual advances after he threatened to return her to the detention home if she refused. He was convicted on two counts: (1) corrupting the morals of a minor; (2) rape "by forcible compulsion."[50] Allowing the former conviction to stand, the court reversed the conviction on the rape charge, holding that the "forcible compulsion" provision required the use or threat of physical compulsion "sufficient to prevent resistance by a person of reasonable resolution." It rejected the definition on which the jury had been instructed to rely, namely, that forcible compulsion referred to "any threat... by physical, moral or intellectual means or by the exigencies of the circumstances."

It is not entirely clear whether the court was primarily concerned with the vagueness of this definition or that it might criminalize an excessively wide range of threats. The court implies that no sensible statute could seek to treat a woman's decision to engage in sexual intercourse in response to a threat to foreclose a mortgage as a case of nonconsensual sexual relations. Still, assuming statutes could be written and applied with sufficient precision, this case illustrates the question of precisely what sorts of threats *should* support an accusation of rape or sexual offense (whether subsumed under "forcible compulsion," "without consent" or some other phrase).

Returning to *Rusk*, we see that the case illustrates an issue that is arguably of particular importance in sexual crimes, namely, the relevance (if any) of the parties' beliefs. Pat claimed that she was scared by Rusk's behavior

---

[47] *Corpus Juris Secundum*, 482.
[48] I assume that he would be liable to prosecution for theft of her keys.
[49] *State v. Thompson*, 792 P.2d 1103 (1990).   [50] 498 A2d 395 (1985).

and facial expressions, that she feared for her life. Suppose this is true, but that Rusk had not used physical force, had made no explicit threats, and had not taken Pat's car keys. Rather, Rusk simply ignored her refusal, undressed her, and then penetrated her. Or suppose that Pat was afraid to *voice* her desire not to engage in sex just as any person might refuse to say no to a group of young males who said "may we please have your wallet?"[51] It is not particularly difficult to imagine cases in which a man does not threaten to cause physical harm if a woman resists his sexual advances, but to imagine that a woman fears that he would.[52] We could say that a woman is raped whenever she genuinely fears the relevant physical or nonphysical harm if she refuses.[53] The problem is that this approach would render defendants liable in cases where the woman is unreasonably although genuinely fearful or where the defendant may reasonably be unaware of the woman's unreasonable fear. On the other hand, we could follow *People v. Evans* and say that the defendant's statements or intentions should be controlling – "if he utters words which are taken as a threat . . . but are not intended as a threat . . . there would be no basis for finding the necessary criminal intent to establish culpability . . ."[54] The problem is that this view would exonerate defendants in cases where their statements or behavior would reasonably, even if falsely, be regarded as a threat and in which they are or should be aware that the woman may be acquiescing out of fear.[55]

If we look more closely at this controversy, it appears that we can distinguish between two questions: (1) has A engaged in nonconsensual sexual relations with B? and (2) is A culpable for engaging in nonconsensual sexual relations with B? The law typically distinguishes between (1) the *actus reus*

[51] Robin West argues that for sexual penetration to be successful "in spite of a woman's expressed 'no,' there must be an implied threat that the man would use a very real weapon, namely, his fists," a threat that looms large in the face of the typical differential in size and strength. Even if West is right, this leaves open the question of from whose perspective the threat is implied. See Panel Discussion, "Men, Women and Rape," 63 *Fordham Law Review* 125 (1994), 150.

[52] Mary Gaitskill reports on an encounter in which she asked a date what he was thinking and he responded "That if I wasn't such a nice guy, you could really be getting screwed." She subsequently had intercourse because she could not face the idea that "things might get ugly" if she refused; "On Not Being a Victim" from *Harper's*, March, 1994, reprinted in Adele Stan (ed.), *Debating Sexual Correctness* (New York: Delta, 1995), 259.

[53] As Joan McGregor puts it, "There are many circumstances where . . . many women would feel threatened and fearful, without displays of excessive physical force or explicit threats and in which women would submit to a sexual relationship against their will. A genuine violation or wrong would occur, one which the law ought to protect against." See "Force, Consent, and the Reasonable Woman" in Coleman and Buchanan (eds.), *In Harm's Way*, 340.

[54] 379 N.Y.S.2d 912 (1975), 921.

[55] As a Massachusetts court has said, it seems clearly wrong to define "non-consensual intercourse on the basis of the subjective (and quite likely wishful) view of the more aggressive player in the sexual encounter," *Commonwealth v. Sherry*, 437 N.E.2d 324 (1982), 326.

(the act itself) conditions of a crime, the overt conduct that is proscribed by the criminal law and (2) the *mens rea* (guilty mind) conditions of culpability, the mental states which, when conjoined with an unlawful act, render someone punishable as a criminal wrongdoer.

The distinction between *actus reus* and *mens rea* is neither sharp nor unproblematic. It depends, in part, on whether a crime is defined as a "basic intent" or "specific intent" offense. Suppose that A unintentionally takes B's raincoat from a coat rack because he confuses it with his own. If, as is typical, theft is a specific-intent offense, then A has taken B's raincoat without permission, but has not stolen it. If theft is a "basic intent" offense, then A has committed the *actus reus* of theft, but it might be thought that he should not be convicted because he lacks the relevant *mens rea*. In the final analysis, it does not matter much which definition we adopt if we agree about the moral and legal force of the relevant facts, namely, that it would be wrong to convict A of theft.

Consider the case of coerced prostitution, where C coerces B to engage in prostitution with a minimum number of persons per day. Does A commit the crime of having nonconsensual sexual relations with B? We might say that A does not commit the *actus reus* of rape because *he* does not coerce B into having sexual relations with him. Or, if rape is a basic-intent offense, we might say that A commits the *actus reus* of having nonconsensual sex with B because B's consent is coerced (albeit by *C*), but that A does not have the *mens rea* of rape. If we agree that A is not culpable of rape, then it does not matter much whether we *say* that A has committed the *actus reus* of rape, but lacks the relevant *mens rea*, or that A has not committed the *actus reus* of rape at all.

There are also numerous controversies about the relevant *mens rea* of sexual offenses. What, for example, should we say about mistakes about consent? Consider the infamous *Regina v. Morgan*, in which several defendants claimed that Morgan told them that they should have sex with his wife, that she would probably feign resistance, but that she actually wished to engage in sexual relations with them. The defendants' claim was trumped up, but suppose that Morgan had actually said this and that they believed it. Suppose as well that Mrs. Morgan did not consent, that her resistance was not feigned, and that the men had sexual intercourse with her despite her vociferous denials.[56] If A rapes B only when A intends to have sex with B without B's consent, then there is (arguably) no rape in this case. If A rapes B when B does not consent to sex with A, then the

---

[56] *Director of Public Prosecutions v. Morgan*, 2 All ER 347 (1975).

men committed the *actus reus* of rape, but there remained a question about *mens rea*. Assuming that the men genuinely believed that Mrs. Morgan was consenting, it could be argued that they are innocent even if their belief was unreasonable. Or it could be argued that they are guilty because it was reckless to ignore the possibility that their belief was false.

Returning to *Rusk* once again, we see that the case highlights a set of issues about evidence and proof that apply to all criminal cases, but which are often particularly salient in cases of sexual offenses. Whatever criteria we use to define a sexual offense, there is a distinction between (1) whether the relevant acts occurred and (2) evidence beyond a reasonable doubt that these events occurred. If, as in *Rusk*, force is a necessary condition of the crime, then the court was right to insist that "the evidence must warrant a conclusion" that the requisite force was used. So even if Rusk did use force, it is possible that "the State failed to prove the essential element of force beyond a reasonable doubt."[57]

Unfortunately, much that has been written on rape is surprisingly in-sensitive to the possibility that there are genuine problems of evidence and proof in cases of sexual offense. Many writers assume that the large pro-portion of offenses that do not result in arrests and convictions is primarily due to a misogynistic legal system.[58] Although the need for evidence that meets the relevant standard of proof pertains to any legal action, sexual offenses present special problems. First, unlike robbery (although like bur-glary), rape typically occurs in private, so there are rarely other witnesses. Second, unlike cases in which the victim is beaten, sexual offenders fre-quently use threats rather than actual force to subdue their victims, so there is often no physical evidence that a *violent* act occurred, even when there is evidence that intercourse occurred. Third, whereas few people consent to giving their wallets to strangers who approach them on the street, or to being beaten or killed (boxing and voluntary euthanasia aside), women frequently do consent to sexual relations with acquaintances al-though rarely with complete strangers. Given this, when the alleged rape occurs between acquaintances, it is often reasonable to take seriously the claim that intercourse was consensual. Fourth, defendants lie. And their lies take on particular importance in virtue of the previous factors, which

---

[57] *State v. Rusk* 424 A.2d 720 (1981), 727.
[58] In the words of Catharine A. MacKinnon, "When a rape prosecution is lost because a woman fails to prove that she did not consent, she is not considered to have been injured at all," *Toward a Feminist Theory of the State*, 180. But just as an acquittal on a homicide charge hardly demonstrates that the victim is not dead, we certainly need not believe that a woman has not been injured just because the fact finder concluded that the state did not prove that the defendant is guilty beyond a reasonable doubt.

makes it especially difficult to demonstrate beyond a reasonable doubt that they are lying. If I am right, women are the principal targets of a crime that presents a constellation of evidentiary difficulties that would result in the non-prosecution or acquittal of many guilty persons even in a world in which law-enforcement officials and jurors generally acted in good faith, which is, of course, not to say that they always do act in good faith.

Numerous commentators have argued that the corroboration and resistance requirements that once characterized many statutes stem from a male desire to protect themselves from criminal charges or from a misogynistic distrust of female veracity. Although there may be some truth to that view, these requirements also reflect genuine difficulties of proof. After all, even if a statute does not require corroboration by a witness or physical evidence, it will often be difficult for a jury to find "beyond a reasonable doubt" that a crime occurred solely on the basis of the victim's testimony in the face of a defendant's untruthful but plausible assertion. When the circumstances under which intercourse occurs are *clearly* nonconsensual, such as when the victim is unconscious or is accosted on the street and taken behind the bushes, then fact finders typically do not require much in the way of independent corroboration, or evidence of the use of force or resistance. But when the circumstances under which nonconsensual intercourse occurs are *not* unlike the contexts in which consensual intercourse often occurs, then even if no statute specifically requires physical force or resistance by the victim, fact finders will no doubt continue "to attach great weight...to the degree of force and resistance."[59] This is not because the absence of evidence of a "vigorous act of refusal" is evidence of the victim's positive consent, but because the lack of evidence of a vigorous act of refusal may lead a perfectly well-motivated fact finder to conclude that there is insufficient proof that she did not consent.[60]

Numerous commentators have also drawn special attention to an asymmetry between the way in which the legal system treats sexual offenses and robbery. Linda LeMoncheck notes that whereas rape victims were once routinely asked about their sexual history, "victims of robbery or mugging are not routinely asked such questions as 'Have you ever been robbed before?' 'Why didn't you take precautions?'"[61] Jeffrey Gauthier notes that "in contrast to other violent crimes such as robbery in which...the victim's

[59] Bryden and Lengnick, "Rape in the Criminal Justice System," 1291.
[60] Lani Anne Remick, "Read Her Lips: An Argument for a Verbal Consent Standard in Rape," 141 *University of Pennsylvania Law Review* 1103 (1993), 1111.
[61] Linda LeMoncheck, *Loose Women, Lecherous Men* (New York: Oxford University Press, 1997), 167.

consent . . . is deemed irrelevant," rape trials wrongly focus on the survivor's behavior.[62] Keith Burgess-Jackson asks why a prosecutor should have to prove that a rape victim did not consent, given that "no prosecutor has to prove beyond a reasonable doubt that a *robbery* victim did not consent to the taking of his or her money, or that a *murder* victim did not consent to being killed."[63]

For the most part, this complaint is silly. The absence of consent to a transfer of property is absolutely crucial to the crime of robbery or larceny and may well become crucial to a charge of murder if voluntary euthanasia is legalized. The issue of consent does not generally arise in robbery or murder cases because the circumstances in which robbery is alleged to have occurred are ones in which it is extremely unlikely that the transfer is consensual. A person is unlikely to hand over to a stranger a wallet full of cash, identification, and credit cards. But disputes about the (alleged) victim's consent can arise. If television court shows are any guide, there are frequent disputes among acquaintances about whether property was taken, loaned, or a gift. And if voluntary euthanasia should become legal, then there will no doubt be cases in which prosecutors will have to show beyond a reasonable doubt that the deceased did not give valid consent to be killed, given the defendant's claim that she did.

As I have noted, the claim that the victim consented is generally not regarded as plausible in stranger cases. As the legal system has broadened its conception of sexual offenses and is more open to cases involving acquaintances, there will be more evidentiary problems about consent. There are good probabilistic or evidentiary grounds for thinking that women are more likely to consent to sexual relations with men that they know reasonably well than with strangers or those they have just met. For American women do frequently consent to sexual relations with acquaintances, sometimes happily, sometimes less so, and sometimes when the acquaintanceship has been of very brief duration. It is not surprising, then, that in situations resembling the stereotypical sexual attack by a stranger, fact finders are apt to presume that the woman's submission was not consensual and that "courts hardly ever require resistance to strangers."[64] By contrast, when nonconsensual sexual relations occur in situations similar to those in which women frequently consent to sexual relations, it is not so easy to

---

[62] Jeffrey Gauthier, "Consent, Coercion, and Sexual Autonomy" in Keith Burgess-Jackson (ed.), *A Most Detestable Crime: New Philosophical Essays on Rape* (New York: Oxford University Press, 1990), 74.

[63] Keith Burgess-Jackson, "A History of Rape Law" in Burgess-Jackson (ed.), *A Most Detestable Crime*, 21.

[64] David P. Bryden, "Redefining Rape," 3 *Buffalo Criminal Law Review* 317 (2000), 366.

conclude that sex was nonconsensual, particularly if the defendant lies or is in denial.

We can make a similar point about the long-standing but presently waning tendency of the judicial system to allow inquiries into the sexual history of the complainant. Although there may be very good policy reasons for states to adopt "shield laws" that preclude questions about the complainant's sexual history (principally to minimize the disincentive for victims to come forward), it is by no means clear that a complainant's sexual habits "have no significant probative value in determining whether she consented."[65] For if the defendant maintains that the complainant consented to sexual relations, and there is little corroborative evidence to the contrary, it is not crazy to suppose that the defendant's story is *more likely* to be true when the complainant frequently engages in casual sex than when she does not.

Legal scholarship and the definition of sexual offenses

Legal scholars have spilled considerable ink developing what they take to be improved models for the law of sexual offenses. There are two questions that we can ask about a model or proposed statute: (1) is it conceptually sound? does the model or statute capture or reflect the moral values at stake? and (2) what are its behavioral consequences in terms of those moral values? These are distinct questions. For all we know, statutory language that makes the most conceptual and moral sense is more likely to be misapplied or misunderstood by the relevant parties than language that is conceptually less defensible. It is also possible that differences in statutory language make no significant difference at all, despite the intensity with which legal scholars advocate one view or another. This is an empirical question about which we have little information.

Consider a case in which the defendant approached a woman on a bicycle, engaged her in conversation, told her that his girlfriend was not satisfying his needs, then carried her into the woods, where she was told to unzip her pants, which she did, and to perform an act of fellatio upon him, which she also did.[66] The complainant maintained that she did not resist or scream because she feared for her safety, particularly in light of the defendant's statement, "I don't want to hurt you," the disparity in their size and strength, and the seclusion of the woods. The defendant was convicted,

[65] Bryden and Lengnick, "Rape in the Criminal Justice System," 1295.
[66] *People v. Warren*, 446 N.E.2d 591 (1983).

but his conviction was reversed on the grounds that the state had not proven that he used force or threat as required by the statute.

Stephen Schulhofer has argued that this case demonstrates the inadequacy of a "force"-based definition of sexual offenses and the need for a definition based on sexual autonomy and consent. Maybe yes, maybe no. The jury did convict, and appellate courts rarely reverse convictions in stranger-rape cases on such grounds, so the decision may be quite atypical. Although a consent-based definition of sexual offense may be conceptually superior to a force-based definition, it is also possible that the judges were the problem, not the statute.[67]

Others have argued that a "consent" statute does not necessarily do much better. Consider the infamous Texas case in which a man entered the victim's dwelling and then demanded sex at knife point. Fearful of contracting a sexually transmitted disease, the victim persuaded the assailant to wear a condom. A Texas grand jury initially refused to indict because it construed the victim's request as evidence that the sexual act did not occur "without [the victim's] consent." This prompts Joan McGregor to ask: "What moral work does consent do if circumstances such as this one could be seen as consensual?"[68] That the consent standard was misapplied in this case does not show that the grand jury would have been more likely to indict the offender under a different model or statute.[69]

Because my purposes are philosophical rather than practical, I want to see what we can learn from the debate among legal scholars about how we should conceptualize morally and legally impermissible sex. One finds in the literature five prominent models of sexual offenses: force, consent, autonomy, property, and (what I shall call) consent-plus. There are, of course, important variations within the framework of some of these models, but each puts a central idea or label at the core of its understanding of sexual offenses. I shall argue that the "force" account of sexual offenses is not a serious contender, and that there are no significant distinctions between the consent, autonomy, and property models. So we will be left with a choice between a consent model and a consent-plus model.

As we have seen, the first model purports to limit the scope of sexual offense among competent adults primarily to the use or threat of physical

---

[67] "[W]ith the same judges, in the same eras, analogous bad decisions might have been handed down under any alternative rule," Bryden, "Redefining Rape," 362.
[68] Joan McGregor, "Why When She Says No She Doesn't Mean Maybe and Doesn't Mean Yes: A Critical Reconstruction of Consent, Sex, and the Law," 2 *Legal Theory* 175 (1996), 175.
[69] If the jury did not indict because it disbelieved the complainant's account of the event, then the problem is not with the consent standard.

force. There are few contemporary defenders of this model, but Norman Podhoretz has criticized what he takes to be the misguided feminist-inspired effort to expand the scope of sexual offenses:

The definition of rape, which has in the past always been understood to mean the use of violence or the threat of it to force sex upon an unwilling woman, is now being broadened to include a whole range of sexual relations that have never before in all of human experience been regarded as rape.[70]

As history, Podhoretz is wrong. It has long been regarded a crime to have sexual intercourse with a woman who is unconscious or drugged, severely retarded, or under age. So force has never been a *necessary* condition of a sexual offense, and I doubt that Podhoretz would want to require it. And if one wants to make the linguistic point that we should restrict the term "rape" to those offenses that involve the use or threat of physical force, that leaves entirely open the question whether rape, so defined, exhausts the category of acts that should be regarded as sexual offenses. And while Podhoretz may be right to note that some contemporary proposals seek to criminalize a range of sexual relations that "have never before in all of human experience been regarded as rape," that is precisely the point of those proposals, and is not an (independent) argument against them.

The second model shifts and broadens the focus from the presence of forcible compulsion to the absence of consent. Since I shall be defending and developing this model at great length, I shall say little here about its attractions. Rather, I want to note some of the objections that have been raised against it. It has been argued that "consent" is too vague to be meaningful, that the model fails to specify with sufficient precision just what actions are prohibited. It is also argued that the consent model has untoward consequences, that it wrongly provides "an invitation to put the victim on trial and divert attention from the defendant's misconduct."[71] For if consent refers to a person's beliefs, desires, or intentions, as some have argued, then one cannot determine whether a woman consents to sexual relations without an intrusive investigation into her psychology.[72]

Are these good reasons to reject the consent model? For the most part, I think not. Whether a consent model can overcome the objection that it is too indeterminate or is more indeterminate than other models is a question

---

[70] Norman Podhoretz's response to comments on his "Rape in Feminist Eyes," *Commentary Magazine*, March 1993, page 7.

[71] Schulhofer, *Unwanted Sex*, 22.

[72] Donald Dripps, "Beyond Rape: An Essay on the Difference between the Presence of Force and the Absence of Consent," 92 *Columbia Law Review* 1780 (1992), 1798.

that we will have to resolve. If (as I shall argue) consent – as such – does not refer to a state of mind, the last objection can be set aside. But the claim that a consent model wrongly focuses on the behavior of the victim rather than that of the defendant is twice wrong. First, to the extent that a case raises a serious question as to whether the victim did provide what I shall call a "token of consent," then the contrast between assessing A's culpability and investigating B's conduct is a false contrast. After all, if A is culpable because he had sexual relations with B without B's consent, then we cannot assess A's culpability without inquiring into B's behavior. True, there will be many cases where there is no reason to inquire extensively into the victim's actions or her psychology, as in a violent rape by a stranger, because it is implausible to suppose that she tokened consent or because the defendant's actions essentially *preclude* her (valid) consent. In other cases, however, it may not be obvious whether B tokened consent, and A's culpability will inevitably turn, in part, on whether there was consent or whether it was reasonable for him to believe that there was. This worry about consent is unwarranted for a second reason. I shall argue below that the crucial question in most cases is not whether B tokens consent, but whether A's behavior renders B's consent *invalid*, whether, for example, B's token of consent is offered in response to A's impermissible threat; so the consent model will, in fact, focus attention on A's behavior rather than B's.

In his important book *Unwanted Sex*, Stephen Schulhofer develops a third model of sexual offense. He argues that the law should provide "comprehensive protection" for a woman's sexual autonomy. We should protect her (negative) autonomy to refuse sexual contact and her (positive) autonomy to engage in sexual relations with other willing partners. And we should protect her autonomy in the same way that we protect "property, labor, informational privacy, the right to vote, and every other right that is central to the life of a free person."[73]

Although Schulhofer uses the language of "autonomy" rather than "consent," there is nothing philosophical at stake between the consent model and the autonomy model. In effect, autonomy refers to the *value* that is to be protected, whereas consent refers to the *means* for protecting and promoting that value: we protect a person's autonomy by prohibiting actions to which she does not consent and empowering her to engage in actions to which she does consent. If "an individual violates a woman's autonomy when he engages in sexual conduct without ensuring that he has her

---

[73] Schulhofer, *Unwanted Sex*, x.

valid consent," then the models are not just functionally or extensionally equivalent. They are identical.[74]

To avoid what he takes to be serious defects in the consent model, Donald Dripps has proposed that we understand a person's sexuality as a commodity or self-owned form of property. On this view, a person's "sexual cooperation is a service, much like any other, which individuals have a right to offer for compensation, or not, as they choose."[75] Within the framework of this admittedly "unromantic" view of sexuality, Dripps distinguishes two offenses: one commits "sexually motivated assault" when one uses violence or the threat of violence to engage in sexual acts; one commits "sexual expropriation" when one engages in a sexual act "knowing that the other person has expressed a refusal to engage in that act," or, if one prefers, knowing that the other person has not expressed a willingness to engage in that act.[76]

Dripps argues that the sexual motivation of an assault warrants enhancing what would otherwise be a simple assault to an aggravated assault, and, when accompanied by a sexual expropriation itself, justifies using the penalties "traditionally applied to rape." Just as robbery (force + taking property) might be punished more severely than assault (force or threat of force) or larceny (taking property), a sexually motivated assault (force + sexual expropriation) should be punished more severely than assault *simpliciter* (threat) or a sexual expropriation (a nonviolent sexual taking), and a sexual battery (beating + sexual appropriation) should be punished more severely than a simply battery (beating).[77]

There are several apparent advantages to the property approach. It utilizes and extends legal models (for example, theft and contracts) that are exceptionally well developed. As with the consent and autonomy models, it provides the conceptual space for a broader account of sexual offense. For example, one can use the crime of larceny as a model for some nonconsensual sexual acts that do *not* involve the use of force, such as engaging in a sexual act with an unconscious person.[78] The property model also makes it relatively easy to consider deception as an impermissible strategy for expropriating sexual relations, although Dripps prefers not to go down this road. After all, given that the law criminalizes a "fairly broad range" of deceptive

---

[74] *Ibid.*, 111.   [75] Dripps, "Beyond Rape," 1786.   [76] *Ibid.*, 1804.

[77] *Ibid.*, 1798. On this view, one who threatens violence in order to engage in a sexual act but (for some reason) does not complete the sexual act has committed a sexually motivated assault but not a sexual expropriation. On Dripps's view, such an act should be punished more severely than a (nonviolent) sexual expropriation, just as attempted murder might be punished more severely than successful battery, even though an attempted murder causes no harm to the intended victim.

[78] Although the wording of Dripps's definition of sexual expropriation does not cover this case, this defect is easily correctable.

strategies that are used to expropriate property with another's apparent (but arguably invalid) consent, the model encourages us to consider whether the same principles should apply to sexual acts.[79]

Dripps's model has been critiqued in terms of some of its specific claims and on more general theoretical grounds. I will first consider the distinction between sexually motivated assault and sexual expropriation. Although Robin West acknowledges that there may be a distinction between a sexually motivated assault and sexual expropriation, she rejects the view that the latter is nonviolent. She argues that any penetration of a woman who has expressed a refusal is a violent act, that it always involves (1) the violence and pain of penetration, and (2) the threat of future violence if the victim fails to acquiesce.[80] Both claims seem doubtful. Although there is probably a strong negative correlation between the pain of penetration and the desire for penetration, I see no reason to think that the purely physical act of penetration itself *must* be particularly painful just because sex is unwanted, just as penetration may be quite painful even when sex is wanted.[81] And if we regard sexual acts on an unconscious woman as constituting sexual expropriation or if a man could coerce a woman into sexual relations by means of nonphysical threats (such as blocking graduation or leaving the victim stranded), then sexual expropriation simply does not require a threat of present or future physical violence.

It might be objected that these forms of sexual appropriation should be understood as acts of *violence*, even if not physical violence, because they involve a *violation* of the victim. But this linguistic move solves nothing. Even if we think of all violations as a kind of violence, we still have the distinction between the violence of violations that involve physical violence in addition to the act of penetration and the violence of violations that do not. So the distinction between violent and nonviolent offenses would reappear in other terms.[82]

---

[79] Coughlin, "Sex and Guilt," 19.

[80] Panel Discussion, "Men, Women and Rape," 63 *Fordham Law Review* 125 (1994), 150. West maintains that for a "nonviolent" penetration to be successful, there must be an implied threat that the man would use his fists. I do not know whether this is true.

[81] We can imagine an offender saying: "You and I are going to play a game. We are going to have sex and I want you to act like you are enjoying it. I will do everything I know how to do to make the sex as pleasurable as possible. I'd be happy to provide some K-Y jelly if it will make penetration less painful. Otherwise, I will kill you with this gun." In *New Jersey in the interest of M.T.S*, the court held that the statutory requirement of physical force was met by the force involved in penetration itself; 129 N.J. 422 (1992), 443. Although it might be best to eliminate a force requirement, this interpretation of a force requirement seems odd.

[82] The critique of the distinction between violence and nonviolence has nothing to do with the property model. It would apply to any theory that seeks to distinguish levels of sexual offense. For such a critique, see Kit Kinports, "Rape and Force: The Forgotten Mens Rea," 4 *Buffalo Criminal Law Review* 755 (2001), 795.

The more general criticisms of the property model are principally aesthetic and phenomenological. Joan McGregor argues that the sexual expropriation model paints "a distorted and alienated view of sexual relationships" because sexual relations have little in common with goods that are exchanged in the market.[83] Along similar lines, Robin West says that if we treat sexuality as a commodity, we "objectify our sexual selves," and that the "theft analogy wildly misdescribes the experience of rape."[84] Echoing these sentiments, Elizabeth Anderson argues that by treating sexuality as "just another form of property," we cannot understand the experience of rape as a "deeper violation of the self than robbery."[85]

I would not reject the property model for these reasons. It need not treat a woman's sexuality as "just another kind of property." Just as we distinguish between property crimes in terms of the *amount* of property (grand theft, petty larceny), we can also distinguish between *kinds* of property, and, in particular, between material property and "personal" property. After all, it is often argued that a woman has the right to choose abortion on the grounds that she owns her body, that her body is a form of property over which she should be able to exercise control. When push comes to shove, the distance between the (ugly) property model and the (attractive) autonomy model is not very great. In defending her "autonomy" model of sexual offense, Jane Larson refers to nonconsensual sex as an act of "bodily and sexual dispossession: the aggressor appropriates the victim's body and sexuality for his own purposes."[86] Indeed, when West herself writes that women lack "full contractual autonomy or 'sovereignty' over their own sexuality" she, too, invokes language not dissimilar from the property model she claims to be rejecting.[87]

Although I do not think that the property model is vulnerable to the criticisms that have been advanced against it, I also believe that its supposed advantages are spurious because it is ultimately indistinguishable from the

---

[83] McGregor, "Why When She Says . . . ," 190.

[84] Robin West, "Legitimating the Illegitimate: A Comment on 'Beyond Rape,'" 93 *Columbia Law Review* 1442 (1993), 1448, 1451.

[85] Elizabeth Anderson, *Value in Ethics and Economics* (Cambridge, MA: Harvard University Press, 1993), 155. Anderson's remarks are offered in the context of a general critique of the commodification of sexuality, and are not directed at Dripps's argument.

[86] On Larson's view, sexual autonomy includes "bodily integrity, sexual self-possession, and sexual self-governance"; Jane E. Larson, "'Woman Understand So Little, They Call My Good Nature "Deceit"': A Feminist Rethinking of Seduction," 93 *Columbia Law Review*, 374 (1993), 425.

[87] Dripps himself now suggests that he could have referred to his view as the "entitlement theory." "For a Negative, Normative Model of Consent, with a Comment on Preference-Skepticism," 2 *Legal Theory* 113 (1996), 120. Dripps says, self-mockingly, that he would have used this terminology had he not been such a "blockhead."

consent or autonomy models with which it is sometimes contrasted. Dripps says that a consent or autonomy model requires us to focus on the victim's behavior rather than on the culpability of the defendant's conduct, but that his approach avoids this.[88] There are two problems here. First, I do not see how the property model allows us to ignore the behavior of the victim. Just as we have to determine if a transfer of ordinary property or services is consensual before we can regard it as theft, we must make a similar determination about sexual expropriation. If one engages in sexual expropriation when one knows "that the other person has expressed a refusal to engage in that act," one is not guilty of such conduct unless the other person "has expressed a refusal to engage in that act," that is, has refused to consent. Second, the claim that the consent model focuses on the victim is mistaken. For, as I have suggested (and will subsequently argue at greater length), the crucial question is typically not whether the victim manifests some token of consent ("If I do what you want, will you let me go?"). Rather, the crucial question is whether the *conditions* under which B manifests a token of consent renders her consent valid or invalid, and this turns primarily on the defendant's conduct.

I have argued that there are no significant differences between the consent model, the autonomy model, and the sexual expropriation model. There is, however, a more distinct rival to the consent model. The literature on sexual offenses contains several examples of what I shall call a "consent-plus" model, all of which take the view that what might ordinarily or plausibly be regarded as consent is necessary but not sufficient to immunize a sexual act from wrongness or illegality. By consent-plus, I do not have in mind "right-wing" arguments that would prohibit consensual homosexuality, fornication, sodomy, and the like, although such views fit the structure of the model. Rather, I have in mind "left-wing" arguments that maintain that something like mutuality or equality or communication or the absence of exploitation is needed to legitimize a sexual relationship.[89] A consent-plus model does *not* merely claim that a consensual sexual relationship can be morally unworthy or "bad." A consent theorist could easily grant that. A consent-plus theory maintains that what is ordinarily regarded as a consensual relationship might be justifiably prohibited by law or regarded as morally impermissible.

[88] Panel Discussion, "Men, Women and Rape," 63 *Fordham Law Review* 125 (1994), 163.
[89] Lois Pineau emphasizes the importance of communication in "Date Rape," 8 *Law and Philosophy* 217 (1989), reprinted in Leslie Francis (ed.), *Date Rape* (University Park, PA: Penn State University Press, 1996). Martha Chamallas emphasizes the importance of mutuality and equality in "Consent, Equality, and the Legal Control of Sexual Conduct," 61 *Southern California Law Review* 777 (1988).

What I call the "plus" factor can enter the model in two ways. One could use a modest view of what counts as valid consent and then insist that consent is not sufficient to render the sexual act legally or morally permissible. On this view, for example, one *can* give perfectly valid consent to a sexual act in a highly unequal or exploitative relationship, but such consent is not sufficient to legitimize the act. On a second approach, one builds the "plus" into one's account of consent, arguing that what is regarded as consensual on the modest view of consent should not be so regarded. On this view, significant inequality between the parties makes "genuine" or valid consent impossible.

Ultimately, it does not matter much whether the "plus" conditions are added on to valid consent or built into the conditions of valid consent. The two approaches are extensionally equivalent with respect to the conditions under which sexual relations are morally or legally permissible. But we cannot say whether the view is attractive until we consider what it would mean to consent to sexual relations and what reasons there are for thinking that consent legitimizes a sexual relation. I will return to those questions below. But to adumbrate that discussion, I will argue that if we are to respect people's positive autonomy to engage in sexual relations, we should not require much more than reasonably modest consent, although we may disagree about what counts as reasonably modest consent.

CHAPTER THREE

The psychology of sex

Why start with sex?

The discussion of the law in chapter two helps to frame the issues that motivate the need for a theory of consent to sexual relations. I suppose that one might launch directly into an analysis of consent. I prefer to begin with sex. Not because sex is more interesting than consent, although that is no doubt true. I begin with sex because the principles of valid consent must attend to the object of consent.

Why is there a problem of consent to sexual relations in the first place? Consent to sexual relations is an issue precisely because people do not always want to engage in sexual relations and because unwanted or nonconsensual sex is experienced aversively. If females were virtually always desirous of engaging in sexual relations with any other human being at any time, we would not have a problem of consent. If, as with some animals, males only desired sex when females were receptive, we would not have a problem of consent. If females did not experience undesired sex as acutely aversive, we would not have a problem of consent. To understand why consent is an issue and to understand what might and might not be plausible responses to that issue, we must attend to some fundamental differences between men and women in the way they are disposed to think and act with respect to sex and to the causal basis of those differences. In this chapter, I seek to sketch out some very basic claims about sexual behavior, sexual psychology, and evolutionary psychology.

Sexual desire, sexual activity, and sexual experience

I begin by distinguishing between sexual desire, sexual activity, and sexual experience. Following Alan Goldman, I understand sexual desire in simple terms, as the "desire for contact with another person's body and for the pleasure which such contact produces." I shall refer to sexual activity as activity "which tends to fulfill such desires..."[1] And we can understand sexual experience as the concurrent (and retrospective) phenomenology of sexual activity. One can desire sexual activity that does not occur and one can engage in (or be subject to) sexual activity that one does not desire. In addition, positively desired sexual activity may not produce the expected positive experience and undesired sexual activity can produce positive sexual experience.[2]

We cannot speak about the content of these categories with too much confidence. As Thomas Nagel observes, we have a "limited supply of information" about each other's sexual psychology.[3] The supply of accurate information is limited because our sexual lives are not entirely transparent to ourselves, because we find it difficult to communicate openly about these matters, and because we have a limited capacity to get inside another's experience. Comparative phenomenology is always a tricky business, and it may be especially tricky with respect to sex. I am not sure that anchovy likers can understand the experience of anchovy haters, and vice versa. But even when two persons both like anchovies, we have no reason to think that their experience is identical. So, too, with sexual desire and sexual experience. We know enough to say some things with considerable confidence, but we must be cautious.

Male/female differences

In what follows, I shall make some general remarks about the psychology of sexual relations, but my main objective is to highlight some crucial differences between males and females.[4] For the core problems about consent to sexual relations stem from the fact that some men desire sexual relations with females who do not desire sexual relations with them.

There are two distinct issues. First, we must ask whether there are any general differences between males and females with respect to sexual psychology and behavior. Second, we must try to explain those differences. Texans and Vermonters speak with different accents, but no one claims that these differences are rooted in biology. I shall suggest that biology probably plays an important role in explaining psychological differences

---

[1] Alan Goldman, "Plain Sex," 6 *Philosophy & Public Affairs* 267 (1977), 268.
[2] The canonical illustration is the scene in *Gone with the Wind* in which Scarlett O'Hara appears to have enjoyed being "raped" by Rhett Butler.
[3] Thomas Nagel, "Personal Rights and Public Space," 24 *Philosophy & Public Affairs* 83 (1995), 100.
[4] As Catharine A. MacKinnon remarks "women and men live in different cultures" with respect to sex; *Toward a Feminist Theory of the State* (Cambridge, MA: Harvard University Press 1989), 177.

between males and females and that a sound approach to consent to sexual relations will be responsive both to the fact of difference and to the best explanation for it.

To begin with two truisms: first, sexual desire, behavior, and experience are diverse phenomena. There is a wide range of sexual thoughts, sexual perceptions, sexual motivations, and sexual activities.[5] Males and females may be more alike in some dimensions than in others. Second, although there may be "average" differences between males and females in many dimensions, there is a wide range of differences between individuals. In statistical language, there are overlapping curves on many variables. Men are, on average, taller than women, but many women are taller than many men. Men have, on average, more sexual thoughts than women, but some women have more sexual thoughts than some men. Still, the differences between males and females are important and they account for the fact that consent to sexual relations concerns female consent.

Thinking and perceiving

Schopenhauer no doubt had men in mind when he said that the sexual impulse "constantly lays claim to half the powers and thoughts of the younger portion of mankind," although I do not know whether he had the fraction exactly right. Compared with females, males have more sexual thoughts per day and spend more minutes per day thinking about sex. Males are more responsive to or aroused by visual sexual phenomena than females. Males are more likely to leer or "turn their heads" as women pass by.[6] Males are more prone to be sexually aroused by the sight of female genitals than women are aroused by the sight of male genitals, so it is not surprising that pornography is primarily directed at and consumed by males.[7] There are also differences between males and females with respect to the characteristics that they seek in mates. Males are attracted to the young and the beautiful, whereas females are attracted to older men and

---

[5] See Edward O. Laumann, John H. Gagnon, Robert T. Michael, and Stuart Michaels, *The Social Organization of Sexuality* (Chicago: University of Chicago Press, 1994), 3.

[6] " 'Look out,' Frances said as they crossed Eighth Street. 'You'll break your neck.' Michael laughed and Frances laughed with him. 'She's not so pretty,' Frances said . . . Michael laughed again. 'How did you know I was looking at her?' . . .'Mike, Darling . . .' " See "The Girls in Their Summer Dresses," a poignant 1929 short story by Irwin Shaw.

[7] Donald Symons, *The Evolution of Human Sexuality* (New York: Oxford University Press, 1979), 27. Symons notes that there are fewer differences between males and females with respect to their response to the viewing of an actual sexual encounter.

seek economic resources, relative power, intelligence, and commitment. Both sexes seek trophies, but their trophies have different characteristics.[8]

Sexual desire

It appears that males and females differ less in their psychological and physiological responses *during* sexual activity than with respect to their anticipatory *desire for* sexual activity.[9] It is often noted that females have a capacity for multiple orgasms. True, but misleading. It is misleading because females have fewer orgasms than males, even given their capacity for multiple orgasms and because the enjoyment *of* sexual relations is not identical to the desire *for* sexual relations, and there seems to be no gainsaying the latter difference.[10] It is an interesting question why people's *ex ante* demand or desire for an activity does not entirely track their *ex post* satisfaction from it. But it appears not to do so.

The gap between male and female sexual desire seems to apply across the whole range of sexual phenomena, be it vaginal intercourse, watching one's partner undress, receiving or giving oral sex, group sex, watching other people do sexual things, and so on.[11] This tendency holds for virtually every activity in virtually every age group. It also appears that males have a much greater preference for *variety* among sexual partners than do females.[12] And, of course, there is the well-established male/female difference with respect to autoerotic activity as parodied in the "Contest" episode of *Seinfeld*.[13]

---

[8] Douglas T. Kenrick, Melanie R. Trost, and Virgil L. Sheets, "Power, Harassment, and Trophy Mates: The Feminist Advantage of an Evolutionary Perspective" in David M. Buss and Neil M. Malamuth (eds.), *Sex, Power, Conflict* (New York: Oxford University Press, 1996), 48.

[9] Symons, *The Evolution of Human Sexuality*, 179.

[10] Linda R. Hirshman and Jane E. Larson observe that heterosexual intercourse is "still more satisfying for men than for women," that 75% of men and only 19% of women report always reaching orgasm. *Hard Bargains* (New York: Oxford University Press, 1998), 229.

[11] Laumann et al., *The Social Organization of Sexuality*, 150.

[12] Thus the reference to the "Coolidge effect." The story is told that President Calvin Coolidge and the first lady were being given separate tours of newly formed government farms. Upon passing the chicken coops and noticing a rooster vigorously copulating with a hen, Mrs. Coolidge inquired about the frequency with which the rooster performed this duty. "Dozens of times each day," replied the guide. Mrs. Coolidge asked the guide to "please mention this fact to the president." When the president passed by later and was informed of the sexual vigor of the rooster, he asked, "Always with the same hen?" "Oh, no," the guide replied, "a different one each time." "Please tell *that* to Mrs. Coolidge," said the President. There is some evidence that whereas women have extramarital affairs when they are dissatisfied with their relationship, men who have affairs are no more unhappy with their marriage than men who do not. See Symons, *The Evolution of Human Sexuality*, 90.

[13] Laumann et al., *The Social Organization of Sexuality*, 135. In this episode Jerry, George, and Kramer decide to have a contest as to who can go the longest without masturbating. Elaine asks to enter the competition. The men tell her that this is not fair, that it is not as much of a problem for women as for men. To compensate for the higher probability of victory, they demand that she put twice as much money into the pool as they do.

Male/female differences with respect to oral sex are particularly interesting for analytical purposes, because performing and receiving are discrete activities with their own utilities. It appears that oral sex is a sacrifice for many women, but not for many men. Whereas 45 percent of males like to receive oral sex, only 17 percent of females like to perform oral sex, creating an aggregate deficit of 28 percent.[14] By contrast, whereas 29 percent of females like to receive oral sex, 34 percent of males like to perform it, creating an aggregate surplus of 5 percent.

The general point about male/female differences should not be exaggerated. Females desire and enjoy sexual relations. And some females have a greater desire for sexual relations than do their regular partners. But the problem of consent arises because there are *differences* with respect to sexual desire, and it is those differences that I mean to highlight here. With respect to sexual intercourse, the data are unequivocal. Males desire more sexual intercourse than females. A study of married couples demonstrates that 14 percent of men complain that their wives withhold sex during the first year of marriage, whereas only 4 percent of women voice a similar complaint. Four years later, 43 percent of men complain that sexual intercourse is too infrequent, whereas 18 percent of women voice that complaint. Men consistently evaluate withholding of sex by their partners more negatively than women.[15] Anthropologist Bronislaw Malinowski maintained that young Trobriand Island women enjoyed sex as much as men, but he also reports that Trobriand males give small presents to their lovers, and if they had little or nothing to offer, the women refused their sexual advances.[16] Actions speak louder than words. Among virtually all cultures at all times, "copulation is considered to be essentially a service or favor that women render to men, and not vice versa, regardless of which sex derives or is thought to derive greater pleasure from sexual intercourse."[17]

Perhaps the most compelling evidence about male/female differences is derived from comparisons between heterosexual couples and homosexual couples. Male homosexual couples have sexual relations more frequently than heterosexual couples. And heterosexual couples have sexual relations more frequently than lesbian couples. The claim that gay men behave more

---

[14] Laumann et al., *The Social Organization of Sexuality*, 157. The individual deficits must be greater due to matching problems – at least some women who like to give oral sex are matched with men who do not like to receive it or have no sexual partner at all.

[15] David Buss and his colleagues attempted to measure the distress experienced in a variety of acts including sexual aggression, various forms of nonsexual abuse, and withholding of sex. See David M. Buss, *The Evolution of Desire* (New York: Basic Books, 1994), 146–47.

[16] See John Marshall Townsend, *What Women Want – What Men Want* (Oxford: Oxford University Press, 1998), 214.

[17] Symons, *The Evolution of Sexual Desire*, 27–28.

promiscuously than heterosexual men is, of course, a staple of right-wing critics of the "homosexual lifestyle." But the critics miss the point. Male homosexuals do have, on average, more sexual partners than male heterosexuals, not because gay men are disposed to be more promiscuous than heterosexual men, but because the promiscuous desires of male homosexuals bounce off the promiscuous desires of other males, whereas the (otherwise) promiscuous desires of male heterosexuals bounce off the less promiscuous desires of females.[18]

Prostitution provides additional evidence of male/female differences. Although societies vary greatly in many ways, there are *no* societies in which prostitutes primarily service women, and in the United States, male prostitutes primarily service other males.[19] Although this could partly be explained by differences in economic resources – if women are less affluent, they have less ability to purchase sexual services – there is virtually no demand for prostitutes to service women even where women are prosperous and independent.[20]

There is a greater difference between males and females with respect to their desire for casual sex than their desire for sex within an established relationship. This tendency has been demonstrated in numerous ways, but perhaps the most illustrative study is reported by David Buss. An attractive male approached one hundred females on a college campus and said, "Hi, I've been noticing you around town lately, and I find you very attractive. Would you go to bed with me?" *None* of the females accepted the proposal. When an attractive female approached one hundred males with a similar proposal, seventy-five responded positively. Whereas the females were offended, insulted or puzzled by the proposal, the males seemed rather flattered.[21] When I asked my students to predict the responses, their predictions were extremely close to the actual findings. One might argue that the reluctance of women to accept the proposal reflected fear of social disapproval, pregnancy, or disease rather than a lack of desire for sex with a person that they had never met, but these worries are an element of desire whatever their causes.[22]

This pattern of motivational differences appears in the way in which males and females describe their first sexual encounter. Whereas 92 percent of males say that their first intercourse was something that they wanted to happen, only 71 percent of females say that they wanted their first

---

[18] Richard A. Posner, *Sex and Reason* (Cambridge, MA: Harvard University Press, 1992), 91.
[19] Townsend, *What Women Want – What Men Want*, 239.
[20] Posner, *Sex and Reason*, 91.   [21] Buss, *The Evolution of Desire*, 73.
[22] See Natalie Angier, *Woman: An Intimate Geography* (Boston: Houghton Mifflin, 1999), 336.

intercourse to happen when it did. This does not mean that the other 29 percent were forced to have intercourse, although 4 percent said that they were. Rather, many women said that their first intercourse was neither wanted nor forced, by which they meant that they were not motivated by desire for sex itself, but by a desire to express affection for their partner or to keep their partner in the relationship.[23]

It is frequently claimed that women tend to be coy about sex, that they sometimes say "no" when they really desire sex, that their resistance to sexual overtures is often feigned. Lord Byron:

> A little still she strove, and much repented
> And whispering "I will ne'er consent" – consented.[24]

For present purposes, I understand coyness as declining a proposal when one hopes or expects to later accept that (or a better) proposal. Coyness is not confined to sexual relations. Consider these two cases.

A: Please let me pay for the meal.
B: Absolutely not.
A: I insist.
B: Well, OK, if you insist.

or

C: Would you be willing to serve as Department Chair?
D: I'm really not interested in administration. I'd rather stick with my teaching and research.
C: There's a good deal of support for you. We think you'd make a fine chair.
D: I prefer not, but I'll consider it.

There are many situations in which it seems "unseemly" to be too anxious to accept another's proposal, and there are many situations in which coyness is a standard bargaining strategy.

Thus understood, there is no reason to deny that people can be coy about their desire to engage in sexual relations, and there is considerable evidence that females are more coy than males. One famous survey revealed that 39 percent of female undergraduates had at least once said "no" to a

---

[23] Laumann et al., *The Social Organization of Sexuality*, 328–29. According to Eleanor Maccoby, males are more oriented toward pleasure – "not just to the pleasure of sex, but to the pleasure of having fun with the partner" whereas "girls are more often looking for a committed, long-term, loving relationship." She observes that this difference has been found in a variety of ethnic groups, at all socioeconomic levels and in all of the Western countries in which studies have been done. See *The Two Sexes* (Cambridge, MA: Harvard University Press, 1998), 207.

[24] Quoted in Lois Pineau, "Date Rape" in Leslie Francis (ed.), *Date Rape* (University Park, PA: Penn State University Press, 1996), 5.

proposal for sexual relationships when they were willing to engage in sexual relationships, and that many women believed such "token resistance" was quite common among other women.[25] To anticipate a worry that such evidence might trigger, I do not say that it is permissible to disregard a disingenuous "no." I say only that people sometimes say "no" to a proposed action that they hope will occur.

Sexual strategies and bargaining

The male/female asymmetry of sexual desire accounts for much of the competition, bargaining, negotiation, stress, and conflict that accompanies sexual life. The competition occurs both within and between the sexes. Men compete with each other for the opportunity to have sexual relationships with (the more desirable) women and women compete with each other for the more desirable men. Acquaintances negotiate whether and when to commence a sexual relationship. Those who are in an enduring sexual relationship negotiate the frequency and types of sexual activity in which they will engage.

Although some recoil from the application of "economic" terminology to human relationships, there is something very much like a market for sexual partners and sexual activity. A non-intrusive indicator of people's preferences is contained in personal advertisements. Men seem to seek young attractive women, which means that such women have a greater range of options among possible partners.[26] They can date or marry "up." According to David Buss female attractiveness is (or, at least, was) a better predictor of the occupational status of her husband than her own socioeconomic status, intelligence, or education – a phenomenon that is explained by the preferences of both the women and men involved.[27] Women seem to seek taller, professional, secure, attractive, and (somewhat) older men. Such men have their pick of partners, thus accounting for the phenomenon of (relatively) unattractive but affluent men with young and attractive "trophy wives."[28]

---

[25] Charlene Muehlenhard and Lisa Hollabaugh, "Do Women Sometimes Say No When They Mean Yes? The Prevalence and Correlates of Token Resistance to Sex," 54 *Journal of Personality and Social Psychology* 972 (1988).

[26] We know, for example, that obesity hurts women financially more than men, in part because their employment opportunities are fewer, but mainly because obese women marry men with much lower earnings than non-obese women or do not marry at all. Rhona Mahony, *Kidding Ourselves: Breadwinning, Babies, and Bargaining Power* (New York: Basic Books, 1995), 20.

[27] David M. Buss, "Mate Preference Mechanisms: Consequences for Partner Choice and Intrasexual Competition" in Jerome H. Barkow, Leda Cosmides, and John Tooby (eds.), *The Adapted Mind* (New York: Oxford University Press, 1992), 256.

[28] In another episode of *Seinfeld*, Russell Dalrymple, a somewhat homely NBC executive, wants to date Elaine. She declines, but remarks: "You're the head of NBC. You can have any woman that you want."

Because males are sexually stimulated more often and more intensely than females in the course of everyday life, women should have considerable leverage in their transactions with men.[29] As Camille Paglia puts it, "we have what they want" and therefore men "have to do all sorts of stuff to prove that they are worthy of a woman's attention."[30] Nancy Wilmsen Thornhill maintains that the male mating repertoire consists of three dominant tactics: (1) honest advertisement and courtship, (2) deceptive advertisement and courtship, (3) coercion – a list to which we might add the use of intoxicants, a variety of enticements and pressures that may not rise to the level of coercion, and the outright purchase of sexual activity from prostitutes.[31] Courtship is itself a complex activity, much of which involves quasi-economic transactions, in which men typically "pay" for a variety of activities hoping (in part) to induce women to engage in sexual relations or demonstrate that they have the capacity to provide resources. For present purposes, however, Thornhill's main point is that fraud and coercion can be thought of as substitutes for honest advertisement, and courtship as strategies for obtaining sexual services, just as robbery and fraud are illicit strategies for obtaining money.[32]

I will have much more to say about both perpetrators and victims of nonconsensual sex in subsequent chapters. Here I want to extend briefly the previous discussion into this area. The use of force to obtain sexual gratification is mostly a problem of male perpetrators and female victims. Force is, of course, frequently used in prisons by males against males, but there are very few cases involving the use of force by female perpetrators against male victims or female perpetrators against female victims.[33] This pattern begs an explanation. I suppose one reason is physiological. Although men can be sexually functional with an unwilling partner, it is not easy for a woman to engage in sexual relations with a male who has no desire for sexual relations with her. But physiology can take us only so far. Even if it is physiologically difficult for women to coerce unwilling men into sexual intercourse, there is no physical barrier that prevents women from coercing men to perform oral sex just as men use coercion to get women to perform oral sex on them. And women do not. It simply does not happen.

---

[29] Symons, *The Evolution of Desire*, 264.

[30] Camille Paglia, *Sex, Art, and American Culture* (New York: Vintage, 1992), 62.

[31] Nancy Wilmsen Thornhill, "Psychological Adaptation to Sexual Coercion in Victims and Offenders" in Buss and Malamuth (eds.), *Sex, Power, Conflict*, 98.

[32] Andrea Dworkin agrees: "A man wants what a woman has – sex. He can steal it (rape), persuade her to give it away (seduction), rent it (prostitution), lease it over the long term (marriage in the United States) or own it outright (marriage in most societies)." Quoted in Robert Wright, "Feminists, Meet Mr. Darwin," *The New Republic*, November 28, 1994, 42.

[33] There are cases of "statutory" rape involving female perpetrators and male victims, but I have not learned of any cases that involve the use of physical force.

Some commentators reject the general picture of sexual psychology that I have sketched. Susan Griffin says that it is a "myth that men have greater sexual needs, that their sexuality is more urgent than women's."[34] Joan McGregor says that this claim is "far fetched."[35] And Martha Chamallas insists that men and women have an equal "capacity to experience sexual pleasure and intimacy."[36] Now the truth of any claim about psychology or behavior is an empirical question. Referring to an empirical proposition as a "myth" does not constitute evidence that the proposition is false. It may well be true, as Chamallas says, that men and women have an equal capacity to experience sexual pleasure and intimacy (which are not identical). Even so, it is important to distinguish between the *capacity* to experience pleasure and the *tendency* to experience pleasure. Linda Hirshman and Jane Larson seem convinced that heterosexual sex is more satisfying for males than for females. But whatever the truth about the tendency or capacity to have positive sexual *experience*, it does not follow that males and females exhibit equal *desire for* sexual activity.[37] And all of the survey research, all the experiments, and all the behavior support the general picture I have presented, not to mention that this picture underlies a good deal of popular culture, literature, and humor.

THE EVOLUTIONARY PSYCHOLOGY OF SEX

Introduction

The general description of sexual psychology and behavior that I have offered is, in principle, as compatible with a purely social or cultural explanation as with an explanation that takes biology seriously. For all we know, males are socialized to find young women attractive, to turn their heads when they walk by, to masturbate more frequently, to enjoy receiving and performing oral sex, and to desire sex with anonymous persons, whereas females are socialized to find older and more affluent men to be attractive,

---

[34] Susan Griffin, "Rape: The All-American Crime" in Mary Vetterling-Braggin, Frederick Elliston and Jane English (eds.), *Feminism and Philosophy* (Totowa, NJ: Rowman and Littlefield, 1977), 316.

[35] Joan McGregor, "Why When She Says No She Doesn't Mean Maybe and Doesn't Mean Yes: A Critical Reconstruction of Consent, Sex, and the Law," 2 *Legal Theory* 175 (1996), 190.

[36] Martha Chamallas, "Consent, Equality, and the Legal Control of Sexual Conduct," 61 *Southern California Law Review* 777 (1988), 839.

[37] Donald Symons observes that men and women "differ far less in their potential physiological and psychological responses during sexual activities per se than they do in how they negotiate sexual activities and in the kinds of sexual relationships and interaction they are motivated to seek." See *The Evolution of Desire*, 179.

to have fewer sexual thoughts, to be less desirous of anonymous sex, and to find performing oral sex less enjoyable. For all we know, having an intense negative response to being forced to engage in sexual relations is something that is learned and which could easily have been quite different. Possible, but not very likely.

I believe that a biological or evolutionary explanation of sexual psychology and behavior will help to explain some – not all – of what has been observed about human sexual behavior. With particular reference to the concerns of this book, it will help us understand why there has been a problem about consent to sexual relations throughout human history and across the range of cultures. It will help to explain why women respond to nonconsensual sex in the way that they do, why we do and should regard it as a serious matter. And by helping us to understand why men engage in certain behaviors – what we are "up against" in this area – it will give us some guidance as to why and what moral and legal strategies are both necessary and feasible.

It might be thought that we do not need to *explain* the propensity for males to engage in nonconsensual sex with females or why females have an aversive response to such encounters. In particular, why not just accept women's reports about their experience? Can an explanation of their experience tell us anything about the contemporary importance of consent? I shall not defend the claim that moral and legal theory always stand to gain from the best understanding of human behavior, although I think that is obviously true. I shall focus on the issue at hand. With respect to the law, an understanding of the perpetrator's behavior is clearly important: "Since the extent of the law's ability to prevent rape is a function of its behavioral model of rape – that is, its understanding of what influences rape's incidence – it follows that the more accurate and comprehensive the behavioral model is, the better law can do its job."[38] With respect to what should *count* as a sexual offense, I believe that an explanation of women's experience is of value. To the extent that experience does not have biological roots and is socially constructed, it may be thought that their experience need not be taken at full value. After all, if women need not experience an interaction aversively and if the content of their experience is relatively malleable, it makes sense to ask whether we should seek to change their *experience* as opposed to changing the behavior of males who generate that experience. Moreover, understanding the basis of the female response to

---

[38] Owen D. Jones, "Law and the Biology of Rape: Reflections on Transitions," 11 *Hastings Women's Law Journal* 151 (2000), 151.

forcible rape allows us to understand why other forms of nonconsensual sexual relations should be taken seriously. As Katharine Baker has suggested, "biology's findings can support feminist visions," even though they do not prove that feminist solutions are normatively correct.[39]

Although the intellectual winds may be shifting, most of the legal and philosophical literature on sexual relations either ignores evolutionary psychology or aggressively rejects it as irrelevant, wrong, or pernicious. Much contemporary work in law, social science, and philosophy assumes something like what John Tooby and Leda Cosmides have called the Standard Social Science Model (SSSM).[40] As Steven Pinker puts it, on this view "Biology endows humans with the five senses, a few drives like hunger and fear, and a general capacity to learn."[41] But not much more. Biology may place some minimal "constraints" on human behavior, but society and culture are the primary driving forces. We know, for example, that boys are more likely to play with guns and girls are more likely to play with dolls. That is a fact. If we ask why this is so, a devotee of SSSM will say that the difference in play behavior is primarily caused by socially arbitrary sex-role stereotyping by parents, peers, and teachers. Change the socialization patterns, and the behavior will change. By contrast, an explanation that takes biology seriously would argue that males are disposed to be more aggressive and females are disposed to be more nurturing, and were they placed in roughly identical environments and subject to similar stimuli, we should expect something like this contrast in their play behavior.

SSSM is and can be applied to a wide variety of human behaviors, for example, language acquisition, deviancy, occupational choice, altruism, and status seeking. It is invoked with particular enthusiasm to explain observed differences between males and females, where it is commonly argued that virtually all such differences are socially constructed. If females are more disposed to prefer child-rearing, this is primarily because they have been taught to accept such a role.

This book takes seriously the view that has come to be known as "evolutionary psychology." On this view, just as the physical characteristics of human beings evolved through natural selection, so do certain features of human psychology and behavior.[42] I will start with evolution, then add psychology, and then the psychology of sexual behavior. The theory of

---

[39] Katharine Baker, "Biology for Feminists," 75 *Chicago-Kent Law Review* 805 (2000), 824.
[40] Barkow, Cosmides, and Tooby (eds.), *The Adapted Mind*. See the editors' introduction.
[41] Steven Pinker, *How the Mind Works* (New York: W. W. Norton, 1997), 45.
[42] "Behavior evolves through natural selection, just as anatomy does"; Jared Diamond, *Why Is Sex Fun?* (New York: Basic Books, 1997), 66.

natural selection has three essential elements: variation, inheritance, and selection.[43] These elements work in two stages. Genes and transmission are one stage, phenotypes and their selection are the other.[44] The process goes something like this: (1) species and individual members of a species will vary with respect to some of their genetic information; (2) this genetic variation produces different phenotypes; (3) some phenotypes will produce more offspring than others, thus transmitting the information in their genes to their offspring; (4) the offspring will vary with respect to their genetic information. And the cycle will be continually repeated. Consider the traditional evolutionary story about giraffes. There was genetic variation among giraffes, such that some giraffe phenotypes had longer necks than others. Those with longer necks were able to reach more food and were more likely to survive and reproduce, thus passing their "long neck" genes to their offspring. And the process continued to the point that increasing neck size no longer had an evolutionary advantage. Natural selection is distinctly not "forward-looking" or "intentional." It is not that the species of giraffes somehow managed to grow longer necks in order to better survive and reproduce. Rather, it simply happened that giraffes varied with respect to neck length (natural selection works only on those variations that exist) and those with longer necks were, in fact, more likely to survive and pass their genes to their offspring.

Common misunderstandings to the contrary, when evolutionists refer to the "survival of the fittest," it is the reproductive success of the genes in the reproducing generation and not their bodily condition or individual survival that is at stake. For sure, the survival of individuals is generally correlated with their reproductive opportunities, but when they diverge, it is the reproductive opportunities that count. The brilliant plumage of some species of birds may help them to attract mates and thus reproduce, but may actually be detrimental to the survival of individuals because they alert predators as well as potential mates. If birds with more brilliant plumage outreproduce those with less brilliant plumage and less elaborate songs, then they are more fit from an evolutionary perspective even if they die earlier than birds with less brilliant plumage.[45] It is also important to note that a heritable trait that provides its possessor with only a small reproductive

[43] David M. Buss, Martie G. Haselton, Todd K. Shackelford, April L. Bleske, and Jerome C. Wakefield, "Adaptations, Exaptations, and Spandrels," 53 *American Psychologist* 533 (1988), 534.

[44] Henry Plotkin, *Evolution in Mind* (Cambridge, MA: Harvard University Press, 1988), 225.

[45] "When immediate reproductive gains are so great that they outstrip the countering pressure of ordinary natural selection for survival, lethal traits leading to extinction can arise in sexual selection"; Bobbi S. Low, *Why Sex Matters: A Darwinian Look at Human Behavior* (Princeton: Princeton University Press, 2000), 218.

advantage can come to dominate the species in a relatively short span of time. If genes for more brilliant plumage conferred a mere 1 percent reproductive advantage over contemporaries, organisms with that trait will swell from 1 percent of the population to 99 percent in less than three hundred generations.[46]

Evolutionary biology does not maintain that every feature of every organism has adaptive value. Some features are simply "by-products" of other features and may have no positive functions, what Stephen Jay Gould refers to as "spandrels."[47] The human navel is a good example. Of course features that developed for one purpose may serve other functions as well. I assume that the human mouth developed in the way it did because of its effect on digestion, respiration, and the like. That it can be used to provide sexual pleasure may be a by-product of that evolutionary design but probably played little role in its formation.

Shift from necks and plumage to minds. Evolutionary psychology can be understood as the conjunction of two ideas. First, evolutionary psychology maintains that the human mind is as much the product of the process of evolution as the pancreas, the five-fingered hand with opposable thumbs, the eyes, and bipedalism.[48] Second, evolutionary psychologists typically reject the view that the human mind is best understood as a giant but essentially unprogrammed computer – a "big associative engine." Instead, evolutionary psychologists maintain that the human mind is best pictured as containing an integrated bundle of mental modules, each of which is dedicated to a different intellectual ability, and "each pre-programmed with a substantial body of information about the world."[49] On this view, humans are born, for example, with language-acquisition and face-recognition software. These specific capacities evolved because those who had (more of) these capacities outreproduced those who did not. So, too, with respect to our tastes in foods. Evolutionary psychologists maintain, for example, that

---

[46] Owen D. Jones, "Sex, Culture and the Biology of Rape: Toward Explanation and Prevention," 97 *California Law Review* 827 (1999), 845.

[47] A spandrel is an architectural structure required by the construction of fan-vaulted ceilings. If one mounts a dome on four arches that meet at right angles, one creates four new triangular-shaped surfaces – spandrels. In the cathedral of San Marcos in Venice, artisans decorated these surfaces with detailed mosaics, but the space for these mosaics arose as a side consequence of an engineering requirement. See Stephen Jay Gould and Richard C. Lewontin, "The Spandrels of San March and the Panglossian Paradigm: A Critique of the Adaptationist Programme," *Proceedings of the Royal Society of London* 205 (1979), 581–98.

[48] Plotkin, *Evolution in Mind*, vii. As Owen Jones puts it, "the architecture and function of the brain is as much a product of evolution as the architecture and function of the hand, heart, or stomach"; "Sex, Culture and the Biology of Rape," 842.

[49] "Biology Isn't Destiny," *The Economist*, February 14, 1998, 84.

human beings come programmed to respond positively to some substances and negatively to others because such responses had survival and reproductive value in the environment in which our minds evolved. Because our minds evolved in an environment in which adequate caloric intake was problematic, those with taste buds that responded positively to fats and sweets were more likely to survive and reproduce than those who did not. Similarly, our distaste for foods which are bitter (or, perhaps more accurately, the experience of bitterness) evolved because a negative response to certain substances had survival value if those substances were likely to be toxic.

The taste response to foods or substances illustrates several crucial points about evolutionary psychology. First, evolutionary psychology maintains that human minds evolved to maximize reproductive fitness in the environment of evolutionary adaptation (EEA), that is, *the environment in which those minds evolved* and *not* necessarily within the present environment. The preference for sweets and fat had survival and reproductive value in an environment when obtaining adequate calories was a problem, but may well have negative survival and reproductive value in the contemporary environment, where sweets and fats are easily obtainable.[50] Second, many of our most important psychological dispositions or abilities are entirely unconscious. It is not that our ancestors "figured out" that fats and sweets had survival and reproductive value. Rather, the brains of some individuals were more likely to respond positively to fats and sweets, and those that were so programmed were more likely to survive and produce more offspring.[51] Third, evolutionary psychology does not maintain that we are mindless creatures whose psychology and behavior are easily predictable and somehow inevitable. In addition to mental modules that dispose us to think, feel, and behave in certain ways, we have evolved other mental capacities that enable us to make choices and solve problems in complex and unpredictable environments, including the capacity to make what would otherwise be distinctly "counter-evolutionary" choices.[52] So in addition to being hard-wired to respond positively to sugar, we are also

[50] "Before there was a sugar bowl, salt shaker, and butter dish on every table, and when lean years were never far away, one could never get too much sweet, salty, and fatty food. People do not divine what is adaptive for them or their genes; their genes give them thoughts and feelings that were adaptive in the environment in which the genes were selected"; Pinker, *How the Mind Works*, 208.

[51] "The overwhelming majority of an organism's biological processes and energetic transactions with the external world are unconscious, in fact, it appears that every process – digestion, oxygen transport, breathing, reflex blinking – that can be carried out unconsciously is more efficiently carried out this way, and conscious processes seem to become unconscious whenever possible"; Symons, *The Evolution of Human Sexuality*, 167.

[52] Diamond, *Why Is Sex Fun?*, 62.

hard-wired with the capacity for considerable behavioral plasticity, witness the capacity to choose saccharin over sugar. Why? Because evolutionary processes favored those with the capacity to make choices and solve problems over those who were hard-wired "to respond inevitably to a certain stimulus with a single, corresponding act."[53]

The previous point is crucial. Despite a common misperception, evolutionary psychology does not maintain that human behavior is "determined" in a straightforward way. Biology is not destiny. A disposition is not a requirement. That our brains are programmed to respond positively to fats and sweets does not entail that we *must* eat prime ribs and chocolate bars, or that we are not responsible for our unhealthy behavior when we do. It does mean that biology may generate an "inertial counterweight" against some desirable choices and we ignore such inertial forces at our peril.[54] If we want people to eat more vegetables, it would be a mistake to assume that we can be socialized to like broccoli and tofu just as easily as we can be taught to like steak and ice cream. We are better advised to acknowledge the disposition for what it is and then go about developing individual, social, and medical responses to it.

It is also important to note that the causes and malleability of behavior are entirely different matters. Although the "biological" is often equated with the "inevitable" or "fixed" whereas the "social" is equated with "changeable," those equations are simply false. A person's accent is socially determined but substantially unalterable once it is in place. And much the same may be true of one's values, norms, and attitudes. By contrast, myopia may be substantially genetically caused, but is easily correctable by lenses and may be permanently altered through surgery.

The evolution of our taste modules illustrates another important point, namely, the interaction between genes and the environment – "genetic predispositions cannot operate in a vacuum and environments must have a genetic code to work on."[55] To ask whether a disposition or a behavior is the product of nature (genetic influences) or of nurture (environmental influences) is akin to asking whether the area of a rectangle is determined by its length or by its width.[56] Our taste modules evolved in the way that they did because our environment contained different substances with different effects on survival and reproduction. Moreover, our food preferences are obviously a function of both our genetic disposition and our socialization.

---

[53] Jones, "Sex, Culture and the Biology of Rape," 852.
[54] For the notion of "inertial counterweight," see Maccoby, *The Two Sexes*, 305.
[55] Doreen Kimura, *Sex and Cognition* (Cambridge, MA: MIT Press, 1999), 4.
[56] Jones, "Sex, Culture and the Biology of Rape," 851.

I did not have to be socialized to like the taste of meat. That came naturally. I may have been socialized to prefer beef to pork.

One additional preemptive strike against those who worry about the moral implications of evolutionary psychology: just as evolutionary psychology does not equate the "biological" with the "invariant," it does not equate the "biological" with the "justifiable." If there are evolutionary forces that endow human beings with certain psychological dispositions toward certain behaviors, those forces neither *justify* nor *excuse* one's choices. Consider taste again. If I have reason to lose weight (which I do), I cannot justify my choice of ice cream over carrot sticks by claiming that biology made me do it. If I do not consume fewer calories, then I am to blame for not so doing. Similarly, if there are evolutionary forces that incline men to "turn their heads," as I think there are, that does not justify or excuse such behavior, particularly if it is bothersome to the targets of such behavior or to men's female companions. If human beings had *no* capacity to make counter-dispositional choices, then moral evaluation of their behavior would be irrelevant. We do not have the capacity not to blink for more than a limited period, so it would be silly to criticize someone for blinking during a five-minute period even if they were asked not to do so. By contrast, we do have such capacities across a wide range of behaviors, so there is no reason to think that evolutionary psychology will help to get anyone off the moral hook.

Sexual psychology and reproduction

Although there are serious disputes internal to evolutionary theory and evolutionary psychology, and while there are legitimate questions as to just how much evolutionary psychology can explain, there is little serious debate among scientists about whether "evolutionary processes, including natural and sexual selection, have affected human bodies, brains, and behavior."[57] And if there is anything to the claim that some dimensions of human psychology are the product of natural selection in the EEA, it would be most surprising if there were no connection between our sexual psychology and reproduction, even though the physiological connection has become rather attenuated in the contemporary world of accessible contraception and abortion. Individual humans are driven by three primary biological imperatives: (1) to survive to reproductive age; (2) to reproduce; (3) to rear offspring

---

[57] Owen D. Jones, "Realities of Rape: Of Science and Politics, Causes and Meanings," 86 *Cornell Law Review* 1386 (2001), 1388.

until *they* reach reproductive age.[58] *Any* surviving species must have adaptive characteristics that fulfill imperatives (1) and (2), otherwise those species would not survive. The third imperative becomes important with respect to those species in which the young are not self-sufficient at birth or hatching.[59] If the genes (or traits produced by genes) of Generation-1 are going to find their way into succeeding generations, it is necessary not only that those genes find their way into Generation-2, but that the genes of Generation-2 find their way into Generation-3. And in a species in which members of Generation-2 are not self-sufficient at birth, this requires that at least some members of Generation-1 enable their progeny to survive to reproductive age. To illustrate, suppose that there are two kinds of mothers in Generation-1: (a) high reproducers, unreliable caregivers; (b) low reproducers, diligent caregivers. Type (a) mothers have many progeny, but few survive to reproductive age. Type (b) mothers have fewer progeny, but virtually all survive to reproductive age. Suppose that three progeny of type (b) mothers survive to reproductive age for every two progeny of type (a) mothers. If there are genes that (partially) account for the disposition to be an unreliable or diligent caregiver (there may or may not be), then the genes that motivate individuals to be type (b) parents would have greater survival value and would quickly come to dominate the species, even though type (b) mothers have fewer children.

It is not just mothers that count. Infants are also more likely to survive if the father stays around to provide resources for the mother and protects the mother and children from predators. So the story gets quite complicated. Whether a father is likely to care for a woman's children is a function of both her traits and his. On the one hand, whatever maternal traits increase the probability that the father (or other males) will help out will also evolve to be more prevalent among the species. On the other hand, a paternal disposition to provide for one's progeny has some adaptive value for males but must be counterbalanced by a male's motivation to spend his time and resources trying to spread his genes around and hope that a reasonable proportion of his progeny will survive without his continual attention.

Before care there is mating. Although the human mating system cannot escape the genetic and evolutionary laws that have been documented in hundreds of species, it also displays some special features. First, human females are characterized by concealed ovulation and constant receptivity,

---

[58] Maccoby, *The Two Sexes*, 91.
[59] Maccoby adds: "The longer the period of vulnerability of the young, the more important the third imperative becomes"; *ibid*.

a combination that makes possible "our unique combination of marriage, coparenting, and adulterous temptation."[60] Unlike other species that mate only during ovulation, humans copulate throughout the reproductive cycle.

Second, a human female has relatively few – approximately twenty – reproductive opportunities over the course of her life whereas a male has virtually unlimited reproductive potential over the course of his life. And unlike female fertility, which declines steeply with age and typically ends by forty, men can remain fertile through their sixties and seventies. Males and females also differ with respect to their investment in these reproductive opportunities. In physiological terms, the mature human egg has approximately one million times the mass of the sperm that fertilizes it. In behavioral terms, the female invests nine months and a good deal of distress and risk in the production of a newborn, whereas the male's contribution takes but a few minutes and carries no risk to his health or longevity. It is not surprising, then, that the disposition to care about one's offspring is more likely to have evolved among women than men.

Third, whereas a woman knows that she is the mother of her child, a man has no readily available method of determining that a woman's child is his. All this adds up to the following sort of story about parenting. Children are most likely to survive if they receive the combined labor and support of a mother and a father, although both mother and father may be tempted to copulate with other fertile adults. A woman's genes are more likely to survive and be reproduced if she has male assistance in providing for her and her progeny. And while a male has some genetic reason to spend his time and resources providing for his own progeny, it is genetically counterproductive for him to invest in another male's progeny. As Steven Pinker puts it: "Any gene predisposing a male to be cuckolded, or a female to receive less paternal help than her neighbors, would quickly be tossed from the gene pool. Any gene that allowed a male to impregnate all the females, or a female to bear the most indulged offspring of the best male, would quickly take over."[61]

The evolution of sexual psychology

Recognizing that I have provided only the barest sketch of evolutionary psychology, I will now try to connect the previous discussion to several observed features of human sexual psychology. I start with the fact that human beings find (consensual) sex to be pleasurable. That humans are predisposed to respond positively to a stimulus is a psychological fact that

---

[60] Diamond, *Why Is Sex Fun?*, 70.   [61] Pinker, *How the Mind Works*, 467.

must be explained. As Jared Diamond has observed, we must ask "Why is sex fun?," just as we have to explain why we respond positively to sugar or lake views or harmonious music. From a phenomenological point of view, sexual desire is the individual's desire to get the pleasures of sex. At the genetic level, however, sexual desire is the result of our genes' strategy to reproduce themselves.[62] Sexual desire is the "*proximate* cause of behavior . . . the mechanism that pushes behavior buttons in real time," whereas reproduction is the "*ultimate* cause . . . the adaptive rationale that led the proximate cause to evolve."[63] Think of it this way: if some humans were predisposed to find sexual relations more enjoyable than others (and if that predisposition has a [partial] genetic basis), then the genes of those who were predisposed to find sex enjoyable would quickly come to dominate the species.

All this leaves open the question of why humans evolved to enjoy sex without regard to fertility. Dogs seem to like sex, but only when it does some reproductive good, and female rats are physically incapable of mating when not in estrus.[64] If human beings enjoy sexual relations even when a woman is not ovulating, this too is probably a consequence of natural selection. We would expect that male behavior must be responsive to the fact that female ovulation is well concealed from men and partially concealed from women themselves. So men who were indiscriminate with respect to timing would outreproduce those who (like dogs) tried to get the timing right. Although there is some evidence that women are more likely to be receptive to sexual relations during ovulation, there might be adaptive value to a disposition to enjoy sex throughout the cycle, for such a disposition would be more likely to keep a male around.[65]

It should now be clear how the evolutionary psychologist would explain the marked difference in the way in which males and females are attracted to members of the opposite sex. We can, for example, explain why age is more crucial to males than to females. If, over time, some males were predisposed to be attracted to females of fertile age whereas other males were less age-sensitive (and, of course, if these dispositions were partially inherited), the genes of the second group would quickly disappear. It is not that older men are attracted to women who are *younger* than them, say by ten years, but that men are attracted to women in the eighteen to thirty-five age range regardless of their own age (and so wives are known to say to their leering husbands – "you have a daughter her age").

---

[62] *Ibid.*, 44.

[63] Steven Pinker, *The Blank Slate* (New York: Viking Press, 2002), 54.   [64] Angier, *Woman*, 193.

[65] Angier reports that women are more likely to initiate sex and have orgasms at the mid-point in their cycle; *ibid.*, 199.

But why should men care about beauty as well as age, or, more accurately, why are men predisposed to respond positively to certain physical features or have a particular conception of beauty? The standard evolutionary explanation is that attractiveness, as defined by appropriate body weight, clear skin, lustrous hair, and symmetrical facial features trigger sexual desire because they are proxies for good health and, therefore, fertility. Although standards of beauty vary somewhat from time to time and place to place, they are pretty much universal and cross-cultural. Thinness may be in this year while voluptuousness (but not obesity) may be in next year, but "that fact is no more than noise slightly complicating but not invalidating the main conclusion: that men at all places and times have on the average preferred well-nourished women with beautiful faces."[66]

It might be objected that one does not need to explain why men prefer attractive women, that men prefer attractive women because they are attractive, just as we prefer a view of the ocean to a view of a parking lot because ocean views are prettier. But that simply begs the question *why* we respond positively to certain human features and why we respond more positively to ocean views than parking lots. The evolutionary psychologist would argue that our aesthetic sensibilities can be explained in much the same way as other psychological mechanisms, that is, by their adaptive advantages in EEA.[67]

What sorts of males should be found attractive by females? From an evolutionary perspective, youth and physical attractiveness should play a smaller role in female mate preference than in male mate preference. Female reproductive success is not significantly limited by the need to find fertile mates, if only because a few males could fertilize numerous females. In addition, male fertility is much less steeply age-graded than female fertility, and thus male fertility cannot be accurately assessed from physical attributes.[68] From a woman's genes' eye view, getting pregnant is not the problem. The survival of her children is the issue, and that will be influenced by the capacity and willingness of her mate to provide for and protect her and her offspring. Evolutionary psychology would predict that women are predisposed to respond positively to men who demonstrate a commitment to

---

[66] Diamond, *Why Is Sex Fun?*, 141. It appears that the hip to waist ratio (1.4:1) that is judged most attractive seems to remain constant, even when the absolute weight judged to be most attractive may vary somewhat.

[67] See G. H. Orions and J. H. Heerwagen, "Evolved Response to Landscapes" in Barkow, Cosmides, and Tooby (eds.), *The Adapted Mind*, 555–80.

[68] Buss, "Mate Preference Mechanisms" in Barkow, Cosmides, and Tooby (eds.), *The Adapted Mind*, 250.

them and who possess the intellectual, economic, and physical resources to provide for and protect them and their offspring.

To reemphasize a previous point, evolutionary psychology does *not* claim that our feelings of sexual attraction are part of any conscious strategy to maximize our reproductive opportunities, any more than our taste sensations are part of a conscious strategy to maximize our chances of survival. A male does not say, "she is twenty-four and healthy, she is likely to be fertile, and so I am attracted to her." A female does not size up a man and say, "he seems likely to stick around, to provide for our children, and to protect me from others, and so I find him attractive." Phenomenologically, both males and females size up the other person and feel attracted to them or they do not. People may have dispositions *because* of natural selection; they do not choose their dispositions in order to promote the survival of their genes.

These dispositions can be very strong indeed. Why do contemporary intelligent, well-educated, professional males often prefer to mate with attractive but less intelligent and lower-income-producing females rather than with less attractive, but more intelligent and higher-income-producing females, particularly when most women are in the labor force and these men do not want large families? One might respond, "Because men are superficial." Precisely so, but why? Evolutionary psychology would say that men are superficial because they have dispositions that were adaptive in the era in which those dispositions were formed.

Evolutionary psychology also offers a plausible explanation for other observed differences between male and female sexual desire. Males prefer quantity and variety while females prefer quality. Because males can produce large numbers of offspring, the most genetically successful males will be those who are able to get more genes into the next generation, *assuming* that a reasonable proportion of their progeny survived, even without their assistance.[69] Because women can produce no more than about twenty offspring during a lifetime, there is little adaptive advantage in having sex with a large number of males, unless they were thereby able to entice non-fathers to support their offspring or could increase the likelihood of getting better genes. It makes more sense for women to try to provide for each of their offspring by selecting mates who are likely to help in child-rearing.[70]

---

[69] The latter assumption is, of course, of some importance. If offspring had little chance of survival without paternal assistance, then males who get females pregnant but do not assist in child-rearing would have no adaptive advantage.

[70] Neil M. Malamuth, "The Confluence Model of Sexual Aggression: Feminist and Evolutionary Perspectives" in Buss and Malamuth (eds.), *Sex, Power, Conflict*, 275.

From an evolutionary perspective, it is also not surprising that females respond less positively to opportunities for casual sex. Males do not lose any reproductive opportunities by a casual sexual encounter. By contrast, women would be using one of their precious and costly reproductive opportunities with a male who is unlikely to provide for his offspring. Contraception changes these calculations in our present environment and the calculations have no doubt affected the psychology and behavior of women. But our psychologies evolved in an era in which contraception was not readily available. And while the sexual revolution has exerted some force against that inertial counterweight, it has not overwhelmed it.

Even in a time when seemingly anything goes, most people do not partake in sex as casually as they partake in food or conversation . . . The reasons are as deep as anything in biology. One of the hazards of sex is a baby, and a baby is not just any seven-pound object but, from an evolutionary point of view, our reason for being.[71]

There is also an evolutionary explanation why men are sexually aroused more quickly and easily than women.

If a successfully reproducing male needs to inseminate a lot of females, he'd better be wired for response – instant response. It shouldn't take much; by theory we should see a rapid response to the very sight of a sexually attractive partner. Every study shows that this describes males.[72]

By contrast, a woman who is easily aroused would be more likely to have sexual relations with a male who would not stay around to care for his offspring. Better she should take her time to determine whether this is a male who will devote time to her and her children.

It might be thought that some contemporary social and economic trends are incompatible with the implications of evolutionary psychology. If we hypothesize that females will be disposed to select mates who have the resources and power to provide for and protect their offspring, then more affluent men should have more offspring than less affluent men. And this is not true in contemporary industrialized societies.[73] But a closer look at the data confirms the general hypothesis, for whereas men of high social status do not have more *children* than lower-status men, they do have more *sexual encounters*. But for contraception, affluent men would have more offspring than less affluent men.

---

[71] Pinker, *The Blank Slate*, 253.
[72] Deborah Blum, *Sex on the Brain: The Biological Differences between Men and Women* (New York: Penguin Putnam, 1997), 227.
[73] Plotkin, *Evolution in Mind*, 111.

Evolutionary psychology is also consistent with the "infamous madonna–whore dichotomy," in which men seek sexual encounters with "loose" women but want their wives to be faithful. Whatever can and should be said against this view from a moral perspective, it represents a perfectly sensible genetic strategy for males who invest in their offspring: "mate with any female that will let you, but make sure your consort does not mate with any other male."[74] After all, it makes little genetic sense for a male to invest his time and resources in providing for the offspring of another male, so "genes inclining men to abhor promiscuous long-term mates would do better at getting into ensuing generations than less discriminating genes."[75]

Intersexual and intra-sexual conflict

I will postpone a more thorough discussion of the psychology of nonconsensual sexual relations to the following chapters. Here I want to describe briefly the way in which evolutionary psychology would try to explain the basic structure of intra-sexual and intersexual conflict and competition. Males are in conflict with females because the evolved preferences of each sex tend to interfere with the preferences of the other sex. Men who seek sex without investing in their partners frustrate a mating goal of many women. So it makes evolutionary sense for a woman to demand a relatively long courtship and heavy investment before engaging in sexual relations. Female coyness may have had adaptive value as a method for determining whether the male has sufficient commitment to the relationship. For this reason, men may seek to display their commitment (verbally or behaviorally) and their resources (paying for dinner, fancy cars) or their ability to protect their mates from predators (bodybuilding) as a way of demonstrating their worthiness to a potential mate.

Just as females have a reproductive interest in obtaining support and protection from the father (or, for that matter, any male), males have an interest in not expending their resources on behalf of another male's genes. And this gives rise to conflicts about fidelity. It will help to distinguish between two types of infidelity. A mate engages in *sexual infidelity* when he or she has sexual relations with a non-mate. A mate displays *emotional infidelity* when he or she displays emotional involvement with or commitment to a non-mate. From an evolutionary perspective, males have more reason to worry about sexual infidelity, whereas females have more reason to worry about emotional infidelity. Since, in the absence of modern paternity tests,

<hr/>

[74] Pinker, *How the Mind Works*, 480.   [75] Wright, "Feminists, Meet Mr. Darwin," 40.

a male cannot be certain that a mate's child is his, he has good reason not to waste his resources on another male's child. By contrast, females have little *reproductive* reason to be jealous of male sexual infidelity. By contrast, females have considerable reproductive reason to worry about a mate's *emotional* infidelity. Her offspring suffer if he is committing his resources to another woman. And this is what the data show. Although both males and females are disturbed by both sexual infidelity and emotional infidelity, males have a more intense negative response to female *sexual* infidelity than to their emotional infidelity whereas females have a more intense negative response to male *emotional* infidelity than to sexual infidelity.[76]

Because the opportunity and desire for extramarital sexual relations has "potentially disastrous consequences for parental cooperation in child-rearing," evolutionary psychology has a plausible causal explanation for both reasonable measures and the "host of repulsive practices" that men have historically employed to increase their confidence in paternity, such as intense supervision, jealous rages, and adultery laws.[77] Although adultery laws nominally apply to both sexes, there are many "double standard" societies in which adultery by the wife is regarded as a graver offense than adultery by the husband, but *no* cases of a "reversed double standard of adultery," a finding which suggests that such laws are not arbitrary cultural artifacts.[78]

Just as there is (inter)sexual conflict between the sexes stemming from their different reproductive strategies, there is (intra)sexual competition between members of each sex. Evolutionary psychology would hypothesize that members of each sex would be disposed to compete with each other with respect to those factors that are valued by the opposite sex. For males, the major reproductive problem is limited access to females, so males will typically compete for such access with each other.[79] Males will (consciously or unconsciously) compete for economic, status, political, and physical

---

[76] This theme is beautifully captured in the 1988 French film, *Trop Belle Pour Toi*, in which Gerard Depardieu prefers his frumpy mistress to his beautiful wife – signaling to the distressed wife that there must be more to the relationship than mere sexual desire. For a discussion of a recent dispute, see Erica Goode, "Jealousy, Maybe It's Genetic, Maybe Not," *New York Times*, October 8, 2002, section F, page 1.

[77] Diamond, *Why Is Sex Fun?*, 37.

[78] Martin Daly and Margo Wilson, *Homicide* (New York: Aldine de Gruyter, 1988), 44.

[79] Males may also sometimes cooperate with each other in order to obtain such access as when they band together and raid neighboring villages for access to their women. As Steven Pinker puts it, "The reason that females never evolved an appetite to band together and raid neighboring villages for husbands is that a woman's reproductive success is rarely limited by the number of available males, so any risk to her life while pursuing additional mates is a sheer loss in expected fitness"; *How the Mind Works*, 515.

assets, because of their value to women.[80] This includes a disposition to engage in aggressive behavior – most of which is targeted at other males.

For females, access to reproductive opportunities is not a serious problem. Rather, females will compete with each other for access to those males who promise to be good partners and providers. A good man is hard to find. Evolutionary psychology would predict that females will compete with respect to those assets that are valued by males, such as beauty and youthful appearance, and this is consistent with various data, for example, that 89 percent of plastic surgery patients are female, that women's magazines focus on cosmetics and clothing, that millions of women have received breast implants, that bulimia and anexoria are virtually exclusively female eating disorders.[81]

Criticisms

Even if the theory of evolutionary psychology is *consistent* with a range of observations about sexual psychology and behavior, it does not follow that the theory is true. Are there good reasons to reject the theory? Needless to say, this is a large issue that I cannot hope to resolve here. Although I think that evolutionary psychology must be at least part of the truth, it will be useful to consider the sorts of objections that have been raised to the theory. In this chapter I will consider some general objections. In the subsequent chapters I will consider objections to its account of the psychology of perpetrators and victims of nonconsensual sexual relations.

Three lines of criticism have been levelled against evolutionary psychology: (1) the theory is empirically false; (2) the theory has unattractive normative implications; (3) widespread *belief* in the theory would have unattractive normative implications. These are distinct criticisms, although I suspect that worries about (2) and (3) supply much of the motivation for (1). Although I think the evidence in support of the theory is quite convincing, I am not a scientist, so I will mostly set (1) aside. Here I want to attend to (2) and (3). Clearly, whether a theory has attractive or unattractive normative implications (2) has no bearing on its empirical validity (1). But a theory might, in principle, have no unattractive normative implications or no implications at all (2), and yet belief in the truth of the theory might have unattractive normative implications (3).

---

[80] Physical prowess may be an asset in two ways. Stronger men are able to fight off weaker men for access to females, and stronger men are more attractive to women because women predict that they are more likely to be able to protect them.
[81] *New York Times*, July 12, 1998, section 9, page 1.

Critics of evolutionary psychology sometimes worry that it is excessively deterministic, that if humans are "hard-wired" to behave in specific ways, then we cannot hold individuals responsible for their behavior and we are powerless to redirect behavior in more desirable directions. Hirshman and Larson write, for example, that on the evolutionary story "to criticize or attempt to reshape these sexual arrangements thwarts natural desires and is doomed to fail as contrary to human nature and biological imperative."[82] This line of criticism rests on several related mistakes. First, it wrongly assumes that determinism is incompatible with responsibility. This is difficult philosophical territory, which I shall not enter here. Suffice it to say that the truth of determinism does not entail that we are not justified in holding people responsible for their behavior.

Second, this view wrongly assumes that if humans exhibit biological dispositions, it follows that efforts to restrain or control behavior are doomed to fail. But, as I have suggested, a disposition is not a compulsion. Evolutionary psychology does not deny that human beings are capable of counter-dispositional choices in sexual behavior any less than with respect to eating chocolate. Indeed, as I have noted, evolutionary psychologists offer an evolutionary explanation for the human capacity to make what would otherwise seem to be counter-dispositional choices.

Third, it is worth noting that sociological or cultural explanations for human behavior are no more (or less) compatible with individual moral responsibility than biological, genetic, or evolutionary explanations. An individual who is "socialized" into "macho norms" is no less "driven" to behave that way than a person who is "genetically disposed" to behave in a certain way. So those who reject evolutionary psychology in favor of sociocultural explanations for behavior gain precisely nothing with respect to validating individual moral responsibility.

Setting the previous issue aside, there is something quite odd about the structure of sociocultural explanations of human behavior, namely, that they regard social processes as independent variables by which we can explain individual behavior but they offer no causal explanation of how these social processes came to be.[83] We can say that a woman's concern about beauty is "just a carbuncle on the ugly back of the sexual division of labor," but

---

[82] Hirshman and Larson, *Hard Bargains*, 238.
[83] An independent variable in one explanatory scheme can generally be recast as the dependent variable in another explanatory scheme. For example, we may regard individual smoking behavior as an independent variable which is then used to explain risk of lung cancer as the dependent variable. We can also regard smoking behavior as the dependent variable which must then be explained by a set of independent variables.

what explains the virtually universal sexual division of labor on which that carbuncle grows?[84] We can use the socially constructed double standard of sexual morality to explain why promiscuous men are regarded as "studs" whereas promiscuous women are regarded as "sluts," but what explains the ubiquity and persistence of the double standard itself?

In addition, it seems that the social-conditioning thesis is typically offered as an explanation only for those behavioral patterns of which people disapprove. It is difficult to understand how socialization could be so powerful in some contexts (sex-role stereotyping) and so relatively unsuccessful in achieving other broadly accepted social goals, for example, teaching citizens not to use drugs, to obey the law, to shun violence, and so on. It is possible that we simply do a better job of socialization in some contexts than in others, but it is more likely that socialization is less powerful than some suggest.

Putting aside these theoretical concerns, there is the crucial issue of evidence, about which those who critique biological explanations often invoke their own double standard. It often seems as if one can attribute behavior to a set of socially constructed variables without providing evidence for such hypotheses at all. Consider the following typical claim: "*In this culture*, males are supposed to pursue sexual contact, and thus all strategies for having sex are stereotypically masculine; women are responsible for limit setting and thus all strategies for avoiding sex are stereotyped as feminine."[85] Evolutionary psychology will, of course, concede that males are supposed to pursue sexual contact in this culture. But if the claim is not to be trivial, it must be read as hypothesizing that this pattern of male behavior is caused by special features of this culture that might well have been different. And minor perturbations to the contrary notwithstanding, the American pattern of behavior is found in virtually all cultures at all times – including some where scholars expected not to find it (and, in the case of Margaret Mead, wrongly thought she had found it).[86]

Consider violence. American males are more violent than American females. One might attribute this to socialization patterns in North American

---

[84] Mahony, *Kidding Ourselves*, 20.

[85] Barry Burkhart and Mary Ellen Fromuth, "Individual Psychological and Social Psychological Understandings of Sexual Coercion" in Elizabeth Grauerholz and Mary A. Koralewski (eds.), *Sexual Coercion* (Lexington: Lexington Books, 1991), 84.

[86] Margaret Mead's description of Samoa as a sexual paradise free of restrictive norms was decisively refuted by Derek Freeman in *Margaret Mead and Samoa: The Making and Unmaking of an Anthropological Myth* (Cambridge, MA: Harvard University Press, 1983). See Margaret Mead, *Coming of Age in Samoa* (New York: W. Morrow, 1928).

culture, but this implies that men would not be more violent than women if they were conditioned by some other culture. Although the amount of male violence varies considerably from culture to culture – evidence that environmental variables are *very* important – there is *no* known culture in which women are more violent than men.[87] Consider play. Boys and girls tend to play with different sorts of toys. Why? It has been argued that boys are socialized into playing with "male-appropriate" toys and girls are socialized into playing with "female-appropriate" toys. This is a plausible story, but it turns out that there is little evidence in its favor. Eleanor Maccoby writes that "numerous studies have found that sex-typed toy preferences develop *before* children have acquired the gender stereotypes that they presumably could use to guide such preferences."[88]

Male/female differences are not ubiquitous across the full range of human behaviors. According to Murdock's World Ethnographic Sample, men do most of the farm work in 125 societies whereas women do most of the farm work in 83 societies. In 133 societies, men and women make roughly equal contributions.[89] Here we have considerable cross-cultural variability, suggesting that the division of farm labor is not significantly driven by innate psychological dispositions. If male and female sexuality were entirely "socially constructed," we might expect to find something like this variability in sexual behavior. But we do not. To take but one example, it is primarily men who pay for the services of prostitutes in all societies at all times. I suppose that universality is not knockdown proof that biologically driven dispositions play a significant role, but it does seem to render that thesis much more plausible.

There is, then, a good deal of evidence that some of the well-established differences between males and females with respect to sexual psychology and behavior can be partially explained by the process of natural selection. And there is a good deal more. I have not, for example, even mentioned the vast body of evidence that is based on hormonal differences between males and females and evidence that can be drawn from the behavior of other animals. But the problem with the strong anti-biological view is not just that there is so much evidence against it. On analysis, it is wildly implausible. Given the reproductive differences between males and females, a sexually undifferentiated psychology would be theoretically improbable.[90]

---

[87] Daly and Wilson, *Homicide*, 156.   [88] Maccoby, *The Two Sexes*, 171–72.
[89] See Townsend, *What Women Want – What Men Want*, 240.
[90] As Martin Daly and Margo Wilson put it – "no theoretical framework has yet been proposed within which a sexually *undifferentiated* psychology would be anticipated, or even explicable," *Homicide*, 160.

Why is there so much resistance to evolutionary explanations of sexual psychology? That is a question for the sociology of knowledge (even if the resistance were correct!). I suspect that there is much less resistance to evolutionary psychology when (1) the phenomena to be explained do not concern human beings or (2) do not concern male/female differences or (3) the human male/female differences do not concern ideologically sensitive psychological traits or (4) it is thought to have attractive normative upshots. Bobbi Low observes that whereas few of us are bothered by the possibility that there are innate male/female differences in other species, we find it "unsettling to ask about sex differences in ourselves [although] humans are one of the most sexually dimorphic of all the primates in behavior."[91] I have detected little resistance to an evolutionary explanation of the disposition to like sweet foods, where there is little distinction between males and females. And I have detected less resistance to the claim that males and females differ with respect to spatial abilities than with respect to a disposition to find parenting emotionally satisfying.[92]

It is sometimes argued that the observed psychological and behavioral differences between males and females must be a function of social conditioning because they are not evident at birth. Putting aside the fact that some differences (such as female superiority in facial recognition) do appear early on, the argument is clearly fallacious. Lactation does not occur in male or female children, but we would hardly conclude that lactation is determined by differences in social conditioning.[93] Similarly, bipedal locomotion does not appear until about one year after birth.

Let us assume, arguendo, that there is at least *something* to the empirical claims of evolutionary psychology. It might nonetheless be thought that the theory has unattractive moral implications. Although the truth of an empirical theory has nothing to do with the attractiveness of its moral implications, people are more receptive to an empirical theory when they are not disturbed by what they take to be its normative implications. Few left liberals resist biological explanations of sexual orientation, because such explanations are now commonly regarded as having progressive rather than

[91] Low, *Why Sex Matters*, 113–14.
[92] Consider this example. Whereas males seem to respond to stress according to the syndrome known as "fight or flight," females seem to show a very different reaction to stress, "one that revolves around nurturing and seeking the support of others," one in which a hormone – oxytocin – seems to play a prominent role; Erica Goode, "Scientists Find a Particularly Female Response to Stress," *New York Times*, May 19, 2000, section A, page 20.
[93] Kimura, *Sex and Cognition*, 1.

conservative implications, although I do not think this is so.[94] By contrast, left liberals are decidedly less receptive to evolutionary explanations of sexual psychology. One scholar writes, for example, that many branches of feminism contend that evolutionary psychology "serves only to justify and promote the oppression of women by perpetuating the notion that male dominance and female oppression are natural outcomes of human evolutionary history."[95] Hirshman and Larson say that "Sociobiologists offer a disrespectful vision of sexual harmony that calls for females to be natural slaves."[96]

Is this so? As I noted above, we should distinguish between two arguments: (1) evolutionary psychology entails unattractive normative implications; (2) the promulgation of or belief in evolutionary psychology is likely to result in morally undesirable outcomes. As far as I can see, there is absolutely nothing to (1). Evolutionary psychology *entails* precisely nothing with respect to what is morally required or morally permissible. I need not rehearse well-trodden ground about the impossibility of deriving an "ought" from an "is." If, for example, natural selection predisposed men to select mates on the basis of their physical attractiveness, it does not follow that this is a morally desirable method of selection, any more than it would render violence morally desirable.[97] We must be careful. I do not deny that evolutionary psychology may be relevant to moral theory. Quite the opposite. I believe that evolutionary psychology lends *support* to some moral views about the principles of valid consent in both morality and law and that is precisely why I discuss it at some length. But it does not and cannot mean that any action is morally required or permissible.

In any case, if we take a commitment to the equal moral worth of men and women to be at the core of feminism, then I cannot see that a feminist moral perspective has *anything* to fear from evolutionary psychology. As Leah Cosmides puts it:

---

[94] The question is whether homosexual behavior is wrong, not whether it is biologically or socially caused. For if it is wrong, then it would be wrong even if it were biologically caused, just as aggressivity is wrong whether or not it is biologically caused. See Edward Stein, *The Mismeasure of Desire: The Science, Theory, and Ethics of Sexual Orientation* (New York: Oxford University Press, 1999).

[95] Zuleyma Tang-Martinez, "The Curious Courtship of Sociobiology and Feminism: A Case of Irreconcilable Differences" in P. Gowaty (ed.), *Feminism and Evolutionary Biology* (New York: Chapman and Hall, 1997), 117.

[96] Hirshman and Larson, *Hard Bargains*, 251.

[97] It appears that sickle-cell anemia can be explained as the result of natural selection. Although the disease is life threatening, those who are passive carriers of the gene for sickle-cell anemia have some protection against malaria. But the fact that sickle-cell anemia can be explained by natural selection hardly shows that it is desirable.

If you want to change the relationship between men and women, you want to understand the cognitive mechanisms that govern how we interact. If you don't understand that, you don't have a prayer of changing it. It's completely wrong to say that if something is a part of our evolved architecture, then it cannot be changed.[98]

Suppose I am wrong. Suppose that the empirical claims of evolutionary psychology do render some otherwise attractive normative views highly implausible. If evolutionary psychology is more or less true and if that truth is incompatible with some normative claims, then so much the worse for those normative claims. The truth is the truth. If there are dimensions of human behavior that are not particularly malleable – as there are – then that would be a truth with which any plausible moral theory would have to deal. If "ought implies can," then morality cannot demand that we behave in ways in which we are incapable of behaving.[99]

Fortunately, the truth is that evolutionary psychology is quite compatible with a view of human behavior as significantly malleable, and certainly no less so than the view entailed by SSSM. As I noted earlier, evolutionary psychology holds that the mind contains multiple "modules," each of which gives us specific capacities and dispositions, and so "one module could subvert the ugly designs of another one."[100] Evolutionary psychologists have maintained that our "moral sense" may itself be explained in evolutionary terms.[101] So if people have sexual dispositions that incline them to behave badly but have a moral sense that is designed to rein in their behavior or have a "cost-avoidance module" that calculates the risks of one's behavior, then we can try to strengthen the power of the moral module or increase the costs of behavior we hope to deter.

The critic might argue that I have erroneously conflated two different connections between causation and malleability. For even if the previous argument is correct at the *individual* level, it does not follow that it is correct at the *social* level. It may be conceded that social processes leave no more room for change in individual human behavior than do genetic processes, once those social processes are in place. Yet, it may be maintained, these social processes are themselves changeable by human design in a

[98] Maia Szalavitz, "Eve Psych," www.mega.nu:8080/ampp/evepsych.html. The publisher has endeavored to ensure that URLs for external websites referred to in this book are correct and active at the time of going to press. However, the publisher has no responsibility for the websites and can make no guarantee that a site will remain live or that the content is or will remain appropriate.

[99] We cannot be morally required to stop blinking for ten minutes, although we can imagine a case in which one might be morally required to not blink for five seconds.

[100] Pinker, *How the Mind Works*, 51.

[101] See, for example, Robert Wright, *The Moral Animal* (New York: Pantheon Books, 1994).

way that genetic processes are not. Certainly the rapid and far-reaching social changes in the status of women that we have witnessed over the last century do much to demonstrate the power of human culture and social institutions to "override what many have seen as deep-seated 'natural' differences between the sexes."[102] Still, understanding the ways in which people may be predisposed to behave can help us evaluate the sorts of institutions and mechanisms that are necessary to control those dispositions and to evaluate the costs of imposing them.

As I noted above, even if biology or evolutionary psychology does not entail or imply any unattractive moral implications, it may be thought that the promulgation of or belief in evolutionary psychology would have undesirable consequences if it is more likely to be misused than other theories.[103] That is an empirical question. At this point, we have no reason to think that is so. Even if it were so, that would not be a reason to believe that an evolutionary account of sexual psychology and behavior theory is false or that it has unattractive moral implications, *per se*. It would only be a (nondispositive) reason to restrict its promulgation. At this point, I think this worry can be set aside.

---

[102] Maccoby, *The Two Sexes*, 313.

[103] A well-known argument along these lines has been made about utilitarianism. Even if utilitarianism is the correct moral theory and does not have objectionable implications when correctly applied, it is possible that people are more likely to misuse utilitarianism than other (and, arguendo, less valid) ethical theories. If that were so, it might be better (on utilitarian grounds!) that people not believe in utilitarianism. See, for example Bernard Williams's contribution to J. J. C. Smart and Bernard Williams, *Utilitarianism, For and Against* (Cambridge: Cambridge University Press, 1973).

CHAPTER FOUR

The psychology of perpetrators

Introduction

In this chapter, I propose to consider the psychology of nonconsensual sex from the perspective of the perpetrator. It might be thought that we cannot understand the experience of nonconsensual sexual relations without first defining its contours so that we know what range of cases we should consider. I disagree. We can start with the paradigmatic case of forcible rape, about which there is little doubt as to its nonconsensuality. We will then be better positioned to consider the host of theoretical issues that motivate this project.

Sex or violence?

It might be thought, however, that I have begged another crucial question by referring to rape as nonconsensual *sex*. For it is frequently said that "rape is about violence, not about sex."(RVNS). Unpacking RVNS will set the stage for the discussion to follow, so I want to consider it in some detail. Here are some typical statements chosen almost (but not quite) at random.

In rape... the purpose of the attack is precisely to demonstrate contempt for the victim's autonomy and dignity.[1]

... rape is more a crime of violence than of sexual passion...[2]

...a major contribution of radical feminism is the debunking of the [sexual frustration] theory – A consensus is emerging among both feminists and

---

[1] Jennifer Nedelsky, "Violence against Women. Challenges to the Liberal State and Relational Feminism" in Ian Shapiro and Russell Hardin (eds.), *Nomos XXXVIII: Political Order* (New York: New York University Press, 1996), 474. This quotation is from Judith Lewis Herman, *Trauma and Recovery* (New York: Basic Books, 1997), 53.
[2] Rosemarie Tong, *Women, Sex, and the Law* (Totowa, NJ: Rowman and Allanheld, 1984), 112.

criminologists that rape is quintessentially a crime of aggression and hostility, not a form of sexual release.[3]

In recent years it has been suggested that rape is first and foremost a crime of violence. What is essential to the act is the infliction of pain and humiliation.[4]

The defining core of rape is the use of sexual intercourse as an expression of hatred or rage, as a way of debasing and humiliating someone.[5]

... research ... demonstrates very clearly, from a sociological point of view, that rape is a crime of violence. It is a crime of control, it is a crime of power, not a crime of passion.[6]

Despite the frequency with which RVNS is advanced, it is not entirely clear how it should be understood, much less whether it is true (given a certain understanding). There are at least three ways in which RVNS might be understood: (1) as an empirical claim about the motives or experience of the perpetrators; (2) as an empirical claim about the experience of the victims; (3) as a political or programmatic claim about the conception of rape that best serves the goal of reducing rape.

I think that (1) is the most plausible construction of RVNS, in which case RVNS is empirically false. But first look at the other interpretations. If RVNS is advanced as a claim about the experience of rape as the victim, it would be uncontroversially true on one account of "sex" and false on another. It is uncontroversially true that rape is typically experienced as a violation and certainly not as a pleasurable sexual encounter. So if one identifies "sex" with "pleasure," then RVNS, so understood, is certainly true. Yet the contrast between "sex" and "violence" that RVNS seems to assume is misleading because it does not allow us to distinguish between *sexual* violence and *nonsexual* violence. And, from the perspective of the victim, it is clear that *sexual* violence is a unique and particularly damaging form of violence.

I think that (3) might well describe the motives of some who advance RVNS.[7] Susan Estrich says that RVNS "has always seemed to me the better

---

[3] D. Kelly Weisberg (ed.), *Applications of Feminist Legal Theory to Women's Lives* (Philadelphia: Temple University Press, 1996), Introduction to section on rape, 412.

[4] Philip Kitcher, *Vaulting Ambition* (Cambridge, MA: MIT Press, 1985), 188.

[5] Naomi Scheman, "Rape" in Lawrence Becker and Charlotte Becker (eds.), *Encyclopedia of Ethics*, second edition (New York: Routledge, 2001), 1445.

[6] This statement is attributed to Kim Gandy, Executive vice-president of the National Organization for Women, in a critique of Randy Thornhill and Craig T. Palmer, *A Natural History of Rape* (Cambridge, MA: MIT Press, 2000), "The Men Can't Help It," *The Guardian*, January 25, 2000.

[7] For example, Charlene L. Muehlenhard, Sharon Danoff-Burg, and Irene G. Powch say that "feminist theorists ... argued for the utility of conceptualizing rape as violence." See "Is Rape Sex or Violence? Conceptual Issues and Implications" in David M. Buss and Neil M. Malamuth (eds.), *Sex, Power, Conflict* (New York: Oxford University Press, 1996), 123.

approach both theoretically *and strategically.*"[8] Scully and Marolla state that "in an effort to change public attitudes that are damaging to the victims of rape...many writers...discount the part that sex plays in the crime."[9] And Katharine Baker says that *"In order to alter the belief* that nonconsensual sex is a substitute for consensual sex, we need to move toward a recognition that it is truly 'other.'*"*[10] It is possible that these claims are true. But the claim that it is better for people to believe RVNS *cannot* be an account of the meaning of RVNS itself.

If we take RVNS seriously, it is best understood as claiming that rapists are not motivated by sexual desire, but by the desire for power, dominance, and control or by emotions such as contempt, hostility, and hatred. Thus the entry on "Rape: Behavioral Aspects" in *The Encyclopedia of Crime and Justice* mentions three patterns of rape: anger rape, power rape, and sadistic rape.[11] Rape for sex is not even on the list. For reasons that are difficult to understand, some feminists seem to believe that their normative views are more defensible if they deny "that sexual motivation on the part of the perpetrator plays any important role in rape behavior."[12] But the question of what motivates sexual offenders is precisely the sort of issue that should not be a "subject of debate between radical feminists and others."[13] For it is not a matter for debate. It is a matter for empirical investigation.

To clear some ground, there is no reason to think that the effect of A's act on B always tracks A's motivations for engaging in the act. If A burglarizes B's house in order to take B's jewelry, B may feel that her space has been invaded or violated. But there is no reason to think that A burglarizes B's house in order to make B feel that her space has been violated. Similarly, it is entirely possible that rapists seek sexual satisfaction from nonconsensual intercourse whereas the victim experiences the intercourse as painful, humiliating, and traumatic. The experience of the victim tells us little about the motivations of the perpetrators.

The failure to distinguish between the perpetrator's motive and the effects on the victims has led some commentators to make some dubious claims

---

[8] Susan Estrich, *Real Rape* (Cambridge, MA: Harvard University Press, 1987), 82.

[9] Diana Scully and Joseph Marolla, " 'Riding the Bull at Gilley's': Convicted Rapists Describe the Rewards of Rape" in Patricia Searles and Ronald J. Berger (eds.), *Rape and Society* (Boulder: Westview, 1995), 66.

[10] Katharine Baker, "Sex, Rape, and Shame," 79 *Boston University Law Review* 663 (1999), 664 (emphasis added).

[11] (New York: Free Press, 1983), 1353.

[12] Michael Studd, "Sexual Harassment" in Buss and Malamuth (eds.), *Sex, Power, Conflict* (New York: Oxford University Press, 1996), 56.

[13] Weisberg (ed.), *Applications of Feminist Legal Theory to Women's Lives*, 412.

about the alleged collective or class basis of rape. Susan Brownmiller has famously written that "from prehistoric times to the present...rape has played a critical function. It is nothing more or less than a conscious process of intimidation by which all men keep all women in a state of fear."[14] In stating that rape is nothing "more" than a process of intimidation, Brownmiller dismisses its sexual component. In stating that rape is nothing "less" than a conscious process of intimidation, she claims that all men engage in this behavior or that rapists act on behalf of non-rapists. Although none of these claims is worth taking seriously at face value, they contain two small kernels of truth. First, the fact that some women are raped may place something close to "all" women in a state of fear, even though this is not anyone's intention. Second, it is possible that many men benefit from the fact that women are in this state of fear, even though they have done nothing to create it.[15] Claudia Card maintains that without "the continual fear of rape, women would lose one significant motivation for heterosexual cohabitation," an institution from which men have historically benefitted.[16] There may be some truth to this. How much is not clear.

Rae Langton and Keith Burgess-Jackson advance a different class-based claim.

> To call [sexual] violence simply "crime" without remarking upon the interesting fact that the perpetrators are nearly always members of one class of citizens, and the victims members of another, would be to disguise its systematically discriminatory nature.[17]

> Where the [victim] is chosen on the basis of her sex, [the rapist] further implies that women *as a class* are inferior to men as a class.[18]

I believe these claims are also dubious. To say that male rape discriminates against women or implies that women as a class are inferior makes no more sense than to say that men's consensual heterosexual behavior discriminates in favor of women or implies that women as a class are superior. Think of it this way. Auto thieves do not steal expensive cars in order to discriminate against their owners. They steal expensive cars because they are more

---

[14] Susan Brownmiller, *Against Our Will* (New York: Simon and Schuster, 1975), 15.

[15] For example, a woman might be more likely to agree to sexual relations with a man not because he threatened or used violence, but because the behavior of other men has caused her to fear that he might.

[16] Claudia Card, "Is Penalty Enhancement a Sound Idea?," 10 *Law and Philosophy* 195 (2001), 212.

[17] Rae Langton, "Whose Right? Ronald Dworkin, Women, and Pornographers," 19 *Philosophy & Public Affairs* 311 (1990), 334–35.

[18] Keith Burgess-Jackson, "A Theory of Rape" in Keith Burgess-Jackson (ed.), *A Most Detestable Crime: New Philosophical Essays on Rape* (New York: Oxford University Press, 1990), 102.

valuable. If Willie Sutton robbed banks "because that's where the money is," I suspect that at least some men rape women because that's where the (desired) sex is.[19]

Why do rapists rape?

With these preliminaries set aside, what do we know about the motivations of rapists? First, and most obviously, different people have different motives, and one person may have several motives. There is no more reason to assume a single or narrowly specified set of motivations for rape than there is to assume homogeneous motivations for murder or arson. Second, and also I think quite obviously, men rape because they get *some* psychic benefit from doing so, be it sexual satisfaction, enhanced self-esteem, a sense of power, or the venting of rage.[20]

Although I regard the previous statement as almost tautologically true, Debra Satz has argued that we should be "loath to follow" the view that "rape can be seen as a 'benefit' to the rapist…"[21] But why? To say – as an empirical matter – that the rapist expects a psychic gain from his act does not entail that this psychic gain should carry *any* weight in our moral calculations about the wrongness of rape, as if the benefit to the rapist partially offsets the harm to the victim. Indeed, we may think that it is worse when someone benefits at his victim's expense than when he does not benefit at all. But suppose, for example, that we assume a consequentialism in which the psychic gain to the rapist is counted as a positive outcome that is to be weighed against the cost to the victim. Would that be so disturbing? I think not. It is improbable to the extreme that the expected gain will be sufficient to yield a positive net outcome in the face of the harm to the victim. And if the world were such that women experienced rape as a trivial matter while men gained great benefits from it, then we might well have a different moral view of what we now call rape.

To sharpen the discussion, I will distinguish two theses about rape. The first thesis maintains that rapists generally use violence as a means to obtain sexual satisfaction. Call this the *instrumental violence* thesis. The second thesis maintains that men typically use violence to express hostility (or some other negative emotion) towards women or the particular victim. Call this the *hostility* thesis. Consider muggers and spousal abusers. Muggers

---

[19] Camille Paglia, *Sex, Art, and American Culture* (New York: Vintage, 1992), 62.
[20] Catharine A. MacKinnon has said, "Men often rape women, it turns out, because they want to and enjoy it"; *A Feminist Theory of the State* (Cambridge, MA: Harvard University Press, 1989), 145.
[21] Debra Satz, "Markets in Women's Sexual Labor," 105 *Ethics* 63 (1995), 69.

typically use violence instrumentally, as a means to obtain money, although they may also gain psychic satisfaction from their power over their victims. By contrast, many perpetrators of spousal abuse use violence noninstrumentally, simply to express anger or to inflict pain.

What about rape? The fact that rape involves the use or threat of violence does not tell us whether the rapist is using violence instrumentally or noninstrumentally. Patronizing a prostitute is an act of "giving money," but no one claims that customers are motivated by the desire to give money to the prostitute.[22] And there is considerable evidence that the instrumental-violence thesis is at least part of the truth, that rapists are at least partially motivated by the desire for sexual satisfaction. Moreover, to say that rapists seek sexual satisfaction is emphatically *not* to say that rape is a crime of "passion," that rapists are motivated by some sort of uncontrollable lust, any more than robbers are motivated by an uncontrollable passion or lust for money.[23]

There are several sorts of evidence for the instrumental-violence thesis. One survey of college men found that those who were more likely to commit rape thought that women were *less* aversive to rape than those who were less likely to commit rape.[24] If the hostility thesis were true, one would expect that those most likely to commit rape would think that women were more aversive to rape than those less likely to commit rape. In a laboratory study, male subjects were shown fictitious depictions of rape. In some depictions, the female victims were aroused by the attack. In other depictions, the victims abhorred the attack. The subjects were consistently more aroused by the former depictions than by the latter.[25] This does not mean that such men are unwilling to use force instrumentally to get sex. It suggests that it is the sex and not the force that they find appealing.

In a very different sort of study, Diana Scully interviewed convicted rapists in prison. She found that some rapists used rape as a method of revenge, for others it was a "bonus added while committing another crime," while for many others, rape was used to gain sexual access to unwilling or

---

[22] Thornhill and Palmer, *A Natural History of Rape*, 149.

[23] For such rapists, "rape appears to be primarily a substitute for consensual sexual intercourse rather than a manifestation of male hostility toward women or a method of establishing or maintaining male domination"; Richard A. Posner, *Sex and Reason* (Cambridge, MA: Harvard University Press, 1992), 384.

[24] Margaret Hamilton and Jack Yee, "Rape Knowledge and Propensity to Rape," 24 *Journal of Research in Personality* 111 (1990), 111. They conclude that "rape is more likely to be an act of instrumental aggression than an act motivated by hostility toward women."

[25] Neil M. Malamuth and J. V. P. Check, "Sexual Arousal to Rape and Consenting Depictions: The Importance of the Woman's Arousal," 89 *Journal of Abnormal Psychology* 763 (1980).

unavailable women.[26] From the perpetrator's perspective, Scully writes, "rape is a low-risk, high-reward act" and the reward appears to be sex.[27]

Although Scully seems to endorse the thesis that many perpetrators view nonconsensual sex as an inferior substitute for consensual sex, she thinks that this claim is "inconsistent with the observation that almost half of the rapists... were either married or cohabiting at the time of their offense."[28] Not so. First, if more than 50 percent of men are married or cohabiting and about half of the rapists are not married or cohabiting, then rape would be *more* prevalent among men who are not married or cohabiting and who therefore lack easily available consensual sexual opportunities. Second, the instrumental-violence thesis does not claim that perpetrators are without consensual sexual opportunities, any more than the claim that robbers use violence instrumentally assumes that robbers have no money. To say that a married man does not rape for sex because he is married is no more self-evident than to say that a married man does not commit adultery or visit prostitutes for sex.

There is some sociological evidence that supports the instrumental-violence thesis. Because rapists are disproportionately unattractive and unemployed, it is plausible to suppose that such men "have a greater incentive to bypass the market in sexual relationships" and resort to the use of force.[29] Precisely because such men have fewer opportunities for consensual sex, they are also more likely to consume more pornography than attractive males, using pornography as an aid to masturbation. So the use of pornography and rape may be correlated, not because the consumption of pornography has some causal effect on the propensity to commit rape (although that might also be true), but because the same sorts of men have more reason to consume pornography and commit rape. Rape is higher where there are more divorced and separated people and where there are more men than women.[30]

[26] Diana Scully, *Understanding Sexual Violence: A Study of Convicted Rapists* (Boston: Unwin Hyman, 1990), 137. The distinction between "unwilling" and "unavailable" is of importance. In some cases, a woman is socially available to a rapist, but she is not willing to have sexual relations with him, so he uses force. This, of course, is the standard story in "acquaintance rape" or "date rape." In other cases, a woman may have no social connection with a man. In these cases, men may use violence to obtain sex because they "believed that these women would not be sexually attracted to them"; *ibid.*, 144.

[27] *Ibid.*, 137.   [28] *Ibid.*, 72.

[29] Posner, *Sex and Reason*, 183. As a general proposition, "it is consistently found that rapists and their victims come mainly from lower classes or low status groups," Menachem Amir, *Patterns in Forcible Rape* (Chicago: University of Chicago Press, 1971), 14.

[30] Larry Baron and Murray A. Straus, *Four Theories of Rape in American Society* (New Haven: Yale University Press, 1989), 10, 55.

Perhaps the most important evidence in support of the instrumental-violence thesis comes from data about the victims of rape. Those who endorse the hostility thesis typically maintain that rapists are relatively indiscriminate with respect to the characteristics of their victims. Here are some examples of this view.

Any female may become a victim of rape. Factors such as extreme youth, advanced age, physical homeliness and virginal lifestyle do not provide a foolproof deterrent or render a woman impervious to sexual assault.[31]

We do know some things about rape in humans. It frequently takes place on juveniles, on women past the age of menopause, and on members of the same sex.[32]

In reality, victim selection is determined primarily by availability and vulnerability rather than sexual desirability, and anyone could be a victim of sexual assault. Rape happens not only to young adult women but to both sexes and all age groups, from infants to the aged.[33]

Each of these statements contains a grain of truth. It is true, as Brownmiller writes, that age and unattractiveness are not "foolproof" deterrents. And, given the large number of rapes, it is safe to say that rape "frequently" takes place on juveniles and women past the age of menopause, and that men are victims of rape. That said, these sorts of statements are *highly* misleading. First, the age distribution of victims "corresponds almost perfectly to the age distribution of women's reproductive value" which, as has also been noted, corresponds to the age distribution of sexual desirability.[34] Eighty percent of the victims of rape are under thirty years old.[35] Interestingly, although women between forty and forty-nine are just as likely to be victims of aggravated assault as women between twenty and twenty-nine, the older women are far less likely to be raped.[36] The data collected on "child" victims show a heavy concentration toward the early puberty years.[37] Young children are raped, but it is very rare. And while same-sex rape does occur, it is a rare phenomenon outside prison, an environment in which same-sex intercourse is the only form of intercourse available. So the age and sex distribution of victims gives more support to the instrumental-violence thesis than to the hostility thesis.

---

[31] Brownmiller, *Against Our Will*, 348.   [32] Kitcher, *Vaulting Ambition*, 187.

[33] "Rape: Behavioral Aspects" in *Encyclopedia of Crime and Justice*, 1352.

[34] David M. Buss, *The Evolution of Desire* (New York: Basic Books, 1994), 164.

[35] The mean age of rape victims in most data sets is twenty-four years old. Owen D. Jones, "Sex, Culture and the Biology of Rape: Toward Explanation and Prevention," 97 *California Law Review* 827 (1999), 861.

[36] Buss, *The Evolution of Desire*, 164.   [37] Jones, "Sex, Culture and the Biology of Rape," 866.

The infrequency with which rapists inflict physical injuries on their victims is, perhaps, the most important evidence against the hostility thesis. Data from the National Victim Center suggest that over two-thirds of rape victims report no physical injuries whatsoever, 24 percent report minor physical injuries, and only 4 percent sustain serious physical injuries.[38] Rape typically involves little *gratuitous* violence above and beyond the violence necessary to achieve sexual intercourse or involved in intercourse itself. It is extremely rare for raped females to be killed. All this suggests that rapists are primarily motivated by a desire to *gain* sexual intercourse rather than to *inflict* suffering on their victims.

If the instrumental-violence thesis is plausible in cases in which men use violence, it is even more plausible in cases of acquaintance rape when the physical violence (penetration aside) is usually quite minimal, and when males typically turn to the use of force only when seduction fails (recall *Rusk*).[39] There is a deep tension between the emphasis on acquaintance rape and RVNS. Indeed, the more we broaden our conception of what counts as nonconsensual sexual relations, the more we have reason to accept the instrumental-violence thesis rather than the hostility thesis. A man may lie to his date or ply her with alcohol in order to obtain sexual intercourse, but it is not plausible to suppose that he is motivated by the desire to defraud or intoxicate her.

Put the question this way: what is the evidence *for* the hostility thesis? Despite the confidence with which RVNS is advanced, the answer is – not much. Diana Scully thinks that her interviewees confirm the hostility thesis when they say that their purpose "was conquest, to seize what was not offered."[40] Fair enough. But it is sex that was not offered and was therefore seized. Martin Schwartz and Walter S. DeKeseredy argue that acquaintance rapists are concerned with "sexual force and domination," but then go on to say that such men rarely find sexual pleasure in the pain they inflict: "these are men who have learned that women's feelings do not count."[41] But there is a crucial difference between egocentric or amoral indifference to a woman's feelings in the course of attaining sexual satisfaction and a specific desire to express hostility towards her.

---

[38] Murder occurred in 7 out of 1223 rapes in one study, and 1 of 646 in another study; *ibid.*, 861.

[39] Mark Cowling, *Date Rape and Consent* (Brookfield, VT: Ashgate, 1998), 19.

[40] Scully and Marolla, " 'Riding the Bull at Gilley's' " in Searles and Berger (eds.), *Rape and Society*, 66.

[41] Martin D. Schwartz and Walter S. DeKeseredy, *Sexual Assault on the College Campus* (Thousand Oaks, CA: Sage Publications, 1997), 50.

It is no doubt true that rapists are often angry at women in general or at their particular victims, but this is not incompatible with the view that rapists desire sex. On the one hand, it is well known that anger can give rise to sexual arousal, although the sexual arousal is no less sexual for that. In other cases, men may be angry at women not because they are hostile to women, but because it is women (not men) who "incite ungratifiable sexual desire."[42] And a man may be angry at a particular woman because she does not consent to having sexual relations with him, particularly when he believes that she *should* consent to do so.

Just as it is often claimed that rape is about violence, not sex, it is also claimed that "sexual harassment is about power, not sex." But despite the mantra-like quality with which these claims are advanced, whatever commonalities there are between sexual harassment and rape suggest that sexual motivations are very important indeed. First, single males are much more likely than married males to use more overt and more persistent forms of sexual harassment, a finding that is consistent with the instrumental use of power.[43] Second, given that there are many ways to harass others, we must explain why men engage in *sexual* harassment. I know of no evidence that suggests that men resort to sexual harassment because they believe that this is the form of harassment that women dread most rather than because this is a form of harassment that gets them what they want. Third, if people use sexual harassment as a technique for expressing their power over others, then we would expect that powerful women would use sexual intimidation as a means to maintain and promote their professional and economic positions.[44] But novels and movies to the contrary notwithstanding, women do not do this.[45]

It is sometimes said that the atrocious behavior of military personnel during war exemplifies the use of rape to dominate and humiliate rather than to obtain sexual satisfaction, that "war provides men with the perfect psychologic backdrop to give vent to their contempt for women."[46] It is true that military leaders have been known to encourage their troops to commit rape as a method to subdue the conquered populace. But while it would be silly to deny that the hostility thesis has relevance to wartime behavior, rape is at least partly sexual even during war. War is, after all, a context

---

[42] Donald Symons, *The Evolution of Human Sexuality* (New York: Oxford University Press, 1979), 284.
[43] Studd, "Sexual Harassment" in Buss and Malamuth (eds.), *Sex, Power, Conflict*, 67.
[44] *Ibid.*, 57.
[45] See, for example, Michael Crichton's *Disclosure* (New York: Knopf, 1994) and the movie, *Disclosure*, based on that novel.
[46] Brownmiller, *Against Our Will*, 32.

in which men lack normal consensual sexual opportunities, prostitution is rampant and women are often enslaved and forced to service the troops. War is also a context in which normal social controls are extraordinarily weak and the risks associated with some illicit behaviors may approach zero.[47] Just as conquering forces loot their victims' property with little risk, war sometimes enables men to use force to obtain sex with virtual impunity. Survey research indicates that a disturbing number of "normal" men would be more likely to commit rape if they knew that they could get away with it. War provides them with a perfect opportunity.

Evolutionary psychology

I am now in a position to extend the evolutionary-psychology model to the propensity for men to engage in rape or other forms of nonconsensual sexual relations. The publication of Randy Thornhill and Craig Palmer's *A Natural History of Rape* in 2000 was a major media event. The furor quickly died down, as it well should have. The book did not present much new evidence for the theory, but summarized findings that had been available for some time. Properly understood, I do not think that their argument is particularly controversial. Although the evidence for the theory may not be as strong as the authors would like, it is clear that many of the criticisms were not motivated by concern over the quality of the evidence, but by what I regard as the misplaced fear that the theory had untoward consequences for women.

I begin with a major caveat. Evolutionary psychology does *not* hold that there is a "gene for rape" any more than there is a gene for walking, learning language, or liking chocolates, although few doubt that humans are "programmed" to walk upright, learn language, and respond positively to chocolate. Evolutionary psychology holds that there are psychological dispositions the behavioral consequence of which is that some men choose to engage in rape and that these dispositions are the product of natural selection in the environment in which they developed. By contrast, SSSM maintains that the dispositions that cause men to rape are the product of particular social processes. There are rapists because males are socialized in the wrong way, and the task is to change the character of these social processes. There is no need for society to work against a biological disposition that is not there. On the evolutionary model, "the rapist is a man with too

---

[47] "[M]any normally risky behaviors can be performed at little or no risk"; Symons, *The Evolution of Sexuality*, 280.

little socialization rather than too much."[48] Society is the only solution to the problem of rape because these "natural" impulses must be changed or controlled.

Thornhill and Palmer suggest that there are *two* versions of the evolutionary-psychology explanation of the ultimate causes of rape. On the *adaptation view* (or proximate-causation view), the disposition to rape is a specific adaptation that was favored by selection because it increased male reproductive success by increasing the number of mates. On the *by-product view* (or ultimate-causation view), there is no specific disposition to use coercion to gain sexual access to females. Rather, the disposition to rape is a by-product or correlate of other dispositions that were favored by selection, principally the intense sexual desires of human males and the sexual choosiness of human females.[49] Thornhill and Palmer do not themselves agree whether the evidence now best supports the adaptation view or the by-product view, but they both maintain that *some* sort of evolutionary account is necessary to explain the fact that human males have always been willing to use coercion to secure sexual access and, for that matter, that males in other species have also been prone to do so.[50]

We have already seen that the evolutionary account of rape begins from the conflict between the male disposition to seek quantity and variety in sexual relations, a disposition which has been selected for its reproductive value, and the female disposition to limit sexual access to healthy men who promise to be good partners and providers, a disposition which has also been selected for its reproductive value.[51] The conflict between these sexual strategies will be experienced by males who have a reasonable number of sexual or reproductive opportunities, but the conflict will be particularly acute for those males who are not chosen by females and would be "left out of the reproductive cycle unless they forced the issue."[52]

There is no reason to think that a special disposition to use coercion to obtain sexual access would have evolved unless it served the perpetrator's reproductive aims. To engage in rape is to risk loss or death at the hands

[48] Camille Paglia, *Sexual Personae* (New Haven: Yale University Press, 1990), 23.
[49] Thornhill and Palmer, *A Natural History of Rape*, 59–60.
[50] It seems that a male scorpion fly obtains mating by offering the female a "gift" – a mass of hardened saliva that he has produced or a dead insect. Females flee when approached by a male that lacks a gift. "A male without a gift approaches a female, grabs here with his genital claspers . . . and positions the anterior edge of one of her forewings in his notal organ, where he then holds it throughout mating"; *ibid.*, 63.
[51] Deborah Blum, *Sex on the Brain: The Biological Differences between Men and Women* (New York: Penguin Putnam, 1997), 224.
[52] *Ibid.*

of one's victim, her mate, family, or community.[53] But if the competition among men for access to females becomes intense, natural selection would favor dispositions to take considerable risk in securing access to females, just as it might favor the evolution of brilliant plumage that does not serve the survival of the individual organism.

It might be objected that the occurrence of oral and anal rape demonstrates that rapists seek physical contact, not propagation. On the by-product view, there is a general disposition to seek sexual pleasure that was favored by selection, but the disposition can culminate in behaviors that do not themselves have reproductive consequences, for example, oral sex, anal sex, masturbation, and sex with contraception. On this view, the fact that rape often takes non-vaginal forms of penetration does not show that reproduction is unimportant to the general psychology of rape, any more than the fact that consensual sex often involves non-vaginal penetration shows that reproduction is unimportant to the psychology of consensual sex. If we assume that the sensory pleasure that males receive from vaginal sex is the result of natural selection, it is probably just an accident of bodily design that men get sensory pleasure from the use of their hands or from penetrating female orifices that primarily serve other purposes.

But rape is not just about sex or reproduction. It is also about the use of violence. And evolutionary psychology maintains that male aggressiveness is also best explained by the process of natural selection. I will not here attempt to document the general proposition that males are, in fact, more aggressive than females, or cite the evidence that this difference is at least partially explained in biological terms. Suffice it to say that from an early age into adulthood, "a robust sex difference in rates of direct (overt) aggression is reliably seen."[54]

Now males typically choose other *males* as the targets for their aggression.[55] Why would natural selection favor a male disposition to fight other males when doing so may well cost them their lives? Evolutionary psychologists maintain that a male disposition towards intra-sexual aggressiveness survived because males compete with other males for access to females. Although male size and strength may have enabled them to subdue many females without resort to the sort of violence that risks injury and death,

[53] As David Buss remarks, "conflict per se serves no evolutionary purpose"; *The Evolution of Desire*, 143.
[54] Eleanor E. Maccoby, *The Two Sexes* (Cambridge, MA: Harvard University Press, 1998), 36.
[55] The proportion of violence directed at females increases with age, in part because in the environments in which it is feasible for men to use violence (principally, outside the work place), adult men spend proportionally more time in close proximity to females than younger men.

they had to be prepared to endure riskier behaviors if they were going to best other male rivals for access to females or to protect themselves against them, a disposition that may even help to explain war.

In foraging societies, men go to war to get or keep women – not necessarily as a conscious goal of the warriors . . . but as the ultimate payoff that allowed a willingness to fight to evolve. Access to women is the limiting factor on males' reproductive success . . . For a man who is not at death's door, *no other resource has as much impact on evolutionary fitness.* The most common spoils of tribal warfare are women. Raiders kill the men, abduct the nubile women, gang-rape them, and allocate them as wives.[56]

From an evolutionary perspective, it is not surprising that men resort to rape during war – not because men are using rape to humiliate the females on the opponent's side, but because access to females was an (unconscious) goal of war all along.[57]

From an evolutionary perspective, it is also not surprising that men commit more violent crime than females. Despite greater sexual equality, the female proportion of arrestees for violent crime has actually declined over the last thirty years.[58] But it is not just that males engage in more interpersonal violence than females. They also engage in much more theft, burglary, and robbery. Indeed, *robbery* homicide is *more* male dominated than non-property-related homicide.[59] Women do not use violence to steal even in an era when the availability of weapons should compensate for their smaller size and lesser physical strength. Why do men commit more property crime than women? It is certainly not that males need more resources simply to live, particularly given that females are more likely to be providing for their children. But there is another sense in which males do have greater need for resources than females. Whereas women do not need financial resources to gain sexual access to males, males may feel the need for resources that exceed their own subsistence needs in order to gain sexual access to females.[60] Once again, evolutionary psychology does not claim that males are consciously engaging in aggressive and risky activities in order to spread their genes around. It says only that the disposition to engage in such activities would probably not have survived unless it did

[56] Steven Pinker, *How the Mind Works* (New York: W. W. Norton, 1997), 510 (emphasis added).
[57] As Bobbi Low notes, "even in the Judeo-Christian heritage, women were a valued profit from warfare. Consider Moses: 'Now, therefore, kill every male among the little ones, and kill every young woman who has known man by lying with him. But all the young girls who have not known man by lying with them, keep alive for yourselves.'" Numbers, 31:15, 17, 18; *Why Sex Matters: A Darwinian Look at Human Behavior* (Princeton: Princeton University Press, 2000), 228.
[58] Martin Daly and Margo Wilson, *Homicide* (New York: Aldine de Gruyter, 1988), 149.
[59] *Ibid.,* 179.　[60] *Ibid.*

tend to spread a male's genes around. We should not get carried away. Evolutionary psychology can easily become the proverbial hammer for which every phenomenon becomes a nail. Still, evolutionary psychology may go some way toward explaining why males are disposed to engage in the use of violence in a world in which dispositions that once contributed to reproductive opportunities no longer do so.

All that said, what is the evidence that rape is even unconsciously related to reproductive opportunities? First, and as I have noted, males rarely inflict physical injuries on their victims and rarely kill them. This is consistent with the hypothesis that rapists will be inclined to avoid actions that would preclude conception and birth. Second, forced copulation is virtually exclusively a male activity, and this is true in all species in which forced copulation has been observed, including species in which males are not significantly bigger or stronger.[61] Third, the victims of rape are likely to be in their peak reproductive years. Fourth, the probability that a victim will be raped penile-vaginally (as contrasted, for example, with oral rape or anal rape) is higher for victims within their fertile years than for victims of non-fertile age, a datum that one would not expect if rape were entirely unrelated to reproduction.[62]

Of course most men do not commit rape, because they do not find it appealing or because the expected social or legal costs outweigh the expected gains or because they are restrained by their moral beliefs. A common picture of our psychic economy includes positive psychic forces that move us in one direction and negative psychic restraints – moral beliefs – that try to keep those forces in check. Yet our moral sense is only partially effective. It often fails to constrain when it should. I believe that evolutionary psychology can help to explain both the failures of our moral sense and its successes. David Hume must be at least partially right in maintaining that our moral sense is rooted in our capacity for sympathy or empathy with others. And he must also be right in maintaining that the more we can identify with the other person, the stronger the restraint.[63] Unfortunately, precisely because males and females have different sexual psychologies, males may not adequately empathize with the female aversion to coercive sexual relations, thereby weakening the strength of the moral restraint.

The problem is this. Almost all humans understand what it is like to be punched, and thus we can easily imagine how another person would

---

[61] Jones, "Sex, Culture and the Biology of Rape," 862.   [62] *Ibid.*, 866.

[63] "The stronger the relation is betwixt ourselves and any object, the more easily does the imagination make the transition, and convey to the related idea the vivacity of conception with which we always form the idea of our own person"; *A Treatise of Human Nature*, book II, section II.

feel if he were hit by us. If males punch females, it is not because they do not fully appreciate what being punched is like. By contrast, males and females are decidedly not alike when it comes to the experience of sexual aggression and sexual coercion. When asked to evaluate the level of distress associated with various actions, females rate male sexual aggression to be close to the maximum of distress whereas males rate female sexual aggression as relatively innocuous.[64] Interestingly, whereas males tend to think that rape is less serious when there is little resistance, females had the opposite reaction, perhaps interpreting nonresistance as complete capitulation and domination of the will.[65] This suggests that at least some men may fail to restrain their aggression not because they have no moral sense at all, but because they do not fully appreciate the pain that is caused by their aggression.

It makes perfect evolutionary sense that males and females would have different reactions to coercive sex. For men, being coerced into sex would not have been a major issue in evolutionary terms. First, unlike women, males can not have sex unless they are sexually aroused. Second, if men were coerced into sex, this would have no significant genetic ill effects on them. At best, the female would get pregnant and the male would have more progeny. At worst, the female would not get pregnant and "spending fifteen minutes failing to get a woman pregnant is hardly a major Darwinian disaster."[66] Given this, we can expect that evolution would have instilled in males a stronger aversion to female infidelity (which can be genetically costly to the cuckolded male) than to coerced sex with women.

Critics

In the previous chapter I discussed several general criticisms of evolutionary psychology and its attempt to explain sexual psychology and behavior. Here I shall discuss but a few arguments that have been directed at its analysis of rape. There are general questions about the adequacy of the evidence in favor of the thesis, and these are serious concerns. Here I want to consider two different sorts of arguments that have been advanced against the theory, because I think they can be quite readily set aside.

It has been argued that evolutionary psychology cannot explain important phenomena such as homosexual rape in prison or the rape of post-menopausal women, that neither behavior fits the thesis of "men spreading

[64] "No other kinds of acts that men can perform, including verbal abuse and nonsexual physical abuse, are judged by women to be as upsetting as sexual aggression"; Buss, *The Evolution of Desire*, 146.
[65] Estrich, *Real Rape*, 22.
[66] Robert Wright, "Feminists, Meet Mr. Darwin," *The New Republic*, November 28, 1994, 37.

their seed."[67] Mark Cowling writes that "rape is not usually seen as a direct strategy to maximize offspring," that women who say they are infertile do not become unattractive to rapists.[68] These sorts of data pose little general challenge to the theory. First, and most generally, the theory does not claim to explain all behavior by all persons all the time. So citing particular bits of behavior that run counter to the theory are hardly damaging to its general claims. Second, evolutionary psychology does not maintain that rape – or even consensual sex – is a "direct strategy" to maximize offspring. Rather, it maintains that male minds have been selected for dispositions to engage in a set of behaviors that may culminate in rape. Consider homosexual rape in prison. If male minds have been hard-wired to seek sexual satisfaction, that disposition will result in consensual heterosexual intercourse in favorable environments, but may result in nonconsensual or homosexual intercourse in less favorable environments. Andrew Hacker's critique of evolutionary psychology similarly fails to understand the distinction between proximate and ultimate causation. He notes that since unwanted pregnancies can now be easily terminated in much of the world, "it is hard to see how coerced sex contributes more than marginally to the size of the population."[69] But a strong disposition that evolved because of its reproductive value is unlikely to disappear just because it has diminished reproductive value in the contemporary environment. Third, *pace* Brownmiller, the evidence suggests that men do not tend to rape post-menopausal women.

Some critics have argued that evolutionary psychology holds that males are "compelled" to rape, a claim that they take to be empirically and normatively false. Katharine Baker thinks that the evolutionary psychology of rape is contradicted by the fact that most men do not engage in rape: "if men are biologically compelled to pursue sexual encounters with potentially reproductive mates, why do most men refrain from raping?"[70] And Larry May suggests that evolutionary psychology wrongly implies that men are not responsible: "After all, if rape is an adaptive response to differential sexual development in males and females, individual males who engage in rape are merely doing what they are naturally adapted to do."[71]

This line of criticism is off the mark. Evolutionary psychology does not maintain that people are "compelled" to engage in any form of sexual

[67] "The Men Can't Help It," *The Guardian*, January 25, 2000. This article is a critique of Thornhill and Palmer, *A Natural History of Rape*, 4.
[68] "Any biological imperative would thus seem to be heavily socially mediated, giving the evolutionary theory at best a background role"; Cowling, *Date Rape and Consent*, 19.
[69] Andrew Hacker, "The Unmaking of Men," *New York Review of Books*, October 21, 1999, 26.
[70] Baker, "Sex, Rape, and Shame," 669.
[71] Larry May, *Masculinity and Morality* (Ithaca: Cornell University Press, 1998), 85.

behavior any more than we are compelled to eat sweets. Second, evolutionary psychology does not maintain that we have only one disposition. As I have argued, evolutionary psychology readily acknowledges and attempts to explain why we have the capacity to make counter-dispositional choices. So putting moral capacities aside, given that men who rape may be punished or killed, it is not surprising that humans display a capacity to be responsive to those threats to their survival and hence choose not to rape when the potential costs of doing so are significant. Third, evolutionary psychology simply does not maintain that humans are not morally responsible for their behavior. It is possible that some people may wrongly think that any theory that seeks to explain behavior may have some such implication, but that is hardly a strike against the theory or its proponents.

Prevention

Can anything be drawn from the previous analysis about the prevention of rape? I think so. First, and most importantly, if our goal is to reduce the prevalence of rape, then "we have to be honest about everything that might lie behind it," including the desire for sex.[72] Second, although sexual offenders are frequently depicted as biologically or psychologically driven to commit their acts, there is no reason to think that the decision to commit a sexual offense is not willful and subject to rational calculations.[73] And the evidence suggests that rapists are no less responsive to the disincentives of the criminal law than persons who commit property offenses such as auto theft.[74] Third, at least some (potential) rapists do have moral capacities that can be tapped and strengthened. One study found that both formal sanctions and moral inhibitions played a significant role in predicting whether men were likely to commit rape, although formal sanctions were important only when moral inhibitions were weak.[75] Given a capacity for moral inhibition, educating males about the way in which rape is experienced by women may help to decrease its prevalence.[76] Just as some people steal from the electric company because they believe it does not hurt anyone

---

[72] Blum, *Sex on the Brain*, 226.
[73] Ronet Bachman, Raymond Paternoster, and Sally Ward, "The Rationality of Sexual Offending: Testing a Deterrence/Rational Choice Conception of Sexual Assault," 26 *Law and Society Review* 343 (1992), 344–45.
[74] Posner, *Sex and Reason*, 386.
[75] In this study, the dependent variable is not the actual behavior of the subjects but their self-reported likelihood of committing an offense; Bachman, Paternoster, and Ward, "The Rationality of Sexual Offending."
[76] Hamilton and Yee, "Rape Knowledge and Propensity to Rape," 120.

whereas they would never steal from another individual, it is possible that some men rape because they believe it does not hurt (as much as it does) and getting them to know better might well make a difference.[77]

Thornhill and Palmer suggest that women need to be educated about the psychology of males, that women will be better positioned to avoid victimization if they understand that rape is partially rooted in male sexual desires. They maintain that women should be informed that males are "quickly aroused by signals of a female's willingness to grant sexual access" and that men may be predisposed to interpret ambiguous signals as more positive than intended.[78]

Critics of evolutionary psychology have been particularly prone to attack these sorts of suggestions as "absolutely, perfectly, unacceptable" on the grounds that they place the burden of preventing rape on women rather than men.[79] It may be argued, for example, that a woman should be able to dress as she pleases without being subject to nonconsensual sex. No doubt. In a better world, women would feel free to walk alone when and where they like, just as we would feel free not to lock our cars or bikes. In this world, however, we do lock our cars and bikes. In principle, advising women about the possible effects of their behavior or dress is no different.

Conclusion

This chapter has sketched an account of the motivation of those who commit sexual crimes. I do not think this account directly entails a specific view about the principles of valid consent to sexual relations. It does suggest that in formulating such principles, we must keep male psychology in mind, and, in particular, that some males have a strong desire to have sex with females who may not desire sex with them. To the extent that we deny the sexual component of that motivation and emphasize its "violent" character, we may inadvertently teach men that so long as their behavior is not violent, it is relatively unproblematic. I shall argue that this is wrong and incompatible with the experience of women, the topic to which I shall now turn.

---

[77] Those who said that they were more likely to commit rape were prone to think that women were *less* aversive to rape than those who were less likely to commit rape; *ibid.*

[78] Thornhill and Palmer, *A Natural History of Rape*, 181.

[79] Erica Goode, "What Provokes a Rapist to Rape?," *New York Times*, January 15, 2000, section A, page 21.

CHAPTER FIVE

The harm and wrong of rape

Introduction

In this chapter I seek to understand the ways in which nonconsensual sexual relations are harmful or wrong. Harm and wrong are not identical. I begin with harm. This analysis will, of necessity, be philosophical as well as empirical. The question as to how women experience their victimization is, in principle, a straightforward empirical question, although our information may be quite incomplete. But the question of what constitutes the harm of rape or nonconsensual sexual relations is philosophical. In particular, we want to ask whether the harm to the victim is best understood as primarily experiential (or subjective) or whether it is best understood as objective (or moral). Deborah Rhode says, for example, that date rape "*is no less harmful* than other assaults, because it calls into question a woman's behavior, judgment, and sense of trust in ways that random acts by strangers do not."[1] Rhode may be right, but we cannot say without an account of harm.

Why ask the question? Given that rape is uncontroversially harmful and wrong, why do we need to know *why* rape is harmful? Purely philosophical concerns aside, if we were only interested in violent rape, we would not need to know – for violent rape is harmful and wrongful on any plausible view. But nonconsensual or marginally consensual sexual relations may be harmful on some accounts of harm and less harmful on others, or not harmful at all. What counts as morally and legally sufficient consent to sexual relations will be sensitive to the harm consequent to allowing sexual relations in marginal cases and the cost or foregone benefit of not allowing sexual relations in such cases. So we need to know how to understand that harm.

In this chapter I seek to understand the way in which rape is harmful to the individual victim. I shall not be primarily concerned with the *prevalence*

[1] Deborah L. Rhode, *Speaking of Sex* (Cambridge, MA: Harvard University Press, 1997), 123 (emphasis added).

of rape. Still, it will be useful to provide some general background. The prevalence of rape significantly depends upon one's definition of the offense. In a finding that has attained mantra-like status on college campuses, Robin Warshaw reports that 25 percent of women have been raped, although only 27 percent of these women *regarded themselves* as victims of rape.[2] Government data, which rely on a narrower account of rape, portray a different story, although the details depend on whether the data come from law enforcement agencies or from victimization surveys. The FBI Uniform Crime Reports indicate that in 1995, there were 72 forcible rapes of female victims per 100,000 females (about 1 per 1,400 females aged twelve or over). The National Crime Victimization Survey reports one rape or sexual assault for every 300 females, of which about one-third were reported to the police.[3] If the data were roughly correct, about 3 percent of twenty-four-year-old women would have experienced a rape or attempted rape in the previous twelve years.[4]

As is well known, most (about 75 percent) rape victims know the perpetrator. Here we should distinguish between *acquaintance* rape, where the victim knows the offender but has had nothing like a "dating" relationship with him (as, for example, in virtually all incest cases), and *date* rape, where the victim and perpetrator have at least some level of social interaction.[5] The age of the victim and acquaintanceship are highly correlated. In 90 percent of the cases involving children under twelve, the victim knew the offender, whereas two-thirds of the victims aged eighteen to twenty-nine knew their assailants. A sizeable proportion of rapes involve multiple perpetrators, although this is much more common when the offender is a stranger.[6]

Approximately 6 percent of victims reported that a firearm was used, and another 10 percent report that some other weapon was employed. But the overwhelming majority of victims (84 percent) report that no weapon was used by the offender. The majority of victims do not endure

[2] Robin Warshaw, *"I Never Called It Rape": The MS report on Recognizing, Fighting, and Surviving Date and Acquaintance Rape* (New York: Harper and Row, 1988), 2, 26.
[3] "Sex Offenses and Offenders: An Analysis of Data on Rape and Sexual Assault," US Department of Justice. This report was retrieved from the internet at http://www.ojp.usdoj.gov/bjs/pub/ascii/sco.txt.
[4] It also seems that the means by which respondents are surveyed make some difference. When women living in three cities were asked in telephone interviews if they had ever been raped or sexually assaulted at some time in their lives, 2% said yes. When women were asked the same question in person, 11% said that they had been raped or sexually assaulted at some point in their lives. Margaret T. Gordon and Stephanie Riger, *The Female Fear: The Social Cost of Rape* (New York: Free Press, 1989), as cited in Sanford Kadish and Stephen Schulhofer (eds.), *Criminal Law and Its Processes: Cases and Materials* (New York: Aspen Law and Business), 316.
[5] Mark Cowling, *Date Rape and Consent* (Brookfield, VT: Ashgate, 1998), 1.
[6] Over one-quarter of victimizations by strangers involved multiple offenders, less than 3% of victimizations by non-strangers involved multiple offenders.

what we might call "gratuitous physical injuries" that go beyond those consequent to unwanted penetration itself. Rape-murders are exceedingly rare. One survey reports that over two-thirds of rape victims report no physical injuries (apart from penetration), 24 percent report minor physical injuries, and only 4 percent sustain serious physical injuries.[7] Perpetrators sometimes use drugs to render their victims unconscious or take advantage of a woman's intoxication, but such cases rarely involve physical injuries.

What do victims do when they are attacked? Although the data do not distinguish between cases involving strangers and non-strangers, it appears that about 18 percent take no self-protective action, whereas about 72 percent take some positive action. Some victims resist, capture, warn, or scare the offender. Some try to persuade the offender to refrain. Interestingly, only 4 percent scream from pain or fear. As Susan Estrich puts it, the most common reaction of victims is not to fight, but to cry.[8] It appears that some victims do nothing because they are effectively paralyzed by the event, whereas others make a conscious decision to make "a deal with the devil" and choose to submit rather than risk further physical injury or death.[9]

Violence, not sex: again

In the previous chapter I argued that rape is often about sex, from the perspective of the perpetrator. The question now arises whether rape is about violence, not sex, from the perspective of the victim. Although rape is hardly about *sexual pleasure* to the victim, rape is violence that is *sexual* in the straightforward sense that it targets the victim's sexual organs or, as in some cases, the perpetrator uses the victim's body in ways that involve *his* sexual organs, as in oral or anal rape.

First, many cases of nonconsensual sexual relations do not involve the use of an explicit threat of violence. As Dorothy Roberts has put it, "If rape is violence as the law defines it (weapons, bruises, blood), then what most men do when they disregard women's sexual autonomy is not rape."[10] True, in many cases the perpetrator threatens physical violence, but does not have

[7] Owen D. Jones, "Sex, Culture and the Biology of Rape: Toward Explanation and Prevention," 97 *California Law Review* 827 (1999), 861.
[8] Susan Estrich, *Real Rape* (Cambridge, MA: Harvard University Press, 1987), 61. Estrich is here commenting on *State v. Alston*, 310 N.C. 399, 312 S.E.2d 470 (1984), where the victim had recently ended a six-month "consensual" but abusive relationship with the offender. The victim acquiesced because she feared she would otherwise be beaten.
[9] Nancy Venable Raine, *After Silence* (New York: Crown Publishers, 1988), 222.
[10] Dorothy E. Roberts, "Rape, Violence, and Women's Autonomy," 69 *Chicago-Kent Law Review* 359 (1993), 362.

to use it because the victim acquiesces. Still, most date rape victims say they did not fear serious physical injury if they resisted. We cannot explain why nonconsensual sexual penetration is so traumatic except on the assumption that the invasion of one's sexual organs or the use of one's body for another's sexual pleasure is experienced as a special sort of violation.[11]

Second, equating rape with violence makes it difficult to take seriously those (arguable) violations of the victim's sexual autonomy that do not involve the use or threat of physical violence, for example, when the victim is coerced by nonviolent threats, or drugged, or deceived, or intoxicated, or retarded. As Gardner and Shute remark, "Assimilation of rape to the category of 'violent crime'...[perpetuates] the public myth that rapists are strangers waiting in dark alleys who subdue their victims by force."[12] I suppose one could say, "*Rape* is about violence, but other offenses are about nonconsensual sex." The general point remains that anyone interested in *broadening* society's conception of what should count as a sexual offense to include such cases should be reluctant to equate sexual offenses with the use of violence, *per se*.

Theories of harm

Step back from the issue of rape and consider the general issue: what is harm? Joel Feinberg's four-volume series on the moral limits of the criminal law provides the contemporary *locus classicus* of a theory of harm.[13] Feinberg's project seeks to answer the question, "what sorts of conduct can a society rightly make criminal?"[14] His answer is roughly Millian. With exceptions and qualifications that we can now ignore, it is legitimate for society to criminalize behavior if and only if it causes harm.

But what is harm? Feinberg argues that *for the purposes of applying the harm principle*, we need a two-pronged account of harm. A harm is (1) a wrongful act that (2) sets back or invades the interest of another person.[15] Both conditions are necessary, because one can harm without acting wrongfully, as when A's superior product drives B's business into bankruptcy or when A kills B in self-defense, and one can act wrongfully without causing harm,

[11] Richard A. Shweder, review of Nancy Venable Raine, *After Silence* in *New York Times Book Review*, September 20, 1998.
[12] John Gardner and Stephen Shute, "The Wrongness of Rape" in Jeremy Horder (ed.), *Oxford Essays in Jurisprudence*, fourth series (Oxford: Oxford University Press, 2000), 212.
[13] Feinberg's four volumes are: *Harm to Others* (New York: Oxford University Press, 1984); *Offense to Others* (New York: Oxford University Press, 1985); *Harm to Self* (New York: Oxford University Press, 1986); *Harmless Wrongdoing* (New York: Oxford University Press, 1990).
[14] *Harm to Others*, 3.   [15] *Ibid.*, 34–35.

as when one acts rudely.[16] On analysis, however, it is provision (2) that appears to provide the criterion of harm, whereas (1) is meant to screen out those harms that the harm principle would not want to prohibit. To rise to the level of harm, Feinberg argues that A's act must set back B's *interests* and the criminal law should not prohibit wrongful acts that do not rise to that level.[17]

Unfortunately, to define harm in terms of set-backs to interests seems only to push the question back one step, and begs the question whether one's interests should be understood in purely experiential terms or also in objective or moral terms. One can distinguish between two types of interest: (a) *well-being interests*, and (b) *rights-based interests*. Let us say that A sets back B's well-being interests when A's act causes B's life to go less well, as when A breaks B's arm, or steals B's money, burns B's house, or kidnaps B's children. Let us say that A sets back B's rights-based interest if A's action violates B's rights (even if A's action does not set back B's well-being interests). If, for example, B has a right to the exclusive use of his property, then A sets back B's rights-based property interest if he trespasses on B's property even though he does not otherwise damage B's property. If B has a right not to be fondled without her consent, then A's nonconsensual fondling sets back B's rights-based interest in her bodily integrity, even though he does not harm B (in any other way).[18]

Three points about the category of rights or rights-based interests. First, I do not claim that A does harm B if A violates B's rights but does not set back B's well-being interests. I say only that some advance a conception of harm on which A does so. Second, the category of rights is completely neutral with respect to the substance of those rights. For example, B may or may not have a right that A not smoke in her presence. Third, the category of rights is also neutral with respect to the grounding of those rights. B's rights might be grounded in a deontological or Kantian view or they might be grounded in consequentialist considerations such as their likely impact on well-being interests.

Let us consider the general category of well-being interests in a bit more detail. Feinberg suggests that we can distinguish between one's *welfare*

---

[16] Indeed, as Derek Parfit has argued, it is possible that one can act wrongfully without affecting for the worse the interests of an identifiable person. See *Reasons and Persons* (Oxford: Clarendon Press, 1984), chapter 15.

[17] For present purposes, I set aside the question whether society can prohibit acts that are offensive to others. Feinberg supports a version of the "offense principle."

[18] Judith Thomson suggests that precisely because we can think of people as well as their property as having boundaries, we can think of claim-infringing bodily intrusions as a form of trespass; *The Realm of Rights* (Cambridge, MA: Harvard University Press, 1990), 205.

interests and one's *ulterior* interests. A person's ulterior interests derive from his particular goals and aims, such as being a successful poet or raising a family. Given his aims, this person's life goes better if those aims are realized, less well if they are not. Not all wants or desires give rise to ulterior interests. I may want scientists to find a cure for sickle-cell anemia, but it does not follow that my life will go better if such a cure is found. Wants generate an ulterior interest only if they are stable, durable, and closely connected to oneself, perhaps through one's own efforts or through a deep personal connection (thus it may be in my interest for my adult children to succeed even though I can do little at this point to further that aim).[19] By contrast, a person's welfare interests are those general all-purpose interests the satisfaction of which is a precondition for the realization of one's ulterior interests. Life, health, adequate intellectual capacity, the absence of absorbing pain, and emotional stability are examples of welfare interests.[20] Unlike ulterior interests, which vary with the individual and culture, we all have similar welfare interests.

What is the relationship between set-backs to one's well-being interests and one's *experience*? This is a complicated and important matter. Although we all have an interest in the quality of our experience, is an aversive experience a necessary condition of being harmed? The answer to this question is an unproblematic *no* with respect to rights-based interests – if there are such interests. If, for example, people have a rights-based interest in privacy, an invasion of one's privacy violates that right even if one is unaware that the invasion has occurred. But the present question is whether aversive experience of some sort is a necessary condition of a set-back to one's well-being interests? Here, too, the answer seems to be no. It seems, for example, that one's welfare interest in one's health can be set back by an asymptomatic disease. And whereas one's ulterior interests derive from one's aims, and are in that sense necessarily subjective, the realization or frustration of those aims does not require that one experience that realization or frustration. If my life goes better if my children succeed, that interest is set back if they fail, even if I do not know that they have failed.

We can frame the issue of the relationship between a person's well-being and her experience in more general terms. Roughly speaking, there are three basic types of theories about the quality of a person's life: experiential theories, desire theories, and "objective list" or "substantive good" theories.[21] An *experiential* theory holds that the quality of a person's life is determined

[19] Feinberg, *Harm to Others*, 45.   [20] *Ibid.*, 37.
[21] See Thomas M. Scanlon, "The Status of Well-Being" in Grethe B. Peterson (ed.), *Tanner Lectures on Human Values*, volume XIX (Salt Lake City, UT: University of Utah Press, 1998), 99.

solely by her experience. A desire or preference theory holds that the quality of a person's life depends (in part) on whether one's actual subjective desires are fulfilled, but it does not require that one actually *experience* the fulfillment of the desire. An objective-list theory holds that one's life goes better when certain goods are achieved, such as moral goodness, rational activity, or attaining knowledge, whether or not one desires those goods.[22] An objective-list theory can certainly grant that experience and desire fulfillment are important components of the quality of a person's life, but the quality of a person's life is not reducible to such components. Does my life go better if my children succeed if I do not know this? On an experiential theory, the answer must be no. On a desire-fulfillment theory, my life goes better if my children succeed if but only if I *care* that they succeed, whether or not I know that they have succeeded. On an objective-list theory, my life may go better if my children succeed, whether or not I know or care that they succeed. This is not the place to explore the choice between these views in any detail.[23] The present point is that if we accept either the desire theory or an objective-list theory, A's action may set back B's well-being interests even if B does not experience a set-back to her interests.

Another distinction about harm cuts across the distinctions I have just considered. Let us say that A causes a *direct* harm to B when the harm to B is not mediated by the behavior or mental states of other persons and that A causes a *socially mediated* harm to B when A's actions cause others to have mental states or to act in ways that set back B's interests. Many harms are at least partially socially mediated. If A slanders B, A sets back B's interests in her reputation by causing *others* to have untrue and negative beliefs about B. If A disfigures B by slashing B's face, the harm is both direct and socially mediated. B's facial scar may set back her economic and social interests because she is perceived as less attractive by others even though it poses no threat to her health. A socially mediated harm is no less objective than a direct harm, even though it is mediated by the subjectivities of others, for the subjectivities of others are facts about the world. Beauty may be in the eye of the beholder, but the eyes of the beholders are what they are, and given those eyes, A's act of disfigurement may cause an objective and socially mediated harm to B.

---

[22] The term "objective list" is introduced by Derek Parfit, *Reasons and Persons*, 499.

[23] It does seem that a purely experiential view cannot be right, that "it makes sense to say that the life of a person who is contented and happy only because he is systematically deceived about what his life is really like is for that reason a worse life, for him, than a life . . . where this happiness was based on true beliefs"; Scanlon, "The Status of Well-Being" in Peterson (ed.), *Tanner Lectures* XIX, 97.

Another preliminary distinction: it is absolutely crucial to distinguish between *wrong* and *harm*, between the wrongness of A's action and the harm to B in a particular case. As a first approximation, we might say that the wrongness of an act is a function of three factors: (1) its *expected* or *ex ante* harm to a victim, (2) A's culpability for that act, and (3) the actual harmful consequences of A's act, although (3) is controversial, as it turns on the right view about moral luck. We might think of the expected harm of an act as the average harm caused by the act. Robbery is more wrong than burglary, because the average harm of robbery (which includes the experience of the victim) is greater than the average harm of burglary, even though many robberies cause less harm than many burglaries. A's culpability for his act is a function of his intentions or capacities. So while murder is more wrong than robbery, negligent homicide may be less wrong than armed robbery, even though the expected harm of manslaughter is greater than the expected harm of armed robbery.

The distinction between "A's act is wrong" and "A's act harms B" opens up some theoretical space. In particular, it makes it more plausible to accept a predominantly experiential account of harm without fearing that such an account will have unacceptable moral implications. Although I am not prepared to argue here for a *purely* experiential account of harm, I believe that experience is at least a major component of harm. And by distinguishing between wrong and harm, we can say – if we want to – that some cases of nonconsensual sexual relations may not involve a particularly serious harm to B, even though A's action is still seriously wrong.[24]

We can similarly distinguish between a conception of rights violations that is experientially *defined* and one that is experientially *justified*. If we say that A's action violates B's rights when it is the type of action that *generally* causes experiential harm, our conception of B's rights is experientially justified or grounded, but not experientially defined. I am not here arguing for an account of rights that is experientially justified, although I am sympathetic to that view. Indeed, I suspect that the notion of harm to B's rights-based interests (such as a trespass of which B is unaware) is just another way of arguing that A's action is wrong even though B has not been harmed experientially. The present point is that we have little to fear from a largely experiential account of harm. We can grant that B has not been

---

[24] "It is possible, although unusual, for a rapist to do no harm. A victim may be forever oblivious to the fact that she was raped, if, say, she was drugged or drunk to the point of unconsciousness when the rape was committed, and the rapist wore a condom"; Gardner and Shute, "The Wrongness of Rape" in Horder (ed.), *Oxford Essays*, 196.

harmed in a particular case without being required to say that A has done nothing wrong or that A has not violated B's rights – "acts which never come to light are not rendered innocent by that fact alone."[25]

Harm and distress

Setting the previous point aside for the moment, assume that nonconsensual sexual relations might involve three sorts of harm to the victim: (1) a set-back to her rights-based interest in her bodily integrity or her sexual autonomy, an "objective" or "dignitary" harm; (2) palpable physical injuries and enduring psychological harm that impair the victim's ability to function; (3) psychological *distress*. In this section, I want to consider the question posed by (3). Should we regard distress itself as a harm? If so, can we distinguish between the distress that justifies legal and moral prohibitions on that account and the distress that does not?

We can learn about the moral status of distress by focusing on cases that do *not* involve physical contact, where distress seems to stand alone as a possible reason for proscribing conduct. Consider offensive conduct and hate-speech. In the first case, we want to know whether we can justifiably prohibit conduct (including speech) on the grounds that the behavior offends others, as exemplified by laws prohibiting public nudity, obscenity, loud noise, desecration of the flag, and public drunkenness. In the second case, we want to know whether a liberal society (or institution) can justifiably prohibit people from making utterances that exhibit discriminatory attitudes on the grounds that the utterances cause distress.[26]

Why should we draw an important distinction between the causation of physical pain and the causation of distress? It might be thought that physically caused pain is typically much more severe than non-physically caused distress in terms of its intensity or duration.[27] The problem is that there is simply no reason to think that this is true. The pain caused by a blow to the stomach may be over in a minute; the distress caused by a humiliating remark may last for days, months, or years. Moreover, it is arguable that there is no fundamental physiological distinction between the site and character of physical pain and mental distress. One experiences

---

[25] *Ibid.*, 197.
[26] See, for example, Andrew Altman, "Liberalism and Campus Speech: A Philosophical Examination," 103 *Ethics* 302 (1993). I set aside other possible reasons for prohibiting such actions, such as promoting equality.
[27] See Frederick Schauer, "The Phenomenology of Speech and Harm," 103 *Ethics* 635 (1993).

psychological distress because physiological events occur in the brain and when one experiences pain from a blow to the stomach, the pain is also experienced in the brain.[28]

Judith Thomson suggests a different approach. Rather than press on the distinction between physical injury and psychological distress, she distinguishes between *belief-mediated distress* and *non-belief-mediated distress*.[29] When you punch me in the stomach, or shout in my ear, or scratch your fingers on the chalk-board, you cause non-belief-mediated distress. These things hurt all on their own. By contrast, when you cause me to feel embarrassed, afraid, humiliated, or insulted, I experience belief-mediated distress. If I did not believe that being called stupid is an insult (say, because I did not understand the language), I would not feel insulted. Thomson argues that we have a "claim" that others not cause us non-belief-mediated distress, but we do not have a claim that others not cause us belief-mediated distress. Thomson argues that causing non-belief-mediated distress is akin to violating a person's right to bodily integrity, and is exemplified by nuisances such as loud noise, dust, and noxious smells. By contrast, we have no claim not to be caused the sort of belief-mediated distress that is often consequent to hate-speech or obscenity.

Why do we not have a claim not to be subject to belief-mediated distress? First, Thomson notes that B's beliefs may be irrational, and it seems odd to think that B's irrational beliefs would justify constraining A's behavior.[30] Second, unlike non-belief-mediated distress which simply happens, Thomson suggests that people bear "some responsibility" for their beliefs, even when they are not irrational.[31] Because one could choose not to be (as) insulted by an ethnic slur, this weakens or negates one's claim not to be caused to feel insulted. Third, Thomson argues that counting B's mental distress is unfair to those who do *not* experience belief-mediated distress. Suppose that A fondles both B and C without their consent. Although B is distressed by A's act, C has learned to steel herself against such behavior and is only mildly annoyed ("men who get their jollies that way are pathetic"). If one has a right not to be caused belief-mediated distress, then A would violate two claims of B (a right to bodily integrity and a right not to be caused belief-mediated distress), but only one claim of C (a right to bodily integrity). And this, Thomson says, "can hardly be right."[32]

I disagree. Consider the crime of assault. If one has a distinct right not to be put in a well-founded fear of bodily injury, then there *can* be a distinct

---

[28] See Susan Brison, "Speech, Harm, and the Mind–Body Problem in First Amendment Jurisprudence," 4 *Legal Theory* 39 (1998).
[29] *The Realm of Rights*, 250ff.   [30] *Ibid.*, 253–54.   [31] *Ibid.*, 253.   [32] *Ibid.*, 255.

right not to be caused belief-mediated distress.[33] Second, Thomson makes two mistakes about controllability. Controllability and belief dependency are only imperfectly correlated. It is not true that one's susceptibility to non-belief-mediated distress is uncontrollable or that one's response to belief-mediated distress is (easily) controllable. An airline baggage handler can avoid the non-belief-mediated distress of loud noise by wearing ear plugs, but it may be difficult to steel oneself against one's belief-mediated fear of Doberman pinschers or anger at an ethnic slur.[34] And even if B *can* reduce her level of distress, it does not follow that the burden of such reduction should fall on B, rather than A.

Third, Thomson's unfairness argument also misfires. Thomson argues that it is unfair to treat C's claim as weaker than B's if C is thick-skinned and B is a (relative) wimp. I do not see why this is a problem. First, even if we say that B is harmed more than C, there may still be reason not to reduce the relative force of C's claim. We may think it unfair to C to treat her claim as less serious if she has taken steps to steel herself against harm or we may worry that doing so would reduce people's incentives to mitigate harm. So we can treat C's claim as comparable to B's claim without denying that B is *harmed* more than C. Second, it seems hard to deny that whether and how seriously A harms B can depend upon what B does.[35] If A shoots at both B and C, but only C is wearing a bullet-proof vest, we do not deny that B has been more seriously harmed than C or that B might have a claim of compensation for injury against A that C lacks.

For these reasons, I believe that belief-mediated distress *can* constitute a morally and legally cognizable harm. What determines whether such distress *should* be so regarded? Note, first, that the question is whether B's distress *provides a reason* to constrain A's behavior, not whether we *should* constrain A's behavior all things considered. Whether we are justified in constraining A's behavior is a complicated matter, because it involves not only the character of B's distress, but the strength of A's right to engage in his behavior or social benefits from deciding not to intervene. We may think, for example, that Holocaust deniers should be free to speak not because the distress which they cause does not rise to the level of a morally or legally cognizable harm, but because there are positive benefits to robust freedom of speech.

---

[33] As Anthony Ellis observes, it seems reasonable to suppose that "if someone makes my life a misery by constantly threatening me with violence, secretly having no intention of carrying out the threats, but purely with the intention of making me live in fear, then he has infringed my rights"; "Thomson on Distress," 106 *Ethics* 112 (1995), 113.

[34] See Schauer, "The Phenomenology of Speech and Harm," 649–51.

[35] See Ellis, "Thomson on Distress," 118.

In determining when B's distress qualifies as a potential reason for constraining A's behavior, we need to consider its *controllability* and *legitimacy*.
Thomson is right to think that controllability matters. If distress (such as
experiencing scratching a chalk-board) is relatively uncontrollable (or is
controllable only at very high cost), then the question whether it is legitimate does not arise. It may not be seriously wrong to cause such distress,
but we cannot ask people not to be distressed.

The moral legitimacy of belief-mediated distress also matters. It is not
that the distress experienced by the target of a racial insult is necessarily
more intense than the distress experienced by the homophobe who observes
a homosexual couple embracing. It is arguably legitimate to feel insulted
if one is the target of an ethnic slur and to expect that one's feelings give
others a reason to refrain from their behavior. By contrast, it is arguably
less legitimate to be upset at the sight of a homosexual couple embracing,
or, more importantly, it is certainly less reasonable to expect that such
distress gives others a reason not to so act. As Simester and von Hirsch have
argued, to prohibit an act under the offense principle, the offensive conduct
must be wrong.[36] I cannot offer an adequate account of the distinction
between legitimate and non-legitimate distress. I do maintain that some
such distinction is necessary if we are going to regard distress as a reason
for others not to cause such distress.

Rights violations and experience

I now want to suggest that there is a deeper connection between experiential
harm (which includes belief-mediated distress) and rights violations and
that the latter are largely, if not entirely, parasitic on the former. I do not
believe that we should understand rights violations as objective harms that
are independent of human experience. I believe that we regard many acts
as rights violations or violations of autonomy precisely because such acts
typically give rise to experiential harm even when they do not do so in a
particular case.

Consider the prohibitions against inflicting bodily harm. In his well-
known discussion of the "minimum content of natural law," H. L. A. Hart
observes that the very content of both morality and law is rooted in certain
facts about human beings, for example, that humans are "prone to, and
normally vulnerable to, bodily attack."[37] If humans were constituted like
turtles, which are immune from certain sorts of attack, there would be

---

[36] A. P. Simester and Andrew von Hirsch, "Rethinking the Offense Principle," 8 *Legal Theory* 269
(2002).
[37] H. L. A. Hart, *The Concept of Law* (Oxford: Clarendon Press, 1961), 190.

no point to the moral principle that it is wrong to attack other humans. Consider the rights of prisoners. As Simon Blackburn notes, "Keeping prisoners in the cold, or the dark, or deprived of sleep, or fed on rotten meat, is abominable because of our biological need for warmth, light, sleep, and a proper diet. If we had other natures, like polar bears or cockroaches, it might not be so bad."[38] Similarly, if humans did not typically experience distress in response to invasions of our privacy or sexuality, then there would be no point to insisting that we have a right that others not engage in such behaviors.

There are two ways in which experiential harm and a right to bodily integrity might be linked. On one view, there is an important right against violations of bodily integrity because women characteristically experience distress when their bodily integrity is violated. In this case, the distress precedes and motivates the right. Consider the right to privacy. Thomas Nagel suggests that humans seem to be the only animals that "don't as a rule copulate in public" and that suffer from "inhibition and embarrassment brought on by the thought that others are watching them."[39] If, contrary to fact, human beings were psychologically constituted such that being observed while naked or copulating did not bother us, there would be no point to such a right. I do not mean that we would have such a right, but that we would not care about its violation. I mean that there would be no such right in the first place.

Rights violations are often linked to distress in a second way, what we might call "second-order" or "theoretical" distress, by which I refer to the distress that derives from the *belief* that someone is violating one's rights, as when people experience distress not solely from someone else's smoke but rather because they believe that the smoker is violating their rights.[40] Similarly, a woman may experience distress at being fondled nonconsensually precisely because she believes that such behavior violates her rights. And a victim of nonconsensual nonviolent sexual relations may feel violated not just because there has been unwanted penetration, but because she believes that her assailant's behavior demonstrates a disregard for her rights.

Second-order distress plays an important supporting role for rights that are rooted in first-order distress by increasing the costs of violating such rights. That said, a right cannot be grounded in second-order distress. We

---

[38] Simon Blackburn, *Ruling Passions* (Oxford: Clarendon Press, 1998), 151.

[39] Thomas Nagel, "Concealment and Exposure," 27 *Philosophy & Public Affairs* 3 (1998), 18. Darwin claims that blushing is a trait that distinguishes humans from other species. See *The Expression of the Emotions in Man and Animal* (New York: D. Appleton, 1872), chapter XIII.

[40] As Mill put it (in a slightly different context) – "It makes a vast difference . . . in our feelings . . . toward [another] whether he displeases us in things in which we think we have a right to control him or in things in which we know that we have not"; *On Liberty*, chapter IV.

cannot bootstrap a right that is grounded in the avoidance of distress by positing the right and then noting that people experience distress when that right is violated.

There are several reasons to regard rights violations as a serious matter even when they do not cause (experiential) harm. Positing a right not to be subject to nonexperienced violations serves as a prophylactic device against those violations that are experienced because the world is such that people frequently do discover that such actions occurred. As Gardner and Shute put it, "the harm principle's standard is met if the class of criminalized acts is a class of acts which tend to cause harm," and this is true even if the act itself does not cause harm under special conditions.[41] On this view, police have reason to arrest a peeping Tom whose target is unaware of his activities not because he has caused harm to this particular target, but because his actions are likely to cause experiential harm to others in the future or because we want to deter other offenders whose acts are likely to cause experiential harm. Second, the wrongness of A's action is principally a function of his culpability and the _expected_ harm of his act, and not the actual harm that ensued. Put another way, the distinction between harmful and non-harmful rights violations tracks the distinction between successful and (unsuccessful) attempted crimes. Attempted crimes cause less harm (to individuals) than successful crimes, but may not be (much) less wrong on that account.[42]

The harms of rape

We are now in a position to consider the harms of rape and nonconsensual sexual relations. We want to understand what is _special_ about the harm of rape. We want to know whether and why the nonconsensual insertion of the penis into the vagina (or another orifice) is a particularly grievous harm.

Some have argued that rape is not a special sort of harm. Susan Brownmiller has written that we should view rape as akin to aggravated assault, "as an injury to the victim's bodily integrity, and not as an injury to the purity or chastity of man's estate."[43] Jeffrie Murphy suggests that rape should not be regarded as anything "more than an assault or an unlawful touching," that "there is nothing intrinsic about sexual assault that makes it objectively

---

[41] Gardner and Shute, "The Wrongness of Rape" in Horder (ed.), _Oxford Essays_, 216.

[42] See Lawrence Becker, "Criminal Attempts and the Theory of the Law of Crimes," 3 _Philosophy & Public Affairs_ 262 (1974). Becker argues that unsuccessful attempts may cause as much _social_ or _criminal_ harm as successful crimes.

[43] Susan Brownmiller, _Against Our Will_ (New York: Simon and Schuster, 1975), 379.

more serious than nonsexual assault."[44] Harriet Baber thinks that it is sexist to view rape as a particularly grievous harm, to assume that rape victims are more traumatized than victims of other crimes or to assume that a woman's most important interests are tied to her sexuality rather than to her intellectual, economic, and (nonsexual) personal interests.[45]

I believe that rape and nonconsensual sexual relations are special harms, and they are special harms largely because they are experienced as special harms. As Ann Cahill puts it, "few women would agree that being raped is essentially equivalent to being hit in the face or otherwise physically assaulted."[46] I also think it likely that the distress to women caused by sexual violations is deeply implanted in the human psyche, that it is not "essentially cultural," nor is it principally a "second-order" or theoretically loaded form of distress. Here we will get support from evolutionary psychology; for just as evolution has given us a vulnerable exterior of skin rather than the less vulnerable exterior of turtles, evolution has also produced a female psyche that is acutely aversive to nonconsensual sexual relations. To the extent that the distress experienced by rape victims is variable and socially constructed, it would be an open question whether we should try to prevent rape or "socialize women to accept it."[47] True, even if we regard the distress as socially constructed, we might still regard it as a form of distress that should weigh heavily in our moral and legal calculations. Still, I believe that the weight we attribute to the distinctive response to sexual violations receives additional support from evolutionary psychology.

Harm to well-being interests (impairment)

Violent rape frequently involves some harm to the welfare interests of the victim or what we might call impairments. It frequently involves some physical injury to the body. It imposes the risk of pregnancy, disease, and, consequently, the risk of death. Nonconsensual sex is not just about sexual violations. It is also about the possible consequences of such violations and it would be experienced as a different sort of violation if it were not.

Now the *extent* to which rape involves these and other palpable harms or impairments is an empirical question. As we have seen, rape does not

[44] Jeffrie G. Murphy, "Some Ruminations on Women, Violence, and the Criminal Law" in Jules Coleman and Allen Buchanan (eds.), *In Harm's Way* (Cambridge: Cambridge University Press, 1994), 214.
[45] See H. E. Baber, "How Bad Is Rape?," from 2 *Hypatia* 125 (1987), reprinted in Alan Soble (ed.), *The Philosophy of Sex*, second edition (Savage, MD: Rowman and Littlefield, 1991).
[46] Ann J. Cahill, *Rethinking Rape* (Ithaca: Cornell University Press, 2001), 3.
[47] Steven Pinker, *The Blank Slate* (New York: Viking Press, 2002), 164.

generally involve the use of weapons or great physical force above and beyond what the assailant believes is necessary to achieve penetration. The strictly physical impairments that result from rape are typically less severe than losing a limb or having one's thumb broken. And if we expand our view of sexual offenses to include cases of unconsciousness, deception, or intoxication, then there is a large category of cases in which victims do not experience any physical impairment (bracketing pregnancy and disease).

Does rape tend to produce long-term psychological impairment (as distinguished from the fear and terror of the experience itself)? Numerous commentators – on different sides of the political spectrum – have opined that the answer is no. Harriet E. Baber says that "there is no evidence to suggest that most rape victims are permanently incapacitated by their experiences nor that in the long run their lives are much poorer than they would otherwise have been."[48] Michael Davis has written that few victims "suffer serious long-term psychic injury."[49] And Camille Paglia writes that "Rape does not destroy you forever. It's like getting beaten up. Men get beat up all the time."[50]

The evidence suggests otherwise. One important study reports that the risk of developing post-traumatic stress disorder (PTSD) is higher for victims of rape (49 percent) than for all other traumatic events except being held captive, tortured, or kidnapped (54 percent), a list that includes severe beating (32 percent), serious accidents or injury (17 percent), or the sudden death of a close friend or relative (14 percent).[51] Rape survivors report more suicidal thoughts and suicide attempts than victims of other crimes.[52] Harriet Baber thinks it is sexist to assume that women are more likely to be traumatized than male victims of violence. But this is not a matter of ideology. If female rape victims are more traumatized than (male and female) victims of other violent crimes, then they are more traumatized.[53] And that is the truth.

Jeffrie Murphy writes that "there is nothing intrinsic about sexual assault that makes it objectively more serious than nonsexual assault."[54] But what do "intrinsic" and "objectively more serious" amount to here? When

---

[48] Baber, "How Bad Is Rape?" in Soble (ed.), *The Philosophy of Sex*, 248.

[49] Michael Davis, "Setting Penalties: What Does Rape Deserve?," 3 *Law and Philosophy* 61 (1984), 71.

[50] Camille Paglia, *Sex, Art, and American Culture* (New York: Vintage, 1992), 64.

[51] Jane Brody, "When Post-Traumatic Stress Grips Youth," *New York Times*, March 21, 2000, section F, page 8.

[52] Judith Lewis Herman, *Trauma and Recovery* (New York: Basic Books, 1997), 50.

[53] It might be argued that the belief that women are more traumatized perpetuates a stereotype of women as weak and vulnerable, and thus it would be better for women if we believed that they are not more traumatized even if they are. That would be a different argument.

[54] Murphy, "Some Ruminations on Women, Violence, and the Criminal Law" in Coleman and Buchanan (eds.), *In Harm's Way*, 214.

Murphy maintains that there is nothing about the penetration of a bodily orifice that makes it "objectively" more serious than a non-sexual imposition on the body, he implies that, by contrast, an attack on the *body* is an objectively serious matter. Why? Just as we can ask whether the penetration of an orifice is "objectively" more harmful than a punch in the nose, we can ask whether a punch in the nose is "objectively more serious" than hurtful speech. If we were so constituted that insulting speech had more severe long-term consequences than physical attacks, we might well regard insulting speech as "objectively" more serious than physical attacks. If the objective seriousness of harm is a function of experience, then sexual assault is objectively more serious than nonsexual attacks.

It is an interesting question why rape victims are at greater risk for PTSD than victims of severe beatings, particularly if Donald Dripps is correct in thinking that most women "would rather be subjected to unwanted sex than to be shot, slashed, or beaten with a tire iron."[55] There are at least three reasons why this might be so. First, people are not always good predictors of how they will respond to various events or conditions. I suspect that most people would choose to be deaf rather than blind, but the evidence suggests that the blind exhibit fewer psychological disorders than the deaf. And while most people think that their lives would be miserable if they were to become paralyzed, the evidence suggests that the paralyzed adjust reasonably well.

Second, unlike victims of some crimes, rape victims see themselves as having made a choice. Reflecting on her victimization, Nancy Venable Raine says "I instinctively 'decided' to live – unlike any number of female saints half-remembered from my childhood who chose death over the loss of their 'virtue.' I did make 'a deal with the devil.' "[56] Victims of rape report that they come to experience a sense of guilt, shame, and self-loathing, feelings that reflect a disposition to second-guess one's decision to succumb.[57]

Third, the socially mediated harms of rape may be greater than the socially mediated harms consequent to other violent crimes. In a society in which non-virgin women are less marriageable or in which raped women are cast off as unclean by their husbands, rape would generate palpable social harms. Although the socially mediated harms of rape are no doubt less severe in contemporary America, victims of rape may well still suffer losses of affection, reputation, and mating opportunities.

---

[55] Panel Discussion, "Men, Women and Rape," 63 *Fordham Law Review* 125 (1994), 141.

[56] Raine, *After Silence*, 222.

[57] Nancy Venable Raine says she wrote a book about her experience as a victim to "drain the swamp of victim-blame" from her mind. As quoted in the review of *After Silence* by Richard Shweder, *New York Times Book Review*, September 20, 1998, 13.

Distress

I do not want to press too hard on the distinction between long-term psychological impairment and what I have called distress, but I think there is a distinction to be made. Even when nonconsensual sexual relations do not have enduring psychological effects, they typically cause distress at the time of the event and for some time thereafter.

Robin West suggests that distress often takes the form of a sense of invasion.

> The fear of sexual... invasion is the fear of being occupied *from within*, not annihilated from without; of having one's self overcome, not ended; of having one's own physical and material life taken over by the pressing physical urgency of another, not ended by the conflicting interests of another; of being, in short, overtaken, occupied, displaced, and invaded, not killed.[58]

I suspect it is precisely this invasion of one's privacy that often triggers victim distress. As Nagel has put it, "the boundary between what we reveal and what we do not, and some control over that boundary, are among the most important attributes of our humanity."[59] Women experience distress at being exposed and (unlike men), at being the targets of "indecent exposure," which is, after all, a criminal offense in itself. Sexual intercourse is a particularly invasive invasion. From a psychological as well as a physical perspective, the penetration of the body, and, in particular, the penetration of one's sexual organs, may be more destructive "than any that stops at the surface of the body."[60] This in no way diminishes the trauma caused by other types of sexual assault, but when we consider the phenomenology of intercourse, writes William Miller, we see that the "vagina is a gateway inside, the gate to the woman's soul by which act of entry property in her body is claimed, whence the notion of possessing and knowing a woman..."[61] And intercourse is not a clean invasion. The male leaves his "nasty slime" in the victim's body, a dimension of rape that may help to explain why it is experienced as "sullying" and "defiling."[62]

---

[58] Robin West, "Jurisprudence and Gender," 55 *University of Chicago Law Review* 1 (1988), 41. I do not see why she thinks that the "harm of [nonconsensual] intercourse is descriptively incommensurate with liberal concepts of harm"; *ibid.*, 95. The control of access to one's self and to information about oneself is a central tenet of liberalism.

[59] Nagel, "Concealment and Exposure," 4.   [60] Cahill, *Rethinking Rape*, 11.

[61] William Ian Miller, *The Anatomy of Disgust* (Cambridge, MA: Harvard University Press, 1997), 102.

[62] Naomi Scheman, "Rape" in Lawrence Becker and Charlotte Becker (eds.), *Encyclopedia of Ethics*, second edition (New York: Routledge, 2001), 1445. As Nancy Venable Raine describes her response, "I want to wash my mouth out with fire. What is in my mouth? Dirt is in my mouth. In my body. His dirt"; *After Silence*, 22.

It is not clear to what extent the form and intensity of a victim's distress is a function of the use of physical violence or the victim's knowledge of the assailant. There are some forms of emotional distress, such as a sense of betrayal, that require familiarity with the assailant. Some victims may experience this distress as worse than a violent attack by a stranger. Mary Gaitskill writes about her attack by a stranger: "The terror was acute, but after it was over, it actually affected me less than many other mundane instances of emotional brutality I've suffered...it had nothing to do with me or who I was, and so, when it was over, it was relatively easy to dismiss."[63] It is an empirical question whether Gaitskill's response is typical. I suspect it is not. Linda Fairstein, a rape prosecutor, maintains that the short-term and long-term psychological effects of nonviolent date rape are typically less severe than those associated with violent rape by a stranger (or a non-date acquaintance).[64]

As evidence of the previous claim, recall Robin Warshaw's finding that only 27 percent of the women whose sexual assault met her definition of rape perceived themselves as victims of rape. Laumann's survey reports that 50 percent of those women who reported that they had been "forced" to have sexual intercourse were "in love" with the men who forced them.[65] Indeed, one study found that almost 40 percent of rape victims date their attacker *after* the rape.[66] We should not minimize the distress experienced by such women, but it seems plausible to suppose that they experience less distress than those who think of themselves as having been raped.

Should we accept the experiential view?

On the experiential view of harm, rape is the "embodied experience of women" and it is a distinctive sort of harm precisely because and only insofar as women experience rape in ways that are not equivalent to other forms of physical assault.[67] On the experiential view, the use of physical violence

---

[63] Mary Gaitskill, "On Not Being a Victim" from *Harper's*, March, 1994, reprinted in Adele Stan (ed.), *Debating Sexual Correctness* (New York: Delta, 1995), 267.

[64] Panel Discussion, "Men, Women and Rape," 63 *Fordham Law Review* 125 (1994), 159. Diana Scully also thinks not: "it is the 'classic' rape by a stranger on the street that women fear most"; *Understanding Sexual Violence: A Study of Convicted Rapists* (Boston: Unwin Hyman, 1990), 172.

[65] Of those who reported that they were forced to have their first intercourse, about 50 percent reported that the intercourse was preceded by kissing and petting. See Edward O. Laumann, John H. Gagnon, Robert T. Michael, and Stuart Michaels, *The Social Organization of Sexuality* (Chicago: University of Chicago Press, 1994), 332–38.

[66] David Bryden and Sona Lengnick, "Rape in the Criminal Justice System," 87 *Journal of Criminal Law and Criminology* 1194 (1997), 1223.

[67] Cahill, *Rethinking Rape*, 109.

or the threat of such violence are not just means by which perpetrators obtain nonconsensual sexual relations, which itself constitutes the principal objective harm of rape, any more than the mugger's gun is just a mechanism for obtaining money. Rather, the victim's response to the perpetrator's acts constitutes a significant component of the harm itself.[68] And where these consequences are less severe, then the aggregate harm of nonconsensual sex is less severe.

It is frequently argued that nonconsensual sexual relations always constitute a serious wrong to the victim whether or not it leads to injury, impairment, and distress, and this because it is a violation of the victim's rights to bodily integrity or sexual autonomy. On this view, rape involves a "dignitary injury" to its victim.[69] It is the violation of the victim's *rights* that is at the core of the wrongness of rape, and not the other sorts of experiential harms that typically come in its trail.

The plausibility of this view turns on the sort of theory of rights we accept. If we view rights as independent moral claims that serve (primarily) as *premises* in a moral argument, then this view makes sense. But on the view I prefer, rights are best understood as moral devices that protect interests that are important to people or that help to shape our social world in a desirable way. If, say, there is a right that others not engage in nondamaging trespass on one's property, it is because we care about such trespass or because a right against all trespass is an efficient prophylactic against the trespass that is damaging. Although many cases of trespass are (otherwise) harmless, we may think it better to have a clear boundary established *ex ante* than to respond to the "actual" harm of a case of trespass *ex post*. Similarly, to say that B has either a right to bodily integrity or a right not to engage in nonconsensual sexual relations is the *conclusion* of a moral argument about the way in which our world should be organized rather than a premise of that argument. That conclusion can, of course, serve as a premise in other moral arguments, but the claim that B has those rights must itself be supported and I believe it is best supported by appeal to the experience of nonconsensual sexual relations. I do *not* say that the appeal to experience must be embedded in a straightforward consequentialist justification of rights. The appeal to experience might well be part of a contractualist argument in which the fact of such experience makes it reasonable to reject

---

[68] Feinberg, *Harm to Self*, 298. Theft by force is more serious than burglary, not because the transfer of property is less voluntary, but because it involves other harms.
[69] Peter Westen, "The Logic of Consent: The Diversity and Deceptiveness of Consent as a Defense to Criminal Conduct," unpublished manuscript.

any moral and legal regime which does not respect such rights.[70] Either way, experience will play a role in the grounding of such a right.

Consider the right to bodily integrity. We cannot simply assume that *any* crossing of a bodily boundary is a serious matter, an important violation of our rights. On one view, bodily integrity is important because "the body houses the free will and is the organ of its purposes"; we must protect the body insofar as it is necessary to protect a person's rational capacities.[71] On a less complicated view, bodily integrity is important because we *experience* crossings of our bodily boundaries as important. On both views, violations of bodily boundaries are less grave matters when they do not threaten the value at stake. When crossing a bodily boundary does not threaten an agent's will or is not likely to cause injury or distress, then they are, in principle, less serious matters.[72] It may be wrong to kiss someone without their consent (or, perhaps, without giving them an opportunity to avoid it), but as Donald Dripps remarks – "A kiss is just a kiss. Vaginal intercourse is something different."[73] Although nonconsensual kisses and nonconsensual intercourse both involve nonconsensual crossings of one's bodily boundaries, nonconsensual vaginal intercourse is different, and it is different because the synchronic *experience* and potential consequences of intercourse are different.

It might be thought that the experiential view of the harm of rape has unacceptable implications. John Bogart says this: "It is not clear that the experience of rape, as a psychological state, remains stable across historical and social distance. It is clear that even within a locality, rape is experienced differently by victims. That fact alone should lead us to be wary of making experience an intrinsic harm of rape."[74] Bogart is concerned that the experiential view implies that rape is more harmful in some societies than others. I do not share his concern. If, in some societies, victims of rape are regarded as "damaged goods" and cannot marry or are forced to marry their assailants (if the perpetrator is willing!), then such women do endure a harm that women in other societies do not. Why should we want to deny that? By contrast, if, as is claimed, sexual coercion does not result in

---

[70] See T. M. Scanlon, *What We Owe to Each Other* (Cambridge, MA: Harvard University Press, 1998).

[71] Ernest J. Weinrib, *The Idea of Private Law* (Cambridge, MA: Harvard University Press, 1995), 128.

[72] "[I]f violating sexual self-determination *never* did anyone any obvious harm, then rape would surely not be seen as any more harmful than the minor interference involved in, say, pressing a leaflet advocating a particular point of view into someone's hand . . ."; Cowling, *Date Rape and Consent*, 30.

[73] Panel Discussion, "Men, Women and Rape," 63 *Fordham Law Review* 125 (1994), 146.

[74] John H. Bogart, "Reconsidering Rape: Rethinking the Conceptual Foundations of Rape Law," 8 *Canadian Journal of Law and Jurisprudence* 159 (1995), 169.

severe trauma, shame, or dishonor among the Mihinaku Indians of Brazil, then the Mihinaku women do endure less of *these* dimensions of harm than women in most other societies.[75] If, in some societies, kissing an unmarried woman will severely damage her reputation and render her unmarriageable and is experienced as a grave affront, then there are societies in which a kiss is not just a kiss. As Gardner and Shute remark, "the justification of the penetration condition in the modern law of rape does involve some attention to social meaning."[76]

This raises the question whether it would be a better world in which women experience less distress from rape. Other things being equal, it must be better that fewer women undergo PTSD, or severe depression, or commit suicide, or simply experience less distress. But other things are not always equal. The possibility of certain "goods" such as intimacy entails the possibility of certain "bads" such as the violation of privacy. We can imagine a world in which people run around naked as a matter of course. There are violations of privacy that cannot occur in this world, but the good of a certain sort of intimacy cannot occur there either. Similarly, a world in which nonconsensual sex is not a big deal is likely to be a world in which consensual sex is also not a big deal. So even if women could be socialized to regard nonconsensual sex as a trivial matter – and that strikes me as implausible – there may be good reason not to prefer such a world.

Those who reject the experiential view can advance a more general worry. There are numerous cases in which we think it is wrong for A to have sexual relations with B but where B does not have an aversive experience at the time. It might be argued that the experiential view cannot account for the wrong of nonconsensual sex by deception, or when the victim is unconscious (and may even remain unconscious), or for the wrong of sexual intercourse with minors who experience no regret.

Now the experiential view certainly does not maintain that the *synchronic* experience of distress is necessary to harm. If A's act at Time-1 results in distress at Time-2, then A's act results in a *diachronic* experiential harm to B. If and when B discovers that A had sexual relations with her while unconscious, she is likely to experience considerable distress.[77] If the typical woman were to say "If I don't know about it when it's happening, then it's

---

[75] Shweder, review of Nancy Venable Raine, *After Silence* .

[76] Gardner and Shute, "The Wrongness of Rape" in Horder (ed.), *Oxford Essays*, 201.

[77] In a *Seinfeld* episode, Jerry tells (his friend) Elaine that he suspects that something sexual occurred while he was unconscious at the dentist's office. Elaine remarks, "So you were violated by two people while you were under gas. So what? You're single"; "The Jimmy," episode first aired on March 16, 1995.

no big deal" – then I think our view of such cases would and should be different, although I find it hard to imagine such a world. Similarly, if sexual relations with minors that were otherwise consensual did not frequently result in aversive experiences, then I believe we would and should say that they are not particularly harmful. That is not the world that we know.

At this point it is useful to invoke the distinction between wrong and harm. Suppose, for example, that A has sexual relations with B while B is unconscious and that B never discovers that this occurred and that A's act has no other aversive consequences for B (such as pregnancy or disease). We can say that A's behavior is wrong because it is *likely* to result in harm to B without having to insist that B was harmed in this case. The experiential view of *harm* may or may not be correct, but there is no reason to think that it will exonerate those who should not be exonerated from doing *wrong*.[78]

Bogart also objects to the experiential view because he thinks it would have unacceptable implications for the legal system – "If an essential feature of rape is that it feel a certain way, it is natural to think it appropriate to inquire into related experiences by the victim."[79] Not so. There is a crucial difference between the best measure of *harm* to a particular victim and the best *legal practices* for the criminal law. A poor person who is robbed of $500 may be harmed more than a rich person who is robbed of $500, but it does not follow that the criminal law does or should investigate the wealth of victims. Similarly, even if the rape of a prostitute is less likely to cause PTSD than the rape of a non-prostitute, say because a prostitute does not regard her sexuality "as a sacred and mysterious aspect of her self-identity," there may be good reason for the law not to be sensitive to or to reflect that fact.[80]

The civil law is different. The compensation owed by a wrongdoer to his victim does turn on the harm to the particular victim. If A slugs B and C with a bat, but B has fewer injuries because she is wearing a helmet, it seems

---

[78] An episode on the television show *Law and Order* poses a difficulty for this view. A mother pays a hospital orderly to impregnate her daughter who is in a permanent coma so that the mother can have a grandchild. The orderly is charged with rape. In this case, the victim has no synchronic experience of rape and will never have any experience at all. Has she been harmed? My intuition is to say yes, but I think the correct answer is no. We do not need to say that she has been harmed in order to regard the perpetrator's behavior as morally or legally objectionable.

[79] Bogart, "Reconsidering Rape," 169.

[80] Murphy, "Some Ruminations on Women, Violence, and the Criminal Law" in Coleman and Buchanan (eds.), *In Harm's Way*, 126. "Even if we assume that prostitutes do place lesser value on their sexuality than do other women, we still might want to punish the rape of a prostitute severely to reaffirm the value that *we* place on sexuality. We often punish to uphold *systems* of rights and values that we will sometimes maintain by punishing offenses even if a particular victim, because of idiosyncratic preferences and values, has less than a normal interest in the values at stake"; *ibid.*

perfectly reasonable to think that A owes C more than B. In principle, rape is no different. If one wants to press a case for compensation, then one must be prepared to show one's injuries, although it is hard to see why a victim's sexual history should ordinarily be relevant to this. In any case, the possibility of such an inquiry is certainly no reason to reject the theoretical claim that the experience of the victim is not relevant to the harm of rape. That practical tail should not wag this theoretical dog.

The psychology of rape: culture and evolution

I have argued that the harmful dimensions of rape that are specifically sexual are rooted in the distress and psychological damage to which it gives rise. If this is roughly correct, we must ask two questions: (1) is this distress a function of social factors which might just as easily have been different? and (2) does the answer to (1) matter?

I will consider the second question first. Assume, for the sake of argument, that Jeffrie Murphy is right to argue that "the importance of sex is essentially cultural..." and that we regard the nonconsensual penetration of an orifice as a special wrong only because our culture surrounds "sexuality with complex symbolic and moral baggage..."[81] Would that be a reason for regarding the penetration of an orifice as a less grievous harm than it is now regarded? Perhaps, but certainly not necessarily. Forcing Orthodox Jews to eat pork would be the source of great distress to them. We do not say, "What's the fuss? The nonconsensual penetration of your orifice generates distress only because you surround your dietary choices with complex symbolic and moral baggage." No, we think it legitimate for people to organize their lives around religious beliefs and the distress consequent to violation of those beliefs is an inevitable outcome of the role of those beliefs in people's lives. It seems similarly reasonable for people to regard their sexuality as a particularly important dimension of their self-identity even if it is not necessary for them to do so and even if many others do not. So even if the "specialness" of sexual assault were primarily cultural and highly variable, there might still be good reason for those societies to take such distress seriously, particularly given that taking such distress seriously does not impose serious costs on others.

That said, we can raise questions about the notion of an "objective" harm against which "culturally driven" harms are contrasted. Why is an attack on the body a paradigm form of objective harm? Not because it is "objectively"

---

[81] *Ibid.*, 214.

harmful in a sense that is independent of our experience, but because our bodies and brains are so constructed that we are instinctively averse to bodily impositions. And it is a good thing. Although our sensations are a source of pain, they are of considerable survival value. They motivate us to avoid bodily impositions that may cause impairment and to treat injuries to the body that would otherwise lead to impairment. For similar reasons, it is, shall I say, improbable to the extreme to think that the "importance of sex is essentially *cultural*," if that is taken to mean that societies display wide variety with respect to the general importance of sexual experience in individual and social life, and with respect to aversion to nonconsensual sexual relations.[82] That we must search high and low for anthropological counter-examples suggests that such societies are the proverbial exceptions that prove the rule – if there actually are any exceptions.

Interestingly, despite the popularity of "social constructionism" among feminist scholars, it is rarely suggested that women's aversion to nonconsensual intercourse is "simply the result of social and cultural conditioning," an aversion that could just as easily be otherwise and that we could or should work to alter.[83] No, we assume that intense female aversion to nonconsensual sexual relations is a deep fact about the psychology of women. That this aversion may display individual and social variability in form and intensity does nothing to dispel the importance of this general truth.

Suppose that the female aversion to nonconsensual sexual relations is at least partially hard-wired. Why might this be so? Here, once again, evolutionary psychology may be of help. Nonconsensual sexual relations are a threat to a female's genetic fitness in several ways. First, rape may lead to death or to injury to the victim's reproductive capacity. Second, when rape leads to pregnancy, it reduces a woman's ability to choose the male who will father and provide for her offspring. Third, a woman who is raped may receive less protection and parental care from her mate because *he* is now unsure about who is the parent of her child. Fourth, rape victims may be perceived as less desirable mates – "damaged goods" – and this reduces their long-term opportunity to reproduce.[84]

---

[82] *Ibid.*

[83] Michael Studd, "Sexual Harassment" in David M. Buss and Neil M. Malamuth (eds.), *Sex, Power, Conflict* (New York: Oxford University Press, 1996), 84. This is not quite right. Some feminist scholars have argued that rape need not and should not be viewed as a particularly grievous harm.

[84] Nancy Wilmsen Thornhill, "Psychological Adaptation to Sexual Coercion in Victims and Offenders" in Buss and Malamuth (eds.), *Sex, Power, Conflict*, 92. Thornhill also observes that rape may circumvent a woman's ability to trade sex for material benefits and that it may also "damage the status of a woman's kingroup by causing the appearance of failure on their part to protect her."

Evolutionary psychology maintains that if women who are raped are likely to have fewer children survive to reproductive age, women who experience intense psychological distress at the prospect of or in response to rape will have an evolutionary advantage. From an evolutionary standpoint, psychological pain is an important and positive adaptation "that helps people guard against circumstances that reduce their reproductive success; it does so by spurring behavioral changes aimed at preventing future pain."[85] Just as the (psychological) experience of physical pain has evolutionary value because it leads us to "avoid situations that may lead to similar injury," the experience of intense distress at the prospect of or in response to rape would lead women "to consider circumstances that resulted in the pain more carefully and to avoid them in the future."[86] If some women are more averse to rape than others, and if the aversion to rape has some genetic basis, and if the more rape-averse women have more progeny survive to reproductive age, then we would expect an intense aversion to nonconsensual sexual relations to evolve as a fixed feature of female psychology.[87] Ann Cahill makes the following remark about young females: "Girls especially may know that their bodies are inherently dangerous without being clear as to the precise nature of the danger they present. They may only sense that something very bad and very hurtful will befall them should their surveillance falter."[88] Although she does not consider an evolutionary explanation of this generalized anxiety, her observation is consistent with what evolutionary psychology would expect.

Consider the sense of shame. Nancy Venable Raine observes that even though she was the victim of an aggravated rape by a stranger in her own home – "about as blameless as any victim can be" – she was unable to "escape from the shame of having been raped."[89] Sure, she should not have experienced shame. But we still have to ask why she did. Although a sense of shame is morally unjustified and psychologically dysfunctional for the individual victim, the disposition to experience shame may also be eminently functional from an evolutionary perspective. The greater the tendency for

---

[85] Randy Thornhill and Craig T. Palmer, "Why Men Rape?," *The Sciences*, January/February 2000, 30–36, 34.
[86] Thornhill, "Psychological Adaptation to Sexual Coercion in Victims and Offenders" in Buss and Malamuth (eds.), *Sex, Power, Conflict*, 93.
[87] As Robert Wright puts it: "Thus during evolution it was costly (genetically) for a woman to have sex with a man she didn't want to have sex with – often a man who (a) evidently had genes not conducive to viable and fertile offspring or (b) had no evident inclination to stick around and help provide for the offspring. The abhorrence women feel at the prospect of sex with a man they find unattractive is an expression of this logic"; "Feminists, Meet Mr. Darwin," *The New Republic*, November 28, 1994, 36.
[88] Cahill, *Rethinking Rape*, 161.   [89] Raine, *After Silence*, 133.

women to feel responsible for their victimization, the greater will be their tendency to avoid situations in which they are more likely to be raped. To put the point slightly differently, a psychological disposition may be bad for the individual *ex post*, but may be good for the individual *ex ante*.

This is the way an evolutionary explanation for the intense aversion to rape would look. What is the evidence for this view? There is a general answer and then some specific evidence. First, and most important, if evolutionary theory helps to explain other important features of human psychology, there is no reason why this particular disposition should be exempt. Second, this view is not only consistent with what we know about the intense abhorrence of coercive sexual relations, it helps to explain the persistence of these responses in an era in which some of the physical, reproductive, and social costs of rape have declined.

Apart from such general theoretical considerations, there is considerable evidence that is consistent with the hypothesis that aversion to rape is linked to its reproductive costs. Evidence suggests that reproductive-age victims are significantly more traumatized by rape than pre-reproductive- or post-reproductive-age females.[90] Moreover, while reproductive-age women are more traumatized by rape than post-reproductive-age women, they are less traumatized by robbery than are older women.[91] The potential reproductive effects of violence seem to make a difference to the degree of trauma. Although these differences may partly represent a conscious response to the risk of pregnancy, it seems much more likely that reproductive-age women are unconsciously *disposed* to be more traumatized. I know of no evidence, for example, that women who are taking oral contraceptives are typically much less traumatized by rape than those who are not.

Other evidence concerns the relation between the *type* of rape and its psychological consequences. It appears, for example, that penile-vaginal intercourse is associated with greater distress and adjustment problems than other forms of sexual assaults. And age makes a difference. Whereas the greatest psychological trauma was seen in those reproductive-age female rape victims who experienced penile-vaginal intercourse (compared with

[90] Thornhill, "Psychological Adaptation to Sexual Coercion in Victims and Offenders" in Buss and Malamuth (eds.), *Sex, Power, Conflict*, at 94. Catharine A. MacKinnon has ridiculed the systematic study of the psychology of rape victims – "It is tempting to suggest that rape-murder of women after menopause would be less traumatic because their contribution to the gene pool is over, but someone might test it"; "Pornography Left and Right" in David Estlund and Martha Nussbaum (eds.), *Sex, Preference, and Family* (New York: Oxford University Press, 1997), 108. I do not see why this should not be tested or that doing so has any untoward results.

[91] Thornhill, "Psychological Adaptation to Sexual Coercion in Victims and Offenders" in Buss and Malamuth (eds.), *Sex, Power, Conflict*, 97.

reproductive-age victims who experienced other forms of sexual assault), *non*-reproductive-age females tend to be as traumatized by nonconsensual oral sex as by penile-vaginal intercourse.[92]

I argued above that some of the harms of rape are socially mediated. That a harm is socially mediated does not mean that it does not have an evolutionary basis. From an evolutionary perspective, some of the reproductive costs of rape to women are a function of the response to rape by their *mates*, on whose brains evolution has written its own sexual psychology. Because the mate of a rape victim has particular reason to question the paternity of his wife's offspring, he may regard the rape as an attack on him. Rosemarie Tong observes with regret that "like their predecessors some contemporary men have difficulty overcoming emotional reactions to rape," even though society is "slowly changing the way it *intellectualizes* about rape."[93] But this is precisely what evolutionary psychology would expect. Contemporary technologies of contraception, paternity testing, and abortion are not part of our evolutionary history, and the psychological responses to rape that developed in the environment of evolutionary adaptation will persist long after the sources of those emotions have faded.

If a male's emotional response to the rape of his mate is part of male evolutionary history, so would be his mate's reaction to *his* response. Survey research suggests that married reproductive-age women are more traumatized by rape than unmarried victims of reproductive age. Given that males tend to take a proprietary interest in the sexual fidelity of their spouses, the potential change in a married victim's relationship with her mate is one way in which rape is more harmful to married women than to single women. But that begs the question: if a male's mate is raped, why should he be jealous or upset with his *mate*? Well, he may not know whether the sexual relationship was consensual. From his perspective, a single act of unambiguously coercive extramarital sex would be less threatening to his relationship than a more ambiguously nonconsensual act of infidelity, which might raise the specter of future infidelities by his mate. Nancy Venable Raine makes the fascinating remark that she "wanted 'real' wounds" when she was raped – "the kind that bleed."[94] It appears she is not atypical. Post-rape psychological trauma actually tends to be *less severe* when the rape is physically *more brutal*.[95] Why might that be so? Evolutionary psychology might

[92] Jones, "Sex, Culture and the Biology of Rape," 869–70.
[93] Rosemarie Tong, *Women, Sex, and the Law* (Totowa, NJ: Rowman and Allanheld, 1984), 93.
[94] Raine, *After Silence*, 25.
[95] Margo Wilson and Martin Daly, "The Man Who Mistook His Wife for a Chattel" in Jerome H. Barkow, Leda Cosmides, and John Tooby (eds.), *The Adapted Mind* (New York: Oxford University Press, 1992), 306.

hypothesize that male jealousy would be lessened by physical evidence of the lack of consent, thus also reducing the *social* or *relational* costs of rape even if it increases the physical costs.

Setting violent rape aside, I suspect that women experience greater regret than men about sexual relationships in which the consent is defective by means of deception or impaired judgment. As Robert Wright puts it, "Men . . . virtually never feel 'violated' by sex with a woman. A man may feel crushed if a woman he loves leaves him, but it is an odd man indeed who regrets the sex."[96] By contrast, women are more apt to lament sexual encounters in which their decisions were influenced by deception, intoxication, or poor judgment. We do not need an evolutionary explanation as to why one might be angry at those who deceive us, but evolutionary psychology may help to explain the sense of violation here that is experienced by women but rarely by men – whose behavior is also influenced by deception and impaired judgment. When a woman would not engage in sexual relations unless she had false beliefs about her partner's affection or unless her judgment was impaired, she has risked pregnancy with a man who is unlikely to stay around to help to raise her child.

It might be objected that evolutionary psychology misses the point, that the harm of rape has nothing to do with reproduction or with its effect on a victim's mate, that rape cannot be less wrong just because the victim is postmenopausal or because it does not raise questions about a woman's fidelity. I am not arguing that the connection between rape and reproduction explains why rape is wrong or why we think that rape is wrong. I am arguing that evolutionary psychology may help to explain the intensity and character of the experience of victims – why women are disposed to experience fear and distress that is out of proportion to the physical effects. It is the fact of the experience – not the *causes of* the experience – that principally explains why rape is such a grievous wrong.[97]

I say "principally," because the causes matter. When the basis of distress is principally cultural or belief-mediated, then we have to decide how much weight we want to accord to such distress. If people experience distress or offense when they witness a same-sex couple holding hands, we may think that it is "their problem, not the couple's." We should not deny that they experience distress, but when someone could choose not to be (as)

---

[96] Wright, "Feminists, Meet Mr. Darwin," 42.

[97] As Michael Ruse puts it: "Why is non-physically injurious rape put on a par with assault, or murder even? Do not say, 'Because people get upset.' That's the whole point!"; "Is Rape Wrong on Andromeda? An Introduction to Extraterrestrial Evolution, Science, and Morality" in Edward Regis, Jr. (ed.), *Extraterrestrials* (New York: Cambridge University Press, 1985), 67.

distressed by adopting different beliefs, we can ask her to justify asking others to refrain from causing such distress, and we can also ask whether we should be striving to change the culture or beliefs in order to reduce the distress rather than restricting the behavior which gives rise to it. By contrast, when the experience of distress in response to some act is an integral "hard-wired" part of our psyche, the distress itself need not be justified at all.

We must be careful. I believe that the "naturalness" of distress matters, but it is difficult to work out just how it matters. If one is hard-wired to experience distress in response to certain stimuli, one need not be embarrassed about the feeling itself. On the other hand, the "naturalness" of distress does not entail that it is noncontrollable nor immunize it from moral evaluation. Even if one is disposed to feel distress in response to a certain stimulus, one can try to work against it. Although evolutionary psychology may explain why males are "naturally" predisposed to experience distress at spousal infidelity, the intensity of that response is not written in stone. More importantly, the "naturalness" of the feeling does nothing to justify the (often violent) *behaviors* to which it gives rise, the various "repulsive practices" by which men have long sought to restrict their wives' opportunities for extramarital relations.[98] But unlike this male predisposition, which can be quite costly to women, the female experience of acute distress in response to nonconsensual sexual relations does not give rise to any untoward cost to men, so there is no reason not to give it – more or less – full rein in our justificatory schemes.

---

[98] Jared Diamond, *Why Is Sex Fun?* (New York: Basic Books, 1997), 37.

CHAPTER SIX

The value of consent

Up to this point I have not hesitated to use "consent" pre-analytically. We have a rough and serviceable idea of what it is to consent to sexual relations that is adequate for ordinary purposes. But we want a deeper analysis of consent, one that will enable us to understand the moral importance of consent, one that will help us to think about what counts as giving consent, and one that will distinguish valid from invalid consent; so it seems that we should turn to an analysis of the concept of consent.

A standard picture about the role of conceptual analysis goes something like this. We start with the principle that it is morally and legally impermissible to engage in sexual relations without the other party's consent. To determine which specific behaviors should be regarded as impermissible, we analyze the concept of consent (and related concepts). We ask, in effect, "when is it proper to say that someone consents to do X"? Given an answer to that question and given the premise, we can then say when sexual relations are morally and legally permissible.

This picture greatly exaggerates what a certain kind of conceptual analysis can do. The concept of consent provides a template that organizes and focuses our attention on a set of relevant moral issues, but it cannot do much more. The question as to when we should regard it as morally or legally impermissible to engage in sexual relations will be settled by moral argument informed by empirical investigation, not metaphysical inquiries into the meaning of consent. The important question is not what consent "is," but the conditions under which consent is *morally transformative* in the relevant way.

Consent as morally transformative

I begin with a reminder that we are not interested in consent as a free-standing concept or word. We are interested in consent to sexual relations because consent "is an act in which one person alters the normative relations in which others stand with respect to what they may do," that is, their rights, duties, obligations, privileges, and the like.[1] B's consent may provide moral or legal *legitimation* for an action by A that would not be legitimate without B's consent, as when B's consent to surgery transforms A's act from battery to a permissible medical procedure, or when B's consent to A's use of her land absolves A of trespass. Put somewhat differently, B's consent can render A's action morally or legally *permissible*. B's consent to A's doing X may also transform the obligations and rights of third parties. In some cases, B's consent to A's doing X may curtail C's right or duty to interfere with A's conduct. If B consents to allow A to tattoo her, C may continue to think tattooing a disgusting activity. But C should not think that A is committing battery or intervene on those grounds.[2]

George Fletcher claims that consent can transform (what would otherwise be) a harmful action to a non-harmful action. In other cases, it does not remove the actual harm, but it negates B's right to complain about the harm. If B consents to a taking of property or gives a gift, then, says Fletcher, there is no harm at all. But if B consents to box with A and is knocked out, B's consent blocks the complaint but not the harm, as captured by the expression "volenti non fit injuria" (to one who consents no harm (or wrong) is done).[3] I am not sure that Fletcher is correct. If one consents to a taking of property, one still *loses* the property, just as one who consents to be boxed in exchange for a fee still suffers the pain and bruises of the beating. So the property and boxing cases may be closer than Fletcher seems to think.[4] In any case, the moral and legal force of any economic or physical injuries that B might suffer is negated or weakened by B's consent and that is what is crucial.

Consent can also work as a promise or a way of acquiring an obligation to do something, as when B consents or promises at Time-1 to do X at Time-2. In general, it is desirable that people be able to make binding commitments on grounds of both autonomy and utility, but it is not clear whether this applies to sex. Alan Soble argues that the Antioch College policy, which requires contemporaneous explicit consent to any initial form of sexual contact, effectively trivializes consent because it does not allow people to promise to perform and because it implies that withdrawing consent is not

---

[1] John Kleinig, "Consent" in Lawrence Becker and Charlotte Becker (eds.), *Encyclopedia of Ethics*, second edition (New York: Routledge, 2001), 300.

[2] Carl Wellman, *Real Rights* (New York: Oxford University Press, 1995), 67.

[3] George Fletcher, *Basic Concepts of Legal Thought* (New York: Oxford University Press, 1996), 112.

[4] B's consent (or, more accurately, B's belief that B consents) can also transform the character of her *experience*. If B consents to box with A, she will not experience the blow to her head as a hostile attack on her person, although B may still experience the non-belief-mediated distress caused by such a blow.

prima facie wrong.[5] Soble has misdiagnosed the issue. With the possible exception of paying for a prostitute, people do not ordinarily rely to their detriment on another's promise to engage in sexual activity. To the extent that breaking promises is wrong precisely because others have relied on one's promise to their detriment, reneging on a promise to engage in sex is not particularly wrong. Soble is (or should be) more concerned that the Antioch policy does not allow people to consent at Time-1 to not having to explicitly consent at Time-2.

Default. A asks B if he can kiss B. B says, "For God's sake, I'll tell you if I want you to stop." After some kissing and petting, A removes his clothing. B removes her own clothing, but says nothing. They have sexual intercourse.

It's hard to believe that there is anything problematic here.

Before going further, I must enter an important cautionary remark about the notion of "moral transformation." To say that B's (valid) consent is morally transformative is to say that it alters A's (or C's) reasons for actions. It is not to say that B's consent is either necessary or sufficient to an "all things considered" moral assessment of A's actions. The moral alchemy may change an act from lead to silver but not necessarily to gold – it makes "morally allowable what would not be allowable without consent, or at any rate . . . *so far* allowable, since there may be additional moral impediments to the doing of it."[6] For example, it may be wrong for A to perform surgery on B with B's consent if the procedure is not medically indicated.[7] And even if B's consent renders A's action permissible, consent does not always work "to make an action right when it would otherwise be wrong."[8] Exchanging money for sexual relations may be morally problematic even if the prostitute consents. Still, the prostitute's consent is morally transformative because it removes one important reason for regarding A's behavior as wrong.

The logic of consent arguments

To put the point schematically, we are interested in the following sort of argument.

[5] Alan Soble, *Sexual Investigations* (New York: New York University Press, 1996), 57. The policy requires explicit consent to each new level of intimacy, for example, kissing, fondling, etc.

[6] Edmund Pincoffs, "On Consenting" in Lyman T. Sargent (ed.), *Consent: Concept, Capacity, Conditions, and Constraints, Archives for Philosophy of Law and Social Philosophy*, volume 12 (1979), 108.

[7] It is another question whether performing such surgery would be a wrong *to B* if B asks A to perform the procedure. For example, it may be wrong for a physician to accede to a beggar's request to have his leg amputated so that he can enhance his success as a beggar, but I am not at all sure that it would be a wrong to B.

[8] Larry Alexander, "The Moral Magic of Consent II," 2 *Legal Theory* 165 (1996), 165.

Major premise: If B consents to sexual relations with A, it is (*ceteris paribus*) permissible for A to have sexual relations with B.[9]
Minor premise: B consents (does not consent) to sexual relations with A.
Conclusion: It is (not) permissible for A to have sexual relations with B.

Given the major premise, it seems that we must determine when the *minor premise* is true if we are going to determine if the conclusion is warranted. We may be tempted to think that an analysis of the concept of consent will identify the *criteria* or necessary and sufficient conditions of valid consent, and that empirical investigation can, in principle, determine if those criteria are met. If the criteria are met, then the minor premise is true and the conclusion follows. If not, then the minor premise is false and the conclusion does not follow.

If things were only so simple. Consider the following cases (in these and subsequent cases, assume that A and B have sexual relations):

Abandonment. A and B drive to a secluded spot in A's car. B resists A's advances. A says, "Have sexual relations with me or I will leave you here."
Vasectomy. A makes advances. B tells A that she will accept only if A wears a condom. A falsely tells B that he has had a vasectomy.
Fraternity Party. B is a college freshman. She has never had much to drink. She attends her first fraternity party and is offered some punch. She asks, "Does this have alcohol?" A responds, "Absolutely." She has several glasses, and becomes quite "high" for the first time in her life. When A proposes that they go to his room, she agrees.

No analysis of the meaning of consent will enable us to say whether A's conduct should be illegal in these cases. And modifiers will not help. We can say that it should be a criminal offense if A "fails to obtain *meaningful* consent, and continues to engage in sexual activity," but then we seem to need to know when consent is sufficiently "meaningful" to bar criminalization.[10]

The principles of valid consent (PVC)

To return to phraseology that I have previously introduced, the primary theoretical task is to specify the *principles of valid consent* (*PVC*) for legal or criminal contexts (PVC_L) and for moral but not legal contexts (PVC_M). In my view, PVC is the primary site of the philosophical action about consent. B clearly gives a token of consent in **Fraternity Party**. It is less clear whether

---

[9] A *ceteris paribus* clause is necessary because I do not want to beg the question whether consent is a sufficient condition for legitimacy.
[10] Joan McGregor, "Why When She Says No She Doesn't Mean Maybe and Doesn't Mean Yes: A Critical Reconstruction of Consent, Sex, and the Law," 2 *Legal Theory* 175 (1995), 190.

her consent is valid. Tokens of consent are obviously important. If B does not token consent, then A's act is impermissible. But B's consent token renders A's act morally permissible (insofar as things turn on consent) only if B's consent meets the criteria specified by PVC.

The content of PVC_L and PVC_M may or may not vary from context to context. Consider the following cases.

Mastectomy. A physician tells his patient that she has breast cancer and that she should immediately undergo a mastectomy. He does not explain the risks of the procedure or other options. Because the patient trusts her physician, she signs a consent form.

Gangrene. A patient's leg is gangrenous and she must choose between amputation and death. She understands the alternatives, and because she does not want to die, she signs the consent form.

Dance Studio. A dance studio gets an elderly woman to contract to pay $20,000 for dance lessons by "a constant and continuous barrage of flattery, false praise, excessive compliments, and panegyric encomiums."[11]

Psychotherapist. B is undergoing psychotherapy with A. Under the grip of "transference" and strongly attracted to A, she proposes that they have sexual relations. A accepts.

Has there been valid or morally transformative consent in any or all of these cases? A full resolution would require both more information and moral argument. But setting aside, for now, the distinction between moral and legal contexts, I think that the best account of PVC might generate the following judgments: the consent in **Mastectomy** is not valid because valid consent to a medical procedure must be *informed* consent; the consent given in **Gangrene** is valid even though the patient reasonably believes that she had no choice but to agree; the consent given in **Dance Studio** does not give rise to a legally binding agreement because the dance studio acted illegitimately in procuring the subject's consent; the consent given in **Psychotherapist** does not render it legitimate for the psychotherapist to have sexual relations with his patient, because the therapist has a fiduciary obligation to refrain from sexual relations with his patient that cannot be waived. Period.[12]

These are just intuitions. How do we determine what is the best account of PVC for one context or another? At one level, this will turn on what is the best account of morality or on that part of morality that concerns "what we owe to each other."[13] On a consequentialist outlook, we will examine the

---

[11] *Vokes v. Arthur Murray, Inc.*, 212 So. 2d 906 (1968), 907.
[12] See chapter 6 in my *Exploitation* (Princeton: Princeton University Press, 1996).
[13] T. M. Scanlon, *What We Owe to Each Other* (Cambridge, MA: Harvard University Press, 1998).

costs and benefits of different versions of PVC and adopt those principles that generate the best consequences when all things are considered. I do not mean that the best version of PVC will be settled "case by case." We will want to know in advance whether we can regard consent as valid in one type of situation or another. But it is possible, for example, that the best version of PVC will be different for medical contexts than for sexual contexts. From a contractarian perspective, we can think of PVC_L and PVC_M as the outcome of a choice made under conditions of impartiality, perhaps as modelled by a Rawlsian veil of ignorance or along Scanlonian lines, as the principles that no one could reasonably reject as a basis for informed, unforced general agreement. Here, too, the principles will vary.

For present purposes it is not necessary to opt for one moral theory or another. The crucial and present point is that we should think of the principles of valid consent as themselves the subject or target of moral theorizing. We are used to thinking of consent principally as an "input" to moral thinking, as a factor that generates a moral result. So we might say, "B consents to sexual relations with A" (input) and thus "It is permissible for A to have sexual relations with B" (output). I am arguing that we should shift the focus of our thinking, that we should regard the principles of valid consent as an *output* of moral theorizing, as what we are trying to justify.

The value of consent

Needless to say, we are not likely to resolve the question of what is the best moral theory. Moreover, we are also not able to say with precision what account of PVC would be adopted within the framework of a given theory. We can make some progress, however, because we can identify some moral considerations that will be relevant to what constitutes the best version of PVC on several different theoretical approaches.

We can begin by asking why consent is important or valuable. In a book published just before his death, Robert Nozick argues that the norm of "voluntary cooperation" might be regarded as the "core principle of ethics."[14] He suggests that the point of these norms is to facilitate mutually beneficial interactions. By adopting the principle that consent is (ordinarily) *sufficient* to legitimize interaction, we encourage mutually beneficial interactions. By adopting the principle that consent is (ordinarily) *necessary* to legitimize interaction, we prohibit interactions that are not to mutual benefit. Nozick's approach does not mandate mutual benefit. A person could

---

[14] Robert Nozick, *Invariances* (Cambridge, MA, Harvard University Press, 2001), 263.

choose to interact with others in a way that "benefits them yet is to his own detriment," so long as the choice is clearly voluntary. But the principal aim is to encourage interactions that are mutually beneficial and to discourage those that are not. Of course not every consensual transaction enhances the parties' utility *ex post*. People make mistakes. But if people typically consent only to those interactions that will improve their expected welfare, and if people typically make fairly good judgments about such matters, then consensual interactions will leave both parties better off than they otherwise would be.

We can put the norm of voluntary cooperation in terms of an ethics of *autonomy*, which also has two dimensions. To say that sexual relations are legitimate only if B consents is to protect the *negative* dimension of B's autonomy or control of her life. But that is not sufficient. B is not an autonomous agent if she is not capable of entering into relationships with others when she and they are so willing. So to say that sexual relations are (prima facie) legitimate if (and not "only if") B consents is to endorse the *positive* dimension of autonomy, the notion that people should be permitted "to seek emotional intimacy and sexual fulfillment with willing partners."[15] The distinctiveness of the two dimensions of autonomy is well illustrated by a moral or legal regime that rigorously protects everyone's right to refuse sexual contact, but places extensive restrictions on one's right to engage in sexual contact, such as restrictions on nonmarital sex or homosexual relations. Under this regime, there is extensive negative autonomy, but little positive autonomy. To acknowledge the positive dimension of autonomy is to see that a common critique of liberal morality is thoroughly mistaken. It is sometimes said that a liberal morality or a concern with autonomy assumes a world of "isolated" or "atomistic" or "asocial" individuals. But to respect an *individual's* sexual autonomy is precisely to respect and facilitate her decisions to interact *with others*. It does not assume that she prefers autoerotic activity.

I need to say something more about autonomy. A common view is that autonomy refers to *control* of one's life, to the ability to shape one's life in accordance with one's desires. Some philosophers adopt a more rigorous or Kantian view, one that emphasizes its moral dimension. The Kantian conception of autonomy tracks its etymology (*auto* = self, *nomos* = law). The autonomous person is one who submits to moral laws or principles that one has made for oneself.[16] Living in accordance with one's

---

[15] Stephen J. Schulhofer, *Unwanted Sex* (Cambridge, MA: Harvard University Press, 1998), xi.

[16] See Joel Feinberg, *Harm to Self* (New York: Oxford University Press, 1986), 27.

nonmoral or non-reflective desires is not to live an autonomous life. George Sher advances a somewhat relaxed version of the Kantian line. On his "responsiveness to reasons" view, an agent is autonomous or self-directing only when she is motivated by her appreciation of the *reasons* provided by her situation, but not exclusively moral reasons.[17]

As Sher points out, the "responsiveness to reasons" view can explain what appears to be a disparate set of requirements for autonomy as well as an apparent anomaly. A's coercive threats imperil B's autonomy because A's threats make B responsive to *A*'s reasons or will, not her own. Information is important to autonomy because one's choices cannot reflect one's judgments or values without the relevant information. Psychological compulsions, phobias, and manipulation interfere with autonomy because they weaken the agent's ability to make choices that reflect her reasons, values, or conception of the good. In addition, the responsiveness-to-reasons view can explain why the capacity for a critical attitude toward one's own beliefs, desires, and choices is also a requirement of autonomy. An autonomous person must have the intellectual resources to reason about her reasons. Interestingly, this account also explains the anomalous but important *sense* in which one may act autonomously when making decisions in response to a threat, as when a bank teller hands over money in response to the gunman's threat – "the money or your life." Although there is clearly one sense in which the gunman's threat interferes with her autonomy, the teller is also responding to the relevant reasons for action. She need not deny that she is morally responsible for her decision to turn over the money. Rather, the robber's threat renders her action *justifiable*.

It is not clear how best to understand the value of autonomy. To put the issue arithmetically, we can contrast an additive view with a multiplicative view. On the additive view, the "good" of autonomous choice is added to the value of the choice, so that it enhances the positive value of a good choice and reduces the negative value of a bad choice. On the multiplicative view, the moral value of autonomous choices depends on the value of the choices. The degree of autonomy amplifies the positive or negative value of a choice. A good autonomous choice is more valuable than a good non-autonomous choice, but a bad autonomous choice is worse than a bad non-autonomous choice. Intuitively, the multiplicative view seems closer to the truth. It seems implausible to suppose that an autonomous choice of evil is somehow better than a non-autonomous choice of evil. Even if we accept the multiplicative view, it is still morally desirable that people have

---

[17] George Sher, *Beyond Neutrality* (New York: Cambridge University Press, 1997), 48.

the space to make autonomous unworthy choices since an autonomous worthy choice is possible only when people have the space for autonomous unworthy choices.

The formula of humanity

We can also understand the value of consent and autonomy in terms of Kant's formula of humanity. On the first and most well-known formulation of Kant's "categorical imperative" – The Formula of Universal Law – one must "Act only on that maxim through which you can at the same time will that it should become a universal law."[18] In the second formulation of the categorical imperative, what Kant calls the formula of humanity (FH), one must "Act in such a way that you always treat humanity, whether in your own persons or in the person of any other, never simply as a means, but always at the same time as an end."[19] FH has become a virtual mantra in contemporary philosophical and public discourse and is applied to a wide range of issues such as medical research, the sale of bodily organs, prostitution, and commercial surrogacy.

As with many moral principles, FH is non-determinative, for the question becomes what constitutes treating others as ends in themselves. FH does not require that one treat another person *only* as an end and not at all as a means, or life would be impossible. Rather, one must not treat another *merely* as a means to one's own ends, which means that one can treat another as a means while, "at the same time," treat her as an end.[20] But what does it mean to treat someone as an end? Christine Korsgaard suggests that on Kant's view, to "treat someone as an end ... is to respect his right to use his own reason to determine whether and how he will contribute to what happens."[21] To treat "humanity" as an end is to respect the capacity that distinguishes and gives dignity to human beings.[22] On this view, one does not treat another *merely* as a means if one first obtains her consent to one's actions in a manner that is consistent with respecting her rational power of self-determination. My plumber and I treat each other as ends and not

---

[18] Immanuel Kant, *Groundwork of the Metaphysics of Morals* (London: Random House, 1948), translated by H. J. Paton, chapter II.
[19] *Ibid.*
[20] Indeed, it can be argued that one *cannot* treat another only as an end, for others cannot be our own goals and purposes. "Only what we aim for, including what we desire, can be a goal or purpose ... Others who exist independently of our action can't be subjective ends, but only ends in themselves"; Onora O'Neill, "Between Consenting Adults," 14 *Philosophy & Public Affairs* 252 (1985), 263.
[21] Christine Korsgaard, "The Reasons We Can Share," 10 *Social Philosophy and Policy* 24 (1993), 45.
[22] Christine Korsgaard, "Kant" in Becker and Becker (eds.), *Encyclopedia of Ethics*, 932.

merely as means so long as we respect each other's capacity to choose on the basis of relevant reasons and seek the other's (valid) consent to our respective actions. I do not force him to work for me; he does not deceive me as to what work is required. Similarly, it is arguable that a "John" treats a prostitute as an end in herself if their transaction is consensual.[23]

So conceived, FH has precious little to do with sentiments such as compassion, kindness, and benevolence. We treat others as a mere means when we treat them in a way to which they do not or cannot rationally consent, to wit, actions based on force (in which one has no chance to consent), coercion (where consent is in response to means one would reject), and deception (where one does not know to what one is consenting).[24] Kant regards deception as a particularly serious wrong because the deceiver undermines his target's ability to use the rational capacity that is at the heart of her moral personality.

What about consent given under difficult or desperate conditions, where there is no deception or explicit coercion? Do we treat a person as an end in herself when we respect choices born of dire need? This is complicated. Joseph Raz argues that one can live an "*autonomous life*" only if one generally has an adequate range of options among which to choose.[25] Even if Raz is correct, as I suspect he is, it may also be important to respect a person's capacity to make decisions under the circumstances in which she finds herself. Consider **Lecherous Millionaire**.

Lecherous Millionaire. B's child will die unless she receives expensive surgery for which the state will not pay. A, a millionaire, proposes to pay for the surgery if B will agree to become his mistress.[26]

There may be good reasons why A should not make this proposal, or perhaps, why B should not be held to the terms of the agreement. But it is arguable that A is treating B as an end in herself and not merely as a means, that it is for *B* to decide whether she wishes to make the deal, and given her own ends, she may quite rationally decide to accept A's proposal or even initiate the proposal herself.[27]

---

[23] "It is not true that he acts without regard for her desires. He does not satisfy her sexual desire; indeed, the prostitute does not expect him to do so. But he does satisfy the one desire she has with regard to him: the desire for money"; Igor Primoratz, *Ethics and Sex* (London: Routledge, 1999), 101.

[24] Christine Korsgaard, "The Reasons We Can Share," 45.

[25] See Joseph Raz, *The Morality of Freedom* (Oxford: Clarendon Press, 1986), 374.

[26] See my *Coercion* (Princeton: Princeton University Press, 1987), 229. I borrow this case from Joel Feinberg, *Harm to Self*, 228–29.

[27] "We may grant that poor women do not have enough options and that society has been unjust to them in not extending more options, while nonetheless respecting and honoring the choices they actually make in reduced circumstances"; Martha C. Nussbaum, "'Whether from Reason or Prejudice': Taking Money for Bodily Services," 27 *Journal of Legal Studies* 693 (1998), 721.

Other cases may be more difficult from this perspective. Consider

Intern. A White House intern, who is infatuated with the President, proposes that they have sexual relations. He accepts.

Groupie. B, a devoted eighteen-year-old fan of A's rock band, gladly accepts A's proposal to have intercourse.

Trophy. A is a very wealthy sixty-year-old corporation executive. B is a twenty-seven-year-old fashion model. A proposes marriage, indicating that he expects regular sexual relations. B accepts.

People do not always act rationally in terms of their own settled aims. What then? In general, to show respect for another's rational capacities requires that we treat her "as if" she were using her reason in an appropriate way. In **Trophy**, it is arguable that A and B both understand the situation: A wants a beautiful young wife on his arm; B wants access to A's wealth. A might well think that it is for B to decide whether the relationship is compatible with her ends so long as he does not use coercion or deception. **Groupie** and **Intern** are more difficult from this perspective. FH surely does not require that A engage in sexual relations with B just because B seems desirous of doing so. Does FH *prohibit* A from engaging in sexual relations with B in these cases? It is arguable that A should refuse to engage in sexual relations if A believes or could reasonably be expected to believe that B has highly limited capacities to understand the consequences of sexual relations for her own long-term well-being. A may find himself torn between not wanting to take advantage of what he may (correctly) think are defects in another's rational capacities *and* a commitment to demonstrating respect for her rational capacities.[28] There are several possibilities as to what FH requires under such conditions. First, we might think that when others are "precariously autonomous and rational," we must continue to treat them *as if* they are rational.[29] Even when we have good reason to think that another is acting wrongly or imprudently, we should suppose that she has good reasons for her action because we owe her this attitude as a matter of her right.[30] Second, we could revise our view of what treating others as ends requires when their capacities are clearly limited. We must treat others as "particular men and women with limited and determinate capacities to understand or to consent to proposals for action."[31] Third, we might think that we simply cannot treat others as "ends in themselves" when their capacities are highly limited and that we must use other moral

---

[28] O'Neill, "Between Consenting Adults," 257.   [29] *Ibid.*, 264.
[30] Christine M. Korsgaard, "The Right to Lie: Kant on Dealing with Evil," 15 *Philosophy & Public Affairs* 325 (1986), 335.
[31] If we are to treat others as persons, we must not view them "abstractly as possibly consenting adults," but as the persons they are; *ibid.*, 253.

principles to guide our actions. On this view, it is not that we need to apply FH in a different way, but that the formula itself only applies under certain conditions. There may not be much difference between the second and third options. On both views, there are conditions under which we are morally required not to show full respect for another's expressed wishes. Such cases aside, the important point is that a plausible interpretation of FH implies that we do not violate FH when we obtain another's consent to a proposed interaction.

Consensual minimalism

I will continue to set aside the content of the principles of valid consent. There are two major candidates for a theory of permissible sexual relations. On the first view, what I call *consensual minimalism*, a sexual relationship is permissible if it is consensual in some reasonably straightforward sense of that term (bracketing effects on third parties). Consensual minimalism does *not* hold that the requirements for valid consent are minimal. It means only that within the range of plausible interpretations of PVC_M and PVC_L, B's consent is sufficient to render it permissible for A to proceed. On the second view, what I called *consent-plus*, consent is necessary but not sufficient to render sexual relations permissible.

As a historical matter, the accepted morality and legal status of sexual relations has turned less on questions about the quality of consent than on whether the parties are of the opposite sex, or married, or putting the right bodily parts in the right places.[32] Although the very notion of sexual morality suffers in certain circles from its association with right-wing views, sexual relations do not lie beyond moral evaluation just because they are unambiguously consensual between the parties and do not have adverse effects on others (as with some cases of adultery).[33] Robin West thinks that we need to develop "a language, a way of talking, within which we can subject to moral and political scrutiny our noncriminal, wholly consensual heterosexual practices."[34] Not to worry. We have the language and a way of talking. The problem is to figure out what to say.

Alan Soble objects to the view that we can and should subject consensual sexual relations to moral evaluation. "To claim that a woman's rational, consensual choice [can be] a matter of... 'serious moral inquiry' is to declare that women need to be protected from their own rational choosings and

---

[32] William N. Eskridge, Jr., "The Many Faces of Sexual Consent," 37 *William and Mary Law Review* 47 (1995), 49.
[33] Scanlon, *What We Owe to Each Other*, 174.
[34] Panel Discussion, "Men, Women and Rape," 63 *Fordham Law Review* 125 (1994), 153.

that men who abide by the rational and consensual decisions of adult women engage in morally suspicious treatment of them."[35] Soble is half right. To claim that a consensual choice can be the subject of serious moral inquiry may well entail that a man can abide by the "rational and consensual decisions" of a woman and yet still engage in "morally suspicious treatment" of his partner. But evaluation does not entail protection. We can evaluate the moral worth of A's and B's behavior without claiming that anyone needs to be "protected from their own rational choosings."

We might distinguish between external and internal moral evaluations of consensual sexual activities. From an external perspective, consensual sexual relations may plausibly be regarded as impermissible if they generate negative externalities to identifiable persons or, as in numerous collective action problems, if they would generate such externalities if they were not prohibited or constrained.[36] As Gardner and Shute put it, "It is enough to meet the demands of the harm principle that, if the action were not criminalized, *that* would be harmful."[37] Consider adultery and prostitution in this light. Even when adultery is consensual between the parties, it is typically not consensual with the spouse. In addition, adultery may increase the probability of marital dissolution, thereby harming children. There are probably good reasons not to criminalize adultery, but we need not refuse to criminalize adultery on the grounds that it is consensual. Similarly, even if prostitution were highly consensual between the parties and has no direct harmful effects on others, its permissibility *might* have harmful social effects, say, because it weakens the centripetal forces in a marriage (a man has less need for his wife if he can get sex easily).[38]

An internal moral critique of consensual sexual relations focuses on the moral quality of the relationship itself.[39] Alan Goldman argues that there are no special moral principles that are "intrinsic to sex." Maybe so, but even if he is right, we can still apply non-special moral principles.[40] On some

---

[35] Soble, *Sexual Investigations*, 39.

[36] I set aside whether causing offense or disgust is itself a reason to prohibit an activity.

[37] John Gardner and Stephen Shute, "The Wrongness of Rape" in Jeremy Horder (ed.), *Oxford Essays in Jurisprudence*, fourth series (Oxford: Oxford University Press, 2000), 216.

[38] As Linda R. Hirshman and Jane E. Larson put it, "Where prostitution is curtailed, wives are better suited to force their husbands to bargain with them for sexual access"; *Hard Bargains* (New York: Oxford University Press, 1998), 287.

[39] Martha Chamallas, "Consent, Equality, and the Legal Control of Sexual Conduct," 61 *Southern California Law Review* 777 (1988), 783. From this perspective, even autoerotic activity is an appropriate subject for moral evaluation, for an Alexander Portnoy-like preoccupation with masturbation "could reflect a failure to understand the importance and value of sexual pleasure"; Scanlon, *What We Owe to Each Other*, 175.

[40] He suggests that the moral evaluation of sexual relations is necessarily parasitic on general moral principles about the treatment of other persons. See Alan Goldman, "Plain Sex," 6 *Philosophy & Public Affairs* 267 (1977) 267, 280.

internal theories of the morality of sexual relations, sex is morally worthy only if it occurs within certain emotional, relational, or institutional contexts. Exemplifying this view, Laurence Thomas suggests that when sexual passion has the benefit of mutual love and trust, it defines a most significant moment of goodness between two people.[41] And some consensual sex certainly falls short of that. But I am not concerned with goodness, but with permissibility, and the question is whether we should regard sexual relations as legally or morally permissible only when they occur within certain contexts.

Kant seems to think so. Unlike much of Kant's moral theorizing, his views on sexual morality are distinctly not a priori. They are based on (questionable) empirical claims about human psychology. Kant believes that sexual desire and pleasure are so intense that they temporarily displace or override all other thoughts, including any "endlike" regard for the pleasure or experience of one's partner.[42]

But a love that springs merely from sexual impulse cannot be love at all, but only appetite. Human love is good-will, affection, promoting the happiness of others and finding joy in their happiness. But it is clear that, when a person loves another purely from sexual desire, none of these factors enter into the love. Far from there being any concern for the happiness of the loved one, the lover, in order to satisfy his desire and still his appetite, may even plunge the loved one into the depths of misery. Sexual love makes of the loved person an Object of appetite; as soon as that appetite has been stilled, the person is cast aside as one casts away a lemon which has been sucked dry.[43]

Kant does not say that sex is morally problematic simply because it involves the instrumental use of another's *body*. It is perfectly legitimate to use another's "hands, his feet, and even all his powers . . . for his own purposes" if he has the "other's consent."[44] Sexual impulse is morally problematic because it makes another's body itself an "Object of indulgence" that precludes us from regarding the other as a person.[45]

---

[41] Laurence M. Thomas, "The Good Society and Sexual Orientation" in Laurence M. Thomas and Michael E. Levin, *Sexual Orientation and Human Rights* (Lanham, MD: Rowman and Littlefield, 1999), 59.

[42] Martha Nussbaum, "Objectification," 24 *Philosophy & Public Affairs* 249 (1995), 267.

[43] Immanuel Kant, "Duties toward the Body in Respect of Sexual Impulse" in *Lectures on Ethics*, translated by Louis Infield (Indianapolis: Hackett, 1963), 163.

[44] *Ibid.*

[45] *Ibid.* D. A. J. Richards thinks that this concern with the body is inconsistent with Kant's view that it is our intellectual capacity to order and choose our ends as free and rational beings that are crucial to our moral personality. Kant may be wrong, but he is not inconsistent, for it is the psychology of desire with which he is concerned, not the body, *per se*. See *Sex, Drugs, Death and the Law* (Totowa, NJ: Rowman and Littlefield, 1982), 109.

In more familiar terms, it is frequently argued that it is seriously wrong to objectify another person. While this claim has broader reach, it is frequently advanced with respect to sex. Unfortunately, it is less clear just what objectification amounts to and whether objectification is necessarily objectionable. Martha Nussbaum has shown that objectification is a multifaceted concept that involves at least seven different ideas: instrumentality, denial of autonomy, inertness, fungibility, violability, ownership, and denial of subjectivity. Kant thought that sexual relations were problematic with regard to several of these dimensions.[46] He says that sexual relation involves a denial of the other's subjectivity because immersion in one's own satisfaction displaces any concern with one's partner's thoughts or feelings.[47] Asymmetry is not the problem. If both parties desire sexual satisfaction, each will "volunteer eagerly to be dehumanized in order that they can dehumanize the other in turn."[48] On Kant's view, reciprocal dehumanization is still dehumanization and is therefore impermissible.

What can be done? According to Kant, the objectification that is a "natural and inevitable" part of sexual activity is too deep to be squared with the "formula of humanity" by sexual reciprocity or consent.[49] Only marriage can do the trick.

The sole condition on which we are free to make use of our sexual desire depends upon the right to dispose over the person as a whole – over the welfare and happiness and generally over all the circumstances of that person. If I have the right over the whole person, I have also the right over the part and so I have the right to use that person's *organa sexualia* for the satisfaction of sexual desire. But how am I to obtain these rights over the whole person? Only by giving that person the same rights over the whole of myself. This happens only in marriage.[50]

It is not easy to make sense of this. The central idea seems to be that because sexual activity causes one to temporarily disregard the interests of one's partner, a *secure* regard for his or her welfare is required.[51] Love cannot do the job because love is necessarily sensitive to the particular and changeable qualities of the individuals, so cannot guarantee the required secure regard. Because the marital contract imposes a binding *legal* obligation to provide

---

[46] See Martha Nussbaum, "Objectification." Nussbaum suggests that an instance of objectification may involve one or more of these forms, but they are also importantly distinct.
[47] *Ibid.*, 266.   [48] *Ibid.*, 267.
[49] Barbara Herman, "Could It Be Worth Thinking about Kant on Sex and Marriage?" in Louise Antony and Charlotte Witt (eds.), *A Mind of One's Own* (Boulder: Westview, 1993), 55.
[50] Kant, "Duties toward the Body," 166–67.
[51] Herman, "Could It Be Worth Thinking about Kant on Sex and Marriage?" in Antony and Witt (eds.), *A Mind of One's Own*, 63.

for the other's welfare, it provides the necessary foundation for legitimate sexual relations.

The contrast between love and marriage exemplifies a more general point about FH. As I noted above, it is often thought that to treat others as ends in themselves is to adopt some sort of psychological stance towards them, to treat others with compassion, kindness, and benevolence. As the Kantian maxim is interpreted by its author, that is false. Consider Kant's retributive theory of punishment. Kant famously argues that utilitarianism wrongly regards punishment as a means to a good for society or for the criminal himself. By contrast, to treat the criminal as an end in himself is to treat him as a responsible agent and to impose punishment in accordance with the "lex talionis," the maxim that punishment should fit the crime.[52] Kant says that we treat a murderer as an end in himself when we execute him, while we would wrongly treat him merely as a means to a social good if we offered to commute his death sentence if he agreed to undergo a medical experiment that benefits the community.[53] It is not that Kant is not "precise" about what FH requires "by way of one's attitude to the other." Rather, it is *not* a matter of psychology at all.[54] It is to accept a set of constraints on one's actions.[55] In the present context, it is the constraints of marriage.

Does Kant give us good reason to reject consensual minimalism? Kant's view of permissible sex is the conjunction of (1) a general ethical theory based on the categorical imperative and FH and (2) a special application of that theory to sexual relations. If we want to reject Kant's conclusion about permissible sex, we could reject FH as a general ethical requirement or we could reject the way in which Kant applies that maxim to sexual relations. I do not know if I want to reject FH, although I would do so before adopting Kant's views about permissible sex. There are two ways in which we could accept FH while resisting Kant's rejection of consensual minimalism: (a) we could reject Kant's psychology and argue that sexual relations need not involve the objectification he decries; (b) we could opt for a non-Kantian application of the FH under which such objectification need not violate FH. Although I think that Kant is wrong about sexual psychology and that FH does not require us to reject consensual minimalism, there is a third possibility. One could argue that even reasonably robust consent is

---

[52] "Punishment can only be imposed because he has committed a crime"; from *The Metaphysical Elements of Justice*, translated by John Ladd (Indianapolis: Bobbs-Merrill, 1965), 100.

[53] Execution is compatible with FH because it respects the murderer's "innate personality" while condemning him to lose his "civil personality."

[54] David Archard, *Sexual Consent* (Boulder: Westview, 1998), 41.

[55] Herman, "Could It Be Worth Thinking about Kant on Sex and Marriage?" in Antony and Witt (eds.), *A Mind of One's Own*, 62.

insufficient to render sexual relations morally (and, perhaps, legally) permissible, but disagree with Kant about what is necessary to legitimate them. Contemporary legal and philosophical literature has shown considerable support for this approach, so I want to give it a run for its money.

Strong reciprocity

On what I shall refer to as *strong reciprocity*, what is ordinarily or plausibly regarded as a minimally consensual relationship is morally impermissible and may even be justifiably prohibited by law. On this view, something like reciprocity or equality or communication or non-exploitation is required.

Eva Kittay focuses on reciprocal sexual desire. She argues that one becomes a "sexual object" rather than a "sexual agent" unless both parties desire sexual contact at the very moment of sexual contact. It does not matter whether the parties are married or in love or having a one-night stand – "the recognition of the other's desire... [is] the sole way in which we can engage in sex without reducing the other to an object," and one "*who insists* on the sexual act makes of the partner [only] a means... to one's own pleasure."[56]

There are several questions that we might raise here. First, it is not clear whether Kittay rejects Kant's psychology of sexual desire. She could think that one can experience sexual desire while remaining attentive and responsive to one's partner, or that one can "recognize" the other's desire as an *ex ante* condition for sexual relations even if one is not cognizant of or responsive to one's partner's desires during sex. Second, and more importantly, there is little connection between the question whether B desires sex and the question whether A "insists" upon sex. B might be perfectly prepared to have sexual relations with A for reasons unrelated to sexual desire without making a sexual object of herself and without any untoward pressure from A, as in the following:

Love. A and B are married. A proposes that they have intercourse. B is not "in the mood," but she knows that it's "been a while" and wants to show her love for B and so agrees.
Big Chill. B is a single woman in her thirties who wants to have a child. She proposes to A, an old friend, that he help her out. A accepts.
Ovulation. A and B have been trying to have a child. B monitors her cycle and proposes that they have intercourse because it is the "right time."

[56] Eva Feder Kittay, "My Foolish Heart: A Response to Alan Soble's 'Antioch's Sexual Offense Policy': A Philosophical Exploration," 28 *Journal of Social Philosophy* 153 (1997), 158 (emphasis added).

There is a larger point at stake here. Although strong-reciprocity views typically celebrate mutual sexual desire, this form of mutuality is neither necessary nor sufficient to morally permissible sex. First, sexual relationships motivated by *mutual* sexual desire may not avoid reducing the other to a sexual object if the parties lack commitment or even affection. Second, the contrast between sexual desire triggered by the senses (sight, touch, feel, scent) and other motivational sources is significantly overdrawn. Although male sexual desire tends to be triggered by visual cues, female sexual desire is often triggered by characteristics that predict that a potential partner will be able to provide security for her and her offspring. It's not that women consciously follow their pocketbook rather than their heart, although that no doubt happens, but that the female heart is itself unconsciously responsive to those traits. Third, even when both parties desire sexual relations for purely erotic content, the parties may have quite distinct erotic experiences. If so, there will be less to the distinction between trading erotic experience for erotic experience and trading erotic experience for some other good, and consequently less reason to insist on reciprocity based on mutual sexual desire. Fourth, there is no reason to believe that mutual sexual desire is morally superior to other motivations, such as the desire to get pregnant or show affection.

Advancing a slightly different view, Elizabeth Anderson attempts to locate the "human good of sexual acts" in a more general theory of value.[57] Anderson argues that whereas it is morally permissible and even appropriate to value some goods as commodities, the worth of many "personal" goods depends upon the motives people have in providing or creating them.[58] She argues that commercial surrogacy is seriously wrong because the "work of bringing forth children into the world" should be governed by parental norms rather than money, and because the commodification of procreational labor "reduces the surrogate mothers from persons worthy of respect and consideration to objects of mere use."[59] Similarly, Anderson argues that sexual relations should always involve a "mutual recognition of the partners as sexually attracted to each other and as affirming an intimate relationship in their mutual offering of themselves to each other."[60]

Now it is not clear whether Anderson believes she is offering a theory of (1) morally worthy sex or (2) permissible sex, or (3) morally justified legal regulation of sex. Although she is quite prepared to criminalize

---

[57] Elizabeth Anderson, *Value in Ethics and Economics* (Cambridge, MA: Harvard University Press, 1993), 154.
[58] *Ibid.*, 151.
[59] "Is Women's Labor a Commodity?," 19 *Philosophy & Public Affairs* 71 (1990), 80.
[60] Anderson, *Value in Ethics and Economics*, 154.

(arguably) consensual commercial surrogacy and consensual prostitution on the grounds that they commodify personal goods, I doubt that she would want to criminalize the general category of sex that does not "realize human sexuality as a shared good."[61] Those issues aside, there are at least two related reasons to question whether mutual sexual attraction and intimacy should be the *sine qua non* of morally permissible sex. First, sex based on "mutual sexual attraction" is not identical to sex that affirms "an intimate relationship." To insist on *both* mutual sexual attraction *and* an intimate relationship as prerequisites for morally permissible sex is to be very demanding indeed. Second, Anderson's view is excessively monistic about sexual motivations. Setting aside the genuine possibility that it might not be wrong to trade sex for money, it seems completely acceptable to engage in sex out of "loyalty, sympathy, affection, and companionship," as contrasted with sexual attraction, motivations that she celebrates in other personal spheres.[62] Here, more pluralism is in order.

Lois Pineau ties her "communicative" theory of sex more closely to consent and FH. She argues that anyone who enters an encounter seeking sexual satisfaction has an obligation to help the other attain his or her end – "To do otherwise is to risk acting in opposition to what the other desires, and hence to risk acting without the other's consent."[63] Because it is not "reasonable" for a woman to consent to what she is unlikely to enjoy, it is unreasonable for a man to assume that his partner consents if he encounters negative, bored, or angry responses.[64]

Pineau's goals are too narrow and too high. They are too narrow because many women (as well as men) would reject the view that morally decent sex should be "gentle, "not aggressive," "absolutely equal," "tender, not ambivalent," and "communicate respect."[65] William Eskridge suggests that a recurring theme in domination and bondage literature is that the decision

[61] Prostitution "debases a gift value and its giver"; it, too, should be prohibited; *ibid.* Anderson also argues that understanding sexual relations as a "gift value" is problematic: "where commitment is enforced by women's economic dependency on their husbands, gravely compromising their powers of exit, there is much room to question how much women's sexual, emotional, and reproductive 'gifts' to men are freely given, how much they express women's own valuations rather than men's valuations of them, and how much the gifts they receive in return reinforce their subordination"; *ibid.*, 152.

[62] *Ibid.*, 151.

[63] Lois Pineau, "Date Rape" in Leslie Francis (ed.), *Date Rape* (University Park, PA: Penn State University Press, 1996), 18.

[64] *Ibid.*, 22.

[65] Katie Roiphe, *The Morning After* (Boston: Little, Brown, 1993), 60. As Ellen Willis puts it, sex must be "beautiful, romantic, soft, nice, and devoid of messiness" and should emphasize "*relationships*, not (yuck) *organs*"; "Feminism, Moralism and Pornography." See Willis, *Beginning to See the Light* (Hanover: University Press of New England, 1992) and reprinted in Adele Stan (ed.), *Debating Sexual Correctness* (New York: Delta, 1995), 45.

to give one's body over "to the bonds and whips of another person represents sex at its most deeply consensual" because it is an "act of extraordinary trust that requires an equally extraordinary responsibility."[66] We need not endorse S&M in order to suggest that an array of less "feminine" modes of sexual activity should not be ruled out as morally permissible.

Pineau's goals are also too high. Pineau argues that society would be well within its rights to prohibit noncommunicative sex. If it is feasible to legislate communication, then so much the worse for women who prefer other forms of sex: "If, as a matter of statistical fact, legislating communication as a central component of consensual sex is a good way to protect women from being sexually assaulted, then the interest a relatively few people may have in hazarding noncommunicative sex may just have to be sacrificed."[67] Setting aside the feasibility of such legislation, there are several questions we might raise about this view. Here I mention but two. First, although Pineau says that it is unreasonable for women to consent to sex that they do not enjoy, she produces little argument for that questionable claim. People reasonably consent to all sorts of things that they do not enjoy, and, absent some argument to the contrary, it is not clear why sex should be regarded as an exception. Second, even if "reasonable" consent would always involve sexual pleasure, it does not follow that we should fail to respect consent that does not meet a reasonableness standard. To insist that one can give *valid* consent only to what it is *reasonable* to consent to is to seriously diminish the moral significance of consent and raises the traditional worries about paternalism that are no less important for being traditional.

In an oft-cited article, Martha Chamallas advances an "egalitarian" theory of legitimate sex that contains a "refurbished" notion of consent. When sex is exchanged for external resources, women enter a realm in which males dominate, but when sex is exchanged for pleasure, women enter a realm in which men and women possess "an equal capacity to experience sexual pleasure and emotional intimacy."[68] She then maintains that sex that is inegalitarian, exploitive, or used for other instrumental purposes "such as financial gain, prestige, or power" is fundamentally nonconsensual "regardless of whether the parties have engaged voluntarily in the encounter."[69]

Here, too, there are several questions that might be raised. I will mention three. First, and least important, it is not self-evident that noninstrumental sex is egalitarian sex. It is an empirical question whether males and females

---

[66] Eskridge, "The Many Faces of Sexual Consent," 64.   [67] Pineau, *Date Rape*, 84.
[68] Chamallas, "Consent, Equality, and the Legal Control of Sexual Conduct," 839.
[69] *Ibid.*, 783.

do have an equal capacity to experience sexual pleasure or emotional intimacy, not to mention that sexual pleasure and emotional intimacy are not
identical. Second, and more importantly, Chamallas advances a peculiar
conceptual view of consent. It is one thing to argue that morally worthy sex
is always noninstrumental or non-exploitive, but quite another to advance
a "refurbished" notion of consent on which sex for external purposes is
considered nonconsensual "regardless of whether the parties have engaged
voluntarily in the encounter." This is to override consent, not to "refur-
bish" it. Now I have argued that PVC are themselves the subject of moral
argument. It may well turn out that the best version of PVC_M and PVC_L
will regard tokens of consent as invalid that would be regarded as valid on
less demanding accounts. That said, we cannot pack *all* our moral concerns
into the notion of consent without depriving consent of its moral value.
Third, it is of capital importance to distinguish between the claims that
(1) the background conditions in which people choose should be more
equal and (2) consent given under unequal conditions should be treated as
invalid. As I shall argue in chapter eight, if we are concerned to assist those
who are *less well off* under conditions of inequality, and if we have reason
to think that such persons are capable of acting reasonably in advancing
their own good, then we should go a long way toward treating their choices
with respect, even if we would demonstrate greater concern and respect for
them by attempting to remedy their background conditions.

Weak reciprocity

What I call weak reciprocity requires that the parties expect to benefit
from a sexual relationship in terms of their own preferences and values,
but it relaxes the criteria for morally permissible sex. On this view, reciprocity does not require exchanges that are equal in amount (assuming the
benefits are measurable) or in kind. Weak reciprocity also maintains that
morally permissible and even morally worthy sex is compatible with at least
some forms of sexual objectification.[70] Martha Nussbaum suggests that the
sort of objectification that involves intense focus on another's bodily parts
is not only unobjectionable, but is a positive dimension of sexual experience when undertaken in a context of "mutual respect."[71] In addition,
says Nussbaum, the objectification involved in the surrender of autonomy

---

[70] It is, I believe, a mistake to think that "reciprocity connotes equal sacrifices or transfer of equal
benefits... a type of quantification that conjures images of libertarian contractualism"; Raymond
Belliotti, *Good Sex* (Lawrence, KS: University of Kansas Press, 1993), 117–18.
[71] Nussbaum, "Objectification," 275.

and control during sex can be exciting, fulfilling, and morally acceptable when such objectifying acts are discrete and reciprocated events within the context of a relationship that is characterized by mutual regard.[72]

So we can be a bit less lofty about the sort of reciprocity that is required to render sexual relations permissible. On some versions of strong reciprocity, it would be wrong for a woman to perform oral sex if she finds it unpleasant and wrong for a man to ask. Vanessa Feltz disagrees. She does not particularly enjoy performing fellatio ("it makes my jaw ache") and she cannot overcome feeling that it "is fraught with embarrassment." Why does she do it? Simple. She loves to receive oral sex and "a little quid pro quo makes sense."[73] Suppose that Feltz and her partner both regard performing oral sex as a "cost" that is much lower than the benefit of receiving oral sex. Suppose, as well, that Feltz and her partner agree that oral sex is better when it is not simultaneous and that it is acceptable for the receiver to block out any thoughts about the cost to the "giver" and to focus on whatever enhances one's pleasure. I am hard pressed to see that there is anything objectionable in this sort of diachronic instrumentalization. Moreover, it does not matter whether both benefit *equally* as long as both benefit *enough*.

If weak reciprocity is a plausible view, the question now arises whether there is any space between weak reciprocity and consensual minimalism. I think not. Putting aside cases of altruistic sexual relations, there is, of course, a sense in which virtually all consensual sex is reciprocal: both parties consent to a transaction only because each expects, *ex ante*, to be better off by their own lights, although many perfectly consensual transactions do not render both parties better off, *ex post*.

Consensual minimalism (again)

Consensual minimalism does not involve a minimalist account of consent. It maintains that a suitably but not excessively robust consent is sufficient to legitimize sexual relations. One may treat others ungenerously or be indifferent to their experience or interests, but one does not treat them *merely* as a means so long as we do and should regard them as the appropriate judges of what will serve their ends and they give consent that is consistent with PVC. Although we need to say much more about what PVC requires for moral and legal permissibility, consensual minimalism is pluralistic with respect to one's reasons for consenting to sexual relations. People have

[72] *Ibid.*, 290.
[73] Robert T. Michael, John G. Gagnon, Edward O. Laumann, and Gina Kolata, *Sex in America* (Boston: Little, Brown, 1994), 153.

numerous aims, goals, and projects that give them reason to engage in sexual activity – sensory pleasure, release of tension, the expression of love, making up after a fight, pregnancy, curiosity, attracting a mate, keeping a promise, attaining financial security, earning money.

The argument for motivational pluralism receives support from its application to homosexual relations. There are several important differences between the sexual lives of gay males and gay females, including the greater propensity for gay males to engage in sex with (relative) strangers. It is possible, of course, that gay male sex is simply less morally worthy (on average) than lesbian sex. But if we consider a theory of morally permissible sex in light of its implications for homosexual relations, and if we think that we should regard casual homosexual relations as morally and legally permissible, then we must prefer consensual minimalism to its more rigorous competitors.

We can take motivational pluralism a bit further. It is not just that we should permit people to engage in sexual relations for a wide variety of reasons, but that sex may be an arena which does and should not require that people act on the basis of reasons. Thomas Nagel has argued that sex is a realm of adult life "in which the defining and inhibiting structures of civilization are permitted to dissolve, and our deepest presocial, animal, and infantile natures can be fully released and expressed, offering a form of physical and emotional completion that is not available elsewhere."[74] On this view, there are good moral reasons to provide the moral and legal background which makes such experience possible, a regime which allows people great room for using their sexual capacities as they see fit, a regime that does not put all aspects of sexual relations to the test of reason. There may be good moral reason to weaken the link between autonomy and reason responsiveness or, at least, to make the link at a step removed. As autonomous persons, we have reason not to want to subject all of our lives to the test of reason.

To provide the space for such sexual experiences may require that we be prepared to take what Barbara Herman calls "a moral-time out," that is, we decide not to subject an activity to the normal kind and degree of moral attention that it might otherwise merit: "From the point of view of morality, many sources of pleasure are sources of risk. What we laugh at and what we find exciting or thrilling are often at the boundaries of the acceptable or permissible. Circuses, sports, comedy, pornography: certain

---

[74] Thomas Nagel, "Personal Rights and Public Space," 24 *Philosophy & Public Affairs* 83 (1995), 100.

sorts of pleasure and moral danger go together."[75] Going even further, William Miller suggests that some sexual acts are exciting precisely because they involve "boundary crossing" into the realm of the disgusting. To do and allow things to be done that would normally trigger disgust is "much of what sexual intimacy is" and is entirely unobjectionable when it is mutual, when both partners "offend the gods of purity equally."[76] To the extent that sexual pleasure is sometimes exciting and thrilling precisely because it is at the boundary of the acceptable, permissible, or reasonable, it becomes the task of cultural institutions "to insure that this risk-seeking impulse is expressed in a controlled and safe way."[77]

When we enter the realm of the law, there is another reason to prefer consensual minimalism to strong reciprocity or a consent-plus view of permissible sex. It is important to distinguish three claims: (1) other things being equal, the law should not permit people to engage in sexual relations when their relationship does not meet certain standards; (2) there is *evidence* that the relationship does not meet such standards; (3) such evidence could be *obtained in morally acceptable ways*. Any plausible consent-plus view of legally permissible sex must assume that (2) and (3) can generally be satisfied. That is highly implausible. It is not just that sexual behavior is typically not visible to outsiders, but that much that is important in sexual life (sexual fantasies, for example) is not known by those with whom we are intimate, or even by ourselves.[78] Even if much sex is morally questionable, we may have no basis for knowing that it is morally questionable or would be able to attain such information only in morally unacceptable ways. So there is certainly good reason to stay our legal hand with respect to morally unworthy sex.

Conclusion

I have argued, in effect, that we should reject both sexual piggishness and sexual priggishness. We should reject the piggish view that if a certain sort of sexual encounter should be legally permissible, it follows that it is morally permissible. We should reject the equally piggish view that if a sexual encounter is morally permissible, it follows that it is beyond moral criticism.

---

[75] Barbara Herman, "Moral Literacy" in Grethe B. Peterson (ed.), *Tanner Lectures on Human Values*, volume XIX (Salt Lake City, UT: University of Utah Press, 1998), 352.

[76] William Ian Miller, *The Anatomy of Disgust* (Cambridge, MA: Harvard University Press, 1997), 127 and 138.

[77] Herman, "Moral Literacy" in Peterson (ed.), *Tanner Lectures* XIX, 352.

[78] "People who sleep together do not know everything that is going on, and often they know very little"; Nagel, "Personal Rights and Public Space," 101.

At the same time, we should reject a priggish view about the moral and legal permissibility of consensual interactions. In commenting on Richard Posner's account of consent, Robin West says this: "The morality of any of these consensual transactions depends upon the value of the worlds they create, which in turn depends in part upon the worth of the relationships they contain... It is immoral to participate in such consensual transactions and immoral for the community to tolerate them."[79] Not so. Just because a relationship can and maybe even should be morally criticized, it does not follow that it is morally impermissible. Moreover, even if it is morally impermissible to participate in certain relationships, it simply does not follow that it is also immoral for the community to tolerate it. This for at least two reasons. First, even if we assume that some relationships have negative moral value, there may be wide reasonable disagreement as to when that is so. Second, even when it is clear that relationships have negative moral value, the case for toleration may be quite strong. Just as there is moral reason for the community to tolerate much speech that has negative moral value, there may be considerable moral value to providing a regime in which consensual relationships that lack moral value are allowed. There is good reason to give women considerable authority to render it permissible for others to have sexual relations with them when they give appropriately robust consent. Appropriate respect for a woman's sexual autonomy demands no less. The task is to determine just what appropriately robust consent amounts to.

---

[79] Robin West, "Authority, Autonomy, and Choice: The Role of Consent in the Moral and Political Visions of Franz Kafka and Richard Posner," 99 *Harvard Law Review* 384 (1985), 399.

CHAPTER SEVEN

The ontology of consent

Consensual minimalism states that, *ceteris paribus*, sexual relations are morally and legally permissible if and only if both parties give consent that is consistent with the moral and legal versions of PVC. Although the important issues concern the conditions of validity, we need to ask what consenting amounts to in the first place – valid or invalid. In this chapter, I ask: what sort of phenomenon is the consent that can be morally transformative in the relevant way? In the next four chapters, I consider issues of validity.

Ontology of consent

Roughly speaking, there are three accounts of what we might pretentiously call the ontology of consent. A *subjective* view argues that consent is a psychological phenomenon, that B consents if and only if she has the relevant mental state. A *performative* view argues that consent is behavioral, that B consents if and only if she tokens or expresses consent in an appropriate way.[1] A *hybrid* view maintains that the relevant mental state and relevant consent token are both necessary for morally transformative consent.

Some courts, statutes, and legal treatises appear to adopt the subjective view. Others adopt the performative view, as in a recent Canadian case:

Consent for purposes of sexual assault is found in the communication by a person with the requisite capacity by verbal or non-verbal behaviour to another of permission to perform the sexual act. The actual thought pattern in the mind

---

[1] The word "performative" is taken from J. L. Austin's *How to Do Things with Words* (Cambridge, MA: Harvard University Press, 1962). Austin distinguishes between an utterance's locutionary force, its perlocutionary effects, and its illocutionary force. An utterance's locutionary force refers to its propositional content. An utterance's "perlocutionary effects" refers to its causal effects on the hearer, for example, frightening, inspiring, seducing. Some utterances have "illocutionary force." They do something, for example, advising, warning, claiming, consenting. In the canonical example, to say "I do" at a wedding ceremony is not (just) to make a statement of one's beliefs or intentions (locutionary force), nor to cause others to rejoice ("perlocutionary effect"), but to perform an act within the marriage ceremony that enables one to be married.

of the complainant cannot be the focus of an inquiry into consent in a sexual assault trial.[2]

One finds both the subjective and performative views in ordinary language. And philosophers too array themselves on both sides of the issue.

In companion articles, Heidi Hurd and Larry Alexander defend a strong subjective view of consent. They argue that precisely because consent can "magically" transform the rights and duties of others, we should adopt a subjective view – if "autonomy resides in the ability to will the alteration of moral rights and duties, and if consent is normatively significant precisely because it constitutes an expression of autonomy" then consent must constitute the "exercise of the will."[3] Hurd and Alexander disagree about the content of the relevant mental state. Whereas Hurd believes that the consenter must form the intention that the other party cross what would be a moral boundary in the absence of consent, Alexander maintains that the consenter must form the intention "to forgo or waive one's moral objection to the boundary crossing."[4] According to Hurd, B's consent intends that A do something. According to Alexander, B cannot intend that A do something, so B's mental state looks to what B herself will do. Still, they both agree that no action or performative by B is required. In order to alter the moral rights or obligations of another, one need only entertain the "*mens rea* of consent."[5]

A. John Simmons argues for the performative view. Simmons acknowledges that there are senses of the word "consent" that signify a (subjective) attitude of approval, but he argues that this sense of consent is irrelevant to the sort of consent that generates an obligation or renders another's action permissible.[6] That requires a performative.[7]

Emily Sherwin defends a hybrid view. She argues that consent is both a "subjective decision" and a "social act," although she thinks it is

---

[2] *Regina v. Esau*, On Appeal from the court of Appeal for the Northwest Territories, 1997, file no. 25409.

[3] Heidi Hurd, "The Moral Magic of Consent," 2 *Legal Theory* 121 (1996). Larry Alexander, "The Moral Magic of Consent II," 2 *Legal Theory* 165 (1996). Alexander and Hurd originally intended to write a joint article, but because they disagreed on some details, they went their separate ways.

[4] Alexander says, for example, that one does not, nay cannot, choose that another person act in a particular way; "The Moral Magic of Consent II," 166.

[5] Hurd, "The Moral Magic of Consent," 122.

[6] A. John Simmons, *Moral Principles and Political Obligations* (Princeton: Princeton University Press, 1979), 83.

[7] Along these lines, David Archard writes that consent to sexual relations "is an act rather than a state of mind"; *Sexual Consent* (Boulder: Westview, 1998), 4. Or as Brenda Baker puts it, consenting is "something that we do"; "Understanding Consent in Sexual Assault" in Keith Burgess-Jackson (ed.), *A Most Detestable Crime: New Philosophical Essays on Rape* (New York: Oxford University Press, 1990), 52.

the performative sense that "matters most" and does not indicate what "subjective" decision is involved or what function it serves in rendering sexual relations permissible.[8] Patricia Kazan argues that consent must include a performative component if we are to avoid focus on the victim's attitude towards sex, but the subjective component is necessary if we are to distinguish between valid and invalid consent.[9]

So which view should we adopt? I believe that the answer to that question turns on the purposes for which we ask it. We begin by reminding ourselves that we are not interested in consent as a metaphysical problem, but because it renders it permissible for A to engage in sexual relations with B. If we ask "what could do that?", a suitably qualified (moralized) performative view is closest to the truth. Alexander and Hurd make an ingenious case for the subjective view, but they are ultimately unsuccessful, and they are unsuccessful because there is no moral magic to consent that has to be explained. B's consent is morally transformative because it changes A's reasons for action. If we ask what could change A's reasons for action, the answer must be that B performs some token of consent. It is hard to see how B's mental state – by itself – can do the job. As Joel Feinberg notes, because A does not have "any direct insight into B's mental states... the question of his responsibility must be settled by reference to presence or absence of... authorization by N, not what B's secret desires or hopes might have been."[10]

I do not want to quibble over words. If Hurd and Alexander were to insist that a mental state is sufficient to establish consent, then I should say that B's mental state does not *authorize* or *legitimate* A's doing X in the absence of B's performative or token of consent. If, for example, B has decided to accept A's business proposal and was about to communicate that decision to A when their call was disconnected, it would ordinarily not be legitimate for A to proceed as if B had agreed. If B leaves her car on the street, hoping that it will be stolen so that she can collect the insurance, the person who takes her car is both morally and legally culpable.[11]

Consider the following cases.

Guilt. Unbeknownst to A, B wants A to have intercourse with her without her consent because she feels guilty about saying yes. While B says "No, please don't," A holds B down and penetrates B.

[8] Emily Sherwin, "Infelicitous Sex," 2 *Legal Theory* 209 (1996), 216.
[9] Patricia Kazan, "Sexual Assault and the Problem of Consent" in Stanley French, Wanda Teays, and Laura Purdy (eds.), *Violence against Women: Philosophical Perspectives* (Ithaca: Cornell University Press, 1998).
[10] Joel Feinberg, *Harm to Self* (New York: Oxford University Press, 1986), 173.
[11] If A knows that B wants her car to appear to be stolen, then they will be guilty of fraud, not theft.

Quadriplegic₁. B is a deaf-mute quadriplegic. She would like to have intercourse with A, but cannot communicate her wishes. A penetrates B anyway.
Quadriplegic₂. B is a deaf-mute quadriplegic. She wants A to penetrate her without tokening consent. A does not know this, but penetrates B anyway.[12]

In my view, it is not permissible for A to proceed in **Guilt** or in both versions of **Quadriplegic**. It is possible, I suppose, that B's mental state would be sufficient to cancel *B's right to complain* if A proceeds (although I think it does not), but it is hard to see how it could render it permissible for A to proceed.

The disagreement about whether we should adopt a subjective or performative view is not merely verbal. There are substantive moral issues at stake. Joshua Dressler argues that lack of consent is an element of the *actus reus* of rape and that "if a female 'concurs in mind and spirit' with the act of intercourse, her interest in autonomy has not been violated."[13] Similarly, Douglas Husak would argue that there is no rape in **Quadriplegic₂**, given the more complete description of B's mental state, and perhaps not in **Guilt** and **Quadriplegic₁**, although the latter pose more difficulty.[14]

Are Dressler and Husak right? As a matter of positive law, I do not know. Perhaps A would not be culpable in **Guilt**. It would be impossible to establish whether he was guilty in both versions of **Quadriplegic**, given that, *ex hypothesi*, there can be no evidence of B's mental state. From a moral perspective, I believe that A has acted wrongly in all three cases. Heidi Hurd concedes that there may be "prudential reasons for the law to require observable behavior" that expresses B's mental state before according a defender a *legal* defense of consent. Nonetheless, she insists that observable behavior is *morally* irrelevant to consent – "If the *actus reus* condition is purely evidential of [B's mental state] and not an independent constitutive component of consent, then, as a moral matter, a person *can* consent to another's actions without manifesting her consent in any manner whatsoever."[15] I disagree. It is of the utmost moral relevance to the evaluation of A's behavior whether A *has reason to think* that B wants him to proceed.

In opting for a performative account of consent, I readily grant that tokens of consent are morally significant precisely because they are reliable indications of desires, intentions, choices, and the like. It is the mental states that largely define what the tokens of consent are meant to convey.[16]

---

[12] Arthur Applbaum suggested that I should distinguish between these two versions of the case.
[13] Joshua Dressler, "Some Cautionary Reflections on Rape Law Reform," 46 *Cleveland State Law Review* 409 (1998), 424.
[14] This is my extension of a private communication. Husak does not refer to these particular cases.
[15] Hurd, "The Moral Magic of Consent," 137.
[16] See Peter Westen, "The Logic of Consent: The Diversity and Deceptiveness of Consent as a Defense to Criminal Conduct," unpublished manuscript.

Who can deny that wills are morally significant? Indeed, they may be basic. But if the point of consent is to alter our normative relations with *others*, then I would insist that some public indication of our will is required.

On the version of the performative view that I prefer, B gives valid consent when B's consent token makes it permissible for A to proceed. The hybrid view also claims that a consent token is necessary if B's consent is to be morally transformative, but insists that B must *intend* her token of consent to change A's reasons for actions. As a practical matter, there will rarely be differences between the two views, but they reach different conclusions in cases of unintentional or mistaken consent.

Biopsy. A mammogram reveals suspicious areas in B's breast. A tells B that he wants to do a biopsy under general anesthesia, and, if positive, perform a lumpectomy. B appears to be listening, but is not paying attention. A asks her to sign a consent form authorizing both procedures (if necessary). B pretends to read the form, but thinks that A will only be doing a biopsy. She signs.

B has clearly given a consent token to the surgery. Has she given valid consent? That is a different question. I believe that the best version of PVC may hold that B has given valid consent to the lumpectomy, even though B did not intend by her action to do so. That will depend upon whether we think A has done enough. Assume, arguendo, that the best version of PVC will hold that A has done enough, that A need not quiz B to establish that she understands what she is signing. If one wants to say that unintentional consent is not consent, then so be it. The question is whether B's consent token renders it permissible for A to perform the lumpectomy if the biopsy is positive. I believe that it might.

It is an advantage of the performative view that it enables us to understand why A's conduct can be wrong even when it is based on a substantively correct view of B's mental state and morally innocent when based on a substantively incorrect view of B's mental state. Consider **Kinky** (a variation of *Morgan*).[17]

Kinky. A truthfully tells three drinking buddies that his wife, B, likes kinky sex, that she wants to have sex with them but will "feign" resistance. They have intercourse with her while B screams and struggles.

Unlike Mrs. Morgan, B actually welcomed the "attack," while giving every indication that she did not. I believe that the men would still be morally and legally culpable, that B had not consented to their actions. A woman's

---

[17] *Director of Public Prosecutions v. Morgan*, 2 All ER 347 (1975). See the description of the case in chapter 2.

secret desires have little bearing on whether A's action is permissible. One could argue that A had given a proxy consent for B in this case. But then things would turn on whether PVC would hold that the buddies would be entitled to proceed on the basis of A's token (of proxy consent), and I am inclined to think they would not be so entitled.

By contrast, consider the true but sad case of Rebecca Burnham.

Burnham. Rebecca Burnham's husband (Victor) severely beat Rebecca until she agreed, under threat of further beating, to stand on the street in front of their house and entice motorists (such as A) to have sex with her while Victor photographed her. Although Rebecca feared physical injury from Victor, she feigned expressions of desire to the motorists.[18]

A lot of ink has been spilled in arguments about how best to describe such cases (which are but a form of coerced prostitution). On the performative view, we could say (1) the motorist is not guilty of rape because there was consensual sex as between A and Mrs. Burnham (bracketing her complaint against Victor). On a subjective view, we could say (2) this was a case of rape because Mrs. Burnham did not desire sex with A, although A should not be convicted (of rape) because it was reasonable for him to believe that Mrs. Burnham consented. Even here, things are more complicated. There is a genuine sense in which Mrs. Burnham does desire that A have sex with her given her fear of the alternatives. It does not seem to matter much whether we opt for (1) or (2), so long as we reach the same conclusion about A's culpability. But I think that the performative view gives the more attractive description. After all, it is not quite right to say that the motorist should be *excused* for the crime of raping Mrs. Burnham if her consent token justifies A's belief that he is authorized to proceed. In the words of a recent New Jersey case: "Permission is demonstrated when the evidence, in whatever form, is sufficient to demonstrate that a reasonable person would have believed that the alleged victim had affirmatively and freely given authorization to the act."[19]

A suitably qualified performative view – one in which a consent token is subject to PVC – also better accommodates questions of deception.

Single. A and B meet in a night class, and have several dates. B makes it clear that she refuses to have sex with married men. A falsely tells B that he is not married.

---

[18] *People v. Burnham*, 176 Cal. App. 3d 1134, 222 Cal. Rptr 630 (1985). I thank Peter Westen for bringing this case to my attention.

[19] *New Jersey in the interest of M. T.S.*, 609 A.2d 1266 (1992), 129 N.J. 422, 445. The court's holding was controversial because the relevant statute requires that the perpetrator use force. The court held that the required force need be no greater than the force involved in penetration itself, even if no use or threat of additional force is involved.

Setting legal issues aside, B's consent does not render A's behavior morally permissible. If B's consent is morally transformative when A's statement is truthful, but not when A's statements are deceptive, then consent cannot be (purely) subjective, for B would have identical states of mind at the time of her consent. The subjectivist might reply: "There is consent (because of B's mental state), but there is no *valid* consent because the consent is based on a false belief induced by A's deception." I have no strong objection to this move, but it seems to collapse the distinction between the subjective and performative views. The point of the performative view is that the permissibility of A's behavior depends upon observable or public acts, and this move accepts that basic point.

Still, it might be objected that the performative view has no advantage over the subjective view in a case such as **Single**. After all, just as B's mental state is identical in cases where she is and is not deceived, B's consent token in **Single** is identical in cases where she is and is not deceived or, for that matter, in cases where she is and is not coerced.

Polite Thugs. A group of four large men approach and surround B. The leader says, "Please give us your wallet."

Patricia Kazan argues that in the absence of "any verbal or physical performances which might be construed as threatening, it is difficult to see how the performative model could classify this situation as nonconsensual."[20] Indeed, Heidi Hurd suggests that a performative model gives a morally obtuse result even when A makes an observable threat.

a woman who succumbs to a deadly threat and engages in intercourse with a knife-brandishing defendant may behave identically to a woman who engages in intercourse with her husband out of a desire to express her love for him. If a victim's mental state is irrelevant to assessing whether she has consented to a defendant's conduct, then it is impossible to distinguish the above two cases.[21]

This objection to the performative view is based on a distinctly ungenerous characterization (caricaturization) of the performative view. First, PVC is not blind to the behavioral context in which a consent token occurs. If the thugs cannot reasonably regard the wallet as a gift, then the fact that they have made no physical or verbal threat is irrelevant. Surely, PVC will hold that a woman's expression of acquiescence ("I'll do what you want") in the face of a knife-brandishing attacker should not be regarded as morally

[20] Kazan, "Sexual Assault and the Problem of Consent" in French et al. (eds.), *Violence against Women*, 37.
[21] Hurd, "The Moral Magic of Consent," 136.

transformative consent. Here, PVC might apply to the subjective view of consent as well. But then we must ask whether the subjective view requires a subjective interpretation of PVC. If it does not – and it is hard to see how a purely subjective interpretation of PVC would work – then we are back to a non-subjective view of valid consent. And as I argued above, the emphasis on observable behavior is consistent with the point of the performative view.

Second, one simply cannot distinguish between the coerced consent that invalidates an agreement and noncoerced consent that yields a valid agreement by reference to B's mental state.[22] That B feels "under pressure" to consent or finds the alternative to acquiescence to be distasteful or painful is not sufficient to invalidate her consent. Consider **Dating** and **Lower Grade**.

Dating. A and B have been dating for some time, but have not had sexual relations. A says, "I'm not willing to continue dating you if we don't have sex, so either we have sex or I'm terminating the relationship."
Lower Grade. A, a professor, says "Have sexual relations with me or I will give you a grade two grades lower than you deserve."[23]

Given B's values and preferences, B may feel under much greater pressure to acquiesce in **Dating** than in **Lower Grade**. Nonetheless, I believe that B's consent in **Dating** has more transformative power, a result that can be explained by reference to PVC, which will take account of A's *right* to make the respective proposals, but which cannot be explained by reference to B's mental states.

In defending her hybrid view, Kazan concedes that genuine consent does not require a positive attitude toward the object of consent. But it does, she says, require a positive attitude toward the act of consenting itself: "it is the failure to distinguish between our attitudes toward the act of consenting and the object of consent which leads to the erroneous conclusion that a positive attitude is not an essential component of consent."[24] Kazan argues that consent to painful dental surgery is valid because one wants to consent to surgery (even though one does not want the surgery), whereas consent in response to a coercive threat is invalid because one does not want to *consent* to sex and not just because one does not want sex. But this move does not work. Consider **Charade**.

---

[22] See my *Coercion* (Princeton: Princeton University Press, 1987), chapter 11.
[23] This case is similar, of course, to *Thompson*, the case in which a high school principal threatened to block the student's graduation; *State v. Thompson*, 792 P.2d 1103 (1990).
[24] Kazan, "Sexual Assault and the Problem of Consent" in French et al. (eds.), *Violence against Women*, 34.

Charade. A approaches B on the street, puts a gun to her back, and says, "We're walking up to my apartment." When they arrive, he says, "You and I are going to play a game. You are going to beg me to - - - - you. Do a good job, and I won't hurt you. Resist, and I'll kill you." B takes off her clothes and says, "I want you."

Given the circumstances that motivate B's saying "I want you" in **Charade**, B also wants to perform the relevant token of consent and to engage in sex. True, she cannot want to give *valid* consent, for A's threat makes that impossible. But B does not want to find herself so paralyzed by fear that she is unable to *feign* valid consent. The distinction between dental surgery and **Charade** is not to be found in B's subjective attitude towards the act of tokening consent, but in the *moral* character of the background conditions that motivate B's token of consent.

What about the mute quadriplegic? Hurd thinks that one can adopt a performative account of consent only "on pain of depriving those who have lost their physical autonomy of the only power left to them – namely, their ability to exercise moral magic through subjective will."[25] And this, she thinks, is reason to favor the subjective view. I disagree. I find it difficult to imagine that a person who is capable of enjoying sexual relations cannot find *any* way to token consent. But if that were so, it would be more sensible to regard her inability to token consent to sex as an additional burden that she must bear than as an argument for the subjective view of consent. Interestingly, it is not clear to what extent Hurd ultimately disagrees. She says that if A engages in sex with a mute quadriplegic who is unable to communicate her desire, then he "may be culpable for so doing, because he has no good reason to suppose that she is a consenting partner," although he does not rape her "as a moral matter."[26] This is odd. If it is not a moral matter that A has sexual relations with B even though "he has no good reason to think that she is a consenting partner," then I do not know what a "moral matter" amounts to.

Tokens

I have argued that B consents to sexual relations with A only when she performs some token of consent. Roughly speaking, there are three ways in which B can communicate consent: (a) a verbal act; (b) a nonverbal act; (c) silence or inaction.

[25] Hurd, "The Moral Magic of Consent," 137. Brenda Baker asks: "Can't people consent to things without communicating their consent . . . [if] they can't communicate it because they are paralyzed or unable to communicate generally . . .?"; "Understanding Consent in Sexual Assault" in Burgess-Jackson (ed.), *A Most Detestable Crime*, 66–67.
[26] Hurd, "The Moral Magic of Consent," 137.

Consider the following:

Antioch. A asks if he can kiss B. B says yes. A asks if he can touch B's breasts. B says yes. A asks if he can remove B's clothes. B says yes. A asks B if she wants to have intercourse. B says yes.
Smile. A and B have been dating. They have not had intercourse. A proposes that they go to his apartment. B agrees. Pointing to his bedroom, A says, "How about we go there?" B smiles, follows A into the bedroom, but says nothing.
Coy. A makes advances. B does not want to seem "too eager." She firmly moves A's hand away, but kisses A. A puts his hand on B's leg again. B moves it away. They kiss more. A puts his hand on B's leg. This time, B kisses A, but does not remove his hand. A begins to remove B's clothing. B does not resist and continues to kiss A.

In my view, nothing much turns on the form of the token, so long as it is reasonable to assume that its meaning is understood by the relevant parties. Some argue that verbal permission should be required, as in **Antioch**.[27] Schulhofer argues that we should require that A obtain an affirmative indication of B's consent, as in **Smile**, but that a verbal-permission rule would impose an excessive degree of formality and artificiality.[28] I think that nothing problematic will follow from construing any form of behavior or omission as a token of consent so long as its meaning is clear and so long as B can indicate to the contrary if it is not. If B really did not intend to consent to sexual relations in **Smile**, and says "I'm sorry, I didn't know that you meant *that*, I think I'd better go," then there should be little confusion whether she has consented to sex, even if it was reasonable for A to temporarily believe that she had. So, too, for **Coy**. What constitutes a token of consent is, to use the vernacular, "socially constructed." If "would you like to come up for coffee?" were generally understood to express a desire for sexual relations, I see no reason to deny that the utterance would be sufficient to constitute consent in the absence of any countervailing indicators. I suspect that there are *very* few cases in which there is genuine ambiguity whether B has tokened consent.[29] There may be cases in which it is unclear whether B's token is morally transformative, given the background conditions under which it is provided, but that is a different matter.

---

[27] Lani Anne Remick, "Read Her Lips: An Argument for a Verbal Consent Standard in Rape," 141 *University of Pennsylvania Law Review* 1103 (1993).
[28] Stephen J. Schulhofer, *Unwanted Sex* (Cambridge, MA: Harvard University Press, 1998), 272.
[29] As Linda Fairstein, Chief of the Sex Crimes Prosecution Unit and Deputy Chief, NY County District Attorney's Office, has said, "There are occasionally cases that happen that way, but most of the time the signals that the victim has given, whether verbally or physically, are very clear. There is very little rape that is due to failure to communicate . . ."; Panel Discussion, "Men, Women and Rape," 63 *Fordham Law Review* 125 (1994), 171.

David Archard rightly distinguishes between flirtatious acts (winks) that A can reasonably take as predictors that B will consent to sexual relations and acts that can reasonably be understood as consent tokens themselves (nods).[30] Consider:

Tease. A and B have dated, but have not had sex. On their fourth date, they go to A's apartment, they drink wine, listen to music, and kiss. A suggests that they go to his bedroom. B agrees. When A starts to undress B, B asks A to stop.[31]

Here too it does not matter much whether we regard B's flirtatious acts as consent tokens, so long as it is also understood that a subsequent refusal of consent (ordinarily) trumps any earlier token of consent.[32] It is both imprudent and arguably wrong for B to intentionally create false expectations that she will consent to intercourse, but such wrongness as there might be has no bearing on the permissibility of A's behavior, given that the predicted consent was not forthcoming or given that B has changed her mind.[33]

What about silence or tacit consent? In my view, there is nothing problematic about tacit consent (as in **Coy**), so long as (1) silence is understood by the parties to be a token of consent and (2) the background conditions are such as to render the silence morally transformative. With respect to (1), silence is often a clear indicator of consent. If B's department Chair says, "Unless I hear from you, I'll assume that you can advise students at orientation," B's silence is an indication that she is available, and much the same can be said for B's silence and inaction in **Coy**. What about (2)? A. John Simmons has argued that tacit consent is valid only under special conditions, namely, that the means for indicating dissent must be "reasonably easily performed" and "the consequence of dissent cannot be extremely detrimental to the potential consentor."[34] As stated, I do not think that Simmons's conditions are quite correct. As I shall argue in chapter eight, one can give valid consent even when the consequences of not dissenting

[30] See David Archard, " 'A Nod's as Good as a Wink': Consent, Convention, and Reasonable Belief," 2 *Legal Theory* 273 (1997).
[31] I borrow this case from Mark Cowling, *Date Rape and Consent* (Brookfield, VT: Ashgate, 1998), 36.
[32] " 'A Nod's as Good as a Wink,' " 279. I say "ordinarily" to leave open the possibility that B's subsequent refusal in a Ulysses case does not trump her earlier consent token. As Donald Dripps points out, sexual encounters typically begin at a low level and then escalate: "the transition from penetration of the mouth by the tongue to the penetration of an orifice by the penis is neither instantaneous nor unscripted. The partners will have time to object to sex acts they don't like . . ."; Panel Discussion, "Men, Women and Rape," 63 *Fordham Law Review* 125 (1994), 146.
[33] See David Bryden and Sona Lengnick, "Rape in the Criminal Justice System," 87 *Journal of Criminal Law and Criminology* 1194 (1997), 1336.
[34] Simmons mentions several other conditions, most of which concern the clarity of silence as a token of consent. Here, too, similar conditions would apply to various forms of verbal or behavioral consent (following into the bedroom), although it is possible that silence is more frequently ambiguous; *Moral Principles and Political Obligation*, 81.

are extremely detrimental to the consentor. The present point is that while Simmons is right to insist that certain background conditions are necessary to the validity of B's tacit consent, much the same is true of explicit consent. Consider **Threat?**

Threat? A and B meet in a bar and go back to A's apartment. B rebuffs A's advances. A smiles at B and says, "Look, you're alone with someone you don't know, who's much bigger and stronger, and, for all you know, has beaten and raped several women. Maybe I'm not as nice as I seem." B is very frightened by A's remarks and does not resist A's advances.

It may be unclear whether B gives transformative consent in **Threat?**, but not because she is silent. After all, if B were really frightened, she might give a decidedly unequivocal token of consent, as in **Charade**. It is not the clarity of the token that is at issue, but whether the consent meets the test of PVC_L or PVC_M.

Is a consent token always necessary?

As a general rule, sexual relations are permissible only if B consents, but even here there may well be exceptions. First, we are discussing sexual *intercourse*. It is doubtful that consent should be regarded as a necessary condition of all sexual bodily contact. There are good physical, psychological, and moral reasons to draw a reasonably bright line between intercourse and other forms of sexual contact. Sexual encounters among acquaintances usually begin at a low level and escalate. If A and B have embarked on the kind of relationship in which sexual contact is a normal feature, it is arguably permissible for A to initiate a low-level sexual contact without B's consent and then move to a marginally higher level of intimacy without prior consent if he does not persist when asked to stop.[35] Obtaining prior consent for every action is awkward and can diminish the value of the activity itself. It is not that one should be able to presume consent for such actions, but that the costs of not requiring consent are relatively low compared with the benefits.[36] The precise contours of morally permissible behavior will depend, in large part, upon the psychology of sexual relations in a particular social context. If women experience great distress at being kissed or fondled without prior

[35] This does not apply to contact between non-acquaintances or among acquaintances who have not embarked on a relationship in which sexual contact is a normal feature. It may be permissible to kiss one's date without consent, but not one's co-worker.
[36] As Linda R. Hirshman and Jane E. Larson put it, "Where the conduct interferes minimally with the victim's bodily integrity and decisional autonomy . . . the risk should fall on the side of encouraging more sexual contacts, even at the risk of allowing some undesired intrusions"; *Hard Bargains* (New York: Oxford University Press, 1998), 270.

consent, as they might in some societies or in some social contexts, then prior consent might be required for these acts as well.

There is a small set of situations in which even sexual intercourse might be permissible without occurrent and competent consent. Consider **Sleep**.

Sleep. A and B have been dating for a month and have just begun having sex. On this occasion, they had "wonderful" sex the night before. B, who has been sound asleep, awakens to find A on top of her. A says "Good morning." B smiles back and says "Good morning."

I suspect that reasonable people will disagree, but I believe that the surprise intercourse in **Sleep** may be morally permissible and should not be legally impermissible, if A were to withdraw if B should object. I do not want to suppose that B had somehow consented in advance. And I prefer to avoid appeals to retrospective consent. Rather, given the couple's history, I would assimilate this case to one in which A moves to a marginally higher level of intimacy without prior consent. One might think that the moral status of A's conduct in **Sleep** is permissible if B responds positively and impermissible if she does not. I prefer not to take moral luck so seriously and to think that the permissibility of A's behavior is much the same in both cases, for better or for worse. But while the example is arguably off to the side, I think it illustrates an important point. If A's behavior in **Sleep** is certainly not abhorrent, this shows that it is a mistake to conceptualize the wrong of nonconsensual intercourse purely as a violation of someone's bodily boundaries or one's sexual autonomy. Rather, and as I have argued, the wrong of nonconsensual sexual relations is a function of experience, and when some of the harms associated with more typical nonconsensual sex seem not to apply, nonconsensual sex is much less wrong or not wrong at all.

In other cases, B might give competent *ex ante* consent to sexual intercourse without giving or being able to give competent concurrent consent.

Ulysses. A and B join the "Ulysses" club which hosts events where all parties sign a form indicating that no one will be legally liable for any sexual act, including forced sex. One can ask another to refrain, but one has no recourse if he does not. A approaches B. B resists. A enlists the help of others to hold B down.

Rohypnol Conception. A and B are good friends. B wishes to become pregnant. She wants A to father her child, but does not want to experience intercourse with A. She tells A that she intends to take Rohypnol and that he should have intercourse with her while she is unconscious.

Dutch Courage. A and B have dated. B is a virgin, and feels frightened of and guilty about sex. Believing that she will never agree to sex if sober, she consumes four drinks in an hour. After some kissing and petting, A says, "Are you sure it's OK?" B holds up her glass, smiles, and says "It is *now*."

Some would have no difficulty with any of these cases. Others would have difficulty with all. Still others, like myself, are troubled by **Ulysses**, but not by **Rohypnol Conception** or **Dutch Courage**. In any case, if A's behavior is permissible in any such cases, then we have at least another case in which it is permissible for A to have sexual relations with B without her concurrent or competent consent.

Two unhelpful formulae

Exceptional cases aside, consensual minimalism maintains that sexual relations are (ordinarily) permissible if and only if B gives a token of consent under conditions that are consistent with PVC. This is an inelegant formula that can no doubt be put more pithily. But there are two pithy formulae that are not helpful. The first unhelpful formula relies on the notion of "unwanted sex." The second unhelpful formula maintains that "no means no."

To get a handle on "unwanted sex," one can distinguish between *desire*, *want*, and *will*. For *stipulative purposes only*, say that B *desires* to do X when B has a pro-attitude toward doing X considered (more or less) by itself. Say that B *wants* to do X when B has a pro-attitude toward doing X, *all things considered*. And say that B *wills* doing X when B makes a (more or less) rational decision to do X, that is, B's choice is consistent with B's want. Given this, it is a virtual tautology that B wills to do X if and only if she wants to do X, but there is a good deal of space between B's desires and B's wants. We want, all things considered, to do many things that we do not desire to do, where the things to be considered involve both the benefits and costs of our actions, our long-term interests and moral commitments.[37] Thus we may want (my term) or be most concerned to exercise, work, grade papers, diet, visit relatives, serve as jurors, pay taxes, give blood, cook dinner, change diapers, and pay for products and services, even though we do not desire to do any of these things in and of themselves.

Given this, there will be little space between one's wants and one's consent (except in those cases where what one wants is that something be done without one's consent). Consider the well-worn example in which parents consent to their child's marriage by providing the required approval even though they do not desire that the child marry (or marry the particular person). Although the parents do not desire that the child marry, other

---

[37] As Simon Blackburn puts it, "Sometimes we act not so much in ways that we want [I say "desire"] to act, but in ways we feel we have to act. We are, as it were, *resigned* to acting in some way, rather than actively wanting to do so"; see *Ruling Passions* (Oxford: Clarendon Press, 1998), 123.

things being equal, they want the marriage to occur, all things considered, where the things to be considered may include their respect for their child's autonomy or their future relations with her.

Two points. First, little of moral interest turns on whether sex is either desired (*per se*) or wanted (all things considered). One can desire sex that is not wanted, as when one decides to "wait" until one is married, and one can want sex that is not desired. Some desired sex is morally problematic, as when there are worries about competence or deception. Some undesired but wanted sex is morally unproblematic, as when women engage in sex to get pregnant.

Second, the distinction between desired sex and unwanted sex fails to help us understand the cases in which consent is not morally transformative because of coercion or duress. Recall **Dating** and **Abandonment**. B wants but does not desire to have sex in both cases, but they are by no means morally equivalent. Rather, it certainly seems as if A is legally and perhaps morally permitted not to continue the relationship on terms he finds unsatisfactory, but he is not entitled to condition not abandoning B on her agreement to have sex.

Some suggest that we can resolve the question of when sexual relations are permissible by adopting the principle that "no means no" (NMN). Despite its popularity, this principle is singularly unhelpful. It is not unhelpful because it is incorrect. It is unhelpful because there are many ways of "getting to yes," and NMN does not help us distinguish between them.

Some have argued that NMN is incorrect on the face of it. Husak and Thomas argue that we should reject NMN if we consider NMN as an empirical hypothesis that "when a woman says the word 'no,' she intends to express her lack of consent, and it would be unreasonable for a man to believe otherwise."[38] They (and many others) note that a study of Texas college students found that approximately 40 percent of the women engaged in "token resistance," that they sometimes said "no" when they were willing to have sex.[39] There are many reasons why women might say no when they actually desire sex, including a desire not to appear to be promiscuous. But *none* of these reasons suggest that no does not mean no at the time at which

---

[38] Douglas Husak and George C. Thomas III, "Date Rape, Social Convention and Reasonable Mistakes," 11 *Law and Philosophy* 95 (1992), 113.

[39] Schulhofer, *Unwanted Sex*, 64. Husak and Thomas, "Date Rape, Social Convention and Reasonable Mistakes," 122. As Camille Paglia puts it, "[I]t's ridiculous to think that saying no always means no. We all know how it goes in the heat of the moment: it's 'no' now, it's 'maybe' later, and it changes again"; *Sex, Art, and American Culture* (New York: Vintage, 1992), 58.

no is uttered. It is one thing to say that a "no" at Time-*1* is consistent with intending to say "yes" at Time-*2*, and quite another to say that a "no" at Time-*1* is equivalent to a "yes" at Time-*1*. So despite the fact – and it is a fact – that some women who say no can also intend to say yes during the course of a sexual encounter, a no virtually always means no when it is uttered. Indeed, a woman could not engage in the "game" of token resistance – if that is what it is – *unless* she intended to express her lack of consent by saying no.

Does all this mean that NMN is true but pointless? Not entirely. NMN can also be understood as a normative claim that a verbal no should be sufficient to indicate the lack of consent, as rejecting the view that passive acquiescence accompanied by "mere verbal protests and refusals" constitutes an expression of consent.[40] And while I suspect that there is rarely much ambiguity as to what "no" means when it is uttered, we can understand NMN as a *normative* claim about how men should interpret "no" in the face of any ambiguity about a woman's consent.[41] True, if NMN were generally accepted, some men may mistakenly interpret a "no" as intending to bar all subsequent advances, and that would be a cost, but the whole point of a default rule is to allocate risks in the face of possible misunderstandings and asymmetrical costs of wrongful decisions. All that said, widespread acceptance of NMN will not tell us when a positive consent token should be treated as valid.

Changing minds

As I have noted, B can say no at Time-*1* while intending to say yes at Time-*2* and B can say no at Time-*1* while intending to continue to say no at Time-*2*, but subsequently change her mind. In addition, and while it happens much less frequently, B can say yes at Time-*1* and then say no at Time-*2*. What should we say then?

First consider the latter case. B can consent to sexual relations prior to intercourse and then withdraw that consent still prior to intercourse.

Size. A and B have been dating, but have not had sex. On this occasion, A proposes that they have intercourse and B accepts. They both undress. After seeing the size of A's exceptionally large penis, B gets scared and says, "I'm sorry, but I've changed my mind." A says, "You can't ask me to stop now."

---

[40] *Corpus Juris Secundum* (St. Paul, MN: West Publishing Company, 1936), 474.
[41] Stephen J. Schulhofer, "The Feminist Challenge in Criminal Law," 143 *University of Pennsylvania Law Review* 2151 (1995), 2173.

Politics. A and B go out on their first date. A proposes going back to B's apartment for sex. B accepts. After some conversation, B finds A's political views repulsive and tells him to leave. A says that she agreed to have sex and he's going to collect first.

Reneging. A proposes that A and B have sex. B says, "Let's make a date for tonight." In bed, B says, "I know I promised, but that was then and I'm too tired now." A says, "I don't care, a promise is a promise."

A can consent to sexual relations and then withdraw her consent during intercourse.

Pain. A and B commence what they think will be a normal sexual interaction. B unexpectedly finds intercourse painful on this occasion, and asks A to stop. A does not withdraw until he ejaculates.

Condom. A proposes intercourse, B accepts on condition that A use a condom. A says, "OK" and then penetrates B without a condom. B tells A to withdraw. A refuses until he ejaculates.

All of these cases involve serious wrongs, albeit for different reasons. First, as a general principle, sexual consent does not constitute a promise or prior permission that cannot be revoked. Why not? After all, one is not morally entitled to stop payment on a check that has been received in good faith. But that is because one may have received goods or services in advance or because the other party has relied to his detriment on the payment. By contrast, consent to engage in sex is ordinarily not a form of payment for goods or services nor a basis for reliance to one's detriment. Second, we have to ask just how intercourse occurs in **Size**, **Politics**, and **Reneging**. Once B says no, it seems that A must be forcing himself upon B and forcible penetration is likely to engender its own physical and psychological harms, apart from the simple fact that there is no concurrent consent.

What about those cases in which B changes her mind after intercourse has begun, such as **Pain** and **Condom?** In a nineteenth-century Vermont case, the defendant's attorney argued that his client should not be convicted of rape if his partner changed her mind during intercourse:

When a woman exposes her person, invites sexual intercourse, rouses a man's passions and allows him, in pursuance of such invitation, actually to penetrate her person, the mere fact that the animal passions which have been roused by her own act, refuse to submit to her commands – instantly to cease – has no resemblance to the high crime of rape.[42]

---

[42] Hal Goldman, "'A Most Detestable Crime': Character, Consent, and Corroboration in Vermont's Rape Law, 1850–1920" in Merril Smith (ed.), *Sex without Consent* (New York: New York University Press, 2001), 191.

The state countered that "rape implies violation of the woman's person; and it occurs at any time during the carnal intercourse when the woman withdraws her consent."[43]

Not surprisingly, most contemporary commentators would agree with the state. Lois Pineau rightly argues that agreement to intercourse does not make all subsequent sexual activity legitimate, that if a woman experiences pain or becomes overcome with guilt or fear of pregnancy or simply loses her erotic desire and communicates her wishes to A, then A should stop or withdraw.[44] Is it as wrong not to cease sexual relations as to commence sexual relations without consent? *Ceteris paribus*, probably not, because the latter case involves B's decision as to with whom and when she will have sexual relations as contrasted with the duration of sexual relations.[45] On the other hand, the failure to withdraw is serious enough and the *ceteris* are not always *paribus*. Sex is not just about sex. There is, for example, a risk of pregnancy or disease that might make non-withdrawal seriously wrong even if it is not "as" wrong on the purely sexual dimension.

Let us now consider the cases in which a no is followed by a yes. Consider Schulhofer's example of the Indiana University undergraduate who proudly announced that he had a "three-no rule" – "He thought he was being sensitive and modern because he was willing to desist after a date's third protest, but he saw nothing wrong with disregarding her "no" the first two times."[46] This student appears not to be atypical.[47] Suppose that his date says yes on the third try. Is her consent valid? It is impossible to say without knowing more. Consider this case.

Persistence. A makes advances which B rejects. A repeats his advances five times. On the sixth occasion, B says, "You don't take no for an answer, do you? If it'll make you happy, go ahead."

Unlike **Coy**, in which B ultimately appears to be happy to engage in sexual relations, A's behavior may be morally impermissible in **Persistence**. Nonetheless, and for a variety of reasons that we need not explore here, B's consent probably does meet the criteria of PVC$_L$. A's behavior probably

---

[43] *Ibid.*
[44] Lois Pineau, "Date Rape" in Leslie Francis (ed.), *Date Rape* (University Park: Penn State University Press, 1996), 14.
[45] David Archard disagrees: "It might be thought that the wrong done to a woman who consents to penetration but dissents from 'completion' is considerably less than the wrong done to a woman who does not even consent to penetration. That can be a dangerous assumption." See *Sexual Consent*, 135.
[46] Schulhofer, *Unwanted Sex*, 60.
[47] One study asked men how many times a woman had to say "no" before it was accepted as her final answer, and the average was 2.6 times; Katharine Baker, "Sex, Rape, and Shame," 79 *Boston University Law Review* 663 (1999) 667.

should not be illegal if he made no wrongful threats unless A has reason to think that B might *fear* he will use force if she does not acquiesce. If social norms are such that women rarely offer token resistance or change their minds unless they are frightened, then we would judge A's behavior more harshly. Still, consenting to sex is not akin to confessing to a crime. We have reason to be very skeptical about the legitimacy of police techniques when a suspect first refuses to talk or denies his guilt and then confesses after several hours of interrogation. There is less reason to be skeptical when a woman first says no to sex, but changes to a yes after several hours with her date. In any case, the question whether B's consent token is valid arises whether B's consent token is the first and only expression of B's preferences or follows a prior token of nonconsent. It is to the question of validity that I now turn.

CHAPTER EIGHT

Coercion

The task of the principles of valid consent (PVC) is to provide the criteria by which to determine when B's token of consent to sexual relations is valid or morally transformative. We might put the issue in negative terms, in which case the question is whether B's consent is *invalid* in one respect or another. In this and the following three chapters, I want to consider three sorts of potential defects in consent – coercion, information (or deception), and competence, devoting one chapter to issues of intoxication.

To speak of a "defect" in B's consent is to assume that B does manifest a relatively unambiguous token of consent to sexual relations with A. And so I shall assume. I therefore set aside those cases in which B does not token consent at all, as in cases of pure force and unconsciousness. In a case of pure force, A penetrates B without any willed acquiescence or cooperation on B's part.

Pure Force. A and his accomplices tie B's arms and legs to a bed. A penetrates B while B screams, "No, please stop."

I suspect that rape by *pure* force is relatively rare. The use of force is typically accompanied by coercive threats of *additional* force if B does not acquiesce.

Force. A overpowers B physically, holds her down despite B's attempts to resist and threatens her with additional force if she continues to resist.

Here it is B's response to the threat of additional force – made particularly credible by *A*'s prior use of force – that allows A to penetrate B. As with **Pure Force**, although unlike some cases of **Force**, there is nothing approaching a token of consent when B is unconscious.

Rohypnol. A slips some Rohypnol, the date-rape drug, into B's drink. B passes out.
Anesthesia. A, a dentist, penetrates B while she is unconscious from anesthesia.

Nor is there a token of consent to sexual relations where B consents to a form of penetration but does not consent to sexual relations.

Gynecologist. A tells B that he will be inserting an instrument into her vagina. Instead, he inserts his penis.

Some would refer to **Gynecologist** as a case of fraud in the *factum* (as contrasted with fraud in the *inducement*) because B consents to allow something to be inserted, just not A's penis. That misdescribes the case, because there is clearly no consent to sexual relations. I also set aside cases of *psychological paralysis*, where A's behavior causes B's decision-making capacity effectively to shut down, where B is incapable of saying or indicating *anything*. I suspect that such cases occur with some frequency, but one would have to have a very expansive view of tacit consent to regard B's behavior as tokening consent. In other cases, however, B may manifest some token of consent, albeit without much in the way of deliberate decision-making. Something close to paralysis can occur when A's behavior surprises or confuses B, as when A abuses a position of professional authority, and B loses her capacity to think clearly about alternative courses of action.

Coercion

In this chapter, I focus on the "voluntariness" of B's consent token. We generally think that PVC$_L$ and PVC$_M$ would regard coerced consent token as invalid, although there may be cases that count as coercion for moral purposes but not for legal purposes. The question is when we should reach that conclusion. Consider a small sample of cases, some of which we have already seen.

Weapon. A, a stranger, says "Do not resist me or I will kill you with this gun."
Abandonment. A and B drive to a secluded spot in A's car. B resists A's advances. A says, "Have sexual relations with me or I will leave you here."
Dating. A and B have been dating for some time, but have not had sexual relations. A says, "I'm not willing to continue dating you if we don't have sex, so either we have sex or I'm terminating the relationship."
Indecent Proposal. A, who is very rich, says to B "I'll give you $1,000,000 if you spend the night with me."[1]
Lecherous Millionaire. B's child will die unless she receives expensive surgery for which the state will not pay. A, a millionaire, proposes to pay for the surgery if B will agree to become his mistress.
Lower Grade. A, a professor, says "Have sexual relations with me or I will give you a grade two grades lower than you deserve."

I do not claim that all these cases represent "genuine" cases of coercion of the sort that would violate PVC. I place them together because they all

---

[1] As portrayed in the movie of this name.

have a similar structure, namely, that B must choose between (1) having sexual relations with A and (2) not having sexual relations with A, so not avoiding some consequence that she would (otherwise) prefer to avoid and (3) not having sexual relations with A, so not receiving a good that she would like to have. A crucial task of PVC is to indicate when the structure of B's choices is such as to negate the transformative power of B's consent.

In what follows, I shall generally assume that B makes a *rational* choice to token consent within the situation in which she finds herself. There are cases of coercion in which A's threat so disturbs B's cognitive processes that she tokens consent even though doing so does not serve her long-term preferences, even given the probable consequences of refusal. But that need not be so. Consider

Charade. A approaches B on the street, puts a gun to her back, and says, "We're walking up to my apartment." When they arrive, he says, "You and I are going to play a game. You are going to beg me to - - - - you. Do a good job, and I won't hurt you. Resist, and I'll kill you." B takes off her clothes and says, "I want you."

A might go on to say "I don't want you to make a rash decision. Take your time, consult (by phone) with your friends, and then let me know what you decide." Although B might decide – quite rationally – to play along, her decision is still obviously coerced. Or consider

Texas. A, a complete stranger, enters B's apartment and waits for B to come home. When B arrives, A threatens to stab B unless B succumbs to sexual relations. B pleads with A to wear a condom, falsely telling A that she has AIDS.[2]

That B has the wits to get A to wear a condom in **Texas** does not show that she was not coerced, any more than a prisoner's choice to be executed is voluntary just because he is offered a choice between electrocution and lethal injection.

I begin with a standard case in which A makes an allegedly coercive proposal to B. I will argue that A coerces B into sexual relations when (i) A proposes to make B worse off relative to the appropriate baseline if she does not acquiesce *and* (iia) it is reasonable for B to succumb to A's proposal rather than suffer the consequences *or* (iib) it is not reasonable for B to succumb, but seriously wrong for A to proceed in the face of B's unreasonable behavior. The point of criterion (i) is to establish whether A's proposal is coercive. If it is not coercive, then PVC will generally regard B's token of consent as valid even if (as in iia) it is reasonable for B to succumb to A's proposal rather than suffer the consequences. But PVC will not regard all consent tokens given in response to coercive proposals as invalid or without the morally transformative power to immunize A from moral or legal liability. The second criterion (iia) or (iib) establishes whether A's coercive proposal actually compels B to consent in a way that negates the moral power of that consent. Although the form of the question "Is B coerced into tokening consent to sexual relations?" is that of an empirical question, I shall argue that the two criteria are fundamentally moralized.

Coercive proposals

There are two reasons why it can be ambiguous whether condition (i) is met. First, it can be ambiguous whether A proposes to impose any consequence if B does not comply. We do not ordinarily say that a panhandler threatens B if he says "Do you have any money to spare?" But consider

Polite Thugs. A group of four large men approach and surround B. The leader says, "Please give us your wallet."

The polite thugs threaten B (just like their less polite twin brothers who say "Give us your wallet or we'll smash your face") because their behavior implies that they will make B worse off if she refuses and it is reasonable to expect them to understand this. What about **Threat?**

Threat? A and B meet in a bar and go back to A's apartment. B rebuffs A's advances. A smiles at B and says, "Look, you're alone with someone you don't know, who's much bigger and stronger, and, for all you know, has beaten and raped several women. Maybe I'm not as nice as I seem." B is very frightened by A's remarks and does not resist A's advances.

Everything here depends upon what it is reasonable for B to believe A intends, or, perhaps more accurately, what A can reasonably be expected to think B believes A intends or *might* intend. I say "might" because A makes a coercive proposal when the consequences of refusal are probabilistic. Consider

Revolver. A places one bullet in a chamber of a revolver. He says, "If you refuse to have sex, I'm going to spin the chamber, point the gun at your head, and shoot. You've got a 5/6 chance that the chamber will be empty. It's your call."

If A makes a coercive proposal to B in **Revolver**, as seems evident, then A's statement in **Threat?** can be understood as creating a sufficient fear of harm. And A should know that.

Assume that there is no misunderstanding about the likely consequences of refusal. How should we define the baseline relative to which B may be worse off if she rejects A's proposal? Reduced to essentials, there are four main possibilities: (1) A may propose to make B worse off than B's status quo or pre-proposal baseline; (2) A may propose to make B worse off than what B can "statistically" expect in the normal course of events (which may be better or worse than her status quo if her "expectations" baseline is higher or lower than her present position); (3) A may propose to make B worse off relative to what B subjectively experiences as her baseline; (4) A may propose to make B worse off relative to where B has a right to be vis-à-vis A, what I call B's *moralized* baseline.

These baselines will often converge. If A says "sign this contract or I will shoot you," A proposes to make B worse off by reference to all four baselines. If B rejects A's proposal, B will be worse off than she was prior to encountering A, or than she could expect in the normal course of events, absent A's proposal. The proposal certainly feels like a threat. And A certainly proposes to make B worse off than she has a right to be. So, too, with all of the examples of violent sexual coercion, as in **Force** and **Charade**. Unfortunately, it is precisely this convergence among the various baselines that makes it easy to misidentify the baseline by which PVC should evaluate A's proposal as coercive when they do not converge.

I have argued elsewhere that the single most important factor in determining when proposals nullify the transformative power of consent on grounds of coercion is whether A proposes to make B worse off than her *moralized* baseline, whether A's "declared unilateral plan" – what A proposes to do if B does not accept A's proposal – would violate B's rights or, where "rights" discourse is inapposite, whether A proposes not to do for B what A has an obligation to do for B.[3] Consider two cases in which B's status-quo baseline differs from her moralized baseline. In some cases, A may have an obligation to render B *better off* than her status quo, in which case A's declared unilateral plan – to do nothing – may well be coercive.

Opportunistic Lifeguard. A is a professional lifeguard at B's country club. He sees that B, whom he knows to be very wealthy, is in trouble. He proposes to help B only if B agrees to pay him $10,000. B accepts, and, after being saved, refuses to pay on grounds that she consented under duress.

In this case, A has an obligation to attempt to rescue B. That is his job. Even though he proposes to make B *better off* than her status-quo baseline (drowning), A proposes to make B worse off than her moralized baseline,

---

[3] I borrow this phrase from Vinit Haksar, "Coercive Proposals," 4 *Political Theory* 65 (1976).

where he would attempt to rescue her. So A's proposal is coercive and B's promise to pay $10,000 is not morally transformative. It is not binding on B.

In other cases, it may be permissible for A to propose to render B worse off than her status-quo or phenomenological baseline.

Plea Bargaining. A, a prosecutor, says, "Plead guilty to a lesser offense and take a one-year sentence or I will prosecute you on a more serious charge, for which you will receive five years if you are convicted." B accepts, then claims she was coerced into the agreement.

On my approach, A's proposal is *not* coercive because he has not proposed to make B worse off than she has a right to be, assuming, arguendo, that the prosecutor is acting reasonably in proposing to put B on trial for the more serious charge. Relative to her status-quo and phenomenological baselines, A may be making a threat, but relative to her moralized baseline, he is making what might be a very attractive and generous offer.[4]

Consider a case in which the moralized baseline and statistical baselines diverge.

BIC. BIC had a contract with Sony under which BIC would be paid a commission for securing customers to use Sony products as business incentives. Sony told BIC that it would terminate the relationship if BIC did not agree to new terms. BIC agreed to new terms and then claimed that it had done so under duress.[5]

Although Sony proposed to make BIC worse off than its statistical baseline (and its status-quo baseline), for BIC had reason to think the contract would continue, there was no legal duress because Sony had a right to terminate the relationship. Relative to BIC's moralized or rights-defined baseline, Sony was actually making an *offer* to continue the relationship, albeit on terms that were less attractive to BIC than it expected. And offers do not typically coerce.

It might be thought that all this discussion of "baselines" and "proposals" is unnecessarily complicated, that the issue is really much simpler: threats are coercive whereas offers are not. A coerces B into mowing his lawn if A threatens to break B's arm if she does not, but A does not coerce B into mowing his lawn if A offers to pay B $50 for doing so. Put in slightly different terms, A's credible threat (to break B's arm) reduces B's range of

---

[4] Does it matter whether B is factually guilty? I think not. If A is acting reasonably in prosecuting B, then A is not proposing to violate B's rights if she does not accept the proposal. I thank Arthur Applbaum for raising this question.

[5] *Business Incentives Co., Inc. v. Sony Corp.*, 387 F. Supp. 63 (1975). See the discussion in my *Coercion* (Princeton: Princeton University Press, 1987), 41.

choice whereas A's offer expands B's range of choice.[6] Properly understood, I think this is right. Unfortunately, this move begs the question of how to distinguish between threats and offers, and that puts us back into the sort of baseline analysis I have offered. There is, after all, a sense in which threats and offers are generally "intertranslatable" – virtually any threat can be recast as an offer, and vice versa. The need for a way to set B's baseline is concealed when the baseline is obvious as in the lawn-mowing and gunman cases, but becomes apparent when the baseline is more controversial. One cannot distinguish between threats and offers without reference to a baseline and, for present purposes, it is B's moralized baseline that does the work. The opportunistic lifeguard's "offer" to rescue B in exchange for a fee is coercive because he effectively threatens not to rescue B by reference to B's moralized baseline (assuming he has an obligation to try to rescue her). The prosecutor's "threat" of a more severe punishment if B refuses to plead guilty is not coercive, because he effectively offers a more lenient punishment if she does plead guilty by reference to B's moralized baseline.

To say that we should evaluate the coerciveness of A's proposal by reference to B's moralized baseline is completely *neutral* with respect to the specification of that baseline.

Opportunistic Samaritan. A, a stranger, is walking by B's country club and hears B shout for help. A proposes to rescue B only if B agrees to pay A $10,000. B accepts and then refuses to pay on grounds of duress.

In **Opportunistic Lifeguard**, it is clear that A has an obligation to rescue B. In **Opportunistic Samaritan**, it is not. If A's declared unilateral plan (not to rescue B for free) would violate B's rights or fail to fulfill his obligations to B, then A's proposal is coercive. If not, probably not. Whether A has a duty of mutual aid is a question for moral theory. Still, the moralized-baseline approach is not empty because it tells us to ignore the fact that A's declared unilateral plan would not make B worse off than her status quo. That is not the issue.

The term "moralized" should not be misunderstood. Heidi Malm worries that to define coercion in a way that makes it impossible to give valid consent to immoral offers "is to adopt an incredibly paternalistic attitude towards persons."[7] But A's proposal does not violate B's moralized baseline simply because A's proposal is somehow wrong or morally unworthy. On my view,

---

[6] This is true even if A makes an unattractive offer, as when A offers B $1 for mowing his lawn. Although B will likely reject A's proposal, it is hardly coercive.

[7] Heidi Malm, "The Ontology of Consent and Some Implications for the Law of Rape," 2 *Legal Theory* 147 (1996), 153.

A's proposal is coercive only if it is immoral *in a special way*, namely, that A proposes to violate B's rights (or fails to fulfill an obligation to B) should B reject A's proposal.

Greedy Mechanic. A, a mechanic, is driving along the highway returning home from work. A sees that B's car has broken down. A stops, and ascertains that he could fix the problem in two minutes. He offers to fix the problem for $100. B accepts, but has little cash. B promises to send A a check for $100.

A's proposal is ungenerous, hardhearted, and exploitative. But A does not propose to violate B's rights should B not accept and it is at least plausible to argue that A is making an offer and that B's consent meets the criteria for PVC_L, although it is less clear whether it meets the criteria for PVC_M. We might say that the law should hold that B has an obligation to pay, but that B is not (otherwise) morally required to pay.

As the previous point suggests, rights are not all of a piece. A may propose to violate B's moral rights without proposing to violate B's morally justified legal rights – so we have the distinction between proposals that are "morally coercive" and those that are "legally coercive." Even so, there will be proposals that are arguably wrong but that do not propose to violate B's moral rights. Recall **Dating**. Depending on details that will vary from case to case, A's proposal may be wrong, crude, insensitive. But I do not think it is necessarily morally coercive, for B has no moral right that A continue dating B on terms that B prefers as opposed to those that A prefers. On my view, A's proposal is not morally coercive because it can be understood as an offer ("Have sex with me and I'll continue the relationship") relative to B's rights.

The cases illustrate another point. Many interactions involve bargaining, negotiation, compromise, and what may reasonably be referred to as threats. Our legal and moral principles need to provide some – but not too much – flexibility in these matters. We will not achieve mutually beneficial results if people are deterred from making proposals that may involve some worsening of the other's situation, and it is the point of PVC_L and PVC_M to specify what sorts of proposals we can and cannot make. For the purposes of the criminal law, we may say that A proposes to violate B's moral baseline if A proposes that unless B acquiesces, A will leave B in a "worsened position *as measured by the worst position in which the criminal offense at issue allows a person to leave another as a result of the latter's refusal to acquiesce to x.*"[8] And there may be good reason – good moral reason – for

---

[8] Peter Westen, "The Logic of Consent: The Diversity and Deceptiveness of Consent as a Defense to Criminal Conduct," unpublished manuscript.

the criminal law to allow A to propose to leave B in a worse position than non-legal morality would permit.

I have argued that B's moral baseline is defined by B's rights or what A has an obligation to do for B. There are, of course, many routes to a rights-based moral or legal framework. One can defend a framework of rights or obligations on Kantian or deontological grounds. One might get there via a contractualist or constructivist route in which rights are an outcome of a decision process, such as Rawls's original position or Scanlon's contractualism. Following Mill, one might argue that the recognition of rights is the best way to promote good consequences. I have my sympathies, but I take no position here. The main point is that the moralized-baseline approach requires some reference to a framework of rights, however those rights are ultimately grounded.

Coercive offers?

I have suggested that proposals are properly understood as coercive only when they can be cast as threats by reference to B's moralized baseline. This view is frequently rejected. Some argue that an employer can make a "coercive wage offer" to a starving B who has no reasonable alternative but to accept.[9] Bonnie Steinbock argues that women are coerced when they are offered probation from a prison sentence only if they agree to have a long-term contraceptive implanted.[10] Schulhofer thinks that women must be protected against "powerfully attractive" offers as well as threats.[11] John Bogart suggests that one acts nonvoluntarily when "there are overpowering factors favoring one course over others."[12] Recalling a phrase from *The Godfather*, it is often said that A coerces B when A makes an offer that is "too good to refuse," perhaps forgetting that Don Corleone "offered" (?) the target a choice between (1) signing a contract and (2) having his brains on the contract.

Pseudo-offers aside, B may find A's offer too good to refuse for different reasons, and it is important to distinguish between them. First, A's proposal may give B an option that is so clearly superior to her present options that it would be irrational for B to reject it, as when A offers B a new job that

[9] See David Zimmerman, "Coercive Wage Offers," 10 *Philosophy & Public Affairs* 121 (1981).
[10] Bonnie Steinbock, "The Concept of Coercion and Long-Term Contraceptives" in Ellen Moskowitz and Bruce Jennings (eds.), *Coerced Contraception?* (Washington, DC: Georgetown University Press, 1996).
[11] Stephen J. Schulhofer, *Unwanted Sex* (Cambridge, MA: Harvard University Press, 1998), 136.
[12] John H. Bogart, "Reconsidering Rape: Rethinking the Conceptual Foundations of Rape Law," 8 *Canadian Journal of Law and Jurisprudence* 159 (1995), 162.

would render her much better off than her eminently acceptable status quo. There is nothing problematic about such offers despite the "overpowering factors" favoring B's decision.

Other cases are more difficult. B may find A's offer too good to refuse because the short-term benefits contained in A's proposal may be so tempting or irresistible that they distort B's judgment and motivate B to accept an offer that she is (*ex ante*) likely to regret, as when A offers B a new credit card at a low introductory rate (which will then be raised). Call this a *seductive offer*. A seductive offer gets B to make a choice, *ex ante*, that does not advance her long-term interests, all things considered, whereas an attractive offer does advance B's long-term interests, all things considered. It is not clear, for example, whether **Indecent Proposal** constitutes an attractive offer or a seductive offer. That depends upon a complicated calculation of its long-term consequences. Suppose that it is a seductive offer. PVC may hold that A's "seductive offer" compromises the validity of B's consent in a way analogous to defects in competence and information, particularly when A is intentionally or negligently taking advantage of the likelihood that B will miscalculate its long-term effects. Even so, seductive offers are not helpfully described as coercive, because A does not threaten any adverse consequence if B declines the offer.

Coercive circumstances?

Still, it might be said that I am missing something important. Suppose that A's declared unilateral plan does not violate B's rights and that B's choice is eminently reasonable, given (or precisely because of) the circumstances in which B finds herself. Recall **Lecherous Millionaire**. Although A does not propose to violate B's rights if she rejects his proposal, it may be claimed that A's offer is coercive because B has no reasonable alternative to accepting A's proposal.

I do not deny that there is a *sense* in which one is "forced" to do that which there is no reasonable alternative to doing and that this feeling is particularly intense when the less attractive alternative is highly unsatisfactory. Recall

Gangrene. A patient's leg is gangrenous and she must choose between amputation and death. She understands the alternatives, and because she does not want to die, she signs the consent form.

This is an important case. Although B may reasonably believe that she has "no choice" but to opt for amputation, we do *not* say that B's consent to amputation is not morally transformative because it is coerced by her circumstances. We would hardly charge A with battery on the grounds that he operated without B's valid consent (assuming that B is suitably informed).

Or consider voluntary euthanasia. It is often argued that the right to end one's life in the face of painful disease or disability can be a crucial element of individual autonomy and human dignity.[13] Yet the very circumstances that may make it reasonable for people to choose voluntary euthanasia can also be seen as highly coercive.[14] I am not arguing for voluntary euthanasia. The present point is that *if* PVC could support a practice under which people can authorize voluntary euthanasia, then one must be committed to the position that very stressful circumstances – including the fear of painful death – do not necessarily rob consent of its morally transformative power.

It might be argued that whereas consent to surgery that is motivated by the fear of death can be valid, consent to sex that is motivated by the fear of death must be invalid. I think not. Consider

Cure. A, a hospital employee, calls B and tells her that her blood tests indicate that she has a serious disease, and that it can be cured by expensive and painful surgery or by intercourse with an anonymous donor (who turns out to be A) who has been injected with a serum. A and B meet in a hotel and have intercourse.[15]

The non-fiction case on which **Cure** is based revolved around the issue of fraud. B actually believed A's claim. But suppose that A's claim is truthful, that A's semen has curative powers, but that it cannot be provided by artificial insemination.[16] If B were to engage in sexual relations with A in order to have access to his semen, we would not think that A had committed a sexual offense.

I have argued that neither PVC_L nor PVC_M regard hard choices as inconsistent with valid consent. David Hume thought that the sorts of cases just discussed demonstrate that the morality of practices such as promising and consenting (as generating permissibility) were "mere artificial contrivances

[13] See "Assisted Suicide: The Philosopher's Brief," *The New York Review of Books*, March 27, 1997. This brief was signed by John Rawls, Judith Jarvis Thomson, Robert Nozick, Ronald Dworkin, T. M. Scanlon, and Thomas Nagel.
[14] Alan Soble, *Sexual Investigations* (New York: New York University Press, 1996), 35.
[15] See *Boro v. Superior Court*, 163 Cal. App. 1224; 210 Cal Rptr. 122 (1985).
[16] Or, now that we are on this hypothetical track, let us assume that the semen must be imparted through intercourse if it is to have its curative power.

for the convenience and advantage of society." As Hume observes, we distinguish between promises motivated by fear of death.

A man, dangerously wounded, who promises a competent sum to a surgeon to cure him, would certainly be bound to performance, though the case be not so much different from that of one who promises a sum to a robber, as to produce so great a difference in our sentiments of morality if these sentiments were not built entirely on public interest and convenience.[17]

We need not accept Hume's quasi-utilitarian framework to agree that there is a distinction between the cases. The crucial point is that the doctor does not propose to violate the patient's rights if the patient rejects his proposal whereas the robber does propose to violate B's rights if she rejects his proposal.

Consider Scanlon's contractarianism. Scanlon argues that the principles of morality – which would include what I have called PVC – are understood as those principles that no one could reasonably reject.[18] Scanlon supports the standard view that consent is morally transformative only if it is "voluntary," but then goes on to argue that voluntariness does not refer to psychological pressure or the difficulty of one's choices. Rather, it is what I have called an "output" of moral reasoning.

if we ask what "voluntariness" amounts to here, it turns out that a choice is voluntary in the relevant sense just in case the circumstances under which it was made are ones such that no one could reasonably reject a principle that took choices made under those conditions to create binding or enforceable obligations.[19]

If we were to apply this framework to Hume's examples, no one could reasonably reject a principle that requires one to honor one's agreement to pay a "competent sum" to a surgeon, even though one agreed to do so only because one feared death. By contrast, we could reasonably reject a principle that requires us to honor our agreement to a robber, in part because accepting such a principle would give potential robbers a greater incentive to rob, even though B might be better off – in her particular case – if her promise were to be regarded as binding.[20]

---

[17] David Hume, *A Treatise of Human Nature*, book III, part II, section V. Joel Feinberg makes a similar point when he says that the voluntariness "required for a valid (legally effective) act of consent is at least partly a matter of policy, to be decided by references to a rule itself justified by the usual legislative reasons of utility and social justice"; *Harm to Self* (New York: Oxford University Press, 1998), 261.

[18] T. M. Scanlon, *What We Owe to Each Other* (Cambridge, MA: Harvard University Press, 1998).

[19] T. M. Scanlon, "Promises and Contracts" in Peter Benson (ed.), *The Theory of Contract Law* (New York: Cambridge University Press, 2001), 114.

[20] *Ibid.*, 115.

It might be objected that this approach fails to distinguish between two claims: (1) B's consent *is* valid, and (2) B's consent should be treated *as if* it were valid. This objection maintains that (1) refers to factors that are 'internal' to B's decision, for example, her level of stress or cognitive capacities or information, whereas (2) adopts an 'external' or policy perspective and asks whether it is permissible for A to engage in some action that would be impermissible but for B's consent token. So we might say that internally flawed or deficient consent is generally *in*valid, but it may (sometimes) make sense to treat it as if it were valid.

I do not think much is at stake here. On my view, there is no direct correspondence between "internal" factors and the validity of consent. When I say that B's consent 'is valid' I mean that it is morally transformative, that it renders A's action permissible. I do not deny that valid consent may be internally deficient in one way or another. If one wants to say that internally deficient consent is actually invalid but that we should distinguish the (actual) validity of B's consent from the conditions under which it is morally transformative, then I would say that I am interested in the latter and not the former.

I return now to coercion. On the moralized-baseline view, A does not coerce B in **Lecherous Millionaire**. However unseemly, A's proposal adds to the range of options available to B when measured against her moralized baseline. I do not see how A's proposal can invalidate *all* the transformative powers of B's consent. I say "all" because we can distinguish two ways in which B's consent might be morally transformative: (1) it might immunize A from liability for a sexual offense if B performs; (2) it might give A a moral or legal *right* to specific performance of sexual services from B if B declines to perform. We might endorse (1) without endorsing (2). For reasons that I shall not pursue here, it is frequently permissible for A and B to enter into a contractual arrangement where A agrees to pay B for services, but where the law does not require specific performance by B, although B may be required to compensate A if B fails to perform.

David Archard disagrees. He contrasts a case (a) in which A places B in difficulty and then exploits B's situation with case (b) in which C places B in difficulty and A subsequently exploits B's situation. He argues that if B's consent is invalid in (a) then it should also be invalid in (b) because the pressure on B is arguably identical in both cases.[21] Consider these two cases.

[21] David Archard, *Sexual Consent* (Boulder: Westview, 1998), 57.

Rescue. A, a mechanic, roams the highway offering to help people in distress for money, but when he finds that the rescuee is an attractive woman, he demands "service" for "service." B is stranded and A makes his usual offer, saying, "If you don't want my help, that's fine, I'll be on my way."

Sabotage. A drains most of the fuel out of B's car then follows her. When her car stops on the highway, he offers to help her out if she has sexual relations with him.

Archard is right to think that if "circumstantial coercion" invalidates consent, then there is no distinction between **Rescue** and **Sabotage**. But while it is not clear what PVC would say here, it might well distinguish between them. After all, B is arguably better off because A exists in **Rescue**, whereas she is worse off because A exists in **Sabotage**. Even from within a contractarian perspective, it might be unreasonable for B to reject a principle that would immunize A from rape charges in **Rescue**.

The case for the moralized-baseline view is perhaps best illustrated by cases in which A himself creates B's circumstances.

Testimony. B is on trial for a crime and prefers not to testify in her own defense because she does not want to choose between implicating a friend and committing perjury (for which she may incur additional punishment). When the prosecution has finished its case, B's lawyer says: "Their case is pretty strong and your only hope for an acquittal is to testify." B testifies.

B can hardly say that she has been "compelled" to testify in violation of her Fifth Amendment right, even though the prosecutor's actions motivated her choice. The claim that such testimony is not coerced is difficult to explain on the "unacceptable alternative" view of coercion but is easy to explain on the moralized baseline view. For the prosecutor does not propose to violate B's rights if B fails to testify in her own defense.

Interestingly, it is now settled American (not British) law that a prosecutor *cannot* remind the jury that a defendant did not testify or say that they may draw inferences about her guilt from her refusal to do so. Call this *reminding behavior*. Reminding behavior is regarded as compromising a defendant's constitutional right not to be compelled to testify. So we have a legal situation in which a defendant is not compelled to testify when motivated by the strength of the prosecutor's case, but is compelled to testify if motivated by the prosecutor's threat to engage in reminding behavior; this is so even if she would have a *better* chance of acquittal without testifying if A engages in reminding behavior than in the case where A simply puts on a very strong case. Why? Because defendants have a right not to be exposed to reminding behavior for refusing to testify, but have no right not to be exposed to the risk of conviction consequent to the prosecutor's presentation of the evidence.

The previous lines of analysis might be subject to another objection. For suppose that B has a *right* to a better range of opportunities. Whereas a defendant does not have a right not to be exposed to a legitimate prosecution, the lecherous millionaire's proposal should arguably fall on deaf ears because a just society would provide B's child with the needed medical care. If B has a right to be provided with such medical care, does it not follow that A's proposal to leave B below her moralized – rights-defined – baseline is coercive? It does not. Rights are specific to relationships. Whereas B may have a right that *society* provide her child with medical care, she has no right that *A* do so. To put the point differently, we can ask what B would like A to do, given that society does not provide for her child. If B would prefer that people like A be forthcoming with proposals, then she has reason to endorse principles that would immunize A from criminal charges.

There is an important point about consensual transactions at stake here. In developing the best versions of PVC_L and PVC_M, we must consider what principles should be applied to the *non-ideal* circumstances in which people find themselves. It is entirely possible that the principles will hold that from A's (and B's) perspective, B's circumstances – even if unjust – may properly define the background against which their transactions occur, and from which we must evaluate their moral status.

From coercive proposals to coercion

Assume that A's proposal is coercive because A proposes to violate B's rights if B refuses to acquiesce. B is not coerced just because she chooses to acquiesce in the face of A's proposal. I believe that PVC will maintain that A's coercive proposal actually coerces B to do X only when (iia) it is reasonable for B to succumb to A's coercive proposal rather than suffer the consequences or (iib) although it is not independently reasonable for B to succumb to A's coercive proposal, it is seriously wrong for A to proceed in the face of B's unreasonable succumbing behavior (see pp. 165–66). The move from coercive proposals to coercion is not a straight line. Consider

Modification. A proposes not to fulfill his contract with B unless B agrees to a higher price. B agrees to the higher price.

The law may well treat B's agreement as valid. Why? Because it will often make sense for parties to renegotiate the terms of a contract and because the law provides B with another alternative – to allow A to breach the contract and sue. The law says, in effect, "we provided you with a means of redress, and if you don't take it, then you're on your own." If A proposes to break B's arm unless B signs a contract with A, however, the law will typically treat the contract as voidable on grounds of duress, because we think it reasonable for B to succumb now and try to recover later rather than endure a broken arm and then sue for damages.

Sexual coercion

With this as background, consider some cases which might be thought to involve sexual coercion. Recall **Abandonment** and **Lower Grade**, to which I will now add

Debt. A, who owes B $500, says "Have sexual relations with me and I will repay my debt. Otherwise, ciao."

On the moralized-baseline view, it seems that A makes a coercive proposal because A proposes to violate B's right (assuming she has such a right) not to be abandoned or to receive the proper grade or to be paid. By contrast, recall **Dating** to which I will now add two cases.

Higher Grade. A, a professor, says "Have sexual relations with me and I will give you a grade two grades higher than you deserve. Otherwise you'll get just what you deserve."
Escape. B is in prison for life. A, a prison guard, offers to help her escape if she has sexual relations with him.

In these cases, A's declared unilateral plan does not violate B's rights because B has no right that A continue their dating relationship nor a right to a higher grade than she deserves nor a right not to be executed by the state (bracketing general objections to capital punishment).

Although it is not an infallible guide, PVC will typically treat B's consent as valid if we can imagine that B is happy to receive A's proposal or might make the proposal herself *in a context in which A would not be violating B's rights if he rejected B's proposal.* We cannot imagine that B is happy to receive A's proposal in the first three cases or that B might initiate the proposal in **Abandonment**, **Lower Grade**, and **Debt**, but we can well imagine that B welcomes A's proposal in **Higher Grade** or **Escape**, or that B might initiate the proposal herself.[22]

---

[22] I do not claim that any B would be delighted to receive A's proposal in **Higher Grade**. I claim only that we can imagine that she might be or that she *might* initiate such a proposal herself.

Dating appears to be a counter-example because B is not happy to receive the proposal. But things are actually more complicated. Suppose that B senses A's frustration and believes A might end the relationship if things do not change. Under these conditions, B might welcome A's proposal, as contrasted with a scenario in which he simply walks away. Indeed, B herself might make the proposal to initiate sexual relations and it would be strange to maintain that B is coerced by a proposal that she initiates.

Strange, but not impossible. Here I return to the highlighted words above. We *can* imagine that B might initiate the sexual relationship in **Debt** ("I'll have sex with you if you repay your debt"), but there may be coercion nonetheless. Or consider

Kidnap. A seizes B's child. B tells A that she will have sexual relations with him if he returns her child.

It is arguable that B has been coerced into sexual relations even though B initiates the sexual proposal. Why? Because A would be violating B's rights if he rejected B's proposal (and if he accepts!).

My analysis of **Higher Grade** and **Escape** should not be misunderstood. It is clearly *wrong* for A to make his proposal in **Higher Grade** and **Escape**, even though A does not propose to violate B's rights if B rejects the proposal. A jailer violates his obligation to society if he helps a prisoner to escape and commits an additional wrong if he trades that favor for sexual services. A professor violates his responsibility to his institution and to other students if he trades grades for sex. In addition, A's proposal may insult B by suggesting that she does or might think about her sexuality in ways she may abhor.[23] But insults do not coerce. And if A's proposal should be taken at face value in **Higher Grade** and **Escape**, we should not refuse to treat B's consent as transformative on grounds of coercion.

The first clause of the previous sentence is important. B might reasonably treat A's proposal in **Higher Grade** and **Escape** as a "throffer" (a threat *and* an offer), as proposing to make B better off than she deserves if she accepts A's proposal, but worse off than she deserves (even prisoners on death row may be treated badly) if she rejects A's proposal. Indeed, B might reasonably treat A's proposal as a "throffer" even if A intends it as a genuine offer. How is B to know? In either case, if B reasonably regards A's proposal as containing a threat, we might well regard the sexual relations as coerced, but it is the "threat" component of the throffer that generates this result,

---

[23] By contrast, while B may subsequently regret acquiescing in **Dating**, B cannot complain that A has introduced a sexual component into a relationship from which it should be absent.

not the offer. Some think otherwise. Schulhofer says that to distinguish between **Higher Grade** and **Lower Grade** by reference to the student's academic standing "seems very much beside the point."[24] I disagree (as do most of my students on a survey); for one reason for thinking A's proposal in **Lower Grade** is wrong simply does not apply to **Higher Grade**, namely, that A is not proposing to violate B's rights should she reject his proposal.

It is no part of this analysis to minimize the psychological pressure on B in the offer cases. B may regard the consequences of refusing A's proposal in **Dating** as devastating, as worse than the consequences of refusing A's proposal in **Lower Grade**. The point remains, however, that B has no *right* that A continue his relationship with B on her preferred terms, whereas she does have a right to the grade she deserves. Moreover, B would not *want* her consent in **Dating** to be regarded as invalid. For if A knew that B could charge him with a sexual offense if she agreed to sex, then he might simply stop dating B altogether – the consequence that B most wants to avoid. For the same reason, B might not want A to regard having sex under these conditions as morally impermissible.

Can A coerce B by proposing to harm C or A himself? I believe so. Consider these cases.

Child Killer. A tells B, "I'm going to kill your child unless you have sex with me."
Suicide. A is infatuated with B, but B has rebuffed him. A tells B that he will commit suicide unless B has sexual relations with him.

If we allow for the possibility of vicarious harm in **Child Killer**, as I think we must, then we might also allow for the special form of vicarious harm presented by **Suicide**. Indeed, A's proposal might be coercive in **Suicide**, even if there is a reasonable chance that A will not carry it out, just as A's proposal is coercive in **Revolver**, where there is only a one-in-six chance that B will be shot.

There is a range of cases that seem to lie on the border between sexual harassment and coercive sexual relations. Consider:

Detention Home. A, who has agreed to take B (nineteen years old) into his home, threatens to return her to the detention home unless she has sexual relations with him.
Hiring. A is the sole owner and proprietor of a restaurant, where the tips are very good. B applies for a job as a waitress. A says that he will hire her only if she has sex with him.
Promotion. A, a supervisor at a large corporation, tells B that he will engineer an undeserved promotion for which B has applied if she has sexual relations with him.

[24] Schulhofer, *Unwanted Sex*, 136.

These are difficult cases because it is arguable that A does not propose to violate B's rights if she refuses to have sex with him. I assume (in **Detention Home**) that A is under no obligation to keep B in his home. I assume (in **Hiring**) that A is under no obligation to hire B even if she is the most qualified, that A could hire his daughter if he preferred. A might say, "I'm not proposing to harm B. Having sex with me is just a condition of employment, as is wearing the designated uniform. If she doesn't like the terms, that's fine with me. I'll find others who do." With respect to **Promotion**, it is arguable that A is under an obligation *not* to promote B. These cases suggest that we cannot simply say that such quid-pro-quo harassment "coerces with incentive," for there is a genuine question whether it is coercive at all.[25]

Although others may not share my intuition, I believe that **Detention Home**, **Hiring**, and **Promotion** are in some ways worse than **Lecherous Millionaire** and **Indecent Proposal** (even though **Lecherous Millionaire** involves a worse consequence for B), that PVC are more likely to regard consent as invalid in the first three cases. Why might this be so? Because there are some contexts in which it is unacceptable for people to use their capacity to help another person in order to obtain sexual favors and some where it is acceptable (or less unacceptable), and that this is to be explained, at least in part, in terms of the social consequences of regarding such arrangements as morally or legally permissible.

Consider how B might choose between possible versions of PVC, knowing that she might be in such situations. It seems plausible to suppose that the class of detention-home inmates and potential employees will be *better off* if PVC disallow such deals. If, as in **Hiring**, sole proprietors are not permitted to make such offers, they will still need to hire and promote employees and will probably hire them without the quid-pro-quo. If, as in **Detention Home**, caregivers are not allowed to make such demands, it is likely that they will still continue to provide their services. By contrast, it is not clear that women will be better off if proposers are barred from making their offers in **Lecherous Millionaire** and **Indecent Proposal**. For if A cannot demand a quid-pro-quo, it is unlikely that A will make any offer at all.

There are additional reasons for treating **Promotion** as more problematic than **Lecherous Millionaire** and **Indecent Proposal**. For the *quid* that is exchanged for the *quo* does not belong to the offeror. Just as grades do not belong to the professor, positions and jobs do not typically belong to a supervisor, and A would be violating his obligation to the organization

---

[25] Linda LeMoncheck, *Loose Women, Lecherous Men* (New York: Oxford University Press, 1997), 166.

if he were to promote or hire less than best-qualified persons. In addition, because it is not transparent whether an employee deserves or would receive promotion or a position in the normal course of events, neither the target nor others can tell whether the supervisor is threatening a harm or offering a benefit. An employee who rejects what is presented as an offer cannot be confident of escaping retaliation, given that "the prospect of meticulous oversight or the biased exercise of the supervisor's discretion is always in the background."[26] And it is not just the target employee with whom we must be concerned. To allow employers to make such offers to some employees is to expose other employees to what they may reasonably believe is a threat. For these and other reasons, it may make sense to adopt a *per se* rule that prohibits quid-pro-quo sexual proposals in certain contexts, even when such proposals are genuine offers and are *not* best understood as coercive.

The following case presents a particularly difficult theoretical issue.

IRS. A has information that B has significantly underreported her income to the IRS. He tells B that he will report her to the IRS unless she agrees to sexual relations.

It is not wrong for A to carry out his declared unilateral plan. Indeed, it might be his obligation to do so. Moreover, if B were to discover that A was intending to report her to the IRS, she might make the proposal to A. There are no doubt good public-policy reasons for prohibiting persons from using their ability to trigger prosecutions to extract private benefits. Whether we should try to subsume such reasons under the banner of coercion is, however, another question. We might want to regard A's behavior as criminal without regarding it as a sexual offense against B.

Consider

Reputation. A and B are on their first date. B rebuffs A's advances. A says, "If you refuse me, I'll tell everyone in school that we had sex. If you go along, I'll keep my mouth shut."

In my view, **Reputation** is a case in which PVC_L and PVC_M give different answers. A's declared unilateral plan – to spread lies about B – is a form of moral extortion.[27] At the same time, I think it would be a mistake to criminalize A's behavior. Why the distinction? First, I do not know that we want to make false gossip a legally recognized form of slander, in which case A would not be threatening a *legal* wrong. Second, as a legal issue, there are immense evidentiary problems in the way of establishing that A made such a proposal, so it would probably be pointless to criminalize the behavior.

---

[26] Schulhofer, *Unwanted Sex*, 147.
[27] Of course it is also arguably wrong for A to spread the truth about his sexual relations with B.

Should we distinguish between coercive threats and arguably noncoercive warnings? Consider these cases.

Cocaine. A, a supplier of cocaine to B, tells B that he will no longer supply the drug unless she agrees to sex. B cannot quickly locate another supplier.

Landlord. A owns the apartment that B rents. B is several months behind on her rent. A tells B, "Have sex with me once a week until you pay up, or I'm going to have you evicted."

Although A's declared unilateral plan in **Cocaine** – not to supply B with drugs – is hardly immoral or illegal, it may, nonetheless, be wrong for A to use this declared unilateral plan in this way. But why? Contrast the two cases. Assuming that A is entitled to evict B in **Landlord**, A's proposal is more akin to solicitation of prostitution than to a case of rape or sexual coercion. In **Landlord**, A's proposal is *not* trumped up. He would carry out his declared unilateral plan if he were not in a position to strike a deal with B. In effect, A is *warning* B of what he will do if she does not agree, not threatening her with a consequence he would otherwise not impose in order to induce her agreement. By contrast, A's proposal in **Cocaine** is "trumped up." Were he not in a position to make this proposal, he would continue to sell to B.

Consider the sort of "threatened" consequence that is a part of ordinary life.

Snit. A and B are married. They have not had intercourse for two weeks. A proposes that they have sex. A's past behavior leads B to believe that if she rebuffs A, he will be verbally abusive and generally difficult to live with.

Snit straddles our concern with the coerciveness of A's proposal and the character of B's response. As described, I would be loath to regard this as a case of coercion or a sexual offense. First, it is not clear that A is explicitly or implicitly proposing to violate B's rights. People are sometimes justified in being angry with others, and for all we know, A is so entitled in this case. Moreover, even when expressions of anger are not justified, it does not follow that one's behavior is rights-violating. Some boorish behavior is part of the rough and tumble of life. Moreover, even if we were to regard A's implicit threats as coercive, it does not follow that B is justified in acquiescing first and prosecuting later. It is arguable that she should stand her ground or leave.

But recall **Debt.** Unlike **Snit**, A's declared unilateral plan would clearly violate B's rights. Yet if B succumbs, it is not clear that she has been coerced into sexual relations in a way that should constitute a sexual offense. Why?

Because B has a reasonable alternative, namely, to reject A's proposal and sue for breach of contract.[28] Although A's declared unilateral plan leaves B worse off than she has a right to be, it is not the sort of worse-off position that the criminal law is designed to handle. In addition, if B were to acquiesce, it would seem that the harm to B of engaging in undesired sexual relations must be relatively small – less than the value of A's debt.

The previous point is perhaps better illustrated by this case.

Goldfish. A and B are on their third date and go back to B's apartment. A makes advances. B rebuffs A. Eyeing B's aquarium, A says "It seems that you like your goldfish more than me." A pulls a goldfish out of the tank, holds it up, and says "It's him or me." Becoming scared that A will kill her goldfish, B begins to undress.

A's proposal is coercive because his declared unilateral plan would violate B's rights as owner of the goldfish (I set aside the question whether goldfish have rights). Although PVC_M might regard B's consent as invalid, I suspect that the best version of PVC_L would hold that A commits no sexual offense. Assuming that B chooses the alternative that is least harmful to her, succumbing to A's proposal would suggest that she regards the harm of (putatively) undesired sexual relations with A as *less* than the harm of the loss of her goldfish, and that cannot be the sort of harm in which the criminal law does or should take an interest. I have said that A coerces B only when it is reasonable to expect B to succumb to the threat rather than suffer the consequences or it is seriously wrong for A to proceed in the face of B's unreasonable behavior. Here we can reasonably expect B to suffer the consequences.

But suppose that B were very attached to this particular goldfish. Burgess-Jackson maintains that we should adopt a "subjective" view of coercion on which we should not hold a woman "to a higher standard of 'resolution' than she actually has." On this view a woman who places great weight on harm to her goldfish is "just as much coerced into intercourse as the woman threatened with serious bodily injury or extreme pain."[29] This is exactly right and exactly wrong. It is exactly right because it is at least possible that a particular woman might place great weight on a harm that most people would regard as trivial. It is exactly wrong, because it shows why the subjective view is mistaken.

---

[28] Donald Dripps has suggested in correspondence that **Debt** is a variant on prostitution. In the standard case of prostitution, A proposes to pay B with A's money. In this case, A proposes to pay B with B's money.

[29] Keith Burgess-Jackson, "A Theory of Rape" in Keith Burgess-Jackson (ed.), *A Most Detestable Crime: New Philosophical Essays on Rape* (New York: Oxford University Press, 1990), 107.

Actually, B's subjectivity does enter the coercion equation, but it must enter in the correct way, that is, through the back door. Recall **Child Killer**. Although this is a case of rape, it is *not* B's subjective attachment to her child that does the explanatory work. Rather, A rapes B because – as an objective and normative matter – A has reason to assume that B has such an attachment, or, if one prefers, it is reasonable for the law to expect A to assume that B has such an attachment.[30] By contrast, if B were to acquiesce in **Goldfish**, keeping secret her pathological attachment to the creature (say because she is embarrassed to reveal it), it is arguably reasonable – as an objective and normative matter – for A to assume that B would not engage in strongly undesired sexual relations in order to save her goldfish, or, if one prefers, it is unreasonable for the law to assume that A should have known this. But that is not the whole story. If A were (made) aware of B's pathological attachment to her goldfish, then it would be seriously wrong – as an objective and normative matter – for A to proceed, just as it would be seriously wrong for A to threaten to drive an acrophobic B onto the Golden Gate Bridge unless she has sex with him. We could say similar things about **Threat?** Even if it were unreasonable for B to fear violence by A, "there is no reason to allow a man to obtain sex by playing upon a woman's fears of violence, even when [the fears] are objectively unreasonable."[31]

However these cases should be resolved, two things should now be clear. First, there will be numerous cases in which PVC_M will regard B's consent as invalid, but where PVC_L will reach a different result. Legal permissibility does not entail moral permissibility. Second, no analysis of the concept of coercion will tell us just which cases should constitute criminal offenses and which should not. The concept of coercion provides the conceptual room to regard such cases as **Abandonment**, **Lower Grade**, and even **Goldfish** as sexual crimes. Whether we should so regard them will be settled by moral argument.

It is arguable, of course, that the criminal law should have room for less serious sexual offenses just as it has room for petty theft. I have no objection to such a view. Indeed, I have generally avoided referring to coercive sex as rape precisely because I think the law can and probably should allow for a class of sexual crimes that are more akin to extortion than to paradigmatic rape. That said, there is a danger in widening the realm of criminally coercive sex. There is a negative correlation between the *scope* of the category of sexual coercion and the minimum seriousness of the

[30] Donald Hubin and Karen Haley, "Rape and the Reasonable Man," 18 *Law and Philosophy* 113 (1999), 137.
[31] David P. Bryden, "Redefining Rape," 3 *Buffalo Criminal Law Review* 317 (2000), 440.

offense. If we assume that women will succumb to a threat only when they perceive succumbing as less harmful than suffering the threatened harm, and if the threatened harm (being abandoned or receiving a lower grade) is not that harmful, then it would seem that coerced sex will not always involve a serious harm nor a grave threat to the victim's sexual autonomy.

Nonviolent coercion

With this analysis of sexual coercion in hand, I want to consider the claim that we should expand our conception of sexual offenses to include nonviolent as well as violent coercion. In principle, I agree with this view. I have argued, for example, that **Abandonment**, **Lower Grade**, and **Debt** involve coercive but nonviolent proposals if A's declared unilateral plan violates B's moral or legal rights. But some feminist scholars have something even broader in mind. Charlene L. Muehlenhard and Jennifer L. Schrag argue that women face two general types of nonviolent coercion: (a) "indirect sexual coercion," that is, pressure to be in a heterosexual dating relationship or marriage; (b) "direct sexual coercion," specific nonviolent pressures to engage in undesired sexual activity, a category that includes "status coercion," "verbal coercion," "moral coercion," "psychological compulsion," and "institutional coercion."[32] Although the social phenomena the authors describe may be worrisome, it is another question altogether whether PVC_L or PVC_M would regard A's behavior as legally or morally impermissible.

Consider "indirect sexual coercion." It would be folly to deny that women may be under considerable pressure to be in a heterosexual relationship or marriage. And I suppose that such pressures can be "so subtle and insidious" that women may not realize to what extent their preferences have been "socially constructed." I shall say more about false consciousness in chapter ten. Suffice it to say here that even if some preferences *are* inauthentic, it does not follow that we should prohibit people from acting on such preferences or that we have a reliable procedure for distinguishing between authentic and inauthentic preferences. In any case, I doubt that Muehlenhard and Schrag would want to claim that a male who engages in sexual relations with a woman who suffers from "indirect sexual coercion" has committed a criminal or even a moral offense or even done anything wrong.[33] Is A

---

[32] Charlene L. Muehlenhard and Jennifer L. Schrag, "Nonviolent Sexual Coercion" in Andrea Parrot and Laurie Bechhofer (eds.), *Acquaintance Rape* (New York: John Wiley, 1991), 115.

[33] As Robin West puts it, even if "the only *truly* unforced sex is the unalienated sex that would prevail in a truly nonpatriarchal society," this is not at all helpful as a means of "distinguishing criminal from noncriminal sex or describing the latter"; "A Comment on Consent, Sex, and Rape," 2 *Legal Theory* 233 (1996), 245–46.

supposed to refrain from sex with B on such grounds even though B says that she is desirous?

The various forms of alleged "direct sexual coercion" fare little better. Muehlenhard and Schrag say that A engages in "status coercion" when a woman has sex in order to keep him in a relationship because of the status he conveys. It is, of course, arguable that men should be less concerned with their own sexual satisfaction and more sensitive to the desires of women. Still, it is absurd to think that it is impermissible for A to have sexual relations with B if B agrees to sexual relations because A would otherwise not continue the relationship.

We are said to have a case of "verbal coercion" when a woman agrees "to unwanted sexual activity because of a man's verbal arguments, not including verbal threats of physical force."[34] We can distinguish three sorts of cases that fit this definition: (1) A's words give B reasons that she should engage in sexual activity with him; (2) B acquiesces because she finds A's verbal pressure unpleasant and wants it to stop; (3) B acquiesces because she fears A's verbal pressure will be followed by some other adverse consequence. If B does not want to have sexual relations with A at Time-1, but, as in (1), is persuaded to change her mind at Time-2, there is nothing that looks like coercion at all. To the extent that A appeals to B's reasons for action, but does not propose any consequence for not so acting, a case for coercion does not even get started. A could, after all, persuade B to stop smoking or give blood.

(2) is slightly more difficult. If one has a moral right not to be subject to verbal harangues, then A effectively proposes not to discontinue violating B's rights until she tokens consent. Even so, this hardly seems like the sort of rights violation that should trigger a legal intervention, in which case little follows from referring to (2) as verbal coercion. But (2) may shade into (3). If B tokens consent because she reasonably fears that verbal pressure will evolve into physical force even though no such threats have been made, we may well have a genuine case of coercion, but then it is the prospect of *nonverbal* pressure that constitutes the coercion, not B's words.

Muehlenhard and Schrag are also concerned about what we might call "moral coercion," where B engages in undesired sex because she feels obligated to do so, as when a woman believes that agreeing to sexual relations is the proper way to reciprocate for a nice dinner.[35] Here "coercion" is doing no work at all. We are not coerced into doing X when we do X because we

---

[34] Muehlenhard and Schrag, "Nonviolent Sexual Coercion" in Parrot and Bechhofer (eds.), *Acquaintance Rape*, 122.

[35] These feelings may arise "because she has incorporated society's norms or because the man persuades her that she is obligated to him"; *ibid.*, 120.

believe that we should do X, whether or not our belief is correct. I am not coerced into giving to The United Way if I do so because I correctly believe that I should or even if I am wrong to think that I should (say, because I should give to a more efficient organization). Similarly, a woman is not coerced into sex if she correctly or incorrectly believes that she has moral reason to agree to sex (say, because she said that she would).

Are women subject to "institutional coercion" to have sex? Once again, we need to separate the theoretical wheat from the theoretical chaff. I do not doubt that the "structure of economic and social relations" may encourage women to consent to sexual relations when they otherwise would not.[36] And I suppose one violates no linguistic law by referring to this phenomenon as "institutional coercion," just as we could say that the structure of our economy "coerces" many high-school students to attend college. But that would hardly mean that the colleges are acting wrongly or that a student's agreement to attend a college is invalid. Similarly, the fact that the social and economic structure might encourage women to accept sexual relationships that they might otherwise eschew hardly means that their partners are culpable of wrongdoing.

What about "psychological coercion"? Setting aside cases of *external control*, where B tokens consent but where B's will is under A's control, as in cases of hypnosis, brainwashing, or the philosopher's hypothetical in which A plants electrodes in B's brain, it surely does no good to say that we should understand "nonvoluntary action to include cases where circumstances or events compel conduct, or where the individual acts under a psychological compulsion."[37] For, as stated, this simply begs the question as to when an individual acts under a "psychological *compulsion*" of the sort that would render her consent invalid. Similarly, to say that consensual sex must be "the result of mutual desire [and] must not be the result of unwelcome exchanges or pressures, unacceptable narrowing of alternatives" is unhelpful or false.[38] It is false because consensual sex need not be rooted in "mutual desire" and because one can voluntarily accept a proposal that one would have preferred not to receive (as in **Dating**) if the other party is acting within his rights. It is unhelpful to say that consensual sex must not result from an "unacceptable" narrowing of alternatives because that simply begs the question whether "unacceptable" is defined subjectively from B's point of view, in which case it has little moral force, or from a moral point of view, in which case we are back with the sort of moral analysis I have advanced.

---

[36] Rosemarie Tong, *Women, Sex, and the Law* (Totowa, NJ: Rowman and Allanheld, 1984), 109–10.
[37] Bogart, "Reconsidering Rape," 162.   [38] *Ibid.*, 163.

Economic pressure and inequality

Worries about the effects of economic pressure and inequality on sexual relations represent a recurring theme in much contemporary feminist literature. Martha Chamallas says that we should not consider consent as "freely given" if it is secured through "economic pressure."[39] William Eskridge is puzzled that economic inducements are thought to taint consent in quid-pro-quo sexual-harassment cases as in **Hiring** or **Promotion**, but not in a case such as **Debt**.[40] Dorothy Roberts is similarly puzzled by the contrast between a case such as **Lecherous Millionaire**, which is usually regarded as voluntary, and a case such as **Promotion**, which is often regarded as coercive sexual harassment.[41] More generally, Catharine MacKinnon argues that the law of rape "presents consent as free exercise of sexual choice under conditions of equality of power" and that if we confronted the "underlying structure of constraint and disparity," then we would regard the range of nonconsensual sex as much larger.[42]

As I have argued, it is hard to see how either PVC_L or PVC_M would regard economic inducements or inequality as a general problem for morally transformative consent. It is simply not true that valid consent presupposes equality between the parties. Eskridge and Roberts need not be puzzled about why quid-pro-quo sexual relations are sometimes thought to be coercive and other times not. As I have argued, there are good reasons to circumscribe the discretion of supervisors in employment contexts that do not apply in non-employment contexts such as **Lecherous Millionaire**. Roberts is substantively correct but unnecessarily derisive when she says that the distinction between cases such as **Promotion** and **Lecherous Millionaire** is based on a "value judgment about male prerogatives."[43] First, the value judgment goes to the rights of the parties rather than (mere) male "prerogatives." And it is arguable that whereas the millionaire has a right to give or not give his money as he pleases, the supervisor does not have a right to give or not give promotions as he pleases. Second, the "value judgment" may well be correct.

---

[39] Martha Chamallas, "Consent, Equality, and the Legal Control of Sexual Conduct," 61 *Southern California Law Review* 777 (1988), 814.

[40] William N. Eskridge, Jr., "The Many Faces of Sexual Consent," 37 *William and Mary Law Review* 47 (1995), 50.

[41] Dorothy E. Roberts, "Rape, Violence, and Women's Autonomy," 69 *Chicago-Kent Law Review* 359 (1993), 384.

[42] Catharine A. MacKinnon, from *Toward a Feminist Theory of the State* (Cambridge, MA: Harvard University Press, 1989) as cited in D. Kelly Weisberg (ed.), *Applications of Feminist Legal Theory to Women's Lives* (Philadelphia: Temple University Press, 1996), 474.

[43] Roberts, "Rape, Violence, and Women's Autonomy," 384.

What about inequality of bargaining power? Roughly speaking, there are three ways in which inequality might be troublesome for consent: (1) inequalities of status and knowledge might compromise the rationality of B's decision; (2) A may use the inequality to exploit B; (3) the inequality may reflect a background injustice.

With respect to (1), I have already acknowledged that there is good reason to worry about seductive offers in which A's proposal distorts B's decision process, as might be true in **Indecent Proposal**. If we can reasonably expect A to identify such cases in a reliable way, then it would be desirable to treat B's consent as violating PVC_M and perhaps even PVC_L. But the problem for valid consent in such cases is not the inequality of the relationship, *per se*, but the defect in the rationality of B's decision caused by the inequality.

Moreover, we must be careful not to require too much information for valid consent. Relations between laypersons and professionals are typically characterized by great inequalities of knowledge. That is why we seek their help. If my physician says, "I think you ought to have this procedure," I may well accept her advice. We do not think that I cannot give valid consent to the procedure even though she understands much more about the matter than do I. Of course we worry when B does not understand at all to what she is consenting. If my auto mechanic says, "you need to replace the compressor relay solenoid," what do I know? I will probably consent to the repair and hope that I am not being taken. What *are* the informational requirements of valid consent to an auto repair or surgery or sex? That is an important question, but it is a question about information or competence, not inequality or coercion.

Even when there are *no* problems about information or competence, inequality may give rise to exploitation. In **Greedy Mechanic**, B understands the situation and makes a perfectly rational decision to give in to A's exorbitant demands. Now it is not clear by what standards a transaction actually is exploitative. It is commonly thought that a transaction is exploitative when and because the stronger party gains much more from the transaction than the weaker party. Interestingly, by this measure, many transactions born of inequality are not exploitative *if* we evaluate the outcome of a transaction in terms of the parties' respective utility gains.[44] In general, the stronger party's bargaining position is stronger precisely because he stands to gain less marginal utility from the transaction than the weaker party. He can

---

[44] Amy Wax, "Bargaining in the Shadow of the Market: Is There a Future for Egalitarian Marriage?," 84 *Virginia Law Review* 509 (1998).

walk away from the situation with ease.[45] Who gains more in **Indecent Proposal**? A has gained an evening with B. B has gained $1,000,000. Was Monica Lewinsky exploited by President Clinton? Putting aside the disastrous consequences for everyone and the possibility that Lewinsky actually received more *erotic* gratification than did President Clinton (she claims to have had the first orgasm), the crucial fact is that Lewinsky got to have a relationship with the *President of the United States*, whereas Clinton received oral sex. I do not claim that there is no exploitative sex. I do suggest that it is difficult to identify the criteria by which a transaction is exploitative. Moreover, and as I have argued elsewhere, if the weaker party reasonably believes that she will gain from an exploitative transaction, the best version of PVC will go a long way toward accommodating her decision to enter into such transactions.[46]

Is there reason to worry about the transformative power of consent when the inequality of power is rooted in injustice? For the most part, I think there is not. It is first worth noting that even if we were able to equalize financial or social resources (or to make them just on whatever theory of justice one favors), inequalities in other dimensions – for example, age, beauty, intelligence, and charm – will affect people's sexual opportunities and their willingness to consent to sexual relations.

More generally, it is a mistake to think that difficult circumstances and inequalities should be regarded as invalidating consent in either morality or law. To the contrary. It is scarcity and constraints that explain the need for morally transformative consent: "If everybody possessed all the endowments he needed to pursue any life plan he wished, contracting would be unnecessary."[47] Moreover, second best is often the best that people can do. Some people would rarely masturbate if they had all the intercourse they desired, but we do not think that the lack of such alternatives compromises the voluntariness of their autoerotic activity. I do not doubt that women sometimes agree to sexual relations that they would reject under different or more just or equal background conditions. But we do not enhance their welfare or their autonomy by denying the transformative power of their consent.

To reemphasize an earlier point, an adequate set of principles of valid consent must be applicable to the *non-ideal* circumstances in which people

---

[45] For an extended discussion, see my *Exploitation* (Princeton: Princeton University Press, 1996), chapter 7.

[46] *Ibid.*, chapter 9.

[47] Michael Trebilcock, *The Limits of Freedom of Contract* (Cambridge, MA: Harvard University Press, 1993), 79.

find themselves, whether those circumstances are due to misfortune, injustice, or simply the facts of life (such as aging). There is reason to think that those principles will be reasonably permissive. It is difficult to defend principles that prevent people from consenting to transactions that will move them from an unjust or unfortunate situation to a better situation. I believe this is true with respect to economic transactions, and I see no reason to think that it is not true with respect to sexual consent.

CHAPTER NINE

Deception

Introduction

It is clear that the PVC_L and PVC_M will hold that coercive proposals can often nullify the transformative power of sexual consent. Sexual deception is different. Although deception typically renders agreements voidable in commercial contexts, *caveat amator* has long been the traditional legal principle for sexual relations. Several states criminalize deception with respect to a sexually transmitted disease or impersonation of a husband. But such exceptions aside, the law has been quite permissive with respect to sexual deception. In the words of a recent Canadian case: "Deceptions, small and sometimes large, have from time immemorial been the by-product of romance and sexual encounters. They often carry the risk of harm to the deceived party. Thus far in the history of civilization, these deceptions, however sad, have been left to the domain of song, verse and social censure."[1] I suspect that prevailing moral norms are only somewhat less permissive. We may think it sleazy if a male lies about his marital status, affections, or intentions in order to get a woman into bed, but many do not think that this is a particularly serious matter.

It is not clear why this is so. As a general principle, we might think that A's deception should generally undermine the moral and legal transformative power of consent because it precludes B from being able to decide whether engaging in sex with A is in her interests or compatible with her values. As a moral matter, I think this is basically correct. With respect to the law, things are more complicated. Stephen Schulhofer observes that "good reasons are seldom offered for the law's refusal to protect sexual autonomy from even the most egregious deceptive inducements."[2] Perhaps such reasons can be produced. Perhaps not.

---

[1] *Regina v. Cuerrier*, Supreme Court of Canada, 162 D.L.R. 4th (513; 1998).
[2] Stephen J. Schulhofer, *Unwanted Sex* (Cambridge, MA: Harvard University Press, 1998), 112.

Distinctions

Before going further, it will be helpful to consider three distinctions. First, the distinction between coercion and deception. It is sometimes argued that sexual deception is *as* impermissible as sexual coercion because sexual deception *is a species of* sexual coercion.

1. The "force" or "coercion" that negates consent ought to be defined to include extortionate threats and *misrepresentation of material fact*.[3]

2. Coercion can take many forms. Free choice may be thwarted by compulsion of the body through physical violence, *or more subtly by the creation of false beliefs through deception*.[4]

3. Deceit and violence – these are the two forms of deliberate assault on human beings. *Both* can coerce people into acting against their will. Most harm that can befall victims through violence can come to them also through deceit.[5]

This "assimilationist" strategy should be rejected. Even if we say – somewhat oddly – that deception is a species of coercion, we can still distinguish between the coercion that involves deception and the coercion that involves threats or force, so the distinction will simply reappear under different labels. In addition, it would be a *non sequitur* to assume that if coercion by threat invalidates consent, then coercion by deception also nullifies consent.

There are some important differences between coercion and deception. Women abhor coerced sex, but the synchronic experience of sex is typically not affected by deception (although it is frequently a source of *ex post* distress). Indeed, that is precisely why some commentators argue that the wrong of rape cannot be based on experience. It is also arguable that one has more control over the extent to which one is deceived than over the extent to which one is coerced, and thus there is more reason to place the burden of deception on the deceived party than on the coerced party. Interestingly, however, there is *a sense* in which deception may be worse than force. Whereas force simply overpowers or bypasses B's will, A's deception *uses* B's will against herself, making her an unwitting agent in the violation of her own rights.

Second, we can distinguish between various *forms* of deception. Consider these cases.

---

[3] Susan Estrich, *Real Rape* (Cambridge, MA: Harvard University Press, 1987), 102 (emphasis added).
[4] Jane E. Larson, " 'Woman Understand So Little, They Call My Good Nature "Deceit" ': A Feminist Rethinking of Seduction," 93 *Columbia Law Review* 374 (1993), 414 (emphasis added).
[5] Sissela Bok, *Lying* (New York: Random House, 1989), 18.

HIV-L. A makes advances. B asks A if he has been tested for HIV. A, who tested positive for HIV one month ago, tells B that he had a negative test one month ago.
HIV-D. A makes advances. B, who knows that A uses drugs, asks A if he has been tested for HIV. A, who tested negative three months ago, but who tested positive one month ago, says, "I tested negative three months ago."
Non-Disclosure. A makes advances. A, who has tested positive for HIV, has a "not asked, don't tell" policy. B does not ask. A does not tell.

For analytic purposes, we can distinguish between a lie that is technically false and intended to deceive (**HIV-L**), a deceptive statement that is technically true (**HIV-D**), and a failure to disclose relevant information (**Non-Disclosure**). Are these distinctions of moral importance? That is less clear. In both **HIV-L** and **HIV-D**, A gets B to falsely believe that he is HIV-negative, and both impose a similar risk to B. Perhaps B bears more responsibility for her false belief in **Non-Disclosure**, given that she did not ask. But there is plenty of responsibility to go around and whatever we think about B's responsibility for her false belief, A's behavior may be sufficiently wrongful to merit moral condemnation and perhaps even criminalization. After all, if we were to think of sexual relations along the lines of a medical procedure or the sale of a house, then A has an obligation to disclose information that might be material to B's decision.

But, it will be said, the distinctions between the various forms of deception are unimportant in my HIV cases only because they concern disease and possible death. It is the *consequences* of deception that worry us, not the deception itself. This may be part of the truth. Consider

Harvard. A and B meet at a party. B indicates that she has a "thing" about Harvard men. A falsely tells B that he graduated from Harvard.

It is wrong for A to lie about such matters, but even if A's lie had causal impact on B's decision to have sex with A, we would not think that A had committed a sexual offense. In any case, no analytical distinctions between the forms of deception will resolve the question whether PVC_L or PVC_M would regard deception with respect to some matter or another as invalidating consent.

Third, the literature on sexual deception typically distinguishes between *fraud in the factum*, where the target is deceived about what she is consenting to, and *fraud in the inducement*. Consider the following cases.

Gynecologist. A tells B that he will be inserting an instrument into her vagina. Instead, he inserts his penis.
Twins. A, whose identical twin is married to B, slips into B's bed while she is half asleep. B believes that A is her husband.

Affection. A and B are dating. A makes advances. B says, "I don't want to go further unless you really care about me." A says that he does, but later tells mutual friends that he was lying.

Vasectomy. A makes advances. B tells A that she will accept only if A wears a condom. A falsely tells B that he has had a vasectomy.

Single. A and B meet in a night class, and have several dates. B makes it clear that she refuses to have sex with married men. A falsely tells B that he is not married.

Sister. A has been having sexual relations with B's sister unbeknownst to B. A says nothing, although A correctly believes that B would have rejected A's advances if she had known about this relationship.

Bigamy. A and B have a marriage ceremony. Unbeknownst to B, the marriage is invalid because A is already married.

Cure. A, a hospital employee, calls B and tells her that her blood tests indicate that she has a serious disease, and that it can be cured by expensive and painful surgery or by intercourse with an anonymous donor (who turns out to be A) who has been injected with a serum. A and B meet in a hotel and have intercourse.[6]

The standard view is that A commits *fraud in the factum* when B is deceived about what is done, as exemplified by **Gynecologist**. A commits *fraud in the inducement* when B consents to what she believes to be intercourse, but does so because she is deceived about certain facts, such as (1) the purpose of intercourse (**Cure**), (2) A's nominal identity (**Twins**), (3) A's characteristics (**Single, Vasectomy**, **Bigamy**, **Cure**, **HIV-L**), (4) A's behavior (**Sister**), or (5) A's mental states (**Affection**). The law has typically regarded only *fraud in the factum* as a crime. In the words of a nineteenth-century British case:

> the proposition that fraud vitiates consent in criminal matters is not true if taken to apply in the fullest sense of the word, and without qualification … Many seductions would be rapes, and so might acts of prostitution procured by fraud, as for instance by promises not intended to be fulfilled … The only cases in which fraud indisputably vitiates consent in these matters are cases of fraud as to the nature of the act done.[7]

When an identical twin impersonated his brother, the woman's consent was considered sufficient "because she knew she was agreeing to an act of intercourse."[8] And while bigamy is illegal, the law does not regard sexual relations within an illegal marriage as constituting a sexual offense, *per se*.[9]

---

[6] *Boro v. Superior Court*, 163 Cal. App. 1224; 210 Cal Rptr. 122 (1985). The law does not need bizarre hypotheticals. Real cases will suffice.

[7] *R. v. Linekar*, Court of Appeal, Criminal Division, 3 All ER 69 (1995), quoting J. Stephen in *R v. Clarence*, 22 QBD 13 (1886–90) All ER 133.

[8] Schulhofer, *Unwanted Sex*, 152.

[9] "Thus if a woman consents to sexual intercourse with a man under the belief that she is legally married to him, being misled by his false statements, the marriage being a mere sham, the act is not rape"; *Corpus Juris Secundum* (St. Paul, MN: West Publishing Company, 1936), 483.

In *Boro*, the "truth is stranger than fiction" case on which **Cure** is based, the court dismissed the charge of fraud on the grounds that the woman knew she was consenting to intercourse. And, not surprisingly, cases such as **Single** and **Sister** would never find their way into court. For reasons I shall develop below, I do not find this distinction particularly helpful.

Caveat amator

Why has the law been more permissive with respect to sexual deception than with commercial deception? Richard Posner offers several explanations, although it is not clear whether he regards the answers as historical/empirical explanations or as normative justifications. He conjectures that if a woman is not "averse to having sex with a particular man, the wrong, if any, is in the lies… rather than in an invasion of her bodily integrity."[10] On this view, **Gynecologist** is properly regarded as a crime, for B does not consent to intercourse with A, but **Vasectomy** is not a crime, because B is not averse to having sex with A. Posner also argues that there is less need to protect targets from sexual deception than commercial deception because prospective sexual partners can choose to prolong courtships and investigate the personal qualities of a suitor whereas delay is less viable in the more hurried and impersonal relationships of the marketplace.[11]

Posner's explanation does not work. Consider

Odometer. A sets back the odometer on a car before selling it to B.

We do not say that there is no criminal fraud in **Odometer** because B is not averse to buying this nominal car from A, that it is a mere case of *fraud in the inducement*. No, it is serious fraud precisely because A misrepresents the *characteristics* of the car. Posner might reply that B has suffered an identifiable economic loss in **Odometer**, whereas B got the experience that she sought, say, in **Single**. But that does not show that sexual deception is not seriously wrong nor that it fails to cause harm. Rather, it requires us to determine whether A's action could be wrong or harmful even if it does not cause a different experience.

I also doubt whether Posner's "time constraint" argument is of much more help. First, delay is often viable in the marketplace. A home or car buyer can have the dwelling or car inspected rather than rely on representations. In addition, Posner may underestimate the costs of postponing a

[10] Richard A. Posner, *Sex and Reason* (Cambridge, MA: Harvard University Press, 1992), 392.
[11] See Larson discussing Posner in " 'Woman Understand So Little,' " 422.

decision on sexual relations, where sex delayed is at least that experience denied and may even preclude a long-term relationship.

It is more likely that the permissive approach to sexual deception derives from "line-drawing" or adjudication difficulties. Although such practical arguments are frequently overused, it may, in fact, be difficult to distinguish between those deceptions that are not seriously wrong and certainly should not be illegal and those that are legitimate candidates for prohibition. Cordial interaction among human beings often seems to require that we make statements that are less than fully honest.[12] Moreover, people may be influenced by information to which they have no right or which others have a legitimate privacy-based interest in protecting. The fact is that there are many arenas in which there is no general understanding of when deception is wrong and when it is a justifiable or excusable part of the social, economic, organizational, or political game. Even when deception is seriously wrong, we are reluctant to invoke the law because the damages are difficult to assess and because there are evidentiary issues that would make the cost of demonstrating deception prohibitive. For "administrative reasons," it may be sensible to assign the burden of fraud to dispensers of information in the commercial arena and to the recipients of fraud in the sexual arena.

The law aside, it is not just that we lack a clear view as to when sexual deception is morally wrong. Some forms of deception may be part and parcel of interactions that precede a sexual relationship: "Exaggerated praise, playful suggestions, efforts to impress, and promises intended to reassure and trigger emotions (but not to be strictly believed) are all part of the ritual of escalating erotic fascination that makes up a 'seduction' in the colloquial sense."[13] Is it wrong for the parties to overstate the pleasure that they experience? If A behaves wrongly in **Affection**, does B behave wrongly if she fakes an orgasm?[14] Love, not just sex, may be deeply intertwined with false beliefs – "What is being in love, in fact, if not harboring certain illusions about love, about oneself, and about the person with whom one is in love?"[15]

So the problem is this. If some sexual deceptions are to be regarded as morally and legally permissible whereas others are not, how can we

---

[12] In an episode of *I Love Lucy*, Lucy makes a bet that she can be completely honest, forcing her to tell her friends what she thinks of their clothing, hair styles, etc.

[13] Larson, " 'Woman Understand So Little,' " 449.

[14] Of course it is not clear whether males would forego sexual relationships if they had not been deceived. Do some males take such pride in their love-making that they would eschew sex that is unlikely to produce an orgasm in their partners?

[15] André Comte-Sponville, *A Small Treatise on the Great Virtues* (New York: Metropolitan Books, 1996), translated by Catherine Temerson (2001), 241.

distinguish between those two categories? In addition to the cases I have presented, consider these:

Talent Scout. A meets B, an aspiring actress. A falsely tells B that he is a talent scout for a Hollywood producer. A makes no "quid pro quo" demands, but A believes (correctly) that B accepts his advances only because she believes his story.
Intentions. A and B have been dating for some time, but have not had intercourse. B tells A that she is "saving herself" for her husband. A likes B but is a committed bachelor. A tells B that he intends to marry her.
Pro-Choice. A is a strong "right to life" advocate. B is strongly pro-choice and chooses not to be intimate with those who do not support a woman's right to choose. In response to B's inquiry, A lies about his view.

We can probably draw a bright line around disease (**HIV**), pregnancy (**Vasectomy**), and identity (**Twins**).[16] But while I would regard **Single**, **Sister**, **Affection**, **Talent Scout**, **Intentions**, and **Pro-Choice** as inconsistent with PVC$_M$, they are not easily distinguished from those that are "puffing" or "storytelling."[17] And if we cannot distinguish the serious from the less serious with sufficient clarity, then PVC must either allow for at least some deceptions that may be seriously wrong or prohibit some deceptions that are not seriously wrong.

That said, I think that current social norms may understate the seriousness of sexual deception. Our intuitions about the moral seriousness of sexual deception may not be a reliable guide if they are contaminated by norms that reflect genuine administrative and evidentiary concerns in the law but are not replicated in the moral sphere. Note, for example, that whereas it is possible to produce evidence about A's objective characteristics, (**HIV-L, Vasectomy, Single, Talent Scout**), it is not easy to demonstrate that A's statements were deceptive in **Affection** and/or that A's statements had causal impact on B's decision. Such difficulties may support *caveat amator* as a legal norm, but not as a moral principle.

The harm and wrong of deception

In order to further develop our understanding of how PVC would regard sexual deception, we need to think about the way in which it is wrong or harmful. Consider Martha Chamallas's argument for a new genre of torts for injuries resulting from sexual deception:

[16] We might include marital status (**Bigamy**), but it is not clear that we would want to regard **Bigamy** as involving a sexual offense, *per se*.
[17] Schulhofer, *Unwanted Sex*, 92.

The gravamen of these complaints is that the defendant either lied about or failed to disclose critical facts about his physical condition, consequently physically harming the plaintiff... Plaintiffs in these cases allege that, absent such deception, they would not have agreed to sexual intercourse with the defendant, and therefore their apparent consent should not bar recovery in a tort action.[18]

Such tort actions involve two elements. First, A's deception is harmful to B only when B would otherwise have not chosen to have intercourse with A (*decision causation*). Second, A's deception is harmful to B only when B's decision results in harm or injury to B (*injury causation*).[19]

Consider

Smoking. A, a cigarette company, misrepresented the risks of smoking to B. B smoked A's product for many years and consequently died of lung cancer. If A had not misrepresented the risks, B would have smoked (no less) because B understood the risks of smoking from other sources.

In this case, A wrongfully attempted to deceive B about the risks of smoking and B was actually harmed by smoking. But A's wrongful behavior did not harm B; it had no effect on B's decision, because A did not actually cause B to have a false belief. So consider

Indifference. A and B meet in a bar. B is indifferent to a potential partner's marital status. In the course of conversation, she asks A if he is married. Thinking that a truthful answer would deter B, he lies. B believes A.

Here, too, there is no decision causation. Although A caused B to have a false belief, it did not affect B's decision.

As these cases illustrate, there is a category of cases in which A's deception does not affect B's decision. These include cases in which B does not believe that A is sincere or suspects that he is not. When an automobile salesperson falsely states "$20,000 is the best I can do," he does not typically *deceive* the target, so B's consent is not a product of A's deception. Of course, the mere fact that one is not deceived by disbelieved statements is not to say that one prefers the regime in which such deception occurs.[20] Although B may consent to enter the automobile-purchase game in which she expects misrepresentations, she might well prefer a regime in which honesty was empirically expected. So, too, for sex. B might well prefer a regime in which she can expect A to be honest, but since that regime is not available, she

---

[18] Martha Chamallas, "Consent, Equality, and the Legal Control of Sexual Conduct," 61 *Southern California Law Review* 777 (1988), 811.

[19] Peter H. Schuck, "Rethinking Informed Consent," 103 *Yale Law Journal* 899 (1994), 918.

[20] See Arthur Applbaum, *Ethics for Adversaries* (Princeton: Princeton University Press, 1996), chapter 6.

enters the only game in town and accepts her mother's advice not to believe what men tell her.

It is difficult to measure the causal impact of deception.[21] Although women may be suspicious of male declarations of love, commitment, and marital status, they may also be prone to overestimate the likelihood that such expressions are honestly made in their own case. Just as most people believe that they are better than average drivers (the Lake Wobegon phenomenon), most people may believe that they are particularly good dishonesty detectors, and thus their decisions may be vulnerable to deception even when they are imbued with a healthy dose of skepticism. And even when deceptive statements are believed and have causal impact, it may be difficult to *demonstrate* that this is so. After all, women do often have sexual relations with men who do not say that they love them or intend to marry them.

Now consider *injury causation*. As a matter of common law, a tort claim requires actual damages. If A misrepresents or fails to disclose the risks of a medical procedure but everything goes fine and dandy, then B has no claim to compensation. B has undergone a *risk* of harm, but a risk of harm is not an actual harm. If A drives negligently, but does not strike pedestrian B with his car, B cannot sue A for damages for having put her at heightened risk.

So Chamallas is not quite right to say that "a defendant may be held liable if he fraudulently tells the plaintiff that he is sterile or free from disease." If B does not become pregnant or acquire a disease, she has not suffered the harm she was concerned to avoid. Of course, A's behavior may be *wrong* when it puts B at risk even if B suffers no harm, just as A can be punished for an attempted crime that causes no harm to its intended victim (and thus would not be a basis for a tort). So whereas Chamallas argues that it might be better to treat sexual deception as a less grave civil wrong than a putatively graver criminal wrong, it may make sense to treat some sexual deceptions as criminal wrongs rather than as civil wrongs.

Although we need not accept Chamallas's proposal to limit our interest to physical harm, we must determine if and when deception does cause damage. Unlike commercial fraud (as in **Odometer**), which typically involves some economic loss, sex is "typically pleasurable in itself," and thus

---

[21] Onora O'Neill suggests that some casual sexual encounters and the sexual aspect of faded marriages may exemplify relationships in which women make no positive assumptions about their partner's desires or motives, and are therefore unlikely to believe certain statements even if, for some reason, the men bother to make them. See "Between Consenting Adults," 14 *Philosophy & Public Affairs* 252 (1985), 269.

it is not clear whether deception destroys or reduces "the value of the encounter to the victim."[22] From a psychological perspective, it clearly can. Unlike coerced sex, deception involves no mental distress concurrent with sexual relations. Still, B may experience *ex post* mental distress if she discovers the deception. She may feel used, betrayed, exploited, duped, and even traumatized at the risks that she came close to incurring (the "near miss" phenomenon), in particular, the risk of pregnancy and disease.

Although "deception regret" is a genuine psychological phenomenon, the previous point raises the question whether A's deception is harmful to B if B does not discover A's deception and if it does not lead to other palpable injuries. Here I have a problem. I argued in chapter five that I am sympathetic to an experiential account of harm. At the same time, I understand and feel the intuitive pull of an objective or non-experiential view. As Robert Nozick's "experience machine" famously illustrates, we (believe that we) want to have certain experiences, but we (believe that we) also want those experiences to be "real" or authentic.[23] I want to have the experience of writing a book that is regarded as good, but I also want the book actually to be regarded as good.[24] Consider the following cases.

Museum. A museum puts on an exhibit of what it represents as Vermeer's paintings, but its curator knows that some are excellent forgeries. Thousands of people enjoy the exhibit and never discover the fraud.

Model. A group of males pretend to be artists and recruit a woman who is willing to pose nude and blindfolded (as in the scales of justice). Unbeknownst to the model, the males do no art work and engage in group masturbation.

Fragments. Binjamin Wilkomirski's *Fragments* is presented as autobiographical memoirs of a child who survived the Holocaust. Readers and listeners are deeply moved by his words. Wilkomirski had never been in a death camp. The autobiography is completely bogus.[25]

My intuition is that the targets have been harmed in **Museum**, **Model**, and **Fragments**, even if they never discover the deception, so never

---

[22] David P. Bryden, "Redefining Rape," 3 *Buffalo Criminal Law Review* 317 (2000), 464.

[23] I say "believe that we" because I think we must allow for the possibility that our intuitions deceive us. Although I believe that I want authentic experiences, it is possible that I really care only for the experiences themselves. See Robert Nozick, *Anarchy, State and Utopia* (New York: Basic Books, 1974), 42.

[24] As T. M. Scanlon puts it, "It makes sense to say that the life of a person who is contented and happy only because he is systematically deceived about what his life is really like is for that reason a worse life, for him, than a life would be that was similarly happy where this happiness was based on true beliefs"; "The Status of Well-Being" in Grethe B. Peterson (ed.), *Tanner Lectures on Human Values*, volume xix (Salt Lake City, UT: University of Utah Press, 1998), 97.

[25] See Binjamin Wilkomirski, *Fragments: Memories of a Wartime Childhood*, translated by Carol Brown Janeway (New York: Schocken, 1996). On the fraud, see Blake Eskin, *A Life in Pieces: The Making and Unmaking of Binjamin Wilkomirski* (New York: W. W. Norton, 2002).

experience regret or anger. Interestingly, an experiential account of harm has difficulties even if the targets do discover the deception. For we would then have to ask whether they have been harmed at Time-2 simply because they experience deception regret or whether their deception regret stems from having been harmed at Time-1. If we adopt the former view, it is arguable that they should not experience any regret at Time-2, since, *ex hypothesi*, they were not harmed at Time-1.[26] And if they were harmed at Time-1, then deception regret at Time-2 is parasitic on an independent harm at Time-1, and does not do much work.

If deception gives rise to non-experiential harm, it must be a moral harm, a violation of *autonomy* or rights, or something along those lines. Even if B is unaware that she has been deceived, A's deception thwarts B's interest in controlling access to her body on terms that satisfy her desires and purposes. Consider some nonsexual examples.

Blood. The Red Cross recruits blood donors by falsely stating that the blood will be used locally. In fact, the blood will be shipped to any location that needs it. B gives blood because she wants to help people in her community.

Basketball. B, a professional basketball player, agrees to play without pay in a charity game for what A represents as an organization devoted to breast-cancer research. In fact, the organization is devoted to anti-abortion activities.[27]

The Red Cross has arguably violated B's autonomy in **Blood**, even though its policy is independently justifiable and imposes no enduring loss on B, and **Basketball** involves a serious violation of B's right to decide to what purposes her basketball playing will be put. We do not say – "What's the loss? After all, she enjoyed the activity, and she has lost nothing of permanent value." To the contrary, B's labor has been appropriated on grounds to which she did not consent.

To the extent that we are concerned with the permissibility of *A*'s behavior, it really does not matter whether we say (1) A has acted wrongly because A's action is of a type that is likely to lead to experiential harm even though A's action has not harmed B in this case, or (2) A has acted wrongly because he has caused a non-experiential objective harm to B. It is worth

---

[26] Along these lines, Gardner and Shute suggest that "If nothing was wrong with being raped apart from the fact that one reacted badly afterwards, then one had no reason to react badly afterwards"; John Gardner and Stephen Shute, "The Wrongness of Rape" in Jeremy Horder (ed.), *Oxford Essays in Jurisprudence*, fourth series (Oxford: Oxford University Press, 2000), 197. Of course, we need not insist that B's experience at Time-2 be *rational* in order to give it weight in our moral deliberations. Indeed, evolutionary psychology might imply that women are predisposed to experience distress at having been deceived.

[27] Some organizations once claimed that pregnancy and nursing are negatively correlated with breast cancer and thus abortion increases the risk of breast cancer.

noting that Gardner and Shute seem to opt for (1) because they couch their analysis in terms of the *wrong* of rape rather than the *harm* of rape. In any case, both views have the same moral implication, namely, that PVC_L and PVC_M may well hold that consent that is rooted in deception should not be regarded as valid.

When?

When *should* PVC_L and PVC_M treat consent that is rooted in deception as invalid? As I have noted, the law has traditionally drawn a sharp distinction between *fraud in the factum*, which it takes seriously, and *fraud in the inducement*, which it does not.[28] Recall **Cure**, a bare-bones sketch of *Boro v. Superior Court*. The relevant California statute allows for a charge of rape when the "victim is at the time unconscious of *the nature of the act*, and this is known to the accused."[29] The court struggled to apply the statutory provision in the light of two factors: (1) unlike a case such as **Gynecologist**, the victim knew she was agreeing to intercourse; (2) the victim thought that intercourse was a form of medical treatment. In considering how to understand "the nature of the act," the court observed that precedent was ambiguous as to whether the impersonation of a spouse constitutes *fraud in the factum*. The victim knows she is agreeing to intercourse, in which case there is arguably no violation of the statute. On the other hand, the victim believes she is consenting "to an innocent act of marital intercourse while what is actually perpetrated upon her is an act of adultery."[30] In *Boro*, the court concluded that the victim agreed to intercourse *simpliciter* and not intercourse as therapy, so there was no violation of the statute, despite "the heartless cruelty of [Boro's] scheme."[31]

A recent British case involved a man who had agreed to pay a prostitute £25, but made off without paying.[32] The prosecution charged the defendant with rape on the grounds that the prostitute would not have agreed to intercourse if she had known that the defendant had no intention to pay her. The court held that the woman knew she was agreeing to intercourse and there was therefore no rape. The court argued that whereas *fraud in the inducement* (as in **Odometer**) renders a commercial contract *revocable* if the victim so chooses, only *fraud in the factum* destroys the consent

---

[28] David Archard, *Sexual Consent* (Boulder: Westview, 1998), 50.
[29] *Boro v. Superior Court*, 1225 (emphasis added).
[30] *Ibid.*, 1228, quoting Ronald Boyce and Rolin Perkins, *Criminal Law*, third edition (Mineda, NY: Foundation Press, 1982), chapter 9, section 3, pp. 1080–81.
[31] *Ibid.*, 1231.   [32] *R. v. Linekar*, Court of Appeal, Criminal Division, 3 All ER 69 (1995).

in the manner required for a sexual *crime*. The court approvingly cited a nineteenth-century case that held that because intercourse "cannot... be regarded as the performance of a contract... the woman's consent here was as full and conscious as consent could be. It was not obtained by any fraud... as to the nature of the act or as to the identity of the agent."[33]

A recent Canadian case concerned the application of a revised statute under which no consent is obtained when the victim "submits or does not resist by reason of fraud."[34] The defendant, who had tested positive for HIV and had been instructed to inform all prospective sexual partners of his condition, had specifically assured a woman that he had tested negative. Over the course of an eighteen-month relationship, they had frequent unprotected sex. The complainant stated that she would not have agreed to unprotected sex if the defendant had not lied. The court held that the parliament clearly intended to move away from the "rigidity of the common law requirement that fraud must relate to the nature and quality of the act," that the statute sought to protect "the individual's right to determine by whom, and under what conditions, he or she will consent to physical contact by another."[35] At the same time, the court sought to avoid applying broad commercial-fraud principles under which "failure to disclose virtually any known risk of harm would potentially be capable of vitiating consent to sexual intercourse."[36] The court was concerned that an expansive interpretation could trigger a criminal charge if the accused "lied... as to [his] position of responsibility... or the level of his salary; or the degree of his wealth; or that he would never look at or consider another sexual partner; or as to the extent of his affection for the other party; or as to his sexual prowess."[37] And while the court conceded that such lies are "immoral and reprehensible," it thought it also obvious that such deceptions should not result in a criminal conviction.

In considering these sorts of cases, we can distinguish two issues: (1) how should the relevant *statute* be applied? (2) should sexual deception constitute a *crime*? These are different questions. Even if *Boro* did not commit a crime under the applicable statute, this hardly shows that his act would not be criminal under a more defensible statute. Second, we are not solely interested in whether sexual deception constitutes rape. We want to know if and when sexual deception is incompatible with PVC_L, acknowledging that it might constitute a lesser criminal or civil wrong. And we want to know when sexual deception is incompatible with PVC_M.

---

[33] *Ibid.*, 144–45, quoting J. Stephen.
[34] *Regina v. Cuerrier*, Supreme Court of Canada, 162 D.L.R. 4th 513, (1998).
[35] *Ibid.*, 529.   [36] *Ibid.*, 536.   [37] *Ibid.*, 563.

So setting aside issues of positive law, there are two questions we can ask about the distinction between *fraud in the factum* and *fraud in the inducement*: (1) does the distinction make sense? (2) if so, is the distinction of moral importance?

With respect to (1), it is arguable that *fraud in the factum* is mislabelled because it does not involve fraudulent consent to sexual relations. A paradigmatic case, such as **Gynecologist**, may involve fraud with respect to "insertion," but B gives *no* sort of consent to sexual intercourse. Second, it is not even clear how the factum/inducement distinction is meant to work. If, for example, we analogize **Odometer** to sexual deception, it, too, is a case of *fraud in the inducement*. B knows that she is signing an agreement to buy a *car*, say, as opposed to buying a house. Moreover, B is buying the nominal car she believes she is buying, say, as opposed to a case in which A switched cars before delivery. The not so small problem in **Odometer** is that A deceives B about the characteristics and value of the car. It seems, then, that **Odometer** could be said to involve *fraud in the factum* with respect to B's decision to buy a car with a specified mileage. Similarly we could say that B's decision in **Single** or **Vasectomy** or **HIV-L** involves a decision to have sex with a particular person with particular "objective" characteristics, and B's decision in **Affection** or **Intentions** or **Pro-Choice** involves a decision to have sex with a particular person with particular mental states.[38] Everything turns on the way in which a case is described, and there is no reason to think that the intercourse/non-intercourse distinction is the only plausible factual basis on which to distinguish one case from another.

Bracketing such definitional concerns, the more important question concerns the moral force of deception. Why assume that *fraud in the inducement* is not a serious matter? And if it is at least sometimes serious, how might we distinguish the serious cases from the less serious? We might say that *fraud in the inducement* is not typically serious because it does not typically cause great experiential harm. But that is an empirical question. It is certainly not true with respect to the potential physical consequences of deception in cases such as **Vasectomy** or **HIV-L**. And it is also not true with respect to the mental distress that may ensue from deception in cases such as **Single**, **Intentions**, **Affection**, and **Sister**. Evolutionary psychology tells its own story about such distress.

---

[38] There is a *Seinfeld* episode in which George is deceived into thinking that he is buying a car that had been owned by Jon Voigt (the actor), but was actually owned by John Voigt (a dentist). Assuming that the seller was telling a truthful deception, is this *fraud in the inducement* or *fraud in the factum*? I say the latter.

When a woman has sex under a man's pretenses of enduring affection (Darwinian translation: pretenses of commitment to ensuing offspring) and then he never calls again, the evolutionary source of her anguish is the same as for the anguish following rape: she has had sex with a man she (unconsciously) deemed unworthy of her eggs, even though in this case the deeming was done after the fact, once evidence of his unworthiness surfaced.[39]

Whether or not we accept this account of deception-induced distress, we have no reason to doubt its prevalence or intensity.

Joel Feinberg plays down the harm caused by fraud in the inducement because he wants to say (1) that a woman who consents to sexual relations because of a false promise of a cash gift has not suffered a grievous sexual harm, and (2) that (1) shows that fraud in the inducement is relatively harmless.[40] The premise (1) may or may not be right, but even so, (2) does not follow.

To see this, consider the fact structure of *Linekar*, where A falsely promises to pay B, a prostitute, a sum of money. It might be argued that B has not suffered a serious sexual harm because she does not engage in sexual relations for reasons that she would reject. She is willing to engage in sex for money, so she is short of the money, not the sex. On Feinberg's view, *Linekar* does not present a serious sexual offense because the prostitute's mental state at the time of the transaction is not affected by the fraud, and "the primary 'harm' suffered was disappointment or resentment at the loss of an anticipated benefit, more a matter for contract than criminal law."[41] Moreover, given that B values her sexual services at less than £25, at best the case seems to involve something analogous to petty theft.

I, too, have the intuition that *Linekar* does not present a serious sexual offense, but I think this analysis is insufficient. We need to distinguish between two types of cases. In one type, exemplified by *Linekar*, B views engaging in sex with A as a cost for which she expects to receive a greater benefit. In a second type, exemplified by **Affection** or **Single**, B views sexual intercourse with A as an activity in which she would like to engage.

Given this distinction, it might be argued that **Cure** is much like *Linekar*, for it is a case in which B is prepared to trade her sexuality for the cure of her illness, in which case she might be said to be short of the cure, not the sex. The difference between these two cases is a function of B's reservation price – the lowest value for which B would be willing to engage in sexual relations with A. Whereas the prostitute is willing to trade her sex for as

[39] Robert Wright, "Feminists, Meet Mr. Darwin," *The New Republic*, November 28, 1994, 42.
[40] Joel Feinberg, *Harm to Self* (New York: Oxford University Press, 1986), 300.
[41] *Ibid.*

little as £25, the victim in **Cure** would only be willing to trade her sex for something as valuable as her life. We might say similar things about a false-promise version of **Indecent Proposal**. George Bernard Shaw's (apocryphal?) quip notwithstanding, there is a qualitative (not just quantitative) difference between the motivational structure of a woman who would respond positively only to proposals for something like a million dollars and the motivational structure of a woman who would respond positively to modest offers.[42]

This suggests that we can think of a range of sexual deceptions as akin to theft of services by fraud, where the crime might range from petty theft to grand larceny. It might be objected that we cannot equate the value of life in a case such as **Cure** with the monetary value of *Linekar* or a false-promise version of **Indecent Proposal**. I prefer not to enter the thicket of debates over the incommensurability of values.[43] After all, even if we cannot equate the value of a great work of art with any amount of money, we can still say it is a crime to steal such art. So, too, for sex.

Some believe there is a danger in this approach. Robin West claims that we should not treat sexuality as something that can be traded in ways that "can't be distinguished from other trades of commercial commodities."[44] This is not a problem. First, even if we view sex as something that can be traded, there is no reason to think that we cannot distinguish between trading sexuality and trading other commodities without denying that both involve trades induced by fraud. More importantly, in arguing that we should take sexual deception more seriously, West herself embraces something close to a commodification view of sexuality. She says, for example, that the "state's refusal to criminalize nonviolent fraudulent... sex evidences the state's refusal to grant women full possessory, sovereign rights over their bodies and their labor."[45] But what do such full "possessory" rights involve if not to treat one's body as a commodity? The point remains that the commodification view provides a plausible off-the-shelf theoretical framework within which we can take sexual deception more seriously than has been our wont.

---

[42] There are several versions of the story, but the gist is that Shaw asks a woman if she would go to bed with him for (say) a million pounds. She says, "For a million pounds, yes." He then asks if she would go to bed with him for (say) five pounds. She says, "What do you think I am?" He replies, "We've already settled that, we're just haggling about the price."

[43] While these sorts of "incommensurability" claims are frequently made, they are more difficult to defend than is often supposed. See Ruth Chang's introduction to Ruth Chang (ed.), *Incommensurability, Incomparability and Practical Reason* (Cambridge, MA: Harvard University Press, 1997).

[44] Panel Discussion, "Men, Women and Rape," 63 *Fordham Law Review* 125 (1994), 155.

[45] Robin West, "A Comment on Consent, Sex, and Rape," 2 *Legal Theory* 233 (1996), 246.

I suggested that in the second type of case, B does not view sex with A as a cost which she incurs in exchange for a benefit, but as an activity in which she would like to engage or as part of a valued relationship. B's willingness to engage in sex may be based on certain assumptions about the risk to her physical person (**HIV-L** and **Vasectomy**) or about her partner's identity (**Twins**), characteristics (**Single**), or mental states (**Affection**, **Intentions**). And the character and value of the activity are undermined by A's deception. In *Linekar*, B engaged in sex for money; she just did not receive it. In **Affection**, B engages in sex as part of what she thinks is a caring relationship, but she is wrong. In **Single** or **Pro-Choice**, B may engage in sex for pleasure, but A's deception gets B to act in ways that violate important values, desires, and purposes. Indeed, both **Twins** and **Pro-Choice** raise questions about the identity of the *person* with whom B is engaged in sexual relations. These are serious matters.

The previous analysis is no doubt incomplete. The general point is that we have the conceptual resources to regard sexual deception as behavior that may undermine the transformative power of consent. How serious? I cannot avoid unhelpfully saying that the seriousness of deception will depend upon a range of empirical and moral considerations, including the intensity of the distress to which various forms of deception typically give rise and the value we place on the more abstract autonomy-based right to control the use of one's sexuality. At this point, I think it is very difficult to say just what the most defensible version of PVC_L and PVC_M would say about deception, although I do think it clear that there will be cases in which PVC_M will regard A's behavior as morally impermissible but where PVC_L will stay its hand. That said, I do not think that the traditional distinction between *fraud in the factum* and *fraud in the inducement* will prove to be of much value to that enterprise.

Directions

In considering how the principles of valid consent should handle cases involving deception, there are two strategies that enable us to make a bit more progress. One strategy looks to the principles for *legal secrets*. A second strategy asks what *general model of sexual relationships* we should apply.

By legal secrets, I have in mind the following sort of question: if A determines that B's land has oil deposits, must he so inform B if A's purchase of the land is to be valid? We could consider the issue in terms of utility or fairness. From a utilitarian perspective, it may be thought that we cannot assume that a transaction is utility enhancing if the parties do not know the values they are exchanging. On the other hand, it might be thought that if A is required to disclose such information, there will be insufficient incentive for people to make such discoveries and a full-disclosure policy will promote less utility in the long run. Fairness also cuts both ways. It might be argued that it is not fair for A to take advantage of the asymmetry of information, but it may also be thought that it is not fair to ask A to share the rewards of his discovery with B, that A deserves to take advantage of his investment in the acquisition of information.

Given these sorts of cross-cutting considerations, we are not likely to be able to solve the problem straight away. Kim Scheppele suggests that we step back from the conflict between the various approaches and adopt a contractarian or Rawlsian perspective, that we ask what sorts of rules about legal secrets would be adopted from behind a (limited) veil of ignorance. Assume that the parties do not know whether they would be in A's position of possessing important information, in which case one would benefit from rules that do not require disclosure, or in B's position, where B lacks that information and would benefit from rules that mandate disclosure.[46] Scheppele suggests that the contractors would probably not require full disclosure across the board as a prerequisite for valid consent. Instead, she thinks they would agree to rules that (1) provide relief against catastrophic losses from "secret-keeping"; (2) require disclosure of "deep secrets," where the target of the secret has no reason for imagining the existence of the information in question; and (3) ensure that when secrets are "shallow" (when the target has reason to suspect the existence of relevant information), both parties have equal access to it.[47]

It is not entirely clear whether Scheppele is right to adopt a contractarian approach to the problem or whether that approach yields these principles or whether those principles apply to sexual deception. Still, it is a plausible approach and we can try to map these principles onto the present cases. It would seem that A is required to disclose the truth in the various versions of **HIV**, if B is to be protected from "catastrophic" losses. **Sister** may involve a "deep" secret, although it may be difficult to fashion legal rules that distinguish **Sister** from cases in which requiring disclosure is not warranted. It is not clear whether or how (3) applies to these cases. Whereas the secrets are shallow in **Single**, **Intentions**, **Affection**, and **Vasectomy**, B cannot have equal access to the relevant information when it is essentially psychological.

Now we can try the second tack. There are roughly four ways to model the social relationships in which sexual deception is a problem. First, we

---

[46] Kim Scheppele, *Legal Secrets* (Chicago: University of Chicago Press, 1998).
[47] Michael Trebilcock, *The Limits of Freedom of Contract* (Cambridge, MA: Harvard University Press, 1993), 109.

could view relationships as a competitive game among adversaries in which both parties try to maximize their interests without regard for the interests of the other parties, except as required by the relevant rules. Business and athletic competition fit this model. Burger King is entitled to pursue its own interests, even if doing so hurts McDonald's. The Yankees try to defeat the Red Sox. Second, we could view relationships as a contractual interaction, where there is room for both cooperation and conflict. A home buyer is allowed to try to pay as little as possible and a seller is allowed to charge what the market will bear. The parties may agree to a transaction that is (*ex ante*) mutually beneficial, but there is a "moral division of labor" between them, as they are entitled to advance their own interests without regard for the interests of the other party. Third, a friendship model assumes that the parties have genuinely interdependent interests (each party's interests are advanced when the other party's interests are advanced) and that the parties have some moral reason to prefer the interests of a friend to their own interests when their interests are not interdependent. Fourth, on a fiduciary model, the parties' interests are *not* interdependent, but the fiduciary has a *duty* to promote the interests of the beneficiary rather than his own interests.[48]

The four models have different implications for deception. On the adversarial model, Burger King has no obligation to tell McDonald's about its new product, and may well be permitted to lie if it is asked. Yet it is not the case that "anything goes" even in competition. Many competitive games are conducted under strict rules that are externally or internally enforced. It depends on the game. In poker, it is permissible to deceive through one's voice, expressions, or mannerisms. Such actions are forbidden in contract bridge.

With respect to contractual agreements, the standard view is complex. Fraud and deliberate misrepresentation are generally prohibited, and real estate transactions often require something close to full disclosure of known defects. Interestingly, even when parties are not permitted to deceive each other about the characteristics or value of the goods or services to be exchanged, deception about one's preferences regarding the terms, conditions, and timing of a settlement is considered permissible.[49] A cannot lie as to whether the car has been in an accident, but he can say that he will not accept less than $10,000 when he knows that he would.

---

[48] "The physician must go so far as to *prefer* the patient's interests to her own, acting as the patient's selfless, scrupulous, dutiful agent"; Schuck, "Rethinking Informed Consent," 921.

[49] J. Gregory Dees and Peter C. Cramton, "Shrewd Bargaining on the Moral Frontier: Toward a Theory of Morality in Practice," 1 *Business Ethics Quarterly* 137 (1991), 149: "As it is put in comments on Rule 4.1 of the ABA Model Rules, with regard to representing clients in a negotiation with third parties, 'Under generally accepted conventions in negotiation, certain types of statements ordinarily are not taken as statements of material fact. Estimates of price or value placed on the subject of the transaction and a party's intention as to an acceptable settlement of a claim are in this category . . .'"

Friendship relations are different. In general, it is not permissible to deceive one's friends in order to advance one's own interests. That does not mean that all deception is impermissible. Friends can tell white lies in order to preserve the friendship, and while paternalistic deception is more complex, it may sometimes be permissible for one to deceive one's friend for her own good. In any case, justified deception must include appropriate regard for the interests and autonomy of one's friends.

The fiduciary model can be both more and less demanding than the friendship model. It can be less demanding if and to the extent that a fiduciary's special obligation to promote the welfare of the agent justifies deception on paternalistic grounds, a view that was once commonly accepted in American medicine and is still quite common elsewhere (for example, Japan). It can be more demanding in that a fiduciary typically has a positive duty to disclose information that is or might be of interest to the agent, and not merely an obligation not to engage in explicit deceptive behavior.[50]

Assuming that we can distinguish between relationships along these sorts of lines, we can ask an empirical and a normative question about the application of these models to sexual relationships: (1) which model best describes the way in which we actually understand sexual relations in a given sort of relationship? (2) which model should be adopted?

Consider first the empirical question. Lois Pineau says that prevailing social norms about dating imply "a relationship which is more like friendship than the cutthroat competition of opposing teams."[51] I am not so sure. I suspect that males and females see things somewhat differently. And even if the adversarial model rarely applies, the contractual model is sometimes closer to the (empirical) truth than the friendship model. On this view, it is permissible for men to try to attain sexual gratification for themselves without much regard for the woman's interests, and it is the woman's role to play "gatekeeper" if she so desires.

Empirical considerations aside, can we specify a correct normative model for relationships at their various stages? I am inclined to think that expectations count for a lot, that what might otherwise be a less preferred view of a relationship is acceptable if that view is adopted by both parties. That aside, something like the friendship model is arguably morally superior to the contract model, although the latter may have its moral uses. There may be some contexts in which men and women might enjoy and prefer

---

[50] See Schuck, "Rethinking Informed Consent," 921.
[51] Lois Pineau, "Date Rape" in Leslie Francis (ed.), *Date Rape* (University Park: Penn State University Press, 1996), 22.

a moral and legal regime in which they are entitled to pursue sexual satisfaction without much regard for the interests of the other party, where
thinking of each other as friends would impose burdens that both parties
would prefer to avoid and which would subtract from the sexual experiences they desire.[52] I believe that we should not adopt the fiduciary model
for most sexual relationships. As a general rule, the fiduciary model should
be adopted only when (1) a relationship is highly unequal in terms of the
parties' competence or information and (2) there is good reason to think
that the more powerful party can promote the weaker party's interests more
effectively than the weaker party. I do not know how often (1) is true in
sexual relations, but we have little reason to think that (2) is often true.[53] To
assume that B is not capable of promoting or protecting her own interests
is arguably demeaning to B and is an assumption that B could reasonably
reject. After all, sexual relations are a context in which people may not want
to know a range of facts about their partners, where people may want to
acquire information on a "need to know" basis.

Conclusion

I am painfully aware that I have not indicated how various forms of sexual
deception would be viewed by PVC_L and PVC_M. If I am right to argue that
the principles of valid consent are the output of moral theorizing that is
sensitive to a range of empirical considerations, a high level of definitiveness
is not on the table. But progress has been made. It is certainly difficult to
see why many forms of deception should not generally be understood as
inconsistent with PVC_M. Even here we must be careful. If we consider the
morality of deception from a contractualist perspective, and if the contractors are endowed with a sophisticated understanding of the psychology of
sexual interactions, it is also entirely possible that it would be unreasonable
to reject principles that do not allow some forms of sexual deception.

The law presents a more difficult challenge. Although the positive law
has not historically regarded most sexual deception as a legal offense, we
should not view proposals to expand the range of legal offenses to include
deception as a form of special pleading. As Schulhofer suggests, "no one
ever disparages the rules of contract law, real property, installment sales,

[52] I have in mind what Erica Jong called the "zipless fuck" in *Fear of Flying* (New York: Holt, Rinehart, and Winston, 1973).
[53] I bracket relationships with professionals, such as physicians, teachers, and lawyers, where the professional's fiduciary responsibilities may entirely preclude a sexual relationship with a patient, student, or client.

or informed medical consent as "infantilizing" the men whom these laws protect."[54] In the absence of an argument to show why sex should be treated differently, a similar although defeasible presumption should hold here as well. That said, an attempt to provide civil remedies or criminal sanctions for sexual deception is likely to encounter a range of genuine line-drawing and evidentiary difficulties. Although we should not assume that these difficulties are insurmountable, it is possible that something close to *caveat amator* will emerge as the preferred legal regime.

[54] Schulhofer, *Unwanted Sex*, 263.

CHAPTER TEN

Competence

Introduction

Even if B's consent is given completely willingly and even if there is no deception, B's token of consent is morally transformative only if she is suitably competent, that is, only if she has the requisite emotional and cognitive capacities. As with other issues that have been discussed, we can understand the need for these requirements in terms of both autonomy and utility. An agent's act is autonomous or self-directing when she is motivated by her appreciation of the *reasons* provided by her situation. One who lacks certain cognitive or emotional capacities is not capable of making decisions consistent with those reasons. She may not understand her long-term interests or have the emotional capacity to delay gratification. And she may be unable to make choices that are consistent with her deepest values or preferences because those have not been formed (in the case of children) or perhaps cannot ever be formed (in the case of the severely retarded) or because those values are distorted (false consciousness).

From a utilitarian or "mutual benefit" account of consensual transactions, we cannot assume that B's impaired consent is likely to be of benefit to B. People frequently make competent decisions that are not to their advantage *ex post*, but we can ordinarily assume that they are to their benefit *ex ante*, unless they choose to interact altruistically with others to their own detriment. But when an agent's cognitive and emotional capacities are impaired, we have less reason to assume that her decision will promote her interests.

There are several ways in which B's competence to consent might be suspect. In this chapter, I shall consider age, retardation, and false preferences. In the following chapter, I consider intoxication. One general theme emerges. I will argue that PVC_L and PVC_M do *not* require a consistent set of mental abilities. For example, if PVC_L hold that a retarded adult with a mental age of thirteen can give valid consent to sexual relations, it does not follow that PVC_L should also hold that a normal fourteen-year-old can give valid consent to sexual relations.

Age

Before the early twentieth century, Americans routinely went to work or married by age thirteen or fourteen. In effect, children were on their own before the onset of puberty. Over time, the age of puberty declined, the age of independence went up, and a majority of children remained in school through their mid-teens.[1] The statutes governing sexual relations among children and between children and adults also changed. In the antebellum South, most states treated children ten and older as adults. Unless evidence of force had been established, there was a presumption of consensual sex.[2] The "age of consent" is now somewhat higher, ranging from fourteen to eighteen. In the majority of states, the age of consent is fifteen or sixteen. If we map current teenage sexual behavior onto existing statutes, there are at least 7.5 million incidents of "statutory rape" per year (the statutes do not actually use the phrase "statutory rape").[3] Many states adopt a two-tiered approach which includes an absolute age requirement and an age-span limitation. A female under a specified age (say fourteen) may be unable to give transformative consent whatever the age of her partner. But if the female is within a certain age range (say fourteen to sixteen), she cannot give legally transformative consent to a partner who is significantly older (say five years older).[4]

Positive law aside, when and why should we regard the consent of a young person as invalid? Consider the following cases.

Chat Room. A, thirty-three, and B, fourteen, have met in an internet chat room. They agree to meet in a motel and have intercourse.

Sweethearts. A, fifteen, and B, fifteen, are high-school sweethearts. They frequently have sexual relations.

Spur Posse. A is a seventeen-year-old member of the "Spur Posses," a group in which boys compete to have intercourse with as many girls as possible. B is a fourteen-year-old high-school freshman who does not know about the group. She is flattered by A's attention.

---

[1] Stephanie Simon, "About Kids and Sex," *Los Angeles Times*, June 3, 2002, part S, page 1.
[2] Diane Miller Sommerville, " 'I Was Very Much Wounded': Rape Law, Children, and the Antebellum South" in Merril Smith (ed.), *Sex without Consent* (New York: New York University Press, 2001), 136.
[3] Michelle Oberman, "Regulating Consensual Sex with Minors: Defining a Role for Statutory Rape," 48 *Buffalo Law Review* 703 (2000), 703.
[4] This describes the Maine statute. See Richard A. Posner and Katharine B. Silbaugh, *A Guide to America's Sex Laws* (Chicago: University of Chicago Press, 1996), 53.

Child. B is an eleven-year-old girl. A is an eighteen-year-old friend of B's older brother. A says, "Did you know that it feels good if I put my penis into your vagina? Do you want to try it?" B says, "OK."

Children. A and B are eleven-year-old classmates in sixth grade. A says, "Did you know that it feels good if I put my penis in your vagina? Do you want to try it?" B says, "OK."

Sitter. B is a fourteen-year-old who baby-sits for A's child. B has an enormous adolescent crush on A (thirty-four). When A is driving B home one evening, B says "I'm a virgin, but they say older men are better. Would you teach me about sex?"

In which cases are sexual relations consistent with PVC_L or PVC_M? I am inclined to think that (barring more details) B's consent will be consistent with PVC_M only in **Sweethearts**, but that it is less clear what the law should say about **Spur Posse**, **Child**, **Children**, **Chat Room**, and **Sitter**.

It is not obvious that age, *per se*, should be a worry at all. Age may be a useful *proxy* for psychological capacities that are relevant to the validity of consent, but it is only a proxy. In principle, we could evaluate a person's competence by reference to the mental capacities that are relevant to that decision and there is no reason to think that the relevant mental capacities of many minors are lower than the mental capacities of many intoxicated or retarded adults whom we typically regard as capable of giving morally transformative consent.

The mental capacities required for competent consent are always a function of the subject of consent. We allow youngsters to make many decisions so long as they are not likely to be seriously harmful. Is it harmful for young girls to engage in what would otherwise be described and experienced as consensual sex? Some think not. It might be thought that sex by minors is no big deal, that "coitus occurring after puberty, willingly undertaken by the girl, and representing the fulfillment of a normal physiological need, probably cannot in itself harm her."[5] Nadine Taub and Elizabeth Schneider argue that statutory rape laws "exalt female chastity and reflect and reinforce archaic assumptions about the... weakness and naivete of young women."[6] And in a controversial book that appeared concurrently with the scandal involving Catholic priests, Judith Levine argues that children and teens can safely enjoy the pleasures of the body, that it is the "sexual politics of fear" that is most harmful to minors, not the sex itself.[7]

[5] "Forcible and Statutory Rape: An Exploration of the Operation and Objectives of the Consent Standard," 62 *Yale Law Journal* 55 (1952), 77.
[6] Nadine Taub and Elizabeth M. Schneider, "Women's Subordination and the Role of Law" in D. Kelly Weisberg (ed.), *Feminist Legal Theory* (Philadelphia: Temple University Press, 1993), 18.
[7] See Judith Levine, *Harmful to Minors: The Perils of Protecting Children from Sex* (Minneapolis: University of Minnesota Press, 2002).

Others disagree. Michelle Oberman has argued that sexual interactions are "by definition, serious undertakings," that are fraught with grave risks of injury and harm to the reputation and self-esteem of vulnerable girls.[8] Oberman argues that we should be more – not less – concerned to protect vulnerable girls from sexual encounters for which they are unprepared.[9] When girls consent to sex for "foolish and mistaken reasons," we should conclude that they "lack the capacity for meaningful consent."[10] Along these lines, Luisa Fuentes says "it is neither a privilege nor a right for a person under a certain age having sex with someone substantially older... Rather, it is an abuse that must be halted..."[11] But to say that such relations constitute an "abuse" is to presuppose what is at issue, namely, that such relations are typically harmful to minors, all things considered.

I begin with the worries about age spans. There are several possible justifications for statutes under which A's behavior is legal in **Sweethearts**, but is illegal in **Chat Room** and **Sitter**. We may think that large age spans present a problem of *coercion*, but on anything like the account of coercion that I have advanced, there is no reason to think that age spans have much to do with coercion, *per se*. Are cases such as **Sitter** more coercive than cases such as **Spur Posse**? As Oberman has argued, "the tendency to target cases involving overreaching or wide age ranges turns a blind eye to the coercion and abuse that may infect sexual encounters among peers."[12] Of course, even if wide age spans are not inherently coercive, they might be a good proxy for coercion that is difficult to observe directly: "it is much more efficient to police against relationships that violate a given age-span than it is to inquire into the quality of consent given by the individual participants."[13] Even if **Sitter** is no *more* coercive than **Spur Posse**, it is possible that wide age spans are more *likely* to be coercive, that the proportion of peer relationships that are problematic on these grounds is lower than the proportion of wide-age-span relationships. This may or may not be so. But, absent evidence about the way in which age spans are, in fact, a good proxy for coercion, this argument provides little support for the age-span approach.

Bracketing worries about coercion, it may be argued that young females are more competent to navigate the world of adolescent/adolescent

---

[8] Oberman, "Regulating Consensual Sex with Minors," 783.

[9] Michelle Oberman, "Turning Girls into Women: Re-evaluating Modern Statutory Rape Law," 85 *Journal of Criminal Law and Criminology* 15 (1994), 42.

[10] *Ibid.*, 67.

[11] Luisa A. Fuentes, "The 14th Amendment and Sexual Consent: Statutory Rape and Judiciary Progeny," 16 *Women's Rights Law Reporter* 139 (1994), 151–52. Fuentes also argues against gender-specific statutory-rape law.

[12] Oberman, "Regulating Consensual Sex with Minors," 751.   [13] *Ibid.*, 770.

relationships than the world of adolescent/adult relationships. Although I have not seen systematic evidence along these lines, it is possible that the decision-making of young females is more likely to be distorted by transference or respect for authority or status seeking when they are contemplating relationships with older males, or that the risks consequent to adolescent/adolescent relationships are small compared with adolescent/adult relationships.

Even if large age spans do not typically compromise the *competence* of a minor to consent to sexual relations, it might be argued that such relationships are highly *exploitative* and should be prohibited on that ground alone. I have argued elsewhere that we can and should distinguish exploitative relations that are nonconsensual and harmful from exploitative relations that are consensual and beneficial to the exploitee as well as the exploiter.[14] If, as I think, there may be relationships that would *otherwise* meet the criteria of PVC_L or PVC_M, the question then becomes whether PVC_L or PVC_M should be adjusted to render the relationships impermissible because they are exploitative.

Here we encounter several issues. First, it is not clear by what criteria a relationship should be regarded as exploitative. It is often argued that relationships are exploitative when the exploiter gains much more than the exploitee. As I suggested in chapter eight, this account is mistaken, at least if we measure the parties' gains by the marginal utility they receive from the transaction.

Second, by whatever account of exploitation is involved, I suspect that sexual relationships between "unequals" are often less exploitative than is commonly thought. If one considers the psychic rewards of a relationship, the younger female typically gains more than her partner. Judith Levine suggests that teenagers frequently seek out sex with older men because they make them feel "sexy and grown up, protected and special," not to mention, she says, that the sex itself may be better.[15] Third, to the extent that the relationship is exploitative because the parties begin from a base of social and economic inequality, the significance of those inequalities may be reduced – not magnified – when the parties confront each other as naked bodies and as dispensers and recipients of sexual pleasure.

Fourth, even if we assume that there is something exploitative and morally problematic about a sexual relationship between an older man and a minor female, it is not clear that exploitation, by itself, is reason

---

[14] See *Exploitation* (Princeton: Princeton University Press, 1996), chapter 1.
[15] As quoted in Robert Worth, "Renegade View on Child Sex Causes a Storm," *New York Times*, April 13, 2002, section B, page 7. See Judith Levine, *Harmful to Minors*.

to prohibit a relationship if it is *otherwise* consensual and not harmful. In effect, B might say: "You say that A is exploiting me. Even if you are right, I know what I'm doing and I prefer to be exploited by A than not to have a relationship with him at all." This is a strong argument, and it requires us to revisit the competency requirements for valid consent.

It is difficult to specify what minors must know if they are to be able to give transformative consent. It is easier to evaluate the expected benefits and harms of youthful sexual relationships and then reason backward to the competence to consent. If most minors of a certain age are harmed by sexual activity, however willingly they participate at the time, then that is good reason to think that they do not have the competence to consent to such activity. As I noted above, however, there is considerable controversy with respect to the harmfulness of youthful sex. Moreover, at least some of the harm is "socially constructed." Michelle Oberman claims that underage sex is typically harmful because the females experience a "diminished sense of self and a damaged reputation," but this would not be so if we did not *think* that early sexual relations were improper.[16] Of course, young girls may be biologically disposed to experience considerable psychological distress from early sexual relations. And even if the harm experienced by minors were largely socially constructed, our views as to what is morally and legally impermissible would have to be at least somewhat responsive to the world as it is. If early sexual relations typically give rise to socially constructed harm in this society, then *we* have a reason to be concerned about such harms even if some other societies do not.

Of course sex is not just about sex. It is also about the risk of pregnancy and disease. It is arguable that teenage pregnancy is bad for the mothers, for the offspring, and for society. Here I consider only the first case. I do not think that teenage pregnancy can be bad for the offspring if the offspring have lives worth living.[17] Moreover, even if teenage pregnancy can be bad for the offspring, this is not a reason to question the competence of the mother's consent unless its bad effect on the offspring were also bad for the mothers. And this might not be so. Similarly, while society might be justified in attempting to reduce adolescent teenage pregnancy because it imposes harms on society, that is not a reason to regard the consent as invalid between the parties. Still, there is good reason to think that adolescent girls

---

[16] Oberman, "Turning Girls into Women," 67.
[17] Here I am persuaded by Derek Parfit's argument. If the child has a "life that is worth living," then it is hard to see how the child is harmed by being born, even if such children have lives that go less well than those of children born to older women. See *Reasons and Persons* (Oxford: Clarendon Press, 1984), chapter 15.

may not have the maturity of judgment to anticipate the long-term negative effect of early sex on their own lives. So even if the expected experience of sex itself is likely to be benign, the long-term consequences may be harmful.

Assume, arguendo, that some thirteen- to fifteen-year-old females have the competence to give valid consent and some do not, that sexual activity is likely to be harmless (all things considered) to some but harmful (all things considered) to others. Should we opt for an individualized approach that would assess the validity of consent on a case by case basis or should we opt for the sort of *per se* rule that we see in most states? There are two arguments for an individualized approach. First, it is argued that an "inflexible test of the capacity to understand" is too inclusive, that we should treat a minor's alleged incompetence to consent as a presumption that is rebuttable by evidence that the minor female "understood the significance of the act in question."[18] It has also been argued that a *per se* rule would involve "punishing many blameless men" if they had sexual relations with minors who had the requisite capacities and who did unambiguously token consent.[19] This objection fails. It begs the question to assume that a man who has sexual relations with a minor in violation of a *per se* rule is blameless just because his behavior would have been blameless in the absence of a rule. We do not say that a bartender is blameless for serving liquor to a minor because the minor happens to have the maturity to drink responsibly. Second, if we are concerned to avoid the punishment of blameless men, a *per se* rule enables a male to safely predict that he will not be innocently convicted if he simply refrains from sexual relations as required by the rule.

Oberman objects to a *per se* rule on the grounds that it would exclude too many cases, that "a binary division between consensual sex and rape is a false dichotomy."[20] It is unfortunate, she says, that the law focuses on "readily identified" factors such as age, rather than on the myriad "pressures and constraints that intrude on autonomous choice."[21] Binary divisions and false dichotomies may be severely underrated. In the absence of clear markers of coercion, deception, and incompetence of the sort that have been considered above, I simply do not see how the law could sensibly consider the range of subtle pressures and constraints that intrude on a minor's choices even when those choices give rise to "devastatingly harmful interactions."[22] Oberman is also concerned that a *per se* rule that treats a minor's consent to sexual relations as invalid might have untoward effects on abortion rights: "laws which treat minors as insufficiently mature to

[18] "Forcible and Statutory Rape," 56.   [19] *Ibid.*
[20] Oberman, "Turning Girls into Women," 72.   [21] *Ibid.*, 42.   [22] *Ibid.*, 72.

consent to sex might easily become ammunition for those wishing to restrict minors' access to reproductive health care."[23] She is right to be concerned. It is not easy to say why a fourteen-year-old should be regarded as sufficiently mature to make her own decision about an abortion, but not sufficiently mature to choose to have sexual relations.

Although I am not concerned here to defend this combination of policies, my approach to PVC shows why it is plausible. Consider the distinction between consent and culpability. We may think that a minor does not have the capacity to consent to some transaction, but that she can be held responsible for violating the law or a moral principle. Without seeking to identify the precise capacities at issue, valid consent may require the capacity to understand and act upon one's long-term interests, whereas culpability may require only the capacity to understand and follow a law or principle. And these are different capacities. Similarly, we can argue that the capacities required to make a reasonable decision whether to engage in sex are not identical to the capacities required to make a reasonable decision whether to have an abortion. To paraphrase Tip O'Neill, all competence is local. First, there are practical considerations. It is certainly more feasible to conduct "judicial bypass hearings" that evaluate a minor's ability to consent to an abortion on an individual basis than with respect to sexual relations. Second, the "positive autonomy" costs are different. To refuse to treat a minor's consent to sexual relations as valid is to require her to abstain from sexual relations. To refuse to treat a minor's consent to abortion as valid is, in effect, to require her to carry a fetus to term or to seek her parents' permission or to go to court. So it is arguable that we have more reason to err on the side of positive autonomy with respect to abortion than with respect to sex. Third, minors may make better decisions about abortion than sex. A minor may be more likely to be harmed by a decision to have sex than a decision to have an abortion, given that she is already pregnant.

In the final analysis, it is largely an empirical question as to what the best versions of PVC_L and PVC_M will say with respect to sex by minors. Although I confess to great uncertainty about what rules might make the most sense here, I am quite confident that an individualized approach should be rejected. It is not unduly pessimistic to think it would be a disaster to adopt a legal framework that said, "We'll decide whether the pressures and constraints on the alleged victim were sufficient to intrude on autonomous choice and, if so, then we'll hold the alleged perpetrator responsible for engaging in nonconsensual relations."

[23] *Ibid.,* 75.

Retardation

Teresa was sixteen years old, enrolled in the eighth grade. She was diagnosed as retarded when she was three, and had an IQ of 59. She met Adkins, who was twenty-seven, in a local mall, where they exchanged telephone numbers. Teresa's mother subsequently overheard a telephone conversation between Adkins and Teresa. She took the phone and told Adkins that Teresa was retarded and that he should leave her alone. Teresa phoned Adkins the next day and asked him to meet her at a store. They met, went to Adkins's home, had intercourse twice, ate dinner, watched television, and fell asleep. They were discovered when Teresa's mother notified police that her daughter was missing.[24] Adkins was convicted for having sexual relations with a person who has a mental impairment that prevents the impaired person from "understanding the nature or consequences of the sexual act ... and about which the accused should have known."[25]

Leslie was a seventeen-year-old female with an IQ of 49. She was lured into a basement along with thirteen high-school males, most of whom were popular athletes at an affluent suburban high school in Glen Ridge, New Jersey. Leslie performed oral sex on at least one male. A baseball bat and broomstick were inserted into her vagina while the other boys watched. At trial, a defendant's lawyer asked Leslie whether she had been threatened.

LESLIE: No, they just did it.
LAWYER: Nobody said ... you have to do this?
LESLIE: They said they were going to tell my mother.[26]

Several boys were convicted for aggravated sexual assault, for having committed an act of sexual penetration when "the victim is one whom the actor knew or should have known was physically helpless, mentally defective or mentally incapacitated."[27] I am not interested here in whether Adkins or the Glen Ridge boys should have been convicted under the relevant statutes. I cite these examples because they frame the question of how PVC_L and PVC_M should regard the consent of the mentally retarded.

It is important to distinguish between problems of coercion and problems of competence. There is no evidence that the Glen Ridge boys used physical

[24] *Adkins v. Virginia*, 20 Va. App 332, 457 S.E. 2d 382 (1995).
[25] See "Developments in Mental Health Law," Institute of Law, Psychiatry and Public Policy, University of Virginia, http://www.ilppp.virginia.edu/DMHL/Issues/diminishedv15n1.html. The conviction was overturned on appeal.
[26] See Bernard Lefkowitz, *Our Guys: The Glen Ridge Rape and the Secret Life of the Perfect Suburb* (Berkeley: University of California Press, 1997), 353.
[27] N.J.S.A. 2C:14–2a(5)(a) and (b). See *New Jersey v. Scherzer*, 301 N.J. Super. 363; 694 A.2d 196 (1997).

force or threats beyond the threat to tell Leslie's mother. On the other hand, we could say that A uses something like coercion if he exerts pressures that he knows or should know that B will find it difficult to resist. Many retarded persons are over-compliant, and, importantly, this was *known* to be so of Leslie. An acquaintance testified that Leslie would "do anything that she's asked to do," that she had never heard her say no to any request.[28] Leslie was a very good softball pitcher. Just before the last inning in one game, Gail King, a player on the opposing team asks in a sugar-coated voice: "Les, won't you please, please let me hit one? If you let me hit it, I'll be your best friend forever."[29] Leslie did. Gail did. Gail was not. By contrast, *Adkins* involved a question of competence. There was not a hint of coercion. And it is the competence question that I want to pursue. Consider these cases.

Retardation. A is a somewhat "nerdy" seventeen-year-old virgin who would like to have his first time with someone non-threatening. He is friendly with B, a nineteen-year-old neighbor, who is moderately retarded. A says, "Do you want to see what it's like?" B responds, "OK, if you want to, but don't tell my mother."
Friends. A and B are both moderately retarded and like each other. A proposes that they have intercourse.
Abuse. A is captain of the high-school football team. B is eighteen, has an IQ of 70, and reveres A. A says, "You'll be my girl friend if we have sex and let my buddies watch." B says, "Really?" A says, "Really." B says, "OK."

Should we regard B's consent as valid in these cases? If retarded females typically end up feeling very hurt in such cases because they do not understand how sex will affect them, then there would be reason to regard their consent as invalid. But suppose that most retarded females (at a certain level of retardation) understand the physiology of sexual relationships, that they typically enjoy the sexual encounters which they *experience* as consensual, and that *they* do not typically regret their sexual encounters or undergo aversive psychological effects that are caused by these encounters. We might have reason to protect them from disease and unwanted pregnancy (for their own sake). We might also worry about the social costs resulting from disease, pregnancy, and offspring. But those concerns are external to the reasons to which the principles of valid consent should be sensitive. If allowing retarded females to engage in sexual relations is not bad for *them*, we should expect PVC to regard their consent as valid.

To put the previous point in now familiar terms, we have reason to be concerned to facilitate the positive autonomy of the retarded as well as to protect their negative autonomy. If we say that minors are unable to give

---

[28] *Ibid.*, 212.   [29] Lefkowitz, *Our Guys*, 85.

transformative consent while they are minors, we do not preclude sexual experience over the course of their lives. Minors get older. By contrast, to say that retarded females cannot give transformative consent is to deny them permanently the opportunity to legitimately experience intimacy and sexual pleasure.[30] The cost of zealously protecting their negative autonomy is very high indeed.

Suppose we are sympathetic with an account of PVC_L and PVC_M that leans toward treating a retarded woman's consent as valid. Would PVC_L or PVC_M draw a distinction between **Retardation** and **Friends** or between either of these cases and **Abuse**? In **Retardation**, it is arguable that a non-retarded male is "taking advantage" of the retarded woman, whereas **Friends** contains no hint of exploitation, advantage-taking, or inequality. Moreover, there is no reason to think that A is more responsible for his behavior than is B. That said, I am not sure that we would want to draw a sharp distinction between **Friends** and **Retardation**. We do not want to say that retarded persons are only permitted to have sexual relations with other retarded persons or, unlike non-retarded persons, that the retarded are only permitted to have sexual relations in the context of an enduring relationship.

Although **Abuse** is probably the easiest case, it presents an interesting theoretical problem. We worry about the sexual abuse of minors primarily because we think that the victims are likely to suffer long-term psychological damage, even if they are not hurt by the encounter when it occurs. But suppose, as a thought experiment, that some retarded persons would never come to experience any aversive psychological effects precisely because their capacities will not develop. Bracketing issues such as pregnancy and disease, what *we* call abuse remains a relatively benign event for *them*. There are at least three positions we could adopt: (1) such encounters are not bad for them and we should regard their consent as valid; (2) such encounters are not bad for them but their consent is not valid because they lack the requisite capacities; (3) such encounters are objectively bad for them even though they do not generate any aversive experience. (1) is implausible because the lack of capacities that immunize the victims from an aversive experience also negate their capacity to give transformative consent. I believe that (2) and (3) are both plausible. As I have noted, I have the common

---

[30] In *Adkins v. Virginia*, the court was concerned that statutes designed to protect the retarded "not be interpreted or applied in a manner that . . . would prohibit all mentally impaired or retarded persons from engaging in consensual sexual intercourse without having their partners commit a felony"; 343. Interestingly, some advocates for the mentally retarded were concerned that a guilty verdict in the Glen Ridge case might imply that all retarded citizens were incapable of consenting to sex.

intuition (among philosophers) that these encounters must be objectively bad for B even if B experiences them as good, but I think this view is more difficult to defend than is often supposed. Fortunately, because (2) and (3) are extensionally equivalent with regard to the impermissibility of A's behavior, it is not necessary to resolve that issue here.

The issue of consent by the retarded highlights another sense in which competence is local. It might seem strange that we would consider allowing retarded females to consent to sexual relations, but not allow them to make decisions about medical treatment, schooling, and finances. It might be thought that if they are not competent to make decisions about the latter, then they are arguably not competent to make decisions about something as important as sexual relations. But, as I have argued, the relevant cognitive capacities are decision specific. A retarded person may well understand what she needs to understand about sexual relations without being able to understand what she needs to understand about financial or medical matters. In addition, the validity of a person's consent rests, in part, on a comparative evaluation of who is best positioned to make decisions. Surrogate decision-makers may be better positioned to make positive decisions with respect to medical treatment and finances, but not with respect to sexual relations. Whereas it may be reasonable to empower a surrogate to authorize a medical procedure for B without a consent token from B, we cannot imagine authorizing A to engage in sexual relations with B without at least a token of consent.

False preferences

There are two issues that might be raised under the rubric of false consciousness. Women may believe that they have consented to sex when they have not, for example, because they wrongly accept the view that women do not consent only if they exhibit "utmost resistance" to the use of physical force.[31] This is an important issue, but it is not my present concern. Here I focus on the argument that what we would otherwise consider to be a clear case of valid consent is defective because women are socialized to consent to sex that they do not enjoy or enjoy what they should not enjoy. We can ask two questions here: (1) is it possible that women consent to sexual relations that do not serve their deepest interests? (2) if so, is their consent morally transformative? The general thrust of my view is to answer these questions, yes, yes.

---

[31] See the discussion of Robin Warshaw's study above, p. 90.

What would it mean to say that B's consent stems from false preferences? Preferences can be false in terms of their *substance* and their *authenticity*. To say that a preference is substantively false is to say that what B believes is good for B is not "really" good for B.[32] To say that B's preferences are inauthentic is to say that B's preferences are not really *B's* preferences. These two forms of false preference are not identical. B could autonomously and authentically prefer what is bad for her, and she could non-autonomously and non-authentically prefer what is good for her.

B's preferences can be *substantively* false in two ways. In the first and relatively uncontroversial case, B's false preferences concern means and facts rather than ends and values, as when B wants to use laetrile because she wants to be cured of cancer and falsely believes that laetrile will provide that cure. We all have preferences that are false in this way. The second and more controversial case concerns values and ends. It is difficult to cite non-question-begging examples of such mistakes because many apparent ends can be recast as means to more basic ends. Suppose that B wants cosmetic surgery. We may say that she has a "false preference" about values or ends, namely, that she values her appearance more than she should. But we might also say that her false preference concerns means or facts. B wants to be happy, but is simply mistaken about the means to that end (of course, it is possible that cosmetic surgery does bring happiness to B, in which case her preference would not be false for that reason). Suppose, however, that B believes that she owes it to her husband to look more youthful. Here her desire for surgery is arguably based on a false view regarding what she should do for her husband. We may think that some ends are objectively good and bad for people and that some ways of balancing (otherwise) legitimate ends (such as health, beauty, and the interests of others) are unreasonable.

Setting aside the substance of B's preferences, it may be argued that what appear to be B's preferences are not really *her* preferences or, perhaps, are not her *autonomous* preferences. There are two general ways in which the autonomy of one's preferences might be questioned. One view of autonomous preferences focuses on their internal structure or psychological prerequisites. Some argue that an agent's first-order or occurrent preferences are autonomous only if they are compatible with the agent's higher-order preferences.[33] On this view, B's desire to smoke a cigarette is not autonomous if it does not accord with her higher-order desire not to

---

[32] Jon Elster, *Sour Grapes* (Cambridge: Cambridge University Press, 1983), 22.
[33] See, for example, the classic article by Harry Frankfurt, "Freedom of the Will and the Concept of a Person," 68 *The Journal of Philosophy* 5 (1971).

smoke. On another structural view, B's preferences are autonomous only if they have survived rational or critical reflection.[34] A third structural view focuses on the inputs to B's psychic economy. Jon Elster has argued that both adaptive and counter-adaptive preferences are not fully autonomous, because B's preferences are largely driven by what *others* have or prefer, as when B prefers the "sour grapes" to the sweeter variety that others are eating, because she adjusts her preferences to avoid feeling frustrated or less well off than others.

A second view on the autonomy or authenticity of preferences focuses on the historical or external conditions under which they were formed. It could be argued that B's preferences are not authentic if she does not have an adequate array of options from which to choose, such as when Amish children are raised to know of only one way of life.[35] And even if a range of options is in principle available, one's preferences for some such options are not authentic if one has been "socialized" into having one's specific preferences (as contrasted with some unspecified but supposedly authenticity-compatible process of preference acquisition).

This is a large topic. Without considering the merits of these various claims, let us assume, arguendo, that B's preferences can be false in terms of their substance or their authenticity (or autonomy). With respect to sexual relations, let us say that B's consent is rooted in false preferences if (1) she inappropriately sacrifices her interests for the sake of others *or* (2) her interests are excessively identified with the interests of others *or* (3) her preferences are not authentic or autonomous. What follows? Joan McGregor says that if a woman's choices fail to promote her good, it is evidence that she is choosing without her "full faculties," and that her consent is not legitimate.[36] Strictly interpreted, this cannot be right unless one defines "one's own good" as including everything that it is good or reasonable to do. Morality often requires us to sacrifice our own good for the good of others. And what should we say about religious beliefs? It is entirely possible that some people make religiously motivated "sacrifices" because they falsely believe that there is such a thing as salvation or that such acts will increase the probability of salvation. In addition, these religious beliefs may be inauthentic or non-autonomous because they were acquired

---

[34] This line of argument is more plausible than one that turns on socialization. On this view, B's beliefs may be autonomous if B has the capacity to and actually does reflect upon them, whether or not B was socialized into having those beliefs in the first place.

[35] See, for example, Joseph Raz, *The Morality of Freedom* (Oxford: Clarendon Press, 1986), 372.

[36] Joan McGregor, "Force, Consent, and the Reasonable Woman" in Jules Coleman and Allen Buchanan (eds.), *In Harm's Way* (Cambridge: Cambridge University Press, 1994), 244–45.

under conditions of intense indoctrination or because the believers lack the critical capacity to reflect upon these beliefs. But, and crudely put, so what? To take freedom of religion seriously is to allow people to act on their religious beliefs even when the beliefs are false and their actions do not serve their interests. And if people should be free to make decisions based on false religious beliefs, it would seem that a similar claim can be made about false sexual beliefs or preferences.

I have argued that the criteria for competence required by principles of valid consent are likely to be *comparative*. We need not assume that B has the ability to make every decision correctly or to make every decision better than anyone else. We need only assume that she is generally in a better position than others to make such decisions.[37] And this will often be true even if some of her preferences are false. Here we have a massive "gate keeper" problem. If we are going to prohibit people from giving transformative consent that is rooted in false beliefs and preferences, then "who – *exactly* who – is going to make these choices for them?"[38] Here we can distinguish between PVC_M and PVC_L. As a moral matter, we can expect A to exercise restraint where A has reason to believe that B is particularly vulnerable, where she has mistaken expectations about a relationship, or is bowing to peer pressure. As a moral matter about the law, however, it is a different story. Unlike A, who has local knowledge about the quality of B's beliefs and preferences, the state is not well positioned to evaluate the quality of B's preferences or beliefs.

From this perspective, we can partially resolve what Margaret Radin takes to be a deep tension for feminists. On the one hand, feminists want to treat "all of women's subjective experience with acceptance and respect." On the other hand, says Radin, in order to make progress toward "a so-cial conception of sexuality that is less male dominated," feminists must view "the male-dominated experiences" in which women now take pleasure with "critical suspicion."[39] As a theoretical matter, we can refuse "to accept women's descriptions of their own experience at face value," while treating their preferences with acceptance and respect as a practical matter.[40] We can view a woman's experience with critical suspicion and still regard her consent as morally transformative.

---

[37] Randy E. Barnett, "The Sound of Silence: Default Rules and Contractual Consent," 78 *Virginia Law Review* 821 (1992), 839.

[38] Donald Dripps, "For a Negative, Normative Model of Consent, with a Comment on Preference-Skepticism," 2 *Legal Theory* 113 (1996), 120.

[39] Margaret Radin, *Contested Commodities* (Cambridge, MA: Harvard University Press, 1996), 129.

[40] Tracy E. Higgins, "Democracy and Feminism," 110 *Harvard Law Review* 1657 (1997), 1690.

Consider some cases.

Groupie. B, a devoted eighteen-year-old fan of A's rock band, gladly accepts A's proposal to have intercourse.

Psychotherapist. B is undergoing psychotherapy with A. Under the grip of "transference" and strongly attracted to A, she proposes that they have sexual relations. A accepts.

Submissive. B suffers from extremely low self-esteem. She is and is known to be unwilling ever to say "no" to anyone. A tells B he would like to have sex with her. Although B does not desire sexual relations with A, she says "OK."

Former Professor. B has just graduated from college. A is a former professor on whom she had an enormous crush. A asks B for a date. B is flattered, thrilled, and excited. A proposes that they have intercourse. B enthusiastically agrees.

Dutiful. A and B have been married for some years. B frequently agrees to sexual relations because she has been taught that it is a wife's duty to satisfy her husband's sexual desires, although she often does not enjoy it.

Caring. A and B have been married for some years. B finds such great pleasure and fulfillment in her role as wife and mother that she often does not distinguish between her interests and the interests of her family. B agrees to sexual relations because she cares for her husband and gets emotional fulfillment from the relationship, although she does not get much erotic pleasure.

I believe that B's preferences could reasonably be viewed with critical suspicion in all of these cases, and that PVC_M might require A to exercise restraint in some. On the other hand, it is arguable that **Psychotherapist** is the only case in which we should treat B's consent as violating PVC_L.

Why is **Psychotherapist** special? I see no reason to think that a woman's consent to sexual relations with her psychotherapist is *always* seriously distorted or that such relations are *always* harmful to patients. But the risks are high. To treat a patient's consent as transformative places a potentially positive therapeutic relationship in danger and is quite likely to exacerbate the patient's difficulties. In addition, because psychotherapists often experience counter-transference or other distortions of judgment, they are not well positioned to determine when a sexual relationship is likely to be benign. Given such risks, it may be wrong for them to agree to a relationship even if it would not be harmful in the particular case. Moreover, even when it is clear to the parties that the relationship will not be harmful, such relationships may tend to undermine confidence in the profession. For these sorts of reasons, it is probably best to adopt a *per se* rule that treats all patient consent to sexual relations as invalid.[41]

---

[41] See my discussion of sexual exploitation in psychotherapy in *Exploitation*, chapter 6.

Something *like* the distorted preferences of a psychotherapy patient may occur in **Groupie**, **Former Professor**, and **Submissive**. In the first two cases, B may be infatuated with A and may well end up quite hurt. She may falsely believe that he is genuinely interested in her or may falsely believe that she does not care whether he is interested. In **Submissive**, B is so reluctant to displease anyone that she agrees to relationships that may lead to disease or pregnancy or psychological distress. But while I am prepared to view B's preferences with critical suspicion in these cases, what is A to do? What are we to do? It is wrong for A to exploit B's desire or willingness to have sexual relations if he believes (or should believe) that such relations are likely to be hurtful to B.[42] But we have no reliable way to determine when B's preferences are sufficiently defective to justify intervention.

B's consent in **Dutiful** and **Caring** might also be viewed with suspicion. The preference for altruism is not necessarily false, but it could be false in a particular case.[43] B's moral belief in **Dutiful** is false because women have no such duty to their husbands and her belief is arguably inauthentic, given the process by which it was acquired. **Caring** is more difficult. Unlike **Dutiful**, where B frequently participates in sexual relations that she does not enjoy, B's experience of sexual relations in **Caring** is positive if not exciting. Moreover, B does not feel that she is sacrificing her interests to those of her husband. From her perspective, their interests are too intertwined to make that possible. Some may think that **Caring** reflects an attractive ideal of marriage. Others may think that B's preferences evince a failure to respect her own value and importance as an autonomous person.[44] Still, even if B's preferences were false in these cases, it would be preposterous to think that B's consent should not be regarded as legally transformative.

---

[42] Is this to say that A should refuse to have sexual relations with B on paternalistic grounds? Perhaps. But A is not B's agent. And A can reasonably refuse to engage in actions that B desires on the ground that he does not wish to be the cause of harm.

[43] I do not deny that altruism may be good for the person who acts altruistically. Volunteer workers often say "I get more out of it than they do," and I see no reason to disbelieve them. Still, we should not assume that one who is acting altruistically is acting unreasonably when altruism is not good for her.

[44] Jean Hampton, "Two Faces of Contractarian Thought" in Peter Vallentyne (ed.), *Contractarianism and Rational Choice* (New York: Cambridge University Press, 1991), 54. Also see Thomas Hill, Jr., "Servility and Self-Respect" in Richard Wasserstrom (ed.), *Today's Moral Problems* (New York: Macmillan Co., 1979). I have relied heavily on George Sher's discussion of these issues in "Our Preferences, Ourselves," 12 *Philosophy & Public Affairs* 34 (1983).

CHAPTER ELEVEN

Intoxication

In this chapter I pursue a different issue of competence: is it permissible for a male to have sexual relations with a woman who unambiguously tokens consent while voluntarily intoxicated? The issue is not without its practical importance. The consumption of drugs and alcohol is implicated in many cases of "date rape." Although there is nothing approaching a token of consent in many such cases, others involve what I call intoxicated consent and raise the question as to how PVC would regard such consent.

To facilitate the analysis, I distinguish between five claims. First, it may be argued that B's intoxicated consent does not render it permissible for A to have sexual relations with B even if B's intoxication is self-induced. Call this the *impermissibility claim*. On my stipulative definition, the impermissibility claim represents our all-things-considered judgment about the content of the principles of valid consent with respect to intoxicated consent. Second, it may be argued that if a woman tokens consent while she is intoxicated, her consent is *necessarily* invalid because intoxication undermines the capacity requirements of valid consent. On this view, intoxication entails invalidity (and impermissibility).[1] Call this the *intoxication claim*. Third, it may be argued that if B's intoxication is itself voluntary or self-induced, then we should treat B as responsible for her intoxicated behavior. Call this the *responsibility claim*. By itself, the responsibility claim says little about the validity of B's consent. It is a general claim about one's responsibility for one's intoxicated behavior. The fourth claim extends the responsibility claim to consent. It might be argued that if a woman is responsible for her intoxicated behavior, it follows that her intoxicated consent must be treated as valid. Call this the *responsibility-entails-validity claim*.

---

[1] According to Joan McGregor, the fact that a woman "was drunk or high on drugs should naturally lead to the conclusion that she was not consenting, as she was incapable of voluntary consent"; "Force, Consent, and the Reasonable Woman" in Jules Coleman and Allen Buchanan (eds.), *In Harm's Way* (Cambridge: Cambridge University Press, 1994), 244–45. Laurence Thomas says "it is axiomatic that consent is rendered void if obtained from a person while [s]he was in . . . an utterly inebriated state"; "Sexual Desire, Moral Choice, and Human Ends," 33 *Journal of Social Philosophy* 178 (2002), 183.

If we accept the responsibility claim *and* the responsibility-entails-validity claim, it follows that the principles of valid consent must treat B's intoxicated consent as valid, that is, we must say that it is permissible for A to have sexual relations with B if B consents while voluntarily intoxicated. At the same time, one might accept the responsibility claim without accepting the responsibility-entails-validity claim, in which case one could argue that it is not permissible for A to have sexual relations with B if B consents while voluntarily intoxicated even though B is responsible for her behavior. Fifth, some defend the responsibility-entails-validity claim and oppose the impermissibility claim by drawing an analogy between intoxicated consent and intoxicated criminal behavior. On this view, if people should be held responsible for wrongful acts committed while intoxicated, then we must also treat B's consent as valid. Call this the *consistency claim.*

I lay out these claims in this way because some people think that the right view can be settled by a form of moral logic, that if we accept certain premises, then it inevitably follows that we must either accept or reject the impermissibility claim. I disagree. I will argue that the question whether we should accept or reject the impermissibility claim is not *entailed* by the agent's intoxication or her responsibility for her intoxication or by a (correct) willingness to hold people responsible for wrongful acts committed while intoxicated. In other words, in deciding whether we should ultimately accept or reject the impermissibility claim, I shall argue that we should reject the intoxication claim, the responsibility-entails-validity claim, and the consistency claim. There are no entailments here. Rather, whether PVC_L or PVC_M would regard B's intoxicated consent as valid will be resolved by substantive moral argument informed by empirical investigation. We must decide whether the balance of moral reasons favors a moral, institutional, or legal regime that regards B's intoxicated consent as valid or invalid. We have the space to go in either direction.

As I indicated at the outset, I shall assume that B gives an unambiguous (verbal or behavioral) token of consent. I set aside those cases in which B consumes or ingests a substance which renders her unconscious or semi-conscious, as in the following (not so hypothetical) cases.

Rohypnol. A slips some Rohypnol, the date-rape drug, into B's drink. B passes out.
Passed Out. B attends a fraternity party where she consumes a large amount of beer. She passes out.
Stupor. A and B have dated, but B has rebuffed A's advances. On this occasion, B is severely intoxicated, although she has not passed out. In response to A's advances, B says nothing when A removes her clothes, but is clearly too weak to resist.
Anesthesia. A, a dentist, penetrates B while she is unconscious from anesthesia.

I also mostly set aside a related issue. People can indicate their intention to engage in sexual relations before they become intoxicated (as illustrated by the lyrics to a Jimmy Buffet song, "Why don't we get drunk and screw?"). Consider these cases.

Rohypnol Conception. A and B are good friends. B wishes to become pregnant. She wants A to father her child, but does not want to experience intercourse with A. She tells A that she intends to take Rohypnol and that he should have intercourse with her while she is unconscious.

Partying. A and B have dated, but have not had sex. A says, "Is tonight the night?" B says, "Yeah, but let's have a few drinks first." Later on, B gets quite high and responds positively to A's advances.

I believe that B can give effective *ex ante* consent in **Rohypnol Conception**, and, by implication, in a case such as **Partying**, where B gives sober *ex ante* consent to sexual relations but intoxicated consent at the time of sexual relations. I suppose it might be argued that PVC requires that B give sober consent immediately preceding intercourse. I disagree. In any case, by confining the discussion to cases in which B's only consent is given while intoxicated, I shall bracket this issue as well.

To fix ideas, consider *Brown*.[2] Sara (a pseudonym), a Brown University freshman, consumes approximately ten shots of vodka in her dormitory room one Saturday night. She walks a few blocks to a Brown crew party, then to a fraternity house to see someone she had been dating. Adam Lack finds Sara in a friend's room lying next to some vomit. Adam asks Sara if she wants a drink of water. Sara says yes. Adam gets her some water. They talk. Adam asks Sara if she wants to go to his room. She says yes. Sara follows Adam to his room without assistance, kisses him and begins to undress him. Sara asks Adam if he has a condom. He says yes. They have sex. They talk, smoke cigarettes, and go to sleep. In the morning, Adam asks Sara for her phone number, which she provides. "It took a while for it to actually set in," Sara says. "When I got home, I wasn't that upset. The more I thought about it, the more upset I got." Three weeks later, and after Sara sees a "women's peer counselor" in her dormitory, Sara brings charges against Adam Lack. According to the Brown University Code of Student Conduct, one commits an offense when one has sexual relations with another who has a "mental or physical incapacity or impairment of which the offending student was aware or should have been aware."

---

[2] This account is based on an article at http://www.brown.edu/Administration/News_Bureau/1996-97/ McVicar1.html. For present purposes, I shall assume that this account is correct. Even if it is not correct, we would still have to decide what to say about a case in which something like these facts occurs.

The present question is not whether Adam Lack violated the Brown University Code, although it is arguable that if (as Adam claimed) Sara asked if he had a condom, then she could not have been *so very* intoxicated or that Adam could reasonably believe that she was not. The present question is whether we should accept the animating principle of this provision: should it be regarded as morally, institutionally, or legally impermissible to have sexual relations with a woman who consents to sexual relations while intoxicated?

Intoxication

It will be useful to distinguish between what we might call "substance-affected consent" and "intoxicated consent."[3] By substance-affected consent, I refer to a case in which B tokens consent after consuming a substance and in which B would or might not have tokened consent had she not consumed the substance. By intoxicated consent, I refer to any subset of substance-affected consent in which the substance distorts B's reasoning process or renders B's decisions inconsistent with her higher-order reflective judgments or stable preferences. Consider the following cases.

Inhibitions. A and B have dated. B has said that she is not ready for sex. From her own experience and from other sources, B knows that alcohol consumption distorts her judgment. Still, without thinking much about it, B consumes several drinks at a party. When A proposes that they have sex, she feels much less inhibited than usual, and half-heartedly says "there has to be a first time."
Fraternity Party. B is a college freshman. She has never had much to drink. She attends her first fraternity party and is offered some punch. She asks, "Does this have alcohol?" A responds, "Absolutely." She has several glasses, and becomes quite "high" for the first time in her life. When A proposes that they go to his room, she agrees.
Spiked. B attends a fraternity party for the first time. There is a keg of beer and a bowl of punch that has been "spiked" with vodka, but is labelled nonalcoholic. B has several glasses of punch, and becomes quite high. When A proposes that they go to his room, she agrees.
Dutch Courage. A and B have dated. B is a virgin, and feels frightened of and guilty about sex. Believing that she will never agree to sex if sober, she consumes four drinks in an hour. After some kissing and petting, A says, "Are you sure it's OK?" B holds up her glass, smiles, and says "It is *now*."
Aphrodisiac. An aphrodisiac is developed. A slips a pill into B's drink. Having become excited, B, who has never shown much interest in sex, proposes that they have intercourse.

---

[3] I thank Arthur Kuflik for helping me to see the need for this distinction.

Love Potion (Number Nine).[4] A and B have been dating. B thinks that A is a wonderful person, but does not feel physically attracted to him. Fearful that A will break off their relationship, B consumes an aphrodisiac and now desires sexual relations with A.

Estrogen. A and B have been married for twenty-five years. B has been experiencing a severe decline in libido due to menopause. During the past year, she rarely wanted to have intercourse, but agreed occasionally. She takes hormone-replacement therapy, and finds that her desire for sexual relations has dramatically increased. A proposes that they have intercourse. B happily agrees.

Lactaid. B refuses to have sexual intercourse when she has abdominal pain. After testing positive for lactose intolerance, she begins taking Lactaid pills. B feels much better and happily accepts A's proposal to have intercourse.

On my stipulative definitions, all of these cases exemplify *substance-affected* consent, but **Estrogen** and **Lactaid** are not cases of *intoxicated* consent because B's judgment is not distorted. Because a decision to token consent is often a function of several variables, it may be difficult to determine whether B would have tokened consent had she not consumed a substance. For this reason, we may prefer to understand intoxicated consent as referring to cases in which B's ingestion of a substance increases the probability that she will token consent or will token consent for reasons that do not reflect her stable preferences or, perhaps, her higher-order preferences about her stable preferences.

The last two possibilities are important and help us to understand what is worrisome about intoxicated consent. On the responsiveness-to-reasons view, it is arguable that B is not acting in a fully autonomous manner when intoxication weakens her ability to govern her actions by reasons that she accepts. B might give sober consent to sexual relations with A for reasons that are consistent with her stable or higher-order preferences, while giving intoxicated consent to sexual relations for reasons that she would reject when sober.[5] Such intoxicated consent may well be problematic, even though B would have given consent if sober. On the other hand, B may consume a substance precisely because she has a higher-order desire to suspend, curtail, or weaken some of her stable psychological traits, say, if she regards herself as irrationally fearful of sexual relations (**Dutch Courage**). We can say that such consent is intoxicated, if we like, but it is arguably not intoxicated in an objectionable way.

Because I have extremely limited knowledge of the phenomenology and physiology of mind-altering substances, I shall say only a little about the way

---

[4] After the song by that title. "I didn't know if it was day or night, I started kissin' everything in sight..."

[5] I thank David Christensen for help on this point.

in which substances affect one's desires, beliefs, judgments, and decisions. It does seem that mind-altering substances vary with respect to valence and intensity. With respect to valence, the substance may enhance B's positive desire for sexual relations on a short-term basis (**Love Potion**, **Aphrodisiac**) or long-term basis (**Estrogen**) or it may weaken the force of B's inhibitions (**Inhibitions**, **Fraternity Party**, **Dutch Courage**) or physical discomfort (**Lactaid**). With respect to intensity, a substance may have an "overpowering" effect on B's judgment, whereas in other cases, its effect is moderate or non-distorting. The mere fact that a substance or some other factor has a causal impact on B's decision to consent that does not appeal directly to B's reasons for action does not render her decision morally problematic. If A plays music that tips the balance in favor of B's consent, B's consent is valid. Why? I suspect it is largely an empirical matter. The effect of music on decision-making is ordinarily quite moderate.[6] If, however, A's playing "Unchained Melody" causes B to make decisions that are inconsistent with her stable preferences, then we might regard her music-induced consent as problematic, particularly if A intentionally takes advantage of this effect.[7] On the other hand, B's consent is certainly unproblematic in **Estrogen** and **Lactaid** even if these substances make a *big* difference to the probability of consent, because they do not distort B's reasoning process or cause B's first-order preferences to be inconsistent with stable preferences or reflective judgments about those preferences.

Some sources suggest that there is an important moral distinction between the consent produced by a substance that relaxes sexual inhibitions (**Spiked**) and one that enhances sexual desire (**Aphrodisiac**). *Corpus Juris Secundum* states that when a drug "is used *merely to excite her passions*, the intercourse is not rape if it is consensual."[8] This seems mistaken. A decision to consent to sexual relations is always a function of positive and negative considerations, and a substance that strengthens the positive considerations is not necessarily less worrisome than one that weakens the negative considerations. The above consideration of deceived consent shows that the positive synchronic experience of sexual relations says little about the validity of B's consent. B might *enjoy* sexual relations when A impersonates B's husband, but we might well regard B's consent as invalid.

---

[6] Some disagree. "Music hath charms to soothe the savage breast, To soften rocks, or bend a knotted oak"; William Congreve, "The Mourning Bride," Act 1, Scene 1.

[7] This theme occurred on the television sitcom *Cheers*. Carla's ex-husband Nick seduced her by playing "Unchained Melody." The show's character Rebecca had a similar reaction to "You've Got That Loving Feeling," by The Righteous Brothers.

[8] 75 *Corpus Juris Secundum*, Rape, Sec 11 (St. Paul, MN: West Publishing Company, 1936), 480 (emphasis added). This statement begs the question whether intercourse should be regarded as consensual if a drug is used to excite the passions.

We can learn about intoxicated judgment by focusing on the distinction between voluntary and involuntary substance-affected consent. Some think it unproblematic that PVC_L and PVC_M should regard B's consent token as invalid when A surreptitiously administers a substance that has a causal effect on B's decision to consent. It is not. If A were to surreptitiously put Lactaid or estrogen pills in B's food, I do not think there would be any serious problem about the validity of B's consent (although we might condemn A's behavior on other grounds). Why? Because the substance did not distort B's reasoning process or affect the reasons for which B thinks it appropriate to consent to sexual relations or her sensitivity to those reasons. On the other hand, we are more inclined to think that B's consent is invalid in **Spiked** and **Aphrodisiac** because the substances affect B's ability to govern her actions by reasons that she accepts.[9] So without much confidence that this account is right in all its details, let me suggest that B's consent is intoxicated if the substance renders B indifferent to or substantially alters the weight of reasons that are an important staple of B's psychic economy. For present purposes, let us assume, arguendo, that B's judgment is sufficiently distorted by her consumption of an intoxicant that her consent would be of questionable validity if the intoxicant had been surreptitiously administered to B by A, as in **Spiked**.

Responsibility

Cases of intoxicated consent come in various degrees of voluntariness or self-inducement.[10] In some cases, B consumes the substance with the specific intention that it alter her psychology (**Love Potion**, **Dutch Courage**). In other cases, B intentionally consumes a substance with the knowledge that it may affect her desire or judgment but does not intend this effect (**Inhibitions**) or fully anticipate its effect (**Fraternity Party**, *Brown*). As a matter of positive law, the voluntariness of B's intoxication has generally been regarded as crucial.[11] But the question for us is normative: *should* B's intoxicated consent be treated as valid if B is voluntarily intoxicated?

---

[9] In some cases, substances may be more akin to deception. Suppose that B likes to have sexual relations when she is aroused by a man. She regards that as a good reason for having sex. If A puts an aphrodisiac in her drink, B may have sex with A for reasons that she accepts, but she is deceived as to *why* she is aroused. I thank Arthur Applbaum for help on this point.

[10] I set aside the question whether alcoholism renders the consumption of alcohol involuntary.

[11] For example, the relevant Vermont statute states that one commits a sexual assault if one engages in a sexual act with another person and has "impaired substantially the ability of the other person to appraise or control conduct by administering or employing drugs or intoxicants without the knowledge or against the will of the other person..."; Title 13, V. S. A. Section 3252. *Corpus Juris Secundum* maintains that there is no offense "where the female voluntarily drank the substance

I will start with the responsibility claim. As a first approximation, let us say that an agent is responsible for her behavior, just in case the behavior is properly attributed to the agent, and that we are justified in having certain moral sentiments, and for thinking that praise, blame, punishments, rewards and the like are justifiable.[12] We regard agents as morally responsible only when they have certain cognitive and emotional capacities, that is, only when they are under the control of their "judgment-sensitive attitudes" or are capable of being guided by appropriate reasons.[13] We treat infants and the insane as non-responsible because they lack the relevant capacities. It is precisely because intoxication weakens the capacity to act on the basis of appropriate reasons that there is a sense in which an intoxicated agent is *not* responsible for her behavior, as witnessed by our intuitions about *in*voluntary intoxication. If B has been forced to drink and is then required to walk in a straight line, we would not blame her for her inability to do so.

Why should *voluntary* intoxication be treated differently? Consider responsibility for wrongful behavior. Heidi Hurd suggests that there are two views on which we could refuse to recognize voluntary intoxication as an excuse for criminal liability. On one view, we refuse to recognize voluntary intoxication as an excuse for wrongdoing because intoxication never (or rarely) defeats an agent's "ability to reason about his obligations and to act in accordance with those obligations."[14] Call this the *reasoning view*. On a second view, we refuse to regard voluntary intoxication as an excuse, because doing so would encourage people to become intoxicated as a way of immunizing themselves from responsibility for their behavior or, less strongly, would give people less incentive not to become intoxicated and thereby put others at greater risk. Call this the *incentive view*.

I believe that Hurd is right to accept the responsibility claim, but that the reasoning view and incentive view are only part of the story. Consider first the reasoning view. Although the reasoning view rightly stresses that intoxication does not always significantly impair the agent's responsiveness to the relevant reasons for action, it does not support the responsibility claim if and when intoxication does seriously impair the agent's cognitive

---

alleged to have excited *or* stupefied her"; 483. The (in)famous Antioch College Code also treats A's role in B's intoxication as relevant. It is a violation of the code if "the person submitting is under the influence of alcohol or other substances supplied to her/him by the person initiating"; as reprinted in Robert B. Baker, Kathleen J. Wininger, and Frederick A. Elliston (eds.), *Philosophy and Sex* (Amherst, NY: Prometheus Books, 1998), 643.

[12] For an extended defense of this view, see R. Jay Wallace, *Responsibility and the Moral Sentiments* (Cambridge, MA: Harvard University Press, 1994).

[13] T. M. Scanlon, *What We Owe to Each Other* (Cambridge, MA: Harvard University Press, 1998), 277.

[14] Heidi M. Hurd, "The Moral Magic of Consent," 2 *Legal Theory* 121 (1996), 141.

capacities, so it cannot explain the intuition that we can justifiably hold people responsible for their voluntary intoxicated behavior even when they are incapable of guiding their actions by the appropriate reasons. Moreover, the force of the reasoning view is actually independent of the *voluntariness* of the intoxication. If an involuntarily intoxicated person is capable of acting in accordance with reasons, it is not clear why she should be excused just because her intoxication is *not* self-induced. If A surreptitiously spikes B's drink, but B is aware that she is drunk and that she should not drive while drunk, it would be (almost) as wrong for her to drive as when her intoxication is voluntary.

Consider the incentive view. It is not clear whether the incentive view is offered as a theory of legal (or institutional) responsibility or moral responsibility. On the incentive view, we do not necessarily hold B responsible for her behavior because doing so is the appropriate response to *B*'s behavior, but because a policy of holding B responsible gives both B and others an incentive to behave as we prefer. So we might have reason to 'hold' B legally or institutionally responsible even if we believe that B is (in some deeper sense) not morally responsible.[15] Interestingly, and despite appearances, the incentive view gives little support to the responsibility-entails-validity claim. The incentive argument is, at root, a consequentialist argument. From that perspective, it is an open question whether treating intoxicated consent as valid has better consequences than treating intoxicated consent as invalid.

Although the reasoning view and the incentive view offer only limited support to the responsibility claim, there are two additional arguments for the responsibility claim that should be considered. On what I call the *flow-through* view, we can justifiably ascribe responsibility to an agent for voluntary intoxicated behavior if she had the requisite volitional and epistemological capacities at the appropriate prior time.[16] On the flow-through view, moral responsibility does not chronologically track the

---

[15] Consider insanity. If it is difficult to determine just who has the mental disorders that preclude one from acting on the basis of the appropriate reasons and if many sane criminals might falsely claim insanity as an excuse, then we might be justified on consequentialist grounds in "holding" the insane legally responsible, even though we believe that the insane are not morally responsible in a deeper sense. See H. L. A. Hart, *Punishment and Responsibility* (New York: Oxford University Press, 1968), 19.

[16] See John Martin Fischer and Mark Ravizza, *Responsibility and Control* (Cambridge: Cambridge University Press, 1998), 89. Specifying the "appropriate prior time" can be controversial. We might say that an alcoholic is not responsible for her intoxicated behavior because she could not choose not to become intoxicated. Or we might say that while she did not have the capacity to not become intoxicated at the time that she became intoxicated, she had the capacity not to become an alcoholic in the first place.

agent's psychological capacities. If an agent has a fair opportunity at Time-1 to control or guide her behavior at Time-2, then our moral response to her use of those opportunities at Time-1 flows through to her behavior at Time-2, even if she is unable to guide or control her behavior at Time-2.

To see this, consider behaviors that are manifestations of a general psychological trait such as sloppiness, punctuality, kindness, stinginess, law abidingness, and veracity. Some behaviors are so deeply rooted in an agent's general psychological disposition that they are not significantly guided by the relevant reasons at the time of the act. B does not "choose" to obey the law or tell the truth or throw her clothes on the floor. She does not give it a moment's thought. Are we justified in ascribing responsibility to B? It depends, but probably so. Fischer and Ravizza argue that an agent is morally responsible for actions that are rooted in deep psychological traits if but only if she had "guidance control" with respect to the formation, retention, or expression of that trait "at *some appropriate point* prior to the action."[17] Although an agent's current act of veracity or stinginess may not reflect responsiveness to reasons, she is responsible for her truth telling or her stingy behavior if (but only if) she had a fair opportunity to shape her traits in the appropriate way.[18]

As go traits, so go mind-altering substances. If B intentionally consumes a substance that makes her uncontrollably violent and she could reasonably be expected to anticipate this, we would regard her as a suitable subject for punishment. Our intuitions would be different if we were to discover that someone had injected the substance into B's arm while she was asleep and she became violent when awake.[19] Similarly, although B's mental capacities at the time of intercourse may be identical in **Inhibitions** and **Spiked**, she has a degree of guidance control in **Inhibitions** that she lacks in **Spiked**, so we are justified in holding her responsible in **Inhibitions** but not in **Spiked**.

Finally, what I call the *dual-self* view takes a slightly different tack. Unlike the flow-through view, it maintains that B's responsibility for her behavior

---

[17] *Ibid.*

[18] "The snapshot properties of the agent and the mechanism that leads to certain behavior do not suffice to specify an agent's moral responsibility: what is *also* relevant is the *history* of the relevant behavior"; *ibid.*, 195. As Scanlon puts it, "once an adult has had certain characteristics for some time and shows no tendency to resist or reject them, it is appropriate to attribute those faults to him and to hold him responsible for actions reflecting them"; *What We Owe to Each Other*, 284.

[19] Still, we might think that B should take preemptive action against her own violent behavior if she discovers that she had been injected. If B knows that she is subject to epileptic seizures unless she takes medication, it is wrong for her to drive without taking the medication, even though she bears no responsibility for being epileptic.

chronologically tracks her psychological capacities. If, at Time-1, B_1 chooses to become severely intoxicated, then she is a *non*responsible agent at Time-2 because she cannot then guide her behavior by the appropriate reasons. We may justifiably hold B_1 responsible for the behavior that gave rise to the nonresponsible B_2, but it is B_1 and not B_2 to whom our reactions are directed. On the flow-through view, we hold B responsible for her intoxicated behavior at Time-2. On the dual-self view, we hold B responsible for her Time-1 decision to become intoxicated.[20] B's voluntary intoxication is a form of culpable negligence or recklessness because reasonable people know that they are more likely to do unreasonable things when they are intoxicated.

The dual-self view is somewhat of a misnomer. Although the label is designed to capture the distinction between B's capacities at two different times, it does not require a special metaphysics or view of personal identity. We could simply say that we are holding B to account for what she does while sober, but not for what (the same) B does while intoxicated. I use the label nonetheless because it captures our intuition about the case in which A injects a substance into an unconscious B that renders her uncontrollably violent when she awakes. For we would say that the violent B really is a different "self" than the normal, nonviolent B, and that the normal B is not responsible for what is done by the drug-induced violent B.

I am not sure to what extent the flow-through view and the dual-self view are ultimately distinguishable. Although the flow-through view is intuitively attractive, it is not clear precisely how one's responsibility for one's actions at Time-1 account for one's responsibility at Time-2, given that one lacks the capacities that are presumed by ascriptions of responsibility at Time-2. If we are, in effect, holding people responsible for what they do at Time-1, then we are back with the dual-self view. Although the views seem quite close, they do seem to have different implications in the face of moral luck. On the flow-through view we can say that the agent who drives while intoxicated at Time-2 behaves worse than the agent who does not drive only because the latter has the good fortune to have a friend who takes her car keys. It is more difficult to say this on the dual-self view, for the Time-1 behavior for which we are holding B responsible is the same in both cases.[21]

---

[20] Things become more complicated if B_2's psychology is irrevocably changed. If B_1 were to consume a substance that renders her irrevocably a nonresponsible agent B_2 who commits a criminal act, we may decide that there is no one whom we can justifiably punish (although we may need to incarcerate B_2 if she is dangerous).

[21] I thank George Sher for help on this point.

The previous discussion suggests that there is bad news and good news about responsibility. The bad news is that it is not clear which argument(s) for the responsibility claim is (are) most attractive. The good news is that it is sufficient that at least one of the arguments (or something like it) can be defended. And *if* we are justified in treating B as morally responsible for her decision to become intoxicated or for her (voluntary) intoxicated behavior, then we should reject the intoxication claim. Intoxication does not *entail* invalidity. It is perfectly coherent to claim that if B is responsible for her intoxicated behavior, then PVC can treat B's intoxicated consent as valid. Are we then required to accept the responsibility-entails-validity claim? If it is coherent to say that B's intoxicated consent is valid if she is responsible for her intoxication, does it follow that we *must* treat her consent as valid?

Does responsibility entail validity?

Heidi Hurd believes that we should accept the responsibility-entails-validity claim and that it receives support from the consistency claim. If we hold people responsible for their criminal behavior, then the *consistency claim* requires us to treat B as responsible for her consent:

> On pain of condescension, we should be loath to suggest that the conditions of responsibility vary among actors, so that the drunken man who has sex with a woman he knows is not consenting is responsible for rape, while the drunken woman who invites sex is not sufficiently responsible to make such sex consensual.[22]

Susan Estrich takes a different tack. She argues that we would not say that people who negligently fail to lock their cars thereby render it permissible for others to steal them.[23] Similarly, we should not say that women who token consent to sexual relations while intoxicated thereby render it permissible for others to have sex with them.

Both Hurd and Estrich move too quickly. *Pace* Hurd, accepting the responsibility claim does not require us to treat B's intoxicated consent as valid. First, on the reasoning view that Hurd endorses, it is entirely possible that the mental capacities that are required for responsibility for criminal wrongdoing are different from and less robust than the mental capacities that are required for responsibility for consent. Michael Moore writes that the "intentions required for conviction of rape or murder ... are so simple that if an actor has not become so intoxicated that he has lost consciousness

---

[22] Hurd, "The Moral Magic of Consent," 141.
[23] Susan Estrich, "Palm Beach Stories," 11 *Law and Philosophy* 5 (1992), 10.

he almost certainly possesses the [relevant] intention . . ."[24] If the law is right to require such minimal mental states for a criminal conviction, it does not follow that either PVC_L or PVC_M should adopt a similar view about the requirements of consent. To push the previous point a bit further, it is also standard law that the sort of duress that invalidates a contract does not necessarily provide a defense to a criminal charge.[25] If A threatens to break B's arm unless B kills C, B will be held responsible for killing C. If A threatens to break B's arm unless B signs a contract with A, B will not be held responsible for fulfilling the terms of the contract.[26] Similarly, it is entirely possible that the sort of intoxication that does not excuse one from criminal liability might negate the transformative effect of one's consent token.

There are several reasons why the capacities required for responsibility for criminal wrongdoing might be less robust than the capacities required by transformative consent. While an agent's responsibility for criminal wrongdoing applies solely to the way in which we respond to the agent herself, an agent's (valid) consent transforms what it is permissible for *others* to do. It is arguable that such transformations require a deeper expression of the agent's will than the intentions required for culpability for wrongdoing.[27] In addition, whereas C is not in a position to avoid the effects of B's harmful act, it is relatively easy for A to avoid the effects of B's consent and thus we can more easily justify shifting the burden from B to A.

Second, and more generally, Hurd fails to acknowledge that the normative implications of ascriptions of responsibility are fundamentally open-ended. It is a mistake to think that to be held morally responsible for one's choices is to be required to internalize *all* the consequences of that behavior.[28] If I choose to smoke or ski, I assume an extra risk of cancer or a broken leg, and there is a clear sense in which I am responsible for the consequences. It is a separate question, however, whether I should bear all the medical costs of such conditions, and as a matter of fact, I do not. Similarly, it is coherent to argue that B is responsible for her intoxicated

---

[24] "Liberty and Drugs" in Pablo de Grieff (ed.), *Drugs and the Limits of Liberalism* (Ithaca: Cornell University Press, 1999), 103.

[25] "To overcome the will, so far as to render it incapable of contracting a civil obligation, is a mere trifle compared with reducing it to that degree of slavery and submission which will exempt from punishment"; *McCoy v. State*, 49 S.E. 768 (1887), 769.

[26] See my *Coercion* (Princeton: Princeton University Press, 1987), chapter 8.

[27] I thank George Sher for help on this point.

[28] As Scanlon puts it, it is a mistake to assume "that taking individuals to be responsible for their conduct in the sense of being open to moral criticism for it requires one also to say that they are responsible for its results in the substantive sense . . ."; *What We Owe to Each Other*, 293.

behavior, but not for all of its normal implications, and, in particular, not for the validity of her consent. In retributive terms, treating B's consent as valid may not fit the crime of becoming intoxicated.

Now consider Estrich's argument. If B fails to lock her car, she is not off the moral hook. If B has borrowed C's car and fails to lock it, then C has a complaint against B if it is stolen. Estrich could reply that this observation lends support to her argument. Even if we can justifiably blame B for the harm to C, her action hardly renders A's behavior permissible. This reply would be correct. In some contexts, we can put B on the moral hook without letting A off the moral hook. Under a "dram shop" law, for example, we may hold B responsible for driving while intoxicated while also holding the owner of a bar responsible for selling liquor to an intoxicated B (who then drives while even more intoxicated).[29]

But contexts involving consent are importantly different. Here we do need to assign the burden of B's consent to either A or B. We cannot simultaneously hold B responsible for the validity of her consent and also say that A's behavior is impermissible. If we want to put A on the hook, then we have to take B off the hook with respect to the validity of her consent. Estrich's example is not apt precisely because it does not involve B's consent to A's action. It would be more telling to ask whether A commits a crime if A asks to borrow B's prized Ferrari, about which she is normally quite proprietary, and an inebriated B turns over her keys, or whether a panhandler commits larceny if he asks B for money, and an (obviously) inebriated B turns over her wallet. In these cases our hand is forced: we cannot treat B's consent as valid and also claim that A has committed theft, although we might well treat A's action as morally impermissible. Similarly, we cannot say that B's intoxicated consent to sexual relations is valid and also say that A has committed a sexual offense.

Consent contexts

I have argued that we should reject both the intoxication claim and the responsibility-entails-validity claim. If the previous argument is correct, moral logic does not require us to accept or reject the impermissibility claim. We can go either way. Which way should we go? It will be helpful to step back from sexual relations and consider other contexts of consent. Consider consent to a medical procedure. It seems entirely reasonable that

[29] See Jeffrey C. Hallam, "Rolling the Dice: Should Intoxicated Gamblers Recover Their Losses?," *Northwestern University Law Review* 85 (1990), 244.

a patient's voluntary intoxicated consent to major surgery should not be treated as valid if B's intoxication is or should be evident to the physician, even if the physician provided all the relevant information while the patient was sober. A physician cannot say, "She was drunk when she came in to sign the consent form. She's responsible for her intoxication, not me. End of story." On whatever argument for the responsibility claim one prefers, we need not and do not say that B's responsibility for her intoxication entails that her intoxicated consent to a medical procedure *must* be treated as valid. In this case, I believe that both PVC_L and PVC_M will regard a patient's intoxicated consent as invalid.

Consent to a medical procedure is a particularly good illustration of the way in which PVC are sensitive to two sorts of considerations. First, PVC are always sensitive to the costs – broadly construed – of preventing arguably consensual transactions when they are likely to be beneficial to the parties, and the costs of allowing arguably consensual transactions when they are likely to prove harmful. We worry about the quality of consent to a risky medical procedure, but we do not and probably should not worry much about the quality of consent to a low-risk procedure such as the use of a tongue depressor, where physicians do not and probably should not attempt to secure explicit advanced consent that is informed by a detailed account of possible adverse consequences of tongue depression.

Second, PVC are also sensitive to the possibility or feasibility of "high quality" consent. If an elderly patient's judgment is compromised by medication, stress, fear, or mild dementia, we might still treat her consent to a hip replacement as valid while treating a middle-aged patient's intoxicated consent to a hip replacement as invalid, even when the intoxicated patient's cognitive capacities are no lower than the elderly patient's. It might be argued that the elderly patient's low-quality consent to the procedure should not count. But what are the alternatives? If we do not accept "lower quality" consent, then we either do not go ahead with the procedure (because she cannot give higher-quality consent) or we paternalistically proceed without her consent. Given the alternatives, it may be preferable to accept low-quality consent. By contrast, we are less willing to accept low-quality consent when it is feasible to obtain higher-quality consent, say by waiting for the patient to sober up.

In order to further illustrate this point, consider two additional medical contexts. It has been argued that people have the right to end their own lives through a process such as physician-assisted suicide or voluntary euthanasia. As Ronald Dworkin puts it, "every competent person has the right to make momentous personal decisions which invoke fundamental religious or philosophical convictions about life's value for himself."[30] The claim does refer to "competent" persons, and Dworkin is quick to note that we should protect people from making such decisions impulsively or out of depression. Yet we cannot set the standards for competence too high, for the very circumstances that may make it *reasonable* for people to choose voluntary euthanasia or physician-assisted suicide can also be seen as placing such people under great stress, not to mention that those contemplating these means often have diminished cognitive capacities. If we insist that patients can authorize voluntary euthanasia or physician-assisted suicide only when their capacities are not significantly diminished, then we prevent them from effecting an outcome that they may reasonably prefer. We condemn them to live and suffer. On the other hand, if we allow such patients to authorize voluntary euthanasia or physician-assisted suicide when their capacities are diminished, then we permit them to make decisions that are subject to manipulation and which may not reflect their interests or higher-order preferences. I take no position on voluntary euthanasia or physician-assisted suicide here. I suggest only that if one supports either, then one must accept the position that stressful circumstances or diminished cognitive capacities are not incompatible with PVC_L or PVC_M in this context.

Reconsider consent to abortion. Although some feminists argue for setting high standards for what counts as valid consent to sexual relations, they often argue *against* setting high standards for what constitutes valid consent to abortion, standards that might involve setting age restrictions, requiring "full" information about the development of the fetus, or requiring "waiting periods" that are ostensibly designed to reduce the risk of a hasty decision.[31] It could be argued, after all, that we should zealously protect a woman's negative autonomy not to have an abortion by insisting on "high quality" consent, because she may be pressured to agree to an abortion or fail to understand the psychological trauma she may undergo. On the other hand, insisting on "high quality" consent may encroach on a woman's positive autonomy to choose an abortion that she believes to be in her interests. In this case, we may well think that PVC_L and PVC_M should err on the side of protecting positive rather than negative autonomy. The general point remains that a concern for the decision-maker's autonomy does not require us to set high standards for valid consent.

---

[30] Introduction to "Assisted Suicide: The Philosopher's Brief," *The New York Review of Books*, March 27, 1997. This brief was signed by John Rawls, Judith Jarvis Thomson, Robert Nozick, Ronald Dworkin, T. M. Scanlon, and Thomas Nagel.

[31] If such conditions are not benignly motivated by concern for the woman's autonomy, as seems likely, we must still explain why they should be resisted.

Consider consent in a commercial context. For many years, the traditional legal rule went some distance towards treating voluntary intoxicated
consent as valid. A contract was voidable by the intoxicated person only
if he was "so far under the influence of narcotics that he [did] not understand the nature and consequences of the transaction."[32] Current doctrine
is less rigorous. It holds that a contract made by an intoxicated person is
voidable "if the other party has reason to know that the intoxicated person
is *unable to act in a reasonable manner* in relation to the transaction."[33] The
contract-law approach is revealing. In deciding whether to treat B's intoxicated consent as binding, contract law seems to shift the focus from B's
responsibility for her intoxicated behavior to the question of whether the
ends served by the contract-law regime would be promoted or undermined
if intoxicated agents were held to their bargains.

By way of analogy, consider defects in information. Does B give valid
consent to a sales contract if she lacks information about the object she is
buying? From the law's perspective, it depends. There may be reasons of
fairness and utility that favor treating B's contract as valid if she makes a
bad deal because she does not seek out readily available information, while
the same sorts of reasons favor requiring those selling homes to disclose
known defects in a house, given the deep asymmetries of access to such
information.[34] There may be similar reasons of fairness and utility that
favor treating B's contract as invalid if (1) B is severely intoxicated and
(2) A knows or should know this. If B's intoxication were "sufficient to
diminish the intelligence, and the party dealing with the intoxicated person
knowingly made use of the situation in order to induce the bargain," it may
be better to assign the burden of B's intoxicated consent to A and regard
such contracts as voidable.[35] On the other hand, the law is more likely to
treat B's contract as valid if A could not reasonably be expected to know
that B was intoxicated. If an intoxicated B were to sign an offer that was
not so absurd as to create a presumption that B is incompetent and it was
sent to A at some distance, then, if accepted, B would be bound by the
contract – not because B gave internally 'competent' consent, not (solely)
because B's intoxication was self-induced, but because when we step back
and ask what version of PVC we prefer, we may well decide that given the

[32] Joseph D. Calamari and Joseph M. Perillo, *Contracts*, third edition (St. Louis: West, 1987), 329.
[33] *Ibid.* (emphasis added).
[34] Stephen Morse, "Crazy Reasons," 10 *Journal of Contemporary Legal Issues* 189 (1999), 189.
[35] Samuel Williston, *A Treatise on the Law of Contracts*, third edition (1950), 106 (emphasis added). The
Supreme Court has held that evidence of competency should be "entirely clear" if it is to sustain a
transaction when a drunkard has been "overreached" by a person who is "competent and aggressive";
Kendall v. Ewert, 259 US 139, 147 (1922).

choice between assigning the burden of B's intoxicated consent to A *or* B, it would be unsettling to the general regime of contracts to allow B to undo the contract under these conditions.[36] To put the point slightly differently, the law asks "Who can avoid the cost of B's bad decisions most easily?" If B is the least cost avoider, then the law will treat B's contracts as valid. If A is the least cost avoider, then the law is more likely to treat B's contract as invalid.

Sex is arguably not like surgery or suicide or abortions or contracts. So consider tattoos and gambling. Many states prohibit tattooing of an intoxicated person.[37] These statutes do not distinguish between voluntary and involuntary intoxication. If the client is intoxicated, the tattoo cannot be performed. How might a state justify the distinction between the permissive approach towards intoxicated consent to sexual relations and the prohibitive approach to intoxicated consent to tattoos? It might be argued that whereas a sexual partner is in a position to know whether a woman's intoxication is self-induced, a tattooist is not likely to know the etiology of the intoxication.[38] Or it might be argued that getting tattooed is a more serious matter than having sex. One can have drunken sex and be sober in the morning and arguably no worse off for it. If one gets a tattoo while drunk, one may be sober in the morning but the tattoo will still be there. The *probability* of regret may be higher with tattoos. On the other hand, sex involves the risk of pregnancy and disease, whereas the primary risk from (sterile) tattoos is merely (?) aesthetic; so the *gravity* of the harmful consequences may be higher with respect to sex. I am not concerned to justify the prohibition of intoxicated consent to tattoos or to argue that PVC_L or PVC_M would treat the two sorts of consent in a similar fashion. The present point is that this is a context in which some states have adopted the impermissibility claim.

Consider gambling. It might be argued that an intoxicated gambler should be able to recover her losses on the grounds that a wager between a gambler and a gambling establishment constitutes an implied contract that is voidable on grounds of intoxication.[39] Not surprisingly, the standard

[36] Williston writes that if an "intoxicated person is able to appear to give intelligent assent, he should not be allowed to set up his own misconduct to defeat one who has been deceived in dealing with him"; *ibid.*, 101.
[37] For example, an Alabama statute: "A person shall not tattoo, brand, or perform body piercing on another individual if the other individual is under the influence of intoxicating liquor or a controlled substance"; Ala. Code 1975 Sec 22-17A-2.
[38] Although the statutes make no room for sober *ex ante* consent to a tattoo, perhaps for administrative reasons it is possible that most states would have no objection to tattoos on intoxicated persons if it were clear that they agreed to be tattooed when sober.
[39] Jeffrey Hallam, "Rolling the Dice," 256.

legal view is that the gambler absorbs the risk of her intoxicated judgment. Unlike the tattoo artist, the casino can ply its customers with alcohol and allow them to fill its coffers. Is this the right view?

We might consider what rule would be chosen by gamblers *ex ante*. Suppose that potential gamblers were given a choice between a rule that treats gambling losses incurred while intoxicated as recoverable and a rule that treats them as nonrecoverable and that the consequences of adopting both rules were well understood.[40] What would they choose? I suspect that most would choose the "nonrecoverable" rule, for unless their losses were nonrecoverable, casinos would be reluctant to allow them to both drink and gamble, particularly given that it might be very difficult to monitor a gambler's sobriety or that the costs of such monitoring would be passed on to the gamblers.[41]

Suppose this is right. Is sex like gambling? Sex is not like gambling in some respects that tell in favor of a less permissive approach to intoxicated sex than intoxicated gambling. First, there is the issue of harm. It is arguable that the emotional and physical harms consequent to intoxicated consent to sexual relations are greater than the various harms consequent to intoxicated gambling. Second, there is the issue of intentions. Whereas people who enter a casino and then become intoxicated intend to gamble all along (although perhaps not as much), women who become intoxicated and then token consent to sex do not necessarily intend to have sex all along, although there is evidence that women are more likely to drink when they are willing to have sex.[42] Third, there is a practical issue. While it may be unreasonable to expect casino personnel to monitor a gambler's alcohol consumption, it is arguably not unreasonable to expect potential sexual partners to monitor each other's level of intoxication.

That said, sex is very much like gambling in other respects that tell for a permissive rule for intoxicated consent to sexual relations. People do like to gamble, *ex ante*, even when they regret having gambled *ex post*, and much the same is true for sex. Indeed, whereas most gamblers lose on a given day (intoxicated or sober) and almost all gamblers lose over

---

[40] It may be argued that I have stacked the deck by making this a decision that people will make with respect to their own (potential) gambling activity, as opposed to the effects of that gambling activity on others. I am not here trying to model the choice of the socially optimal rule. I am trying to model what rule would be chosen if we were solely concerned to respect the gambler's autonomy.

[41] If gamblers have different preferences, then perhaps there should be gambling analogues to the choice between "dry" and "non-dry" residence halls. Gamblers who want to protect themselves against gambling while intoxicated could choose to go to a dry casino.

[42] Deborah Davis and Elizabeth Loftus, "What's Good for the Goose Cooks the Gander: Inconsistencies between the Law and Psychology of Voluntary Intoxication and Sexual Assault," www.sierratrialandopinion.com/papers/alcoholandconsent.rtf, 14.

the long run, many intoxicated sexual relationships are pleasurable and do not typically involve significant physical or psychological harm. Without wanting to minimize the risks or the distress experienced by women in cases such as *Brown*, our moral and legal rules should not be driven by the cases that go badly. Moreover, it is not just that some women may wish to engage in sex and drinking simultaneously. Rather, drinking to the point of at least moderate intoxication may be crucial to what some regard as a desirable sexual and social experience. Both men and women report greater subjective sexual pleasure with increasing levels of blood alcohol, even though physiological response actually diminishes.[43] And some women deliberately become intoxicated so that they can engage in sexual relations without experiencing guilt or to excuse themselves *ex post*.[44] Given that a decision to regard intoxicated consent as invalid would limit the positive autonomy of women to engage in sexual relations while intoxicated, we cannot say that something like the Brown University policy enhances women's autonomy, all things considered.

Indeed, the issue of intoxicated consent allows us to reconsider the significance of autonomy, *per se*.

New Year's Eve. A and B, a married couple, get roaring drunk at a New Year's Eve party. They take a cab home, stagger upstairs, fall into bed, and have sex.

It would be crazy to think that A does something seriously wrong because B consents while quite intoxicated, unless B had previously indicated that she does not want to have her intoxicated consent taken seriously. But assuming that husbands can commit sexual offenses against their wives, it is not clear on what basis those who endorse the intoxication claim or the impermissibility claim could reject the view that A's behavior is seriously wrong or even deny that A commits rape. Why would this view be crazy even if B did not give sober *ex ante* consent to this particular instance of drunken sex? Because (in part) there is no "non-autonomy-based" physical or psychological harm in a marginal sexual interaction with a person with whom one frequently has sexual relations. Despite its current popularity, the emphasis on the objective harm or wrong of violations of sexual autonomy can take us only so far. We do not think that the right to control access to one's body on each potential occasion is of monumental moral importance independent of the more tangible physical and emotional harms. The point of respect for autonomy is to give people control over what matters to them. We cannot determine what respecting women's autonomy involves

[43] *Ibid.*, 4. [44] *Ibid.*, 9.

here until we have a better – empirically grounded – understanding of their experience with respect to intoxicated sexual relations.

Given all this, we might try to determine what moral or legal rules about the validity of intoxicated consent would be chosen by women *ex ante*. We need to know whether women are likely to enjoy sexual relations while intoxicated and, more importantly, how they tend to feel about it in retrospect. We must be careful. Neither the moral nor the legal validity of a woman's intoxicated consent to sexual relations is a function of her actual *ex post* regret or satisfaction with respect to a given sexual encounter. She might enjoy sex to which she gave invalid consent or regret sex to which she gave valid consent. But the choice among versions of PVC_L or PVC_M may well take account of the *ex ante* disvalue of her *ex post* regret. If, given appropriate information, women would choose versions of PVC_L or PVC_M that allow them to become intoxicated and engage in sexual relations so long as they actually token consent, then that would tell in favor of a permissive construction of PVC even if some women would have proved to be better off under a less permissive construction.[45] If women would choose a regime in which their intoxicated consent is never treated as valid, then that would tell in favor of a less permissive construction of PVC even if some women would be better off under a more permissive construction.

As a thought experiment, suppose that some fraternity houses have a "tattoo" rule, where men are prohibited from engaging in sexual relations with women who give their first token of consent while intoxicated and some have a "gambling" rule, where men are permitted to engage in sexual relations with women who give their first token of consent while intoxicated. Further suppose that there is reasonable compliance with these rules. Which houses would women prefer? I do not know, but the choices that women now make do tell us something. Given the choice between walking at night alone and staying home, many women choose to stay home because they fear a sexual attack. Given the choice between staying home and attending a fraternity party where they may end up having intoxicated consensual sexual relations, many (often the same) women go to the fraternity parties. This may suggest that they do not regard the prospect of having sexual relations while intoxicated with a strong *ex ante* sense of dread, although that may also reflect a misperception of the risks. It is also possible that many women would prefer tattoo-rule fraternity parties to gambling-rule

---

[45] "Even in many instances in which individuals would ex ante prefer to be governed by some particular rule, it will also be true ex post . . . that some of the individuals would prefer that the rule were otherwise." See Lewis Kaplow and Steven Shavell, "Fairness versus Welfare," 114 *Harvard Law Review* 967 (2001), 1357.

fraternity parties, but may prefer the latter to staying home if the first alternative is not available. When all is said and done, if women would prefer the gambling-rule fraternities, then they have little complaint when men engage in sexual intercourse with them after they give intoxicated consent.

The consistency claim

Suppose we are inclined to accept the impermissibility claim, namely, that the best versions of PVC_L and PVC_M would regard B's intoxicated consent as *in*valid. If we also believe that people should be held responsible for their intoxicated wrongful behavior, then it seems that an intoxicated A might be liable for having sexual relations with B who consents while intoxicated. And some will find that puzzling or downright unfair. In numerous conversations on this topic, I have found that the consistency claim exerts strong intuitive moral pull and may give us reason to reject the impermissibility claim even when other considerations tell in its favor.

Consider the following matrix of eight possible situations, where A is sober or voluntarily intoxicated, B is sober or voluntarily intoxicated, and B unambiguously tokens consent or nonconsent.

		B		
		Sober		**Intoxicated**
		Consent	No consent	Consent	No consent
A — **Sober**		I - Permissible	II - Impermissible	III - Permissible or impermissible	IV - Impermissible
A — **Intoxicated**		V - Permissible	VI - Impermissible or excusable?	VII - Permissible, impermissible, or excusable?	VIII - Impermissible or excusable?

In which cases should we regard A's behavior as permissible, impermissible, or excusable? I take it that I, II, and IV are completely unproblematic. If A and B are sober and B gives consent, then A's behavior is permissible (I). If A is sober and B does not give consent then A's behavior is impermissible whether B is sober (II) or intoxicated (IV).[46] I shall also assume that VI and VIII are relatively unproblematic. One could argue that A's responsibility for his behavior is diminished ("Sorry I got so aggressive, but I was drunk"), but I will assume that A is at least somewhat culpable.

---

[46] I ignore the possibility that it is permissible for A to proceed in IV and VIII if A has reason to think that B would have consented if B had been sober.

Although it might appear that V is also unproblematic, it is actually more complicated because A's intoxication may render him (somewhat) indifferent to whether B consents or whether her consent is sober or intoxicated. It may be argued that the difference between V and VI (and VII) is largely a matter of moral luck from A's perspective, so just as we endorse a general prohibition of driving while intoxicated even though many drunk drivers cause no harm, we could endorse a general prohibition of sex while intoxicated. But I shall set that aside.[47] I also continue to set aside a worry about gender neutrality in V and VII. After all, it could be argued that if PVC treats B's intoxicated consent as invalid, then A's intoxicated consent should also be treated as invalid, that B commits an offense against A in V, when B is sober and A is intoxicated, and that *both* commit offenses in VII.[48]

Now focus on III and VII. As we have seen, the consistency claim maintains that if A is responsible for his intoxicated behavior to his detriment in VI and VIII, then B should be responsible for her intoxicated behavior to her detriment in III. I have argued that while we could say this, we are not required to say this. Suppose we accept the impermissibility claim. Would this mean that B is effectively inoculated from responsibility for the normal moral and legal consequences of giving consent? Yes. It does not mean that she bears no moral responsibility for her action. If, for example, B gives intoxicated consent to adulterous sexual relations with A, it may be fair to blame her for the harm to her family. Still, it does not follow that A is entitled to proceed.

But recall the incentive view of moral responsibility. It might be argued that if we say that A's behavior is institutionally or legally impermissible in III, such a policy would lessen a woman's incentive to avoid intoxication in the first place. In the romantic language of economics, the

---

[47] For similar reasons, I shall also set aside a complication among the cases that involve B's intoxicated consent (III and VII). Whereas B's stable preference in **Inhibitions** is *not* to engage in sexual relations with A, B's settled preference in **Dutch Courage** is precisely to engage in sexual relations with A. And so it might appear that A's behavior is worse in **Inhibitions** than in **Dutch Courage**. But bracketing considerations of moral luck, that depends upon what A has reason to believe. From A's perspective, **Inhibitions** and **Dutch Courage** may look the same.

[48] One might argue that if a man is capable of becoming sufficiently aroused to have intercourse, then he cannot be so intoxicated as to invalidate his consent. This view must be wrong, given that men have erections while sleeping. Although men do not run the risk of pregnancy and are probably less likely to experience intense *ex post* distress about such encounters, it is also true that some men do experience emotional distress about sexual encounters they would have preferred to avoid, and they also run the risk of disease and the economic, social, and psychological consequences of fathering a child they did not intend to sire. Moreover, if the more abstract value of sexual autonomy is at issue (as contrasted with palpable harms), it is arguably the same in both cases.

impermissibility claim would create a "moral hazard."[49] People may be more likely to ride their bicycles recklessly if they are wearing helmets.[50] People may be less likely to lock their car doors if their car is insured against theft. Unemployment compensation may give the unemployed less incentive to look for work. Similarly, women may be less likely to avoid intoxication if A is required to treat B's intoxicated consent as invalid. And, the argument goes, our choice among possible moral or legal rules should take account of such effects.

Three points. First, moral-hazard effects are often real. It is entirely possible that something like the Brown University policy will lead to more intoxication than a policy that treats a woman's intoxicated consent as valid. Second, moral-hazard effects are often quite moderate. Those with theft insurance still wish to avoid the inconvenience of losing their property. Most unemployed persons would prefer a job to unemployment compensation. Similarly, women would have reason to avoid giving intoxicated consent to sexual relations, even if male predators would be liable for taking advantage of their condition. Third, even if a policy does give people less incentive to avoid undesirable behavior, we may accept moral-hazard effects as a tolerable price for achieving some other objective. Better to cushion the blow of unemployment or auto theft than to minimize unemployment or auto theft. Better to reduce the exploitation of intoxicated consent than to strive to minimize its frequency.

If we say that A's behavior is impermissible in III (where A is sober and B gives intoxicated consent), what should we say about VII (where A is intoxicated and B gives intoxicated consent)? Can we say that B's intoxicated consent is *not* morally or legally valid, but that A is culpable for taking advantage of B's intoxicated consent if he is intoxicated? The short answer is – yes. Recall the earlier discussion of consent to a medical procedure. We might treat B's intoxicated consent to a medical procedure as invalid while holding an intoxicated physician responsible for accepting B's intoxicated consent to a medical procedure. Similarly, we can say that when A becomes intoxicated, he culpably puts himself at risk for having sex with a woman who gives consent because she is intoxicated. Does this mean that men would bear a greater burden for intoxication than women? Yes, no, and, perhaps, so what? Yes – men may bear a greater legal and moral burden from intoxication; no – because women would continue to bear greater physical and emotional burdens from intoxicated sexual relations;

---

[49] A "moral hazard" is created when one is more likely to engage in an undesirable behavior because one is insured or protected from its consequences.

[50] "A Bicycling Mystery: Head Injuries Piling up," *New York Times*, July 29, 2001, section 1, page 1.

so what? – because even if men do bear greater burdens for intoxicated sexual behavior, the asymmetry may well be justified.

Although the consistency claim will remain intuitively attractive and will exert considerable practical pull, I do not believe that it provides much philosophical support for regarding intoxicated consent as invalid. I do not say that we should accept the impermissibility claim. I say only that the consistency claim does not give us reason to reject it.

Conclusion

In the final analysis, should we accept the impermissibility claim? Should we endorse something like the Brown University policy as a matter of morality or as a matter of institutional policy at colleges and universities or as a matter of law? The last question is not merely hypothetical. There are several cases in which defendants have been convicted of rape by intoxication,[51] including one where the complainant (who met the defendants at a bar where she was a lap dancer) agreed to make a pornographic film but stated in front of witnesses that she would need to get "*** up" in order to do it.[52] I doubt that these cases constitute a general trend in the criminal law, but the question remains whether this is the direction in which we should be headed.

I continue to think that the right answer to our questions depends upon a range of empirical and moral considerations that we have not entirely resolved. But we have made progress. If my argument is roughly correct, we can say that the best answer to the question is not entailed in a straightforward way by the agent's intoxication at the time of her consent (which would tell against validity) or her responsibility for her intoxication (which would tell for validity) or by our willingness to hold persons responsible for wrongful acts committed while intoxicated (which would also tell for validity). We have the space to go either way.

With the caveat that these thoughts are tentative and revisable in the face of relevant evidence, I am inclined to think that we should *reject* the impermissibility claim as a matter of law, institutional policy, and even morality, in those cases where A can be reasonably confident that B's intoxication is voluntary. The previous condition is important. The salient issue is not whether B's intoxication is voluntary or whether A himself induced B's

---

[51] See, for example, *People v. Giardino*, 82 Cal. App. 4th 454 (2000).

[52] This case is discussed in Davis and Loftus, "What's Good for the Goose Cooks the Gander." By agreement with the defense attorney, the authors do not provide a legal citation. Private communication with Professor Davis.

intoxication. The salient issue is whether A has reason to believe that B's intoxication is voluntary. From that perspective, **Dutch Courage** is an easier case than *Brown*. For even though Sara's intoxication was self-induced, it is arguable that probabilistic evidence aside, Adam had no special reason to believe this.

Why do I suggest that we reject the impermissibility claim? Not to protect predatory males or to hold women to account for their irresponsible behavior, but because it does a better job of balancing the positive and negative autonomy of women than a more restrictive approach. First, the pleasures of alcohol and sex are so closely intertwined for some that to require contemporaneous sober consent would be unduly restrictive. Second, because the disinhibiting effects of alcohol are widely understood, a permissive approach should not produce predatory behavior in which A takes advantage of B's ignorance. Third, to insist on sober *ex ante* consent to subsequent intoxicated consent would preclude many women from doing precisely what they want to do, namely, not to be required to consent before they become intoxicated.

Of course even if a more permissive approach works best in the majority of cases and would be favored by most women, we would have reason to reject it if many women were seriously harmed by sexual relations to which they gave intoxicated consent. Paternalism is more justifiable when the harms are grave and irrevocable. But bracketing the risks of pregnancy and disease, which might be sufficient to tip the scale, I suggest that the harm in such cases as *Brown* is typically not particularly grave. Although it is not dispositive, it is of relevance that Sara did not feel victimized during or even shortly after her encounter with Adam. And we cannot say, "True, but her autonomy was violated because she did not give valid consent"; for the task is to determine whether she did give valid consent. If the conjectures of this section are on the mark, then the answer is that she did.

CHAPTER TWELVE

Sex and justice

Introduction

A well-known scene in Woody Allen's *Annie Hall* depicts split-screen conversations between Annie (Diane Keaton), Alvy (Woody Allen), and their
respective psychotherapists. When Annie's therapist asks how often they
have sex, she says, "Constantly. I'd say three times a week." When Alvy's
therapist asks how often they have sex, he says, "Hardly ever. Maybe three
times a week."

Or consider this *Seinfeld* exchange between Elaine and Jerry after Elaine's
new boyfriend abruptly aborted what promised to be their first sexual
encounter.[1]

ELAINE: Listen, lemme ask you something. When you're with a guy, and he tells
    you he has to get up early, what does that mean?
JERRY: It means he's lying...
ELAINE: Oh, come on...Men *have* to get up early some time...
JERRY: No. Never.
ELAINE: Jerry! I'm sure I've seen men on the street early in the morning.
JERRY: Well, sometimes we do actually have to get up early, but a man will *always*
    trade sleep for sex.

Up to this point, I have asked, in effect, "what constitutes valid consent
to sexual relations?" Although the answer to this question requires moral
judgments, the question is distinct from another moral question: "when
should a woman give valid consent to sexual relations?" The second question
arises in at least two different contexts. First, we might ask when a woman
should first consent to sexual relations in a courtship ("come on, we've
been dating for over a month!"). Second, we might ask when a woman
should consent to sexual relations in the context of an *enduring* relationship,
such as a marriage. I do not know whether moral theory has anything

---

[1] Unbeknownst to Elaine, she had acquired a strong body odor from riding in Jerry's car, which, in
turn, had been "infected" by a parking attendant.

interesting to say about the first question, but it is the second question that I have in mind here. Given an asymmetry of desire for sexual intercourse, should the less desirous party consent to sexual intercourse more often than she would otherwise desire?

The question is about consent to sex, not sex. Setting aside some special cases (such as **Sleep**), we shall assume that it is never morally permissible for A to have sexual relations with B without her concurrent consent.[2] There is no assumption, a la Hale, that the marriage contract includes a blank-check agreement for sexual relations on request. To the contrary, we shall assume that a husband must refrain from intercourse with a wife who does not give valid consent. The present question is whether she should consent or whether it even makes sense to ask such a question.

I will put the problem schematically. Assume that A and B have been married for some years. Both understand that A prefers sexual relations more frequently than B. They understand that there are occasions on which it is frustrating for A to forego sexual relations but when B's desire or pre-moral preference is not to engage in sexual intercourse. Given this situation, there are three possible moral solutions: (1) A should absorb the burden of the asymmetry by foregoing sexual relations whenever B does not desire sex; (2) B should absorb the burden of the asymmetry by consenting to sexual relations whenever A desires sex; (3) A and B should share the burden of the asymmetry by having sexual relations less often than A would (otherwise) desire and more often than B would (otherwise) desire. What should A and B do? I do not know. The main purpose of the chapter is to argue that it is reasonable to ask the question. In particular, I will argue that partners in an enduring relationship can reasonably view the frequency of sexual relations as a matter to be governed by principles of distributive justice.

Why assume that this is a question only for B? In principle, I do not. Advice columnists frequently respond to women who complain of their husbands' dead batteries. The Viagra phenomenon revealed a widespread but previously undiscussed problem for men (although some articles also suggested that many women are less than ecstatic about the drug's effects). I frame the question in non-gender-neutral terms for three reasons: first,

---

[2] Although I have not seen data on American men, it seems that most Canadian men agree, notwithstanding claims about patriarchal hegemony to the contrary. In one survey, when male respondents were asked whether "A man has the right to have sex with his wife/partner when he wants, even though she may not want to," the responses were as follows: strongly agree: 0.9%; agree: 1.5%; disagree: 35.5%; strongly disagree: 62.1%; Walter DeKeseredy and Martin Schwartz, *Woman Abuse on Campus* (Thousand Oaks, CA: Sage, 1998), 98.

simplification; second, it is empirically more typical;[3] third, if "ought implies can," the moral question arises more easily for women than for men,
although it is possible for men to decide to attempt to become aroused in
the face of a prior desire not to do so.

Moral reasons and consent

There is nothing problematic about thinking that B should consent to do
or permit X even though A would not be entitled to take or do X without
B's consent. It is, of course, often impossible for A to obtain something
from B without B's cooperation. Scholars should agree to review their fair
share of manuscripts for journals and scholarly presses, but if they do not,
there is not much anyone can do. In other cases, however, it is practically
feasible for A to take that to which B should consent, but it would be wrong
for A to do so. Perhaps B should agree to cut down a tree on her property
that is blocking A's view, but it would be wrong for A to cut it down if B
says no. If A loans B his lawn mower while B's mower is in the shop, then
B should loan A her mower while A's mower is in the shop, but it might be
wrong for A to take B's mower if B selfishly refuses. Similarly, it might be
wrong for B not to consent to donate blood for a sibling, but it might
also be wrong (although practically feasible) to take B's blood without her
consent.

   Now "should consent" is open-ended with respect to the force and type
of moral reasons. Moral reasons are not all on a par. Judith Jarvis Thomson
maintains that there are important distinctions between the claim that B
"ought" to do X for A, and the claim that B has an "obligation" to do X
or that A has a "right" that B do X or that it would be "unjust" for B not
do X. To use her example, if an older brother (O) ought to share a box of
chocolates with his younger brother (Y), it does not follow that Y has a right
to any chocolates or that O has an obligation to give any to Y or that Y is
acting unjustly.[4] I agree that there is space between general "ought" claims
and more specific claims that invoke "rights," "obligation," and "justice,"
but I do not think that much turns on such distinctions in the present
context. The primary question is whether B has moral reason to consent
to sexual relations with A on some occasions when she does not desire sex,
not whether she has a "conjugal duty" to do so or whether A has a right

---

[3] Whereas 14% of men and 4% of women complain that their spouses have refused to have sex during
   the first year of marriage, 43% of men and 18% of women express this feeling four years later; David
   M. Buss, *The Evolution of Desire* (New York: Basic Books, 1994), 187.
[4] "A Defense of Abortion," 1 *Philosophy & Public Affairs* 47 (1971), 56–57.

that she do so. And while I frame the issue in terms of justice to emphasize the distributive dimension of the issue, I do not assume that justice implies any special moral force.

Sex and justice

Bracketing the issue of sexual relations, partners in enduring and committed relationships often consider how the various benefits and burdens of family life should be distributed between them. They consider the distribution of household chores such as cooking, cleaning, laundry, dish-washing, and the various tasks of child-care such as feeding, changing diapers, transportation, and doctor's visits. They consider the distribution of satisfaction with respect to various decisions, such as where to dine, where to vacation, whose parents to visit, what television shows to watch (or whether to watch any), what radio stations or CDs should be played in the car, how often one should play golf, and so on. Moreover, I suspect that partners frequently discuss such issues in terms of fairness or justice, and, if they do not, say, because the husband's preferences rule the day, then it is arguable that they should.[5]

Consider the "Battle of the Sexes." On one version of the problem, A prefers to go to the opera and B prefers to go to the ballet, but both prefer to go to the opera or the ballet together than going to their preferred entertainment alone or staying at home.[6] A matrix of their payoffs might look something like this (where A's payoffs are to the left of the comma, B's to the right).

		B Home	Opera	Ballet
	Home	0, 0	0, 1	0, 2
A	Opera	2, 0	8, 3	2, 2
	Ballet	1, 0	1, 1	3, 6

A and B might decide to alternate (opera this week, ballet next week) or opt for a more complicated mix (four operas for every three ballets) or introduce another issue that can compensate for their choice on this issue,

[5] Susan Moller Okin maintains that "justice is needed as the primary, meaning most fundamental, moral virtue *even* in social groupings in which aims are largely common and affection frequently prevails"; *Justice, Gender, and the Family* (New York: Basic Books, 1989), 29–31.
[6] See Brian Barry, *Theories of Justice* (Berkeley: University of California Press, 1989), 116–17.

(they always go to the opera, which A strongly prefers, but they always vacation at the shore, which B strongly prefers). There may well be a best method for arriving at principles of justice at the most abstract level (for example, a contractualist approach), but there is no single right principle for resolving such conflicts at the level of application. A just resolution will depend upon the overall context of the relationship and the intensity of the parties' preferences for the various activities. If A has only a slight preference for opera, but B has a great preference for ballet, and if they do not engage in strategic misrepresentation of their preferences, then they might well go to the ballet more frequently than they go to the opera, thereby generating roughly equal long-run entertainment utility.[7] In any case, there is nothing paradoxical about seeing such decisions as the proper subject of a principle of fairness, and much the same could be said about transporting children and visiting parents.

If this is right, there is prima facie reason to think that principles of distributive justice should also apply to sex. Consider the intensity of sexual satisfaction. Suppose that A always has an orgasm whereas B rarely does so because A is not a particularly sensitive or skilled lover (and it is easier for males to reach orgasm). A's behavior is arguably unfair to B and B might well put her complaint in these terms. Suppose that both partners enjoy receiving oral sex much more than they enjoy performing it, just as both enjoy the result of house cleaning more than they enjoy doing it. Suppose that B performs oral sex on A about as frequently as A desires, but A often recoils at performing oral sex on B. It is arguably unfair (and imprudent) for A to take advantage of B's willingness to provide him with pleasure and refuse to reciprocate.

David Archard disagrees.

It is surely true that most of us have freely entered into sexual relationships and activities which did not live up to our expectations or wishes. It was not as good for us as it was for the other. This cannot be described as unfair since there seems [*sic*] no principle of justice which prescribes a fair distribution of sexual pleasures to the participants in a consensual activity. Sex is a mutual giving of each to the other. It is not required that the giving be equally proportioned.[8]

But this is much too quick and begs several questions. Archard is certainly right to say that a sexual encounter is not unfair simply because it does not live up to expectations or because it was better for one party than

---

[7] Needless to say, if the parties want a just resolution, they will not engage in strategic presentation of their preferences.
[8] David Archard, *Sexual Consent* (Boulder: Westview, 1998), 77.

another. On the other hand, that sex involves a mutual giving no more precludes the possibility of unfairness than the fact that a trade is mutually beneficial precludes its being unfair. And while Archard correctly claims that sexual pleasure need not be equal, it is entirely possible that fairness requires something like equal sensitivity or equal concern. What constitutes a just distribution of sexual satisfaction will turn on a number of empirical considerations, including the parties' capacities for sexual pleasure. If, for example, it is much easier for A to reach orgasm than B, it does not follow that a relationship is unfair simply because A has orgasms more regularly than B. If B has a "natural" capacity for multiple orgasms, whereas A does not, then a pattern in which they each have one orgasm per sexual encounter may well reflect A's insufficient sensitivity to B's sexual pleasure.

As with intensity, so with frequency. Suppose that Annie and Alvy try to model their conflict as a decision along the lines of the Battle of the Sexes. Consider a matrix in which the numbers represent the parties' average "utiles" from two options *on the nights when they have different pre-moral preferences.* On some nights, their preferences do not diverge. On some such nights, neither is amorous and both prefer to go straight to sleep. On other nights, both are amorous and both prefer to have sex before going to sleep. On the nights in question, however, they are asymmetrically amorous. A prefers sex then sleep. B prefers sleep.

	Sleep	Sex
A	2	5
B	6	1

It is, of course, very difficult to quantify these experiences for all the standard reasons about the measurement of utility and because the phenomenology of sexual desire is complex. As I noted in chapter two, a women's *desire for* sexual intercourse may not track her *pleasure in* sexual intercourse. Moreover, it is difficult to set a proper "baseline," because the phenomenology of sexual desire is responsive to factors such as the opportunity costs and to the parties' history. Sex is not just about orgasm. It is about desiring to be desired, abhorring rejection, feeling put upon, power, and the like. A's utility from going straight to sleep is higher when sex is not a practical possibility (say, when B is menstruating) than when B's refusal signals a lack of interest. Similarly, although B does not mind sex, *ceteris paribus* (it's a "1"), she does mind having to forego sleep, so she might experience what would otherwise be a positive "1" as a cost. A may feel more frustrated if they did not have sex on several recent occasions on which this situation arose, whereas B may feel more resentful if they did. In any case, let's bracket such concerns and assume, arguendo, that the matrix captures something close to their relative satisfaction.

Suppose that A and B are trying to determine what they should do on the occasions that they face *this* matrix. At this point, it is an open question as to what principles they would adopt. It might be thought that a principle of fairness would demand that the parties treat each party's interests equally, and that this cashes out as some version of sexual utilitarianism – maximize the total amount of pleasure distributed over the two parties. In this case, a principle of aggregate utility will always favor sleep (6+2) to sex (5+1), but B will get the lion's share of that utility. And that does not seem right. If we eschew an aggregative consequentialism, say, because it does not take seriously the "distinction between persons," we may give priority to the party whose experience is worse.[9] In this case, however, a maximin principle would also always favor sleep, which has a minimum of "2", to sex, which has a minimum of "1." But that suggests to me that maximin is not the right principle in this context. We might opt for a principle of "equal utility," in which case the parties would go for sex and sleep on a 50/50 basis over time, as each averages 3.5 utiles when they encounter such occasions.

Suppose that the utilities are different.

	Sleep	Sex
A	−2	5
B	2	−1

Here both parties experience their lesser alternative in negative terms, and A experiences the frustration consequent to the absence of sex as worse than B experiences sex. It might be thought that the subjective experience of frustration consequent to unresolved sexual desire could not be more aversive than the more salient or observable aversive experience of engaging in undesired sex; it is an empirical question whether this is so.[10] If something

---

[9] John Rawls, *A Theory of Justice* (Cambridge, MA: Harvard University Press, 1971), 27.

[10] As the fictional Ted Wallace puts it, " 'Of course women get the itch now and again, we wouldn't be here as a race otherwise. . . . But they are not, lucky, lucky, lucky things, for ever hungry, for ever desperate, for ever longing for the base physical fact of getting their rocks off' "; Stephen Fry's *The Hippopotamus* (London: Hutchinson, 1994).

like this matrix can occur, then a principle of aggregate utility would favor always having sex (4 v. 0), as would a maximin principle (-1 v. -2). If A and B were to aim for long-run equal utility, they would have sex on approximately 40 percent of these occasions, or three times out of seven.[11] So if Annie and Alvy had these utilities every night, they may have stumbled onto the right answer.

The previous matrix illustrates a problem that arises when one party's utility differential is much greater than the other's. Suppose that the utilities look something like this:

	Sleep	Sex
A	1	10
B	2	1

If the parties were to aim for equal long-run utility for each without attention to aggregate utility, then they would have sex on 10 percent of these occasions.[12] A might complain that this is insensitive to the pleasure that he must forego, that they should give equal consideration to each party's *utility potential* (which is just another version of aggregate utility). But to do so renders B's modest preferences hostage to A's intense preferences, an outcome that may not take sufficiently seriously "the distinction between persons." The worry here is that on virtually any principle that gives weight to aggregate utility, A's intense pleasure will overwhelm B's dysphoria.

I do not have a good answer to this case. Perhaps their marriage is doomed. Interestingly, when the disutilities go the other way, the outcome seems much more tractable. Consider this query to Ann Landers:

My husband is in his 80s and refuses to give up on sex. For some time now, he has been unable to complete the act, after trying for up to two hours. By that time, I am totally exhausted and feeling resentful. These weekly attempts are sheer torture for me, especially when my arthritis acts up.[13]

It is hard to know how to model this case. But suppose the matrix looks something like this:

---

[11] If they have sex two times out of seven, then A gets a total of zero ($(2 \times 5) + (5 \times -2)$ and B gets 8 ($(2 \times -1) + (5 \times 2)$). If they have sex three times out of seven, then A receives a total of $+7$ ($(3 \times 5) + (4 \times -2)$), and B gets $+5$ ($(3 \times -1) + (4 \times 2)$). If they have sex four times out of seven, then A gets 14 ($(4 \times 5) + (3 \times -2)$) and B gets 2 ($(4 \times -1) + (3 \times 2)$).

[12] For each ten occasions, A gets 19 ($(9 \times 1) + (1 \times 10)$) and B gets 19 ($(9 \times 2) + (1 \times 1)$).

[13] *Burlington Free Press*, September 29, 1996.

	Sleep	Sex
A	1	3
B	2	−20

It is not easy to argue that B should *ever* have to go through "sheer torture" to satisfy A. If this means that B always gets her way, so be it.

Whatever the best principles for resolving the asymmetric desire for sexual relations, a just resolution of these differences requires that partners step back from their own feelings, a view from somewhere different if not a view from nowhere. Here, as elsewhere, principles of justice require a *form* of impartiality. Such stepping back is not always easy. I have to work to understand that some people do not like chocolate, and empathy for another's sexual desires or lack of such desires may be much more difficult. Consider John Townsend's description of a couple he interviewed:

He said that his wife just didn't understand that he really wanted sex, and he couldn't understand why she didn't want to do it. I asked the wife whether it was true that she did not understand that her husband wanted sex and that it was very important to him. She replied that she understood perfectly but that she didn't want to do it as often as he wanted. He found her attitude incomprehensible... He did not understand that it was sometimes just as important to her *not* to have sex as it was to him to have it.[14]

Given the genuine epistemological difficulties about such matters, not to mention the distorting effects of self-deception and bias, those who strive toward a just resolution of these differences will no doubt make many mistakes even if they accept the right distributive principles. But here, as elsewhere, and despite frequent but entirely misplaced objections, the relevant sort of impartiality does not require a lack of sensitivity to the legitimate and very partial concerns and experience of the persons affected by one's actions.[15] Quite the opposite.

One additional point. A just resolution of the asymmetry of desire will be responsive to the parties' ability to control their desire and sexual experience as well as that experience itself. To the extent that sexual desire is biologically linked to procreation, males and females will typically go

---

[14] John Marshall Townsend, *What Women Want – What Men Want* (Oxford: Oxford University Press, 1998), 249.

[15] "Impartiality comes in at the point where the principles are chosen. Whether or not it comes in at the point where they are applied depends on what the principles themselves prescribe"; Barry, *Theories of Justice*, 291.

separate ways around the age of menopause, and B is hardly responsible for a decline in libido that results from hormonal changes. But biology is not destiny. To paraphrase Rawls, physiological facts are neither just nor unjust. What is just and unjust is the way that we respond to these facts.[16] If hormone-replacement therapy or Viagra would help (and is not otherwise contraindicated), then perhaps she and he should consider those options. If A is (relatively) oversexed, then he could consider drugs that would bring their libidos into greater convergence.[17] I make no claims about what the parties should do. My objective is to render plausible the view that the frequency of sexual relations is an appropriate subject for principles of distributive justice.

Objections

If I have rendered plausible the view that the frequency of sexual relations is an appropriate subject for principles of distributive justice, there are several important objections which can be raised against that line of argument.

Wants

It may be argued that a woman should simply never consent to sexual relations that she does not want. As stated, this objection simply begs the question whether a woman should want to engage in sexual relations for moral reasons. Given the distinction I have drawn between (all things considered) wants and (*ceteris paribus*) desires, it cannot be true, as a general proposition, that it is wrong to consent to sex that one does not desire, as illustrated by non-controversial cases such as **Love** and **Ovulation**. Moreover, it also cannot be true, as a general proposition, that one should not consent to do something for moral reasons that one does not (otherwise) desire to do, for that is precisely the motivational import of moral reasons. Consider the "Battle of the Sexes" matrix as a *pre*-moral representation of the parties' utilities, which must then be adjusted to reflect their desire to be fair. Although A would prefer to go to the opera, *ceteris paribus*, A also believes that other things are not equal. For, given that B really wants to go

---

[16] "The natural distribution is neither just nor unjust; nor is it unjust that persons are born into society at some particular position. These are simply natural facts. What is just and unjust is the way that institutions deal with these facts"; Rawls, *A Theory of Justice*, 102.

[17] Given that some anti-depressants seem to yield a decline in libido (particularly the selective serotonin uptake inhibitors such as Prozac and Zoloft), perhaps low dosages of these drugs might be used for this reason.

to the ballet and given that they most recently went to the opera, A may genuinely *want* to go to the ballet all things considered, when the things to be considered include A's desire "to behave in accordance with principles that can be defended to oneself and others in an impartial way."[18] And much the same can be true for sex.

We could put the point differently. The question whether B wants or should want to engage in sexual relations for moral reasons is a question that B might ask for herself. Suppose that B goes to C for advice:

B: Should I ever consent to sexual relations with A if I'm not in the mood?
C: You should never consent to sexual relations that you do not want.
B: But you're missing my point. I'm trying to figure out if I *should* want to, given that he desires sex much more often than me and given that I also want to be fair. You assume that my wants are a given. I believe they are the outcome of my deliberation about what I have reason to do. I want to do what is right, but its content is not always transparent, and so I'm asking you what fairness requires here.

There is a common but mistaken tendency to view wants as inputs to our decision rather than as the outcome of a reasoning process. On the "input" view, one's all-things-considered want – the winning want – is simply the want with the greatest motivational power (or the decision that represents the best aggregation of those wants). This view is false. As Joseph Raz suggests, "Were this a sensible picture of people's wants, there would be no room for reasoning about what one should most want to do."[19] And we do so reason.

One might think that sexual desire should be regarded as spontaneous and not readily controllable, but that view is completely at variance with the way in which it is ordinarily understood and discussed. Consider the following typical form of advice: "One of the most common disagreements between couples is their differing desires concerning frequency of sex. So, try to figure out what would be acceptable to you, and to him, and see where you can find common ground, or areas for compromise."[20] The standard fare in supermarket check-out-counter magazines is similarly future oriented: "How to put the spice back into your sex life." I am not interested in the details (here). The point is that this line of thought assumes that one can

---

[18] Barry, *Theories of Justice*, 272.
[19] Joseph Raz, "Incommensurability and Agency" in Ruth Chang (ed.), *Incommensurability, Incomparability, and Practical Reason* (Cambridge, MA: Harvard University Press, 1997), 114.
[20] Go Ask Alice, Columbia University's Health Education Program, http://www.goaskalice.columbia.edu/1365/html.

reasonably treat the character of one's sexual life and one's sexual behavior as the object of deliberation and decision.

Given this, if the claim that B should not consent to sex that she does not want is to get off the ground, it must be understood as a more specific claim, for example, that: (1) B should not consent to undesired *sex* with her husband for reasons of justice, although she could certainly consent to undesired nonsexual acts for reasons of justice, or (2) B should not consent to undesired sex for reasons of *justice*, although she could reasonably want to engage in undesired sex for a variety of *non*moral reasons. Consider these two possibilities.

Sex is special

It might be objected that whereas many non-desired activities (ballet, mowing lawns) are legitimate candidates for moral deliberation, sex is different. There is a practical and a moral version of this objection. The practical version claims that, as a matter of psychological fact, sex is experienced as special and that it is therefore self-defeating for (otherwise) morally conscientious partners to openly engage in sexual relations for reasons of fairness.[21] It just does not work. It might be thought that whereas A can enjoy the opera when it is "his turn," although he knows that B would (otherwise) prefer the ballet, A will not enjoy or value sexual intercourse when he believes that B consents because she wants to be fair to A. As Simon Blackburn puts it, "A partner who realizes that the other is meeting them not because they want to, but out of a sense of duty, thereby recognizes that the relationship is lost."[22]

Although I have no data to offer, I strongly suspect that the practical objection is not true. First, even if A will enjoy sex more if he believes that B desires sex for erotic reasons than for reasons of justice, it hardly follows that he will not enjoy morally motivated sex at all. To paraphrase Woody Allen, fair sex may be better than no sex at all.[23] Second, even if A would not enjoy sex to which B consents solely for reasons of justice, I doubt that he will regard his marriage as lost if such motivations play some role in B's psychic economy. Third, and for all we know, some (ordinary decent) people may prefer sex that is motivated by love or fairness as opposed

---

[21] I say no "(otherwise) morally conscientious" because it is obvious that non-decent men can and do get satisfaction from undesired and nonconsensual sexual relations.

[22] Simon Blackburn, *Ruling Passions* (Oxford: Clarendon Press, 1998), 21.

[23] "Empty sex is better than no sex at all, right?"; *Stardust Memories*.

to erotic desire, which they may regard as more animalistic, and which demonstrates less regard for them as a person. Fourth, one's experience changes during sexual relations. Even if B consents to sexual intercourse for reasons of fairness, she may experience sexual pleasure once they are "into it," and A's experience will be responsive to that.

Suppose that the practical objection fails. The moral variant of the "sex is special" objection maintains that one *should* not enjoy sex that one knows to be motivated by reasons of fairness. This is a difficult argument to make. I have argued that we should not tightly constrain what counts as legitimate *non*moral reasons to want to engage in sexual relations as, perhaps, in **Love** and **Ovulation**. If it is legitimate to engage in sexual relations when one's partner is motivated by these sorts of reasons, it is difficult to see why it should be wrong to do so when one's partner is motivated by moral reasons.

Justice and marriage

It could be argued that even if one might properly engage in sex for moral reasons, persons in a loving relationship will or should not be particularly concerned with the distribution of the benefits and burdens of their lives together, be it money, child-care, or sex. Following Hume, Rawls famously argues that questions of justice arise only under what he calls the "circumstances of justice," that is, those objective and subjective circumstances that render cooperation both possible and necessary.[24] The objective "circumstances of justice" include approximate equality, vulnerability, and moderate scarcity. If a good is not scarce (such as air), then there would be no issue about its distribution, but if a good is scarce (as with water in many places), then an issue of justice may arise. The subjective circumstances of justice include the psychological capacity to be motivated by reasons of justice (which makes justice *possible*) and the disposition not to take an "interest in one another's interests" (which makes justice *necessary*).[25] For present purposes, the subjective conditions matter most. A concern with fairness or justice arises only when the parties' conception of themselves and their lives lead them to "make conflicting claims on the natural and social resources available."[26] It is this assumption that is under fire from communitarians.

In his well-known critique of Rawls's theory, Michael Sandel argues that a loving marriage or family is the paradigm context in which justice is irrelevant because the circumstances of justice do not or should not obtain. In a loving family, the parties define – or aspire to define – their own interests

---

[24] Rawls, *A Theory of Justice*, 126–30.   [25] *Ibid.*, 127.   [26] *Ibid.*

in terms of the interests of their loved ones. Call this the communitarian thesis. As Elizabeth Anderson puts it, a commitment to a shared life, such as a marriage, "requires redefining one's interests as part of a *couple*."[27] Perhaps it is acceptable for siblings to invoke concepts of justice because no one assumes that their interests are highly intertwined, notwithstanding the denotation of "fraternity" to the contrary. But relationships between spouses and between parents and children are or should be a different story.

Now it is not entirely clear whether the communitarian thesis is fundamentally normative or empirical. It might be understood as a moral claim about the way in which spouses *ought* to think, that they should aspire to a "spirit of generosity" in which "the question of what I get and what I am due do not loom large..."[28] It might be viewed as an empirical claim that spouses do not, in fact, think about "mine" and "thine." Or it might be viewed as an empirical claim about the effects of justice rhetoric on the quality of family life.

I believe that we should resist the moral version of the communitarian thesis. First, and least important, there is a logical limit to the identity of interests and desires it is possible to achieve. If each party has an all-things-considered want to do what the other has an all-things-considered want to do, there will be no wants for the overall wants to get hold of and they will reach an altruistic stalemate: "I want to do what you want to do." Some differentiation of interests is necessary if the parties are to demonstrate the robust concern for the other that communitarians wish to celebrate.[29]

Second, assuming that even loving spouses can experience different levels of sexual desire, the communitarian view does not provide any help with the problem at hand. Even if a good marriage is characterized by an identity of interests such that issues of justice are irrelevant, this still leaves open the question of how married partners should respond to the asymmetry of sexual desire. The parties must appeal to some principle if they are to resolve such issues. In addition, the communitarian thesis wrongly minimizes the way in which principles of justice serve an important practical purpose. Principles of justice provide solutions to distributional issues among friends and intimates (as well as strangers), and arguably enhance these relationships

---

[27] Elizabeth Anderson, *Value in Ethics and Economics* (Cambridge, MA: Harvard University Press, 1993), 151.

[28] Michael Sandel, *Liberalism and the Limits of Justice* (New York: Cambridge University Press, 1982), 33.

[29] See Alan Soble, "Union, Autonomy, and Concern" in Roger Lamb (ed.), *Love Analyzed* (Boulder: Westview, 1997).

by bracketing issues about which the parties prefer not to have to make decisions, even when there is no deep conflict between them.[30]

Third, it is both unrealistic and undesirable to expect that the desires or interests of intimates will coincide so tightly. The communitarians are right to stress that when parties believe that their interests are deeply interdependent, then the circumstances of justice obtain to a lesser extent. Up to a point, thinking really does make it so. But only up to a point. Our numerical distinctness and our interest in exercising agency as independent beings dictate the need for finding solutions that are mutually acceptable among different persons rather than solutions that do not distinguish between them, even when they are loving partners.[31] Property is the easy case. It is relatively easy for spouses not to strongly distinguish between "mine" and "thine" or, more accurately, for them not to care who has what.[32] It is much more difficult to achieve a communal view with respect to activities. Do loving spouses care how many diapers they change or who stays home with sick children or whether they go to ballet or opera or where they locate? Do loving spouses experience conflict between their own professional goals and those of their spouses? Might they still be genuinely loving spouses if they do care? In my view, the answers are yes, yes, and yes. A good marriage need not represent a "union" in which the circumstances of justice are repealed. It may represent an intimate partnership between autonomous individuals who do and should have interests, goals, and aspirations that can conflict. A form of contractual thinking here is not merely a concession to hard-nosed realism. It may reflect a more attractive view of marital relations, and, it might be said, a view that acknowledges women's rightful claims to moral agency.

Marriage aside, some communitarian thinking exhibits a mistaken view of the relationship between intimacy and morality. Sandel thinks that many traditional moral categories and principles should not apply to friends and intimates and are not, in fact, applied if their feelings are genuine. But friendships between real human beings are complex, and are vulnerable

---

[30] A long-standing tennis partner/friend and I try to alternate supplying tennis balls because taking turns is an easy solution to the issue, and not primarily because we think our interests conflict.

[31] Neera Kapur Badhwar suggests that "the circumstances of justice are far more deeply rooted in the human condition than is generally recognized." See "The Circumstances of Justice: Pluralism, Community, and Friendship" in Robert M. Stewart (ed.), *Philosophical Perspectives on Sex and Love* (New York: Oxford University Press, 1995), 276.

[32] Hume says that justice should have no place among married people who are "unacquainted with the *mine* and *thine*, which are so necessary and yet cause such disturbance in human society"; *A Treatise of Human Nature*, book III, section II. But it is impossible for my wife to regard my shoes as anything but *my* shoes.

to the full range of human frailties such as limited self-knowledge, self-deception, rationalization, and envy. Do *real friends* (perhaps unwittingly) take unfair advantage of their friends? I think so. In two senses of the highlighted words. Friends who are *real* imperfect human beings do such things. And human beings do not cease being real *friends* when they do.

Precisely because relationships between intimates are imbued with feelings of trust and affection, it is arguable that friends do and should relax their moral defenses to the various ways in which they might be mistreated or exploited. But they do not and should not relax their moral commitment to acting fairly towards their friends. If I sell my exercise machine to a stranger, I will be honest, but I will not be particularly concerned that the price is fair, nor will I investigate what is a "fair price" for the item. Within a certain framework, we have a division of moral labor: he looks out for his interests, I look out for mine, and if we can agree on a price, so be it. By contrast, if I were to sell the machine to a friend, both he and I will be quite concerned that the price is fair. I will not want him to pay too much; he will not want to pay too little. This is not because we are obsessed about justice. Rather, precisely because friendship is *not* a contract for economic advantage, we find ways to be sure that we do not exploit each other, thereby taking such matters off the table.

It would be presumptuous in the extreme for this author to sermonize about the proper role of moral concerns within friendships and intimate relations. But I am not convinced that the communitarians have it right. A concern with justice among intimates expresses a recognition that the parties are moral equals, even when affection and generosity are sufficient to defuse conflict and give everyone the resources to which they are entitled.[33] It is not just that "deep and long-lasting love" can *coexist* with standards of justice, as Susan Moller Okin suggests.[34] Rather, the motivations of affection and generosity that characterize an ideal family should arguably be written on a foundation of justice, what Hume describes as "the cautious, jealous virtue."[35]

Second, love does not eliminate the need to make decisions about the distribution of resources or even one's affection. As Charles Larmore observes, "love, once its objects are many, does not place us beyond morality."[36] A

[33] Eamonn Callan, *Creating Citizens* (Oxford: Clarendon Press, 1997), 82.
[34] Okin, *Justice, Gender, and the Family*, 32.
[35] *Ibid.*, 29. The quotation from Hume is found in *An Enquiry Concerning the Principles of Morals*, section III, part I, par. 3.
[36] Charles Larmore, review of André Comte-Sponville, *A Small Treatise on the Great Virtues*, translated by Catherine Temerson (New York: Metropolitan Books, 2001), in *The New Republic*, October 22, 2001, 37–42, 42.

parent's love for all of her children does not solve her problem of where to live or vacation or whether she should pay for one child's music lessons or the other's mathematics tutoring. And, as Larmore also notes, if spouses or partners love themselves as well as each other, then there will be limits to the sacrifices that each will or should be prepared to make.

Sandel might readily grant much of this. He might admit that there is not and should not be a complete identity of interests among loving spouses. And he could grant that, *ceteris paribus*, a just intimate relationship is morally superior to an unjust one. When he says that an increase in justice does not imply an "unqualified" moral improvement in a relationship, he implicitly concedes that it implies a moral improvement on *one* dimension (that may be outweighed by a moral regression on another).[37]

As I suggested above, Sandel could be understood as making an *empirical* claim about the relation between the rhetoric of justice and the quality of intimate relationships. Here we must be careful to distinguish between claims about *evidence* and empirical claims about *causes*. Viewed as a claim about evidence, it may be argued that a conscious preoccupation with fairness demonstrates that the parties have failed to achieve the identity of interests that characterize a good marriage. If a couple were to begin to discuss more features of their lives in terms of justice, this would indicate that things have gone bad. Viewed as a claim about causes, it may be hypothesized that framing issues in terms of justice tends to weaken feelings of intimacy, accelerating the decline of benevolence and mutual identification to which they (should) aspire and which would enhance the quality of their lives as individuals.

I have three responses. First, the causal version of this argument is interesting, whereas the evidentiary version is not. If increasing concern with justice indicates only that things have already gone bad, then there is no reason to regret its appearance, particularly if it will make things more just even if not more intimate.

Second, it is entirely possible that the causal claim is true with respect to sexual relationships, that appeals to the discourse of justice will generate a decline in the quality of their marriage and the parties' sexual lives. Sexual injustice may benefit from "benign neglect."[38] I say this is possible. It is also possible that a concern with justice is a way of demonstrating respect for one's partner and that this reinforces positive feelings. It is possible that

---

[37] Sandel, *Liberalism and the Limits of Justice*, 34.
[38] When Daniel Patrick Moynihan said that "the *issue* of race could benefit from a period of benign neglect," he did not mean that we should neglect racial inequality. He suggested that we would be more likely to achieve that goal if we stopped talking about it so much.

those who feel they are being treated unjustly tend to act out those feelings in ways that move the couple further apart, not closer to a relationship in which worries about justice become irrelevant.

The relationship between justice and intimacy may exemplify what Robert Nozick wryly refers to as "normative sociology" – the study of what the causes of social problems "ought to be."[39] As Nozick observes, we want good things to be caused by good things and bad things to be caused by bad things. If poverty is bad and crime is bad, we would like it to be true that poverty causes crime, in which case reducing poverty (a good thing) will also reduce crime (another good thing). In the present context, communitarians tend to think that a concern with egalitarian justice (of which they disapprove) will make things worse on the love and affection front. By contrast, "impartialists" may think that a concern with egalitarian justice (of which they approve) will make things better. Normative sociology is not empirical sociology. We know, for example, that there is no direct correlation between poverty and crime: crime skyrocketed during the 1960s, a decade of declining poverty and rising income. In the present context, I venture to say that we simply do not know much about the causal relation between justice and intimacy.

Third, we do well to remember that even if it were true that *pressing* claims of injustice on one's spouse (or on oneself) is likely to have negative effects on the character of a relationship, this does not show that sexual life cannot be unjust in the way I have described. It would show only that the parties are better off if they ignore it.

The wrong problem?

In commenting on my earlier "interesting and amusing" (and briefer) discussion of this topic, Robin West agrees that "the distribution of sexual satisfaction within a marriage between spouses with different sexual appetites . . . is a legitimate problem of justice." She also claims that I focused on the wrong injustice.[40] According to West, she and I disagree on two "baseline" facts: (1) whereas I supposedly and wrongly claim that engaging in undesired sex is merely unsatisfying for women, she believes it is actually "quite harmful"; (2) whereas I supposedly and wrongly claim that most couples *do not* have sex when wives are not in the mood, she believes that most wives placate their domineering husbands. I do not believe that my

[39] Robert Nozick, *Anarchy, State and Utopia* (New York: Basic Books, 1974), 247–48.
[40] Robin West, "A Comment on Consent, Sex, and Rape," 2 *Legal Theory* 233 (1996), 249.

earlier foray made the claims that West attributes to me, but that is of no consequence. I take up West's remarks because it enables me to sharpen and clarify the argument of this chapter.

First, I do not know how women experience undesired sex with their husbands. My best guess is that – like most things – it varies, and I do not know what the distribution of their experiences looks like. If undesired sex is, as West asserts, quite harmful, then it is unlikely that a principle of justice will give B reason to consent. But *to the extent that* B's experience is not particularly aversive as compared with male frustration, then the claim that justice requires greater frequency is somewhat stronger.

Second, I make *no* claims about the relative proportions of "chivalrous" and domineering husbands among the married men of this nation or the world.[41] I have not claimed and do not need to claim that the "frustrated husband" is a greater problem than the excessively acquiescent wife. I argue only that it is an interesting question whether the asymmetry of sexual desire gives rise to a problem of distributive justice and, if so, how it should be resolved.

---

[41] West also seems to attribute to me the view that the "frustrated" husband who does not coerce his wife should be described as "chivalrous." I have no idea as to the basis of this attribution.

Appendix:
Alphabetical list of hypothetical cases

This list contains all of the hypothetical cases discussed in the book. In the sexual cases, assume that the parties have sexual relations after the fact description.

Abandonment. A and B drive to a secluded spot in A's car. B resists A's advances. A says, "Have sexual relations with me or I will leave you here."

Abuse. A is captain of the high-school football team. B is eighteen, has an IQ of 70, and reveres A. A says, "You'll be my girl friend if we have sex and let my buddies watch." B says, "Really?" A says, "Really." B says, "OK."

Affection. A and B are dating. A makes advances. B says, "I don't want to go further unless you really care about me." A says that he does, but later tells mutual friends that he was lying.

Anesthesia. A, a dentist, penetrates B while she is unconscious from anesthesia.

Antioch. A asks if he can kiss B. B says yes. A asks if he can touch B's breasts. B says yes. A asks if he can remove B's clothes. B says yes. A asks B if she wants to have intercourse. B says yes.

Aphrodisiac. An aphrodisiac is developed. A slips a pill into B's drink. Having become excited, B, who has never shown much interest in sex, proposes that they have intercourse.

Basketball. B, a professional basketball player, agrees to play without pay in a charity game for what A represents as an organization devoted to breast-cancer research. In fact, the organization is devoted to anti-abortion activities.

BIC. BIC had a contract with Sony under which BIC would be paid a commission for securing customers to use Sony products as business incentives. Sony told BIC that it would terminate the relationship if BIC did not agree to new terms. BIC agreed to new terms and then claimed that it had done so under duress.

Big Chill. B is a single woman in her thirties who wants to have a child. She proposes to A, an old friend, that he help her out. A accepts.

Bigamy. A and B have a marriage ceremony. Unbeknownst to B, the marriage is invalid because A is already married.

Biopsy. A mammogram reveals suspicious areas in B's breast. A tells B that he wants to do a biopsy under general anesthesia, and, if positive, perform a lumpectomy. B appears to be listening, but is not paying attention. A asks her to sign a consent form authorizing both procedures (if necessary). B pretends to read the form, but thinks that A will only be doing a biopsy. She signs.

Blood. The Red Cross recruits blood donors by falsely stating that the blood will be used locally. In fact, the blood will be shipped to any location that needs it. B gives blood because she wants to help people in her community.

Burnham. Rebecca Burnham's husband (Victor) severely beat Rebecca until she agreed, under threat of further beating, to stand on the street in front of their house and entice motorists (such as A) to have sex with her while Victor photographed her. Although Rebecca feared physical injury from Victor, she feigned expressions of desire to the motorists.

Caring. A and B have been married for some years. B finds such great pleasure and fulfillment in her role as wife and mother that she often does not distinguish between her interests and the interests of her family. B agrees to sexual relations because she cares for her husband and gets emotional fulfillment from the relationship, although she does not get much erotic pleasure.

Charade. A approaches B on the street, puts a gun to her back, and says, "We're walking up to my apartment." When they arrive, he says, "You and I are going to play a game. You are going to beg me to ---- you. Do a good job, and I won't hurt you. Resist, and I'll kill you." B takes off her clothes and says, "I want you."

Chat Room. A, thirty-three, and B, fourteen, have met in an internet chat room. They agree to meet in a motel and have intercourse.

Child. B is an eleven-year-old girl. A is an eighteen-year-old friend of B's older brother. A says, "Did you know that it feels good if I put my penis into your vagina? Do you want to try it?" B says, "OK."

Child Killer. A tells B, "I'm going to kill your child unless you have sex with me."

Children. A and B are eleven-year-old classmates in sixth grade. A says, "Did you know that it feels good if I put my penis in your vagina? Do you want to try it?" B says, "OK."

Cocaine. A, a supplier of cocaine to B, tells B that he will no longer supply the drug unless she agrees to sex. B cannot quickly locate another supplier.

Condom. A proposes intercourse, B accepts on condition that A use a condom. A says, "OK" and then penetrates B without a condom. B tells A to withdraw. A refuses until he ejaculates.

Coy. A makes advances. B does not want to seem "too eager." She firmly moves A's hand away, but kisses A. A puts his hand on B's leg again. B moves it away. They kiss more. A puts his hand on B's leg. This time, B kisses A, but does not remove his hand. A begins to remove B's clothing. B does not resist and continues to kiss A.

Cure. A, a hospital employee, calls B and tells her that her blood tests indicate that she has a serious disease, and that it can be cured by expensive and painful surgery or by intercourse with an anonymous donor (who turns out to be A) who has been injected with a serum. A and B meet in a hotel and have intercourse.

Dance Studio. A dance studio gets an elderly woman to contract to pay $20,000 for dance lessons by "a constant and continuous barrage of flattery, false praise, excessive compliments, and panegyric encomiums."

Dating. A and B have been dating for some time, but have not had sexual relations. A says, "I'm not willing to continue dating you if we don't have sex, so either we have sex or I'm terminating the relationship."

Debt. A, who owes B $500, says "Have sexual relations with me and I will repay my debt. Otherwise, ciao."

Default. A asks B if he can kiss B. B says, "For God's sake, I'll tell you if I want you to stop." After some kissing and petting, A removes his clothing. B removes her own clothing, but says nothing. They have sexual intercourse.

Detention Home. A, who has agreed to take B (nineteen years old) into his home, threatens to return her to the detention home unless she has sexual relations with him.

Dutch Courage. A and B have dated. B is a virgin, and feels frightened of and guilty about sex. Believing that she will never agree to sex if sober, she consumes four drinks in an hour. After some kissing and petting, A says, "Are you sure it's OK?" B holds up her glass, smiles, and says "It is *now*."

Dutiful. A and B have been married for some years. B frequently agrees to sexual relations because she has been taught that it is a wife's duty to satisfy her husband's sexual desires, although she often does not enjoy it.

Escape. B is in prison for life. A, a prison guard, offers to help her escape if she has sexual relations with him.

Estrogen. A and B have been married for twenty-five years. B has been experiencing a severe decline in libido due to menopause. During the past year, she rarely wanted to have intercourse, but agreed occasionally. She takes hormone-replacement therapy, and finds that her desire for sexual relations has dramatically increased. A proposes that they have intercourse. B happily agrees.

Force. A overpowers B physically, holds her down despite B's attempts to resist and threatens her with additional force if she continues to resist.

Former Professor. B has just graduated from college. A is a former professor on whom she had an enormous crush. A asks B for a date. B is flattered, thrilled, and excited. A proposes that they have intercourse. B enthusiastically agrees.

Fragments. Binjamin Wilkomirski's *Fragments* is presented as autobiographical memoirs of a child who survived the Holocaust. Readers and listeners are deeply moved by his words. Wilkomirski had never been in a death camp. The autobiography is completely bogus.

Fraternity Party. B is a college freshman. She has never had much to drink. She attends her first fraternity party and is offered some punch. She asks, "Does this have alcohol?" A responds, "Absolutely." She has several glasses, and becomes quite "high" for the first time in her life. When A proposes that they go to his room, she agrees.

Friends. A and B are both moderately retarded and like each other. A proposes that they have intercourse.

Gangrene. A patient's leg is gangrenous and she must choose between amputation and death. She understands the alternatives, and because she does not want to die, she signs the consent form.

Goldfish. A and B are on their third date and go back to B's apartment. A makes advances. B rebuffs A. Eyeing B's aquarium, A says "It seems that you like your goldfish more than me." A pulls a goldfish out of the tank, holds it up, and says "It's him or me." Becoming scared that A will kill her goldfish, B begins to undress.

Greedy Mechanic. A, a mechanic, is driving along the highway returning home from work. A sees that B's car has broken down. A stops, and ascertains that he could fix the problem in two minutes. He offers to fix the problem for $100. B accepts, but has little cash. B promises to send A a check for $100.

Groupie. B, a devoted eighteen-year-old fan of A's rock band, gladly accepts A's proposal to have intercourse.

Guilt. Unbeknownst to A, B wants A to have intercourse with her without her consent because she feels guilty about saying yes. While B says "No, please don't," A holds B down and penetrates B.

Gynecologist. A tells B that he will be inserting an instrument into her vagina. Instead, he inserts his penis.

Harvard. A and B meet at a party. B indicates that she has a "thing" about Harvard men. A falsely tells B that he graduated from Harvard.

Higher Grade. A, a professor, says "Have sexual relations with me and I will give you a grade two grades higher than you deserve. Otherwise you'll get just what you deserve."

Hiring. A is the sole owner and proprietor of a restaurant, where the tips are very good. B applies for a job as a waitress. A says that he will hire her only if she has sex with him.

HIV-D. A makes advances. B, who knows that A uses drugs, asks A if he has been tested for HIV. A, who tested negative three months ago, but who tested positive one month ago, says, "I tested negative three months ago."

HIV-L. A makes advances. B asks A if he has been tested for HIV. A, who tested positive for HIV one month ago, tells B that he had a negative test one month ago.

Indecent Proposal. A, who is very rich, says to B "I'll give you $1,000,000 if you spend the night with me."

Indifference. A and B meet in a bar. B is indifferent to a potential partner's marital status. In the course of conversation, she asks A if he is married. Thinking that a truthful answer would deter B, he lies. B believes A.

Inhibitions. A and B have dated. B has said that she is not ready for sex. From her own experience and from other sources, B knows that alcohol consumption distorts her judgment. Still, without thinking much about it, B consumes several drinks at a party. When A proposes that they have sex, she feels much less inhibited than usual, and half-heartedly says "there has to be a first time."

Intentions. A and B have been dating for some time, but have not had intercourse. B tells A that she is "saving herself" for her husband. A likes B but is a committed bachelor. A tells B that he intends to marry her.

Intern. A White House intern, who is infatuated with the President, proposes that they have sexual relations. He accepts.

IRS. A has information that B has significantly underreported her income to the IRS. He tells B that he will report her to the IRS unless she agrees to sexual relations.

Kidnap. A seizes B's child. B tells A that she will have sexual relations with him if he returns her child.

Kinky. A truthfully tells three drinking buddies that his wife, B, likes kinky sex, that she wants to have sex with them but will "feign" resistance. They have intercourse with her while B screams and struggles.

Lactaid. B refuses to have sexual intercourse when she has abdominal pain. After testing positive for lactose intolerance, she begins taking Lactaid pills. B feels much better and happily accepts A's proposal to have intercourse.

Landlord. A owns the apartment that B rents. B is several months behind on her rent. A tells B, "Have sex with me once a week until you pay up, or I'm going to have you evicted."

Lecherous Millionaire. B's child will die unless she receives expensive surgery for which the state will not pay. A, a millionaire, proposes to pay for the surgery if B will agree to become his mistress.

Love. A and B are married. A proposes that they have intercourse. B is not "in the mood," but she knows that it's "been a while" and wants to show her love for B and so agrees.

Love Potion (Number Nine). A and B have been dating. B thinks that A is a wonderful person, but does not feel physically attracted to him. Fearful that A will break off their relationship, B consumes an aphrodisiac and now desires sexual relations with A.

Lower Grade. A, a professor, says "Have sexual relations with me or I will give you a grade two grades lower than you deserve."

Mastectomy. A physician tells his patient that she has breast cancer and that she should immediately undergo a mastectomy. He does not explain the risks of the procedure or other options. Because the patient trusts her physician, she signs a consent form.

Model. A group of males pretend to be artists and recruit a woman who is willing to pose nude and blindfolded (as in the scales of justice). Unbeknownst to the model, the males do no art work and engage in group masturbation.

Modification. A proposes not to fulfill his contract with B unless B agrees to a higher price. B agrees to the higher price.

Museum. A museum puts on an exhibit of what it represents as Vermeer's paintings, but its curator knows that some are excellent forgeries. Thousands of people enjoy the exhibit and never discover the fraud.

New Year's Eve. A and B, a married couple, get roaring drunk at a New Year's Eve party. They take a cab home, stagger upstairs, fall into bed, and have sex.

Non-Disclosure. A makes advances. A, who has tested positive for HIV, has a "not asked, don't tell" policy. B does not ask. A does not tell.

Odometer. A sets back the odometer on a car before selling it to B.

Opportunistic Lifeguard. A is a professional lifeguard at B's country club. He sees that B, whom he knows to be very wealthy, is in trouble. He proposes to help B only if B agrees to pay him $10,000. B accepts, and, after being saved, refuses to pay on grounds that she consented under duress.

Opportunistic Samaritan. A, a stranger, is walking by B's country club and hears B shout for help. A proposes to rescue B only if B agrees to pay A $10,000. B accepts and then refuses to pay on grounds of duress.

Ovulation. A and B have been trying to have a child. B monitors her cycle and proposes that they have intercourse because it is the "right time."

Pain. A and B commence what they think will be a normal sexual interaction. B unexpectedly finds intercourse painful on this occasion, and asks A to stop. A does not withdraw until he ejaculates.

Partying. A and B have dated, but have not had sex. A says, "Is tonight the night?" B says, "Yeah, but let's have a few drinks first." Later on, B gets quite high and responds positively to A's advances.

Passed Out. B attends a fraternity party where she consumes a large amount of beer. She passes out.

Persistence. A makes advances which B rejects. A repeats his advances five times. On the sixth occasion, B says, "You don't take no for an answer, do you? If it'll make you happy, go ahead."

Plea Bargaining. A, a prosecutor, says, "Plead guilty to a lesser offense and take a one-year sentence or I will prosecute you on a more serious charge, for which you will receive five years if you are convicted." B accepts, then claims she was coerced into the agreement.

Polite Thugs. A group of four large men approach and surround B. The leader says, "Please give us your wallet."

Politics. A and B go out on their first date. A proposes going back to B's apartment for sex. B accepts. After some conversation, B finds A's political views repulsive and tells him to leave. A says that she agreed to have sex and he's going to collect first.

Pro-Choice. A is a strong "right to life" advocate. B is strongly pro-choice and chooses not to be intimate with those who do not support a woman's right to choose. In response to B's inquiry, A lies about his view.

Promotion. A, a supervisor at a large corporation, tells B that he will engineer an undeserved promotion for which B has applied if she has sexual relations with him.

Psychotherapist. B is undergoing psychotherapy with A. Under the grip of "transference" and strongly attracted to A, she proposes that they have sexual relations. A accepts.

Pure Force. A and his accomplices tie B's arms and legs to a bed. A penetrates B while B screams, "No, please stop."

Quadriplegic$_1$. B is a deaf-mute quadriplegic. She would like to have intercourse with A, but cannot communicate her wishes. A penetrates B anyway.

Quadriplegic$_2$. B is a deaf-mute quadriplegic. She wants A to penetrate her without tokening consent. A does not know this, but penetrates B anyway.

Reneging. A proposes that A and B have sex. B says, "Let's make a date for tonight." In bed, B says, "I know I promised, but that was then and I'm too tired now." A says, "I don't care, a promise is a promise."

Reputation. A and B are on their first date. B rebuffs A's advances. A says, "If you refuse me, I'll tell everyone in school that we had sex. If you go along, I'll keep my mouth shut."

Rescue. A, a mechanic, roams the highway offering to help people in distress for money, but when he finds that the rescuee is an attractive woman, he demands "service" for "service." B is stranded and A makes his usual offer, saying, "If you don't want my help, that's fine, I'll be on my way."

Retardation. A is a somewhat "nerdy" seventeen-year-old virgin who would like to have his first time with someone non-threatening. He is friendly with B, a nineteen-year-old neighbor, who is moderately retarded. A says, "Do you want to see what it's like?" B responds, "OK, if you want to, but don't tell my mother."

Revolver. A places one bullet in a chamber of a revolver. He says, "If you refuse to have sex, I'm going to spin the chamber, point the gun at your head, and shoot. You've got a 5/6 chance that the chamber will be empty. It's your call."

Rohypnol. A slips some Rohypnol, the date-rape drug, into B's drink. B passes out.

Rohypnol Conception. A and B are good friends. B wishes to become pregnant. She wants A to father her child, but does not want to experience intercourse with A. She tells A that she intends to take Rohypnol and that he should have intercourse with her while she is unconscious.

Sabotage. A drains most of the fuel out of B's car then follows her. When her car stops on the highway, he offers to help her out if she has sexual relations with him.

Single. A and B meet in a night class, and have several dates. B makes it clear that she refuses to have sex with married men. A falsely tells B that he is not married.

Sister. A has been having sexual relations with B's sister unbeknownst to B. A says nothing, although A correctly believes that B would have rejected A's advances if she had known about this relationship.

Sitter. B is a fourteen-year-old who baby-sits for A's child. B has an enormous adolescent crush on A (thirty-four). When A is driving B home one evening, B says "I'm a virgin, but they say older men are better. Would you teach me about sex?"

Size. A and B have been dating, but have not had sex. On this occasion, A proposes that they have intercourse and B accepts. They both undress. After seeing the size of A's exceptionally large penis, B gets scared and says, "I'm sorry, but I've changed my mind." A says, "You can't ask me to stop now."

Sleep. A and B have been dating for a month and have just begun having sex. On this occasion, they had "wonderful" sex the night before. B, who has been sound asleep, awakens to find A on top of her. A says "Good morning." B smiles back and says "Good morning."

Smile. A and B have been dating. They have not had intercourse. A proposes that they go to his apartment. B agrees. Pointing to his bedroom, A says, "How about we go there?" B smiles, follows A into the bedroom, but says nothing.

Smoking. A, a cigarette company, misrepresented the risks of smoking to B. B smoked A's product for many years and consequently died of lung cancer. If A had not misrepresented the risks, B would have smoked (no less) because B understood the risks of smoking from other sources.

Snit. A and B are married. They have not had intercourse for two weeks. A proposes that they have sex. A's past behavior leads B to believe that if she rebuffs A, he will be verbally abusive and generally difficult to live with.

Spiked. B attends a fraternity party for the first time. There is a keg of beer and a bowl of punch that has been "spiked" with vodka, but is labelled nonalcoholic. B has several glasses of punch, and becomes quite high. When A proposes that they go to his room, she agrees.

Spur Posse. A is a seventeen-year-old member of the "Spur Posses," a group in which boys compete to have intercourse with as many girls as possible. B is a fourteen-year-old high-school freshman who does not know about the group. She is flattered by A's attention.

Stupor. A and B have dated, but B has rebuffed A's advances. On this occasion, B is severely intoxicated, although she has not passed out. In response to A's advances, B says nothing when A removes her clothes, but is clearly too weak to resist.

Submissive. B suffers from extremely low self-esteem. She is and is known to be unwilling ever to say "no" to anyone. A tells B he would like to have sex with her. Although B does not desire sexual relations with A, she says "OK."

Suicide. A is infatuated with B, but B has rebuffed him. A tells B that he will commit suicide unless B has sexual relations with him.

Sweethearts. A, fifteen, and B, fifteen, are high-school sweethearts. They frequently have sexual relations.

Talent Scout. A meets B, an aspiring actress. A falsely tells B that he is a talent scout for a Hollywood producer. A makes no "quid pro quo" demands, but A believes (correctly) that B accepts his advances only because she believes his story.

Tease. A and B have dated, but have not had sex. On their fourth date, they go to A's apartment, they drink wine, listen to music, and kiss. A suggests that they go to his bedroom. B agrees. When A starts to undress B, B asks A to stop.

Testimony. B is on trial for a crime and prefers not to testify in her own defense because she does not want to choose between implicating a friend and committing perjury (for which she may incur additional punishment). When the prosecution has finished its case, B's lawyer says: "Their case is pretty strong and your only hope for an acquittal is to testify." B testifies.

Texas. A, a complete stranger, enters B's apartment and waits for B to come home. When B arrives, A threatens to stab B unless B succumbs to sexual relations. B pleads with A to wear a condom, falsely telling A that she has AIDS.

Threat? A and B meet in a bar and go back to A's apartment. B rebuffs A's advances. A smiles at B and says, "Look, you're alone with someone you don't know, who's much bigger and stronger, and, for all you know, has beaten and raped several women. Maybe I'm not as nice as I seem." B is very frightened by A's remarks and does not resist A's advances.

Trophy. A is a very wealthy sixty-year-old corporation executive. B is a twenty-seven-year-old fashion model. A proposes marriage, indicating that he expects regular sexual relations. B accepts.

Twins. A, whose identical twin is married to B, slips into B's bed while she is half asleep. B believes that A is her husband.

Ulysses. A and B join the "Ulysses" club which hosts events where all parties sign a form indicating that no one will be legally liable for any sexual act, including forced sex. One can ask another to refrain, but one has no recourse if he does not. A approaches B. B resists. A enlists the help of others to hold B down.

Vasectomy. A makes advances. B tells A that she will accept only if A wears a condom. A falsely tells B that he has had a vasectomy.

Weapon. A, a stranger, says "Do not resist me or I will kill you with this gun."

Index

DATE DUE